WRITING POEMS

WRITING POEMS

FOURTH EDITION

Robert Wallace
Case Western Reserve University

Michelle Boisseau
University of Missouri - Kansas City

HarperCollins*CollegePublishers*

Acquisitions Editor: Lisa Moore
Project Coordination, Text and Cover Design: Interactive Composition Corporation
Cover Photograph: Mark Bumgarner
Art Studio: Interactive Composition Corporation
Electronic Production Manager: Eric Jorgensen
Manufacturing Manager: Hilda Koparanian
Electronic Page Makeup: Interactive Composition Corporation
Printer and Binder: RR Donnelley & Sons Company
Cover Printer: Phoenix Color Corp.

Also available for this edition is an impressive array of high quality video and audiotapes of a variety of literary works, which can be used to broaden the students' experience of literature. Instructors are invited to learn more about the HarperCollins video and audiotape library from their HarperCollins representative or the publisher.

Writing Poems, Fourth Edition

Library of Congress Cataloging-in-Publication Data

Wallace, Robert, 1932–
    Writing poems / Robert Wallace, Michelle Boisseau. —4th ed.
        p. cm.
    Includes bibliographical references (p. 381) and index.
    ISBN 0-673-99013-3
    1. Poetry—Authorship   I. Boisseau, Michelle, 1955–
    II. Title.
    PN1059.A9W34   1995   95-3563
    808.1—dc20   CIP

    96 97 98   9 8 7 6 5 4 3

CONTENTS

II ⌒ CONTENT: THE ESSENTIAL SOMETHING

III ☞ PROCESS: MAKING THE POEM HAPPEN

9 FINDING THE POEM: Headwaters

12   BECOMING A POET: A Hand at the Back of the Room 347

PREFACE
To the Teacher

Since poetry happens all at once in writing a poem, as it does in reading one, the book's division into parts on form, content, and process, and of these parts into chapters, is a convenience of exposition. We have organized the material, not the course—or, really, the variety of courses that are possible. We invite teachers and readers to follow their own direction and priorities, skipping around the text freely.

Chapter 1 ("Verse Is") might be a place to begin, as an awareness of what it means to divide sentences into *lines* is basic. So might be Chapter 5 ("Subject Matter"), since the beginning poet often overlooks possibilities, particularly those (as William Carlos Williams would say) close to the nose. Another beginning point might be Chapter 9 ("Finding the Poem"), which looks at the sources of poems in reading, imitation, notebooks, quarreling with ourselves, and so on, as well as at ways of maintaining the poetic impulse. Another teacher might begin with Chapter 7 ("Metaphor") to establish a different emphasis; or with Chapter 8 ("Beyond the Rational"), which explores some of the origins of poetry in word magic and dream. Perhaps an ideal order might be to take in succession one chapter from each part, more or less raising simultaneous matters simultaneously; for instance, Chapters 1, 5, 9 first; then 2, 6, 10; and so on. In a course introducing both fiction and poetry, Chapter 6 ("A Cast of Characters") could provide common ground as it takes up useful elements of voice, point-of-view, irony, and symbol. The section of Chapter 11 on "Tightening," which cites Mark Twain's essay on the sloppy narrative of James Fenimore Cooper, provides another link to fiction.

If instructors allow an extra week or so for the condensed technical information in Chapters 2 ("Free Verse") and 3 ("Meter"), the book's twelve chapters and "A Glossary of Forms" (Appendix I) make a roughly comfortable fit for a semester course. For a shorter course, some chapters could be assigned selectively. The sections within chapters are handy for this purpose. One might choose, for a quarter course, only "Syntax" or "Alliteration and Assonance" from Chapter 4 ("The Sound of Sense") and the first section or two of Chapter 7 ("Metaphor"). Other sections may seem relevant mainly for a particular student—"Rhyme," say, or "Titles"—and can be assigned individually or referred to in conference. In schools with both an Introductory and an Advanced course, some chapters and sections might be delayed by agreement, such as Chapter 12 ("Becoming a Poet") or the section on "Texture" in Chapter 4 or that on "Surreality" in Chapter 8.

Organized by the material, *Writing Poems* may be adapted to a variety of course formats and levels of student training. As one teacher commented tartly, "The book is superb but, as I have been saying, I teach it my way, not the book's way." It seems safe to say that Chapters 1–12 are rarely, if ever, taught in order.

In courses that focus on workshopping, a significant use of the book is to let the teacher put the exposition of fundamentals *on automatic pilot*, letting the book take up the issues. It is frustrating, after an especially exciting semester, for a teacher using only an anthology to recall that a class never really got to metaphor, or to the basics of meter. Explanations in chapters are therefore fairly thorough, as well as eclectic.

Writing Poems can also function as a friendly handbook. Spend a few minutes early in the course encouraging students to think of it that way (and not as something to just put aside when a reading assignment is completed). Point out a lively poem in the "Poems to Consider" section of a chapter you won't be teaching soon, or an exercise among the "Questions and Suggestions" that might help when students are looking for ideas for poems. Have them turn to "A Glossary of Forms," "Select Bibliography," "Index of Terms." Encourage browsing. Students noodling in "Index of Terms" might wonder what for heaven's sake is *stichomythia*, discover Christina Rossetti's "Up-Hill" in "A Glossary of Forms," and be off on shiny, new poems of their own. The section "Po' Biz" in Chapter 12, with suggestions about participating in workshops, may also be usefully pointed out.

As reading poems naturally stimulates and guides writing poems, *Writing Poems* is also a convenient mini-anthology. We have gathered more than 300 poems from the sixteenth century to the present. Rarely are students familiar with much recent poetry—often only Shel Silverstein and pop lyrics—so the selection leans strongly toward the contemporary. We have also included a number of poems by students (whose names are marked in the text by asterisks) as models of what beginning poets can accomplish. While most of the "Poems to Consider" (following each chapter) are intended to exemplify matters raised in that chapter, some, like Henry Taylor's "Barbed Wire" (p. 60), have been placed for contrast; and some are just good poems that might appear anywhere.

All poets write (and learn from) their own weaker poems, so we have rarely used "bad" examples. Early versions of poems, particularly in Chapters 10 and 11 ("Revising"), offer numerous instances of the clumsy or wrongheaded—as well as assurance for aspiring poets that problems can be solved. As Ben Jonson urges,

> No more would I tell a green writer all his faults, lest I should make him
> grieve and faint, and at last despair. For nothing doth more hurt, than to
> make him so afraid of all things, as he can endeavor nothing . . . Therefore a
> master should temper his own powers, and descend to the other's infirmity. If
> you pour a glut of water upon a bottle, it receives little of it; but with a
> funnel, and by degrees, you shall fill many of them.

The "Questions and Suggestions" are intended to supplement, not replace, the instigations a thoughtful teacher can supply. This or that exercise will often be more relevant to a student or two than to a whole class, though many exercises are good for in-class use. Usually, students arrive in creative writing courses eager and strongly motivated; so the challenge is less to inspire than to provide the continuing stimulus of fresh ideas and new information. In workshops especially, a timely exercise can break the trance. On a warm fall day, when the sun is out and the leaves still in color, a class might do worse than be sent on a Metaphor Hunt (make up ten fresh metaphors, copy the three best to turn in by period's end). Or—it's been done—bring *Alice's Adventures in Wonderland* and just read aloud from it till the bell rings; or, better, from Randall Jarrell's *The Bat Poet*.

With many of our colleagues pursuing the hidden political, racial, and sexual biases of "texts"—in what Alan Shapiro has called a "hermeneutics of suspicion" ("Horace and the Reformation of Creative Writing," *American Poetry Review*, March/April 1992)—it is perhaps left more than ever to us to affirm literature's pleasure and delight for students.

A NOTE ON THE FOURTH EDITION

Readers of the third edition will notice that we have revised extensively Chapters 5, 7, 8, 9, and 12; and there are new discussions of poems in every chapter. Examples of revision by Marianne Moore, Wilfred Owen, Don Welch, Donald Hall, and Michael Burns have been added in Chapters 10–11, along with a set of drafts for "Politics" by Miller Williams. Boxed exercises in Chapter 3 will, we hope, engage students more immediately in the complexities of meter. Also new is "Introduction: At the Flying School," which should give students some perspective at the outset.

The most notable innovation is a new section in Chapter 12, "The Growth of a Poet," which follows a student poet through three poems written at different phases of her development.

More than one-third of the poems in *Writing Poems*, fourth edition, are newly added, including poems by or translations of these poets not represented in earlier editions:

Debra Allbery	Pamela Alexander	Renée Ashley
Alvin Aubert	Paul Auster	David Baker
Gerald Barrax	Christopher Buckley	Michael Burns
Alice Cary	Nina Cassian	Henri Coulette
Hart Crane	H. D.	Toi Derricotte
Patricia Dobler	Stephen Dobyns	Norman Dubie
Cornelius Eady	Nancy Eimers	T. S. Eliot
Paul Éluard	Lynn Emanuel	Clarissa Pinkola Estés
Alice Fulton	Suzanne Gardinier	Amy Gerstler
Robert Hass	Linda Hogan	Margaret Holley

Andrew Hudgins	T. R. Hummer	Fleda Brown Jackson
Mark Jarman	Shirley Kaufman	Jane Kenyon
Mary Kinzie	Elizabeth Kirschner	Thomas Lux
Sandra McPherson	Edna St. Vincent Millay	Susan Mitchell
Thylias Moss	Naomi Shihab Nye	William Olsen
Greg Pape	Ricardo Pau-Llosa	Stanley Plumly
Susan Prospere	Claudia Rankine	Adrienne Rich
J. Allyn Rosser	Enid Shomer	Maura Stanton
Timothy Steele	James Tate	César Vallejo
Ellen Bryant Voigt	Marilyn Nelson Waniek	David Wojahn

Also added are poems by, among others, Gerald Costanzo, Elton Glaser, Louise Glück, Langston Hughes, Donald Justice, Yusef Komunyakaa, Philip Levine, William Matthews, Claude McKay, Sharon Olds, Liz Rosenberg, Louis Simpson, Gary Soto, Elizabeth Spires, Chase Twichell, and William Butler Yeats.

The pleasure of adding poems balances the regret of dropping others. For a loss too painful, there remains the copier.

We owe much to teachers and poets too numerous to acknowledge easily—not least our own teachers—and are truly grateful for every correction and helpful notion. A special thanks to Michelle Boisseau's students and colleagues at Morehead State University in Kentucky where she taught while preparing this edition.

We also wish to thank the formal reviewers for this edition: Barry Bauska, University of Puget Sound; Rosemary Cox, De Kalb Community College, Central Campus; William Feeler, Midland College; Edward J. Gleason, St. Anselm College; Jack Hicks, University of California, Davis; Marianna Hofer, University of Findlay; Mark Irwin, Fort Lewis College; and Richard Spilman, Wichita State University.

— R.W., M.B.

INTRODUCTION
At the Flying School

Poetry thrived for a long time before there were creative writing courses, and even before the invention of printing.

Ancient and new mingle in poetry. The road on which the beginning poet stands, when the poet looks back, disappears into the past, where it once wound across the dusty savannah, through ice-age mountains. Civilizations rise and fall. Paint flakes. Stone falls from stone. Languages alter or disappear. "We write in sand," Edmund Waller said in the seventeenth century; "our language grows / And, like the tide, our work o'erflows." The arts, however, even though the works and often the artists' names are forgotten, have been passed along from living hand to living hand. As William Butler Yeats (1865–1939) wrote on the eve of World War II, in "Lapis Lazuli,"

> On their own feet they came, or on shipboard,
> Camelback, horseback, ass-back, mule-back,
> Old civilizations put to the sword.
> Then they and their wisdom went to rack:
> No handiwork of Callimachus°
> Who handled marble as if it were bronze,
> Made draperies that seemed to rise
> When sea-wind swept the corner, stands;
> His long lamp-chimney shaped like the stem
> Of a slender palm, stood but a day;
> All things fall and are built again,
> And those that build them again are gay.

> °*Callimachus*: Greek Sculptor, 5th C. B.C.

Like all poets, Yeats knew the joy of building poems.

Because old poems fade, we need new poems. Even with poems in the successful style of an era, as Mary Kinzie notes, "pretty soon the surprises do not surprise us any more." The human truth, however durable, must always be reimagined and made fresh. The poet lives "in a spring still not written of." "Make it new," Ezra Pound urges. Without change, art stagnates. At the same time, as T. S. Eliot points out in his essay "Tradition and the Individual Talent," a poet "is not likely to know what is to be done, unless he lives in what is not merely the present, but the present moment of the past, unless he is conscious, not of what is dead, but of what is already living."

The writing of new poems, then, seems inevitably to mix both what the beginning poet learns of the craft, the possibilities, of poetry and what only each new writer can bring to the adventure—fresh subjects, fresh attitudes, fresh understanding, fresh insights; "the genuine," as Marianne Moore says in "Poetry," for which a place can be found after all in "all this fiddle." Your teacher, like the authors of this book, can help; but expect to follow them only so far. The image of learning to write as a process of exploration is a good one. Howard Nemerov wryly defined writing poems as a spiritual exercise "having for its chief object the discovery or invention of one's character."

In some schools such courses are called not "Creative Writing," but "Experimental Writing." There's value in that. Faced with the icy Alp of a blank white page, favorite pen in hand, sometimes the poet may well feel intimidated by the injunction: *be creative; create*. But: *experiment, try something out*—this is friendlier. Even on a bad day, one *can* experiment. Put a few words down, think up rhymes for each; re-order them, add a few connecting words, and try to make an arresting sentence. Use it as the first line or lines of a poem. What might the poem's *next* sentence say? Or: write a careful paragraph (full of details) picturing your teacher in third grade, then break the paragraph into lines; then revise, tighten or add to, that version. (Some poets, as Yeats did, find it useful first to write a poem out as prose.)

The resulting poems may be awful, but we expect experiments to fail. What we learn is how to give the next experiment a better chance of success—how to refine the apparatus, how to try for a sharper result by posing the problem more precisely, how to know better what we are looking for. Writing—trying to discover one's deepest feelings and to present one's most serious view of the world—is always an intimate, vulnerable activity. Value the poems that succeed; let go of those that do not.

No more than in science is excellence in poetry democratic. How good, not how many, is the criterion. There are plenty of poems fair-to-middling. The *1995 Poet's Market* (Writers Digest Books) lists 1,700 publishers of poetry, including magazines such as *Joe Soap's Canoe* (which recently published John Ashbery) and *The New Yorker*. Counting all the poems printed each year would be like counting a waterfall. Opportunity, necessarily, becomes challenge.

Try always doing a little more than seems expected. The spark for you, after all, may wait in some unknown place. Maybe writing a *pantoum* (see "A Glossary of Forms," p. 369) will set you going. Have a look at "Select Bibliography" (p. 389). Perhaps find a couple of the books in your library. Does *The Electric Life: Essays on Modern Poetry* sound interesting? Criticism is just talk about poetry (or whatever), and good talk has value. Listen in. Pound was probably too fierce: "Pay no attention to the criticism of men who have never themselves written a notable work." A fine critic himself, C. S. Lewis was at once fairer and fiercer: "It is always better to read Chaucer again than to read the critics."

So we return to what waits always at the center: poems. We learn to write poems from reading poems we like. That's how poems were written before there were creative writing courses, and that remains how it is done. When you discover a poem that truly talks to you, in this book or elsewhere, see what else by the poet you can find in the library or in *Books in Print* at the bookstore.

And always be sure you're having fun. Keep your sense of humor going, as the poet Leonard Trawick (b. 1933) does in "At the Flying School," which is a triptych of wonderful verbal cartoons. The winged horse Pegasus (from Greek mythology) has always been a symbol of poetry. The poem begins with that and imagines the horses trying to perch like birds. In lines 4–5, Trawick is playing with a line from James Wright's famous poem about a bird springing up and down in delight on a branch, "for he knows as well as I do / that the branch will not break." Here, the branch—and the line—break.

At the Flying School

At the flying school the horses
are mastering the take-off,
but there are problems with perching:
even if they find a foothold, the branch
will break. The kiwis and ostriches,   5
enrolled in the workshop on roots,
are rediscovering their heritage.

Down in the Novices' section
an oyster whispers, "I want to soar."
The resident angel folds its wings   10
and touches the rough shell.
"First, learn to feel
your flesh's cool weight
nestled in its silky cup,
the sea pressing against your sides,   15
the brine filtering through your valves.
Now, at your center, find
the gray light sending beams
in all directions smooth as glass,
so smooth—see?—you can slip on them,   20
just a little bit, side to side.
Now your flesh, your valves, the sea
begin to dissolve. Watch the light.
You begin to rise."
"Yes, . . . yes," whispers the pupil,   25
moving its concrete wings.

Don't be fooled. It *will* turn out that you can do it.

— R.W., M.B.

FORM

The Necessary Nothing

1

VERSE IS

Catsup and Diamonds

Shakespeare was seventeen. None of his poems was written, nor even imagined. That year—perhaps a year or two earlier or later—admiring a poem, he wrote one similar to it. Possibly his wasn't a very good poem, but it pleased him. He enjoyed having written it, enjoyed saying it aloud. Soon he wrote another poem, then another. Like him, all poets begin. Like them, Shakespeare chose to write in a form called verse.

What is verse, then?

We may begin to answer by noting the obvious difference between verse and prose. When you open a book, how do you know whether you are looking at prose or verse? Prose always continues across the printed page from left margin to a right margin set arbitrarily, *externally*, by the printer. The printer determines when a new line begins, and the wider the page, the longer the line. On a page wide enough, an entire book of prose could theoretically be printed on one line.

Verse, however, is a system of writing in which the right margin, the line-turn, is determined *internally* by a mechanism contained within the line itself. Thus, no matter how wide the page, a poem is always printed in the same way. The poet, not the printer, determines line length, or measure.

The Greek word for measure is *meter* (as in *thermometer*, "heat measure"). In poetry the word *meter* traditionally refers to the conventions of verse by which poets measure their lines (for instance, iambic pentameter). *All* verse, though, even free verse, has some kind of measure—some rationale or system by which the poet breaks or ends lines. The choice of the measure may be intuitive or trained, but the nature of verse demands that poets have a clear perception of the identity of each line, even if they cannot articulate the reasons.

This crucial aspect of verse is hidden in the etymology of the word itself. *Verse* comes from the Latin *versus*, which derives from the verb *versare*, meaning "to turn." (This root appears in such familiar words as *reverse*, "to turn back.") Originally the past participle, *versus* literally meant "*having turned.*" As a noun it came to mean *the turning of the plough*, hence *furrow*, and ultimately *row* or *line*. Thus, the English word *verse* refers to the *deliberate turning from line to line* that distinguishes verse from prose.

This deliberate turning of lines adds an element to verse that prose does not possess. The rhythm of prose is simply the linear cadence of the voice; the pauses, which break and so determine the rhythm of the flow, merely set off the clauses and phrases that are the units of sentences—and are normally marked in written or printed prose by punctuation. In verse, however, this same cadence plays over the additional, relatively fixed, unit of **line**. Reading verse, the voice also pauses ever so slightly at line-ends, as if acknowledging the slight muscular shifting of the eye back to the left margin. The element of line thus gives verse an extraordinary, complex rhythmic potential of infinite variation.

Line-breaks may coincide with grammatical or syntactical units. This reinforces their regularity and emphasizes normal speech pauses.

> How many times,
> I thought,
> must winter come
> and with its chill whiteness
> slip-cover
> field and town.

Line-breaks also may occur within grammatical or syntactical units, creating pauses and introducing unexpected emphases.

> How
> many times, I thought, must
> winter
> come and with its chill
> whiteness
> slip-cover field and
> town.

When the end of a line coincides with a normal speech pause (usually at punctuation), the line is called **end-stopped**, as in these lines by John Milton (1608–1674) from "Lycidas":

> As killing as the canker to the Rose,
> Or taint-worm to the weanling Herds that graze,
> Or Frost to Flowers, that their gay wardrobe wear,

Lines that end without any parallel to a normal speech pause are called **run-on** or **enjambed** (noun: **enjambment**), as in these lines from *Paradise Lost*:

> Of man's first disobedience, ‖ and the Fruit
> Of that forbidden Tree, ‖ whose mortal taste
> Brought Death into the World, ‖ and all our woe.

A **caesura** (‖), a normal speech pause that occurs within a line, may produce further variations of rhythm and counterpoint not possible in prose.

By varying the use of end-stop, run-on, and caesura and by playing sense, grammar, and syntax against them, the poet may produce fresh rhythms. Note how Milton creates an effect of free-falling with these devices:

> Men called him Mulciber: and how he fell
> From Heaven they fabled, thrown by angry Jove
> Sheer o'er the crystal battlements: from morn
> To noon he fell, from noon to dewy eve,
> A summer's day, and with the setting sun   5
> Dropt from the zenith, like a falling star,
> On Lemnos, th' Aegean isle.

The syntactical pauses, or divisions of the action, occur within the lines; and the line-ends are primarily run-on.

LINE

Line is the essence of verse. The poet's sensitivity to line, an awareness of its interplay with the other elements of a poem, is central to craft. Consider this quatrain written by an anonymous, sixteenth century poet and now called "Western Wind."

> Western wind, when wilt thou blow,
>   The small rain down can rain?
> Christ, if my love were in my arms
>   And I in my bed again!

In love and away from home, the poet longs impatiently for spring when the lovers will be reunited. In prose the poet might have written something like this:

> I long for spring to come, with its westerly wind and its fine, nurturing rain; for
> then at last I will again hold my love in my arms and we will be in bed together!

Compare the poem and its prose imitation. What makes the poem richer?

Speaking *to* the wind, for instance, suggests isolation as well as loneliness. In prose we address inanimate objects only rarely, as someone who has just struck a thumb with a hammer may address the hammer. In the poem both wind and the "small rain" are personified—**personification** is treating something inanimate as if it had the qualities of a person, such as gender or (here) volition—and "can rain" suggests that the rain shares the speaker's impatience for spring. Similarly, the direct address to the wind suggests that the exclamatory "Christ" in line 3 is also, in part, a prayer. The speaker's world is a world of forces—wind, rain, and Christ—as the merely human world of the prose imitation is not. The poem expresses the natural procreativity of the speaker's desire more passionately than the prose version does, so that the human in the poem also seems to be a force among forces. The incomplete conditional of lines 3–4 conveys more by implication than the prose's explicit but flat "we will be in bed together." What is longed for is simply

beyond words. The poem's singular "I in my bed again!" seems at once more vigorous and, because it is in some measure joking, less intimidated by circumstance
than does the rather passive prose.

All of this dramatization might be presented in prose, but it occurs more naturally, more succinctly in verse. The compression of verse calls for an alertness of
attention, word by word, line by line, that we rarely give to prose. More happens in
less space (and fewer words) in verse than in prose, which is habitually discursive
and given to adding yet something further, drawing us onward to what is next and
then next, and next again. We half expect the prose to continue, whereas the
poem seems finished, complete. Prose, like a straight line, extends to the horizon.
Verse, like a spiral, draws us into itself.

This reflexiveness of verse causes us to attend to, hear, *feel*, the poem's rhythm
as we do not the prose's rhythm. Only two syllables in lines 1–2 (the second syllable of "Western" and "The") are not heavy. The lines are slow, dense, clogged,
expressing the speaker's anguish and the ponderousness of waiting. By contrast,
lines 3–4 are filled with light syllables; only "Christ," "love," "arms," "I," and "bed"
have real weight. These lines seem to leap forward, expressing the speaker's eagerness for the eventual release of longing into forthright action. The poet's measuring of lines is also a measuring of feeling. Rhythm is meaning. The "equal" lines of
verse differ more tellingly from one another than the elements of the freer, looser
prose can do. The young lover's desire, carrying its own music with it, is less a
speech than a song.

Verse invites our attention line by line, adding a spatial dimension that prose
cannot imitate. Study the following poem. One of a number of "chansons inno-
centes," it is by the indefatigable experimenter who elsewhere brilliantly wrote
"mOOn," E. E. Cummings (1894–1962).

> in Just-
> spring   when the world is mud-
> luscious the little
> lame balloonman
>
> whistles   far   and wee   5
>
> and eddieandbill come
> running from marbles and
> piracies and it's
> spring
>
> when the world is puddle-wonderful   10
>
> the queer
> old balloonman whistles
> far   and   wee
> and bettyandisbel come dancing
>
> from hop-scotch and jump-rope and   15

it's
spring
and
    the

        goat-footed   20

balloonMan   whistles
far
and
wee

Cummings uses line and word-spacing to choreograph the rhythms visually. Most obvious is the speeding of words run together, "eddieandbill," "bettyandisbel," as the children "come running" or "come dancing"; and the slowing (and so distancing) of words open-spaced, like "whistles   far   and wee" in line 5. This adverbial phrase is repeated twice, spaced differently for increasing emphasis:

    far   and   wee

then, with a line for each word at poem's end:

    far
    and
    wee

This repetition-with-variation seems appropriate for a poem about the cycle of seasons and return of spring. We notice also that "in Just- / spring"—where the strong, hyphenated run-on (and then extra space in line 2) suggests how *barely* it is spring yet—is picked up in lines 8–9 by

            and it's
    spring

and again in lines 15–18 by

              and

    it's
    spring
    and

The poem establishes its own conventions, and, once they are established, is able to vary them. One example is the alternating of four- and one-line stanzas, which suggests a slower, faster, slower pace. The indentations and stanza-breaks of lines 18–21—

    and
        the

> goat-footed
>
> balloonMan   whistles

—suggest a slow, almost dragging gait.

The poem's lack of punctuation (except for apostrophes and hyphens) lets it end without the sense of finality a period might imply. And the convention of using lower-case throughout is significantly varied in "Just-" and "balloonMan." The first perhaps seemed only for added emphasis. At line 21, however, the capitalized words seem intentionally linked to mean that the seller of balloons is *just* a *man*—not, as we suddenly realize that the poem has been quietly suggesting, the goat-footed and licentious god Pan.

"in Just-" is an extreme instance, but the inimitable effect of any poem derives from the *lines* of its verse. Cutting across the sentences, the lines give to every poem its essential difference. Something to say, **content**, and the way of saying it, **form**, are inseparable. As with a diamond, we value not the carbon itself but the form it has taken under pressure.

FORM

Why do we value form? Perhaps the answer lies in the secrets of our musculature, in our dark roots. Why do we live in square rooms? Why do we draw mechanical doodles when we are bored? Why do we tap our feet to music? Perhaps there is a profound link between the meter of verse and the human pulse, the rhythm of life itself— *te* TUM *te* TUM *te* TUM. The rhythmical impulse runs deep in us, and it is the basis of all the arts. We are pleased by symmetry, whether as children delighting in colored blocks of wood or as poets wishing to make words rhyme. Hanging around language, seeing what tricks it can perform, is a crucial fascination for the poet. W. H. Auden says,

> As a rule, the sign that a beginner has a genuine original talent is that he is more interested in playing with words than in saying something original; his attitude is that of the old lady, quoted by E. M. Forster—"How can I know what I think till I see what I say?"

Form is valuable because it preserves content, like the little verse about which months have thirty days. The motive for writing a poem or story may be to keep fresh an experience we care about and, thus, is not unlike the motive for taking photographs. We want to retain the light and the look of the moment. In a poem the thing is fixed, tied down, in the tightness of lines and rhymes. "Form alone," Henry James said, "*takes*, and holds and preserves substance—saves it from the welter of helpless verbiage that we swim in as in a sea of tasteless, tepid pudding."

When we try to express the thought, feeling, or event so well that it lasts as long as language itself, we escape (a little) the unremitting passage of all things into time, and we escape (a little) the endless bombardment of our senses. Works of art are machines for saving and clarifying experience. Robert Frost called the poem "A momentary stay against confusion."

As simply as possible, form is the nothing, the magic or pressure, that is necessary to transform the ordinary carbon of experience into the forever-diamond of art. Consider this simple case:

Going to Extremes

RICHARD ARMOUR (1906–1989)

Shake and shake
   The catsup bottle.
None'll come—
   And then a lot'll.

That catsup bottles are poorly designed and blurt out gobs of the red goo is hardly information. What makes us laugh is Armour's clever rhyme ("bottle-lot'll") with the contraction's surprising imitation of catsup's last-second, unexpected spurting. Form, more than the content, creates the meaning.

Of course, form and content are inseparable in practice. Any utterance has both, and it is impossible to distinguish precisely between them. As consciousness is always embodied, every idea or feeling, when stated, has only the shape of the words used. Even the telephone book has form and rhythm ("Anderson, D. D., Anderson, D. R., Anderson, D. S., Anderson E. B., Anderson, George"); but in a poem that pleases us, what works is the concord of the two, form and content. Often, when a poem "doesn't work," there may be a discord; for example, an elegy written in galloping rhythm is ludicrous:

My old Harry is dead and is gone to his rest,
Who was always in all ways the bravest and best.

FLUID AND SOLID FORMS

Poetic form may be thought of as being of two kinds. In "A Retrospect," Ezra Pound distinguishes between what he calls **"fluid"** and **"solid" forms**. Some poems, he says, "may have form as a tree has form, some as water poured into a vase." Mighty literary quarrels have been fought over a preference, movements have been formed, manifestos hurled. But both sorts of poetic form make good poems. Fluid (or **open**) form is organic, like a tree's growth. Solid (or **closed**) form is symmetrical, like water poured into a vase. Both are natural, and so long as poets are willing not to be theory-bound, they may use whichever form fits a particular poem best.

The idea of fluid, organic form is that the form should somehow express the content. As Emerson suggested succinctly, "Ask the fact for the form." Fluid form has made possible poems as finely wrought as Walt Whitman's "A Noiseless Patient Spider" (p. 12), Charles Simic's magical "Stone" (p. 27), and Margaret Holley's "The Fireflies" (p. 213). But it also, unhappily, justifies sloppy, raggedy, harum-scarum poems, more fluid than form—as many, surely, as there have been sloppy, overstuffed, padded sonnets or villanelles.

The problem with wanting form to be nothing more than the expression of content is that it is impossible. Beginning poets might pin to the lampshades on their desks this poem by Robert Francis (1901–1987):

Glass

Words of a poem should be glass
But glass so simple-subtle its shape
Is nothing but the shape of what it holds.

A glass spun for itself is empty,
Brittle, at best Venetian trinket.   5
Embossed glass hides the poem or its absence.

Words should be looked through, should be windows.
The best word were invisible.
The poem is the thing the poet thinks.

If the impossible were not   10
And if the glass, only the glass,
Could be removed, the poem would remain.

Ideally, form is the necessary nothing.

Whether fluid or solid, form must try to express content. Because every poem is a new creation, one wants to give it the form it needs, without regard to theory. Invented forms are neither better nor worse, in general, than adapted forms, only better or worse for the job at hand.

The sonnet, for instance, is one of the most difficult fixed forms, but its structure may well *help* the poet write a poem, just as a good interviewer's questions draw a coherent account from a witness. Consider how the material of Sonnet 73 by William Shakespeare (1564–1616) fills and fits the three quatrains and single couplet of the Elizabethan sonnet:

That time of year thou mayst in me behold
When yellow leaves, or none, or few, do hang
Upon those boughs which shake against the cold,
Bare ruined choirs° where late the sweet birds sang.
In me thou see'st the twilight of such day   5
As after sunset fadeth in the west,
Which by-and-by black night doth take away,
Death's second self that seals up all in rest.

In me thou see'st the glowing of such fire
That on the ashes of his youth doth lie,   10
As the deathbed whereon it must expire,
Consumed with that which it was nourished by.
    This thou perceiv'st, which makes thy love more strong,
    To love that well which thou must leave ere long.

4 *choirs:* choir lofts.

The theme is the poet's aging. In the three quatrains he compares his age to three things: autumn, the dying of the year; twilight, the dying of the day; glowing ashes, the dying of the fire. The quatrains emphasize the threefold comparison. The couplet at the end, with its difference in tone, presents a resolution of the problem offered in the quatrains. Form and content are in harmony.

Note that the order of the comparisons corresponds to a mounting anguish of feeling. The movement is, first, from a bare winter-daylight scene to a twilight scene, and then to a night scene, the time when a fire is allowed to die. The progression from day to dusk to night emphasizes and supports the image of night as "Death's second self" and possibly suggests night as the time one most fears dying.

Another progression is at work in the three images: each of the *dyings* is shorter and more constricted than the last, as though the speaker were aware of the quickening of death's approach. The first comparison is to a dying season, the second to a dying day, and the third to a dying fire. In its preoccupation with time, the first quatrain looks backward to summer, when "late the sweet birds sang." The second looks forward to "Death" explicitly and inevitably ("by-and-by"). The third imagines the coming night/death, when death is no longer a prospect but a reality: "deathbed." The increasingly narrow, bleak images of the three quatrains enhance the speaker's sense of loss and depletion in growing older. There echoes throughout the poem's images a story of an aging man's death during the night after a cold winter day.

The constraint of the sonnet form dramatically matches that of the speaker. He addresses the trouble of aging only indirectly, through inanimate images, as if to hold its personal implications at a distance. The apparent composure is, however, deceptive. Each of the three images begins with a more positive tone than it ends with. The increasingly self-diminishing revisions in line 2 offer a clear example: "yellow leaves, or none, or few." The yellow leaves, like the "twilight" and the "glowing" of the fire, are attempts at an optimism that the speaker cannot maintain. In each of the images he is compelled to say what he originally seems to have wanted to withhold, even from his own consciousness.

Intended as a compliment to the lover on the strength of her love, the couplet begins on a positive note: "This thou perceiv'st, which makes thy love more strong." But the next line betrays the speaker's fears because he does not say, as we might expect, "To love that well which thou must *lose* ere long"; rather, "To love that well which thou must *leave* ere long." He sees his death as *her* leaving him, not the other way around. Throughout the poem, the speaker has expressed, not his self-image, but what he imagines to be his lover's image of him: "thou mayst in me behold," "In me thou see'st," and "This thou perceiv'st." By "leave" in line 14 he need not mean more than "leave behind," but the bitter taste of jealousy is on the word. He does not say, "To love *me* well *whom*," nor even "To love *him* well *whom*," but "To love *that* well *which*." The poet refers to himself as a thing, as though time had robbed him, in his lover's eyes, of manhood. Thus, the full weight of his fear of being rejected, replaced, falls on his odd choice of the word "leave." The complimentary statement stands, of course, but we feel the swirl of dramatic currents beneath its surface.

Such delicate precision of content in form is equally possible in fluid forms.

A Noiseless Patient Spider

WALT WHITMAN (1819–1892)

A noiseless patient spider,
I marked where on a little promontory it stood isolated,
Marked how to explore the vacant vast surrounding,
It launched forth filament, filament, filament, out of itself,
Ever unreeling them, ever tirelessly speeding them.   5

And you O my soul where you stand,
Surrounded, detached, in measureless oceans of space,
Ceaselessly musing, venturing, throwing, seeking the spheres to connect
    them,
Till the bridge you will need be formed, till the ductile anchor hold,
Till the gossamer thread you fling catch somewhere, O my soul.   10

The spacious lines, unreeling loosely out across the page, correspond to the long filaments the spider strings out into the wind when it is preparing to construct a web. The two stanzas, like paragraphs, one for the spider, one for the soul's "musing, venturing, throwing, seeking," shape the poem's central comparison.

This comparison is not presented mechanically, however. The spider's activities, described in stanza 1, are neither explained nor resolved until the last line of stanza 2. The success of the soul's "gossamer thread," catching and anchoring, implies a similar success for the spider. Notice the verbal echoes between various words in the two stanzas: "stood"/"stand," "surrounding"/"Surrounded," "tirelessly"/"Ceaselessly." Similar links bridge the images, as in the contrast of small to grand scale with "on a little promontory," followed in stanza 2 by "measureless oceans of space." After "promontory" (a headland or cliff jutting out into the ocean), the images of "oceans of space," "bridge," and "anchor" lend unity to the comparison. Like the spider's action, the poem's apparent randomness is in fact careful and purposeful.

Alliteration and assonance give some of the lines a unity of sound and emphasize the linear, filamentlike structure: *m*'s in line 2, *f*'s in line 4, and long *e*'s in "unreeling" and "speeding" in line 5. It is rhythm, however, that completes the effect. In lines 7–10 the *progression* of the caesuras toward the line-ends gives an almost visual impression of the filaments' lengthening toward ultimate contact—confirmed in sound by the half-hidden rhyme (hold-soul) in lines 9–10:

> Surrounded, ‖ detached, ‖ in measureless oceans of space,
> Ceaselessly musing, ‖ venturing, ‖ throwing, ‖ seeking the spheres to connect them,
> Till the bridge you will need be formed, ‖ till the ductile anchor hold,
> Till the gossamer thread you fling catch somewhere, ‖ O my soul.

Although Shakespeare's Sonnet 73 is an example of solid form and Whitman's "A Noiseless Patient Spider" of fluid form, these poems are more alike, as verse, than different. Each demands and rewards careful attention. They illustrate the richness of choice open to the poet concerned with writing his or her next poem. Classic forms such as sonnets are new and contemporary when they are used for fresh purposes, as in Marilyn Nelson Waniek's "Balance" (p. 115) or Robert Frost's "Design" (p. 305). The poet—writing as one must in the language and style of a particular time but keeping an eye on what poets of the past have done—must neither accept the moment's fashions too easily nor fear them.

BALANCE, IMBALANCE

Form is a poem's—a poet's—way of letting us notice things. The packed, heavy syllables of lines 1–2 of "Western Wind," for instance, contrast with the quick, lighter syllables of lines 3–4, showing different tones or elements of the speaker's complex feelings (sadness, expectation). A single line may, in its balance or imbalance, make us aware rhythmically of something unstated or only implicit in its meaning. Recall the last line of "A Noiseless Patient Spider," in its two very uneven parts: the long wavering "Till the gossamer thread you fling catch somewhere" and the short, ending fixity of "O my soul." Imbalances of Milton's lines about Mulciber help give the illusion of falling in space.

A line, as the basic unit of verse, may have its own inner structure of relationships. One feels, for example, the antitheses or strict balancing of parts in these lines from Alexander Pope's "The Rape of the Lock":

> Whether the nymph shall break Diana's Law,
> Or some frail *China* Jar receive a Flaw,
> Or stain her Honour, or her new Brocade,
> Forget her Pray'rs, or miss a Masquerade,
> Or lose her Heart, or Necklace, at a Ball. . .
>
> II, 105–109

The irony of course lies in treating the important and the trivial with equal significance: to lose her chastity or to chip a China jar, to stain her honor or a mere brocade, and so on. The first contrast balances in two lines, but then the madness of misplaced values escalates and each line contains its own pithy contrast. Two heavily accented syllables on each side of the caesuras underline the balance rhythmically:

> Or stain her Honour, ‖ or her new Brocade,
>
> Forget her Pray'rs, ‖ or miss a Masquerade,
>
> Or lose her Heart, ‖ or Necklace, at a Ball…

The balance or imbalance may be—and usually is—a good deal subtler than in Pope's lines; and it may function equally in poems in meter or in poems in free verse. In an elegant essay, "Listening and Making," Robert Hass points out the rhythmical imbalance in these lines (4–5) from Whitman's "Song of Myself":

> I loaf and invite to my soul,
>
> I lean and loaf at my ease ‖ observing a spear of summer grass.

The rhythm of the first line (three accents) is essentially repeated by the first part of the second line (three accents); but the second part not only extends the line but does so by *four* accents. Hass notes the accents by line, with a single slash showing caesura: 3, 3/4. He comments: "Had Whitman written *observing a spear of grass*, all three phrases would be nearly equivalent. . . ; instead he adds *summer*, the leaning and loafing season, and announces both at the level of sound and of content that this poem is going to be free and easy."

As a further example Hass offers this little poem by Whitman:

A Farm Picture

> Through the ample open door of the peaceful country barn,
> A sunlit pasture field with cattle and horses feeding,
> And haze and vista, and the far horizon fading away.

Each line has six accents, divided (by a light phrasal pause or caesura in lines 1 and 2) in this way:

3 / 3
3 / 3
2 / 4

The asymmetry of line 3 (2/4) effectively resolves the pattern (as a 3/3 version of the line might not), releasing the tension, letting the rhythm come to rest in the longer, four-accent phrase, "and the far horizon fading away."

We may take the point further. Lines 1–2 are linked by more than their parallel, balancing rhythms. Mechanically, they make up one of the poem's two sentences; and together they present the speaker's place—the frame of the open barn doorway, "the cattle and horses feeding" seen at a middle distance. The appearance is of order and plenty; the barn is "ample," "peaceful," the pasture sunny. However, if we can intuit the speaker's feelings in the symmetric rhythms of the verbless, action-less sentence, the scene seems also static and unsatisfying.

The asymmetry of rhythm in line 3 suggests what troubles him as his eyes rise to glimpse it: "haze and vista, and the far horizon fading away." He is drawn to the uncertain and far-off, because it represents possibilities either longed for or unreal-ized ("fading"). Perhaps he pauses from his work. His vantage point, within the shade of the barn, suggests an unexpected melancholy. After the very slight caesuras (unmarked by punctuation) in lines 1–2, the decisive caesura in line 3 helps give a sense of incompleteness, of division, as the last and longest phrase, "and the far horizon fading away," ends the poem with a lingering attention to what is both distant and vanishing. The sentence in line 3 also lacks a main verb. "A Farm Picture" is a still life, in more than one sense of the word.

Considering balance/imbalance, look again at the couplet of Shakespeare's Son-net 73. Its peculiar dolefulness no doubt comes in part from the lines' succession of virtually heavy, monosyllabic accents. (It would be hard not to count "thy" and "ere.")

This thóu percéiv'st, ‖ which mákes thý lóve móre stróng,

To lóve thát wéll ‖ which thóu múst léave ére lóng.

The sense of unresolved feeling comes also in part from the pattern of accents:

3 / 5

3 / 5

Both lines pause exactly between the second and third foot. Lack of change leaves the tension unrelieved. A certain grimness of tone, moreover, seems implied in the unrelenting parallel of the two "which" clauses.

In the previous examples, lines are end-stopped. In this daring poem by Louise Glück (b. 1943), however, a number of the lines are strongly run-on. Observe how this technique reinforces the effect of their irregularity and often striking imbalance:

The Racer's Widow

The elements have merged into solicitude.
Spasms of violets rise above the mud
And weed and soon the birds and ancients
Will be starting to arrive, bereaving points
South. But never mind. It is not painful to discuss   5
His death. I have been primed for this,
For separation, for so long. But still his face assaults
Me, I can hear that car careen again, the crowd coagulate on asphalt
In my sleep. And watching him, I feel my legs like snow

That let him finally let him go   10
As he lies draining there. And see
How even he did not get to keep that lovely body.

Full caesuras divide lines 4–9 and 11, and we may count the accents as balancing:
3 / 2, 1 / 2 / 3, 1 / 3, 1 / 2 / 3, 1 / 5 / 3, 1 / 2 / 3, and 4 / 1. (Note that four lines have
two caesuras.) Unmarked by punctuation, a caesura after "And weed," which completes the phrase in line 2, also breaks line 3: 1 / 3. The run-ons, particularly those
that flow from and to caesuras very near the ends or beginnings of lines (like "But
still his face assaults / Me,"), give the poem's rhythm an extreme effect of starting
and stopping, of jerking forward, of careening, like a car out of control.

The widow's assertion that "It is not painful to discuss / His death" is contra-
dicted not only by the jagged rhythms, but by the imagery that suggests how dis-
traught she really is ("Spasms of violets," "I can hear . . . the crowd coagulate on
asphalt") and by the deliberately inexact rhyming. Oddly, the only exact rhyme
depends on "snow," a word that makes little sense in a sentence otherwise less than
fully coherent. The repetition in line 10—"That let him finally let him go"—
sounds natural but of course is not. Everything in the poem works to convey the
widow's repressed but ill-concealed emotional turmoil.

A quite different impression emerges in the rhythm of the following poem by
Elizabeth Spires (b. 1952). The speaker, three months pregnant, meditates lan-
guorously.

Letter in July

My life slows and deepens.
I am thirty-eight, neither here nor there.
It is a morning in July, hot and clear.
Out in the field, a bird repeats its quaternary call,
four notes insisting, *I'm here, I'm here.*   5
The field is unmowed, summer's wreckage everywhere.
Even this early, all is expectancy.

It is as if I float on a still pond,
drowsing in the bottom of a rowboat,
curled like a leaf into myself.   10
The water laps at its old wooden sides
as the sun beats down on my body,
a wand, an enchantment, shaping it
into something languid and new.

A year ago, two, I dreamed I held   15
a mirror to your unborn face and saw you,
in the warped watery glass, not as a child
but as you will be twenty years from now.
I woke, a light breeze lifting the curtain,
as if touched by a ghost's thin hand,   20
light filling the room, coming from nowhere.

I know the time, the place of our meeting.
It will be January, the coldest night
of the year. You will be carrying a lantern
as you enter the world crying,   25
and I cry to hear you cry.
A moment that, even now,
I carry in my body.

The sense of stasis in Spires's poem is very strong. Most of the lines are end-stopped; five of the seven lines in stanza 1 are complete sentences. The run-ons tend to be weak, like the one linking lines 11 and 12, which connects full clauses. Caesuras usually occur mid-line, suggesting balance. One exception, in line 13—"a wand, an enchantment, shaping it"—evokes balance in a different way by framing the central phrase. Only in line 19 does the early caesura start an unsettling rhythm, but this is quickly absorbed by the ensuing end-stops and the symmetrical rhythm of the two phrases in line 21:

light fìllĭng thĕ róom, ‖ cŏmĭng frŏm nówhére.

The poet's control is consummate.

As you write, especially as you revise, be aware of balance or imbalance as a quality of your lines' rhythm. This awareness will often let you sense what's going right, or going wrong, as a passage develops.

SPACE AND OBJECT: LINE-LENGTH, STANZAS

Line-length and whether to use stanzas are among the almost instinctive choices poets make in beginning a poem. Any number of considerations will be involved. One easily overlooked, however, is the poem's visual, or even sculptural, character on the page: space and object. A sense of the possibilities, of the shape the poem will offer to the eye, can often be a subliminal guide in the choices the poet makes in composing.

As to line-length, for instance, the first phrases of the emerging poem may come with a sense of how they want to be deployed in lines. Perhaps in their rhythm the poet already hears a line-break. Usually, shorter lines lend themselves to lightness, ease, speed, wit, delicacy. Longer lines tend toward weight, substance, difficulty, seriousness, sonority. When the lines of a poem are of markedly differing lengths, it may suggest hesitancy, agitation, excitement, or even, as in Robert Frost's "After Apple-Picking" (p. 103), the somnambulance of dream.

The resulting appearance of the poem on the page will be an invitation, conceivably a message, to the reader. Is the poem narrow but longer, wide but shorter? Is it slender, bony, quick? Solid, heavy, full? Are the lines nearly even, smooth, or raggedy, jumpy, mixing long and short? Do its lines get gradually longer, shorter, as it goes along? Will the form give a reader an accurate first impression of the poem, of its tone? Glance at Richard Wilbur's "Hamlen Brook" (p. 27) and Charles Simic's "Stone" (p. 27). The poems have almost exactly the same number of words, but they greet the reader rather differently. Generally, given a text of a certain length, the more lines, the more movement.

The choice to use **stanzas**, and what sort—couplets, triplets, quatrains, and so on—may involve considerations of visual effect. Stanzas, for instance, express a poem's organization. (See Appendix I, "A Glossary of Forms," pp. 369-379, for more about stanzaic types.)

Stanzas may be "closed," ending with a completed sentence, or "open," continuing a sentence across the stanza-break. Closed stanzas may, like paragraphs in prose, correspond to units of meaning (as in Whitman's "A Noiseless Patient Spider"), segments of an argument (as in Francis's "Glass"), or scenes or phases of an action in narrative (as in Gillian Conoley's "The Woman on the Homecoming Float," p. 23). A poem may also mix closed and open stanzas. Such choices, made in the process of writing, have to do with flow or structure, with poise or momentum. For a poem like Marianne Moore's "The Fish" (p. 46), given the fluid and shifting undersea-scapes of its subject matter, open stanzas seem obvious, as do the varying (rather than equal) line-lengths of the stanza form she chose.

The triplets of "Upon Julia's Clothes" by Robert Herrick (1591–1674) present spatially (as the rhymes do in sound) the central contrast:

> Whenas in silks my Julia goes
> Then, then, methinks, how sweetly flows
> That liquefaction of her clothes.
>
> Next, when I cast mine eyes, and see
> That brave vibration, each way free,   5
> O, how that glittering taketh me!

Julia's walking in silks is lovely (stanza 1), but when—"next," for time passes before the speaker looks again—when she goes disrobed, "each way free," the beauty is irresistible (stanza 2). "Brave," as well as meaning fine or splendid (as of clothes), of course suggests daring and boldness. The wonderful coinage "liquefaction," literally making liquid of something, derives from "flows" in line 2, and leads to the fishing image implicit in "cast" and "taketh" in stanza 2. He casts his look like a fishing line and—a witty reversal, the fisherman caught—is "taken" by her naked loveliness, which readily excels the glittering of her silks.

The poem would not be essentially different if the six lines were presented without the stanza-break. But the blank space helps, both by visually anticipating the two-fold idea and by indicating the passage of a bit of time, thus giving emphasis to "Next, when."

Every poem has, for the reader, a visual element. The shape on the page establishes at least a subliminal predisposition as to tone or theme, weight or lightness, fixity or casualness, calm or agitation, and so on. Often, as with "Upon Julia's Clothes," this may seem no more than we should find in the sounds and ideas in any case. But perhaps even with the most predictable form, the quatrains of Updike's "Player Piano" (p. 95), for example, something has been added subliminally—a promise of precision.

Glance at the Poems to Consider (pp. 23-30), indeed at poems throughout the book, and note the variety of shapes. When you come to read them later, consider how the shape of each poem reflects or is appropriate to it. Notice the different "feel" of poems with or without stanzas, of those with regular or irregular stanzas, of those with smaller and larger stanzas; of poems with lines of virtually equal or greatly unequal lengths. Small, perhaps nearly imperceptible things matter—the slight forward-pushing effect of the indentation in lines 2 and 4 of Armour's "Going to Extremes," for instance. Or the suggestion of greater reach and daring in the generally *longer* lines of stanza 2 of Whitman's "The Noiseless Patient Spider."

Consider the use of stanzas in a more complex poem by Thomas Lux (b. 1946). Look at it long enough before reading to form a distinct impression.

Tarantulas on the Lifebuoy

For some semitropical reason
when the rains fall
relentlessly they fall

into swimming pools, these otherwise
bright and scary   5
arachnids. They can swim
a little, but not for long

and they can't climb the ladder out.
They usually drown—but
if you want their favor,   10
if you believe there is justice,
a reward for not loving

the death of ugly
and even dangerous (the eel, hog snake,
rats) creatures, if   15

you believe these things, then
you would leave a lifebuoy
or two in your swimming pool at night.

And in the morning
you would haul ashore   20
the huddled, hairy survivors

and escort them
back to the bush, and know,
be assured that at least these saved,
as individuals, would not turn up   25

again someday
in your hat, drawer,
or the tangled underworld

of your socks, and that even—
when your belief in justice   30
merges with your belief in dreams—
they may tell the others

in a sign language
four times as subtle
and complicated as man's   35

that you are good,
that you love them,
that you would save them again.

Lines are fairly uneven and stanzas strongly run-on, sentences flowing over so that the stanza-breaks do not seem to be ordering meaning. Seven of the stanzas have three lines, creating a sort of norm, but several have four and one has five lines. From its appearance, the poem might seem unfinished—not to have quite resolved itself into regularity. Yet this uncertainty fits the poem's tone. Observing spiders habitually fallen into pools, the speaker is speculating on the possibility of saving them. The statements are tentative, conditional: *if. . .* , *if. . .* , *if. . .* , then you *would . . .* , they *would . . .* , and then they even *may . . . .*

We understand that the speaker does not really believe that the human values of justice and reward and goodness will function in the natural world of the tarantulas. The notion of saving them founders on the fact that the world is as it is, wasteful, often at cross purposes, and not as we might compassionately or tidily wish it. The poem doesn't state this conclusion, but implies it by in effect abandoning the impractical speculation, leaving it incomplete.

The tentativeness, as of thinking still in process, shows also in the syntax. The word "relentlessly" in line 3 might go with "when the rains fall" in line 2 or, ambiguously, with the following phrase, "they fall / into swimming pools." It works equally with both. On first reading, the pronoun "they" in line 3 seems to refer to "the rains," but of course refers to the spiders, as we discover from the added apposition, "these otherwise / bright and scary / arachnids" in lines 4–6. We sense the speaker revising his thought as he goes, for instance, in "and know, / be assured" in lines 23–24, or in the effort at exactitude of "these saved, / *as individuals*," in lines 25–26. The poem is a meditation, precarious, exploring, deliciously displayed.

As always, both line and stanza, breaking the ongoing meaning into fresh units, are ways in which a poem calls for greater attention to facets, to the parts of a statement, and so compresses, focuses, and implies.

QUESTIONS AND SUGGESTIONS

1. Here are two poems printed as prose. Experiment with turning them into verse by dividing the lines in different ways. What different effects can you create? The

originals, as well as all further notes to the Questions and Suggestions, can be found in Appendix II (pp. 381-388).

a) Theology

There is a heaven, for ever, day by day, the upward longing of my soul doth tell me so. There is a hell, I'm quite as sure; for pray, if there were not, where would my neighbors go?

b) Braille

The blind folding their dollar bills in half. Giving the fives a crease on each corner; leaving the tens smooth as a knuckle. There are ways, even in trust among the rank and file of the seeing, not to be bilked. The blind leading the blind is not so bad—how it is lost on us every day that you can learn all of the world you need to know by tapping it gently with a stick.

2. Compare the following poems with Whitman's "A Noiseless Patient Spider" (p. 12). How has what the poets are saying influenced their formal decisions? Perhaps write a poem of your own about a spider, choosing the form with deliberation. Or try an ant, housefly, or other small creature that you can observe carefully.

a)   *Spider*

JAN M. W. ROSE*

Afraid for both of them,
her movements, uncertain,
she lightfoots it between

twelve intersections of thread
and an odd collector's item: 5
a strange dark bug she keeps

knotted in a silk pouch
tight as a cherry pit.
Gnats hover in the moist air

languorous with conversation.   10
"She's strange" they murmur,
riding tiny currents of air.

About her are slung
a dozen males,
bulging in their white hammocks,   15

shimmering in porch light.
Even as she wanders,
legs tapping the wires

---

*Throughout *Writing Poems*, an asterisk following the poet's name indicates that the poem was written when the poet was a student.

like piano strings,
they bob up and down,   20
suspended hard in sleep.

But her long worn Utility
chooses none; the captive males
curl tighter in their nets;

and dropping her blue-white line,   25
for a moment—she fidgets—
then turns into shadow.

b)   *These Heady Flowers*

ELIZABETH KIRSCHNER (b. 1955)

I am living deeply now
like the white spider I spy
among the wild roses. She lifts her legs,
moves her small ghostly body across each flower
like moonlight in a house. She is the snowflake   5
vanishing. Her fall from the dark sky
matters. It is quick and bright.
Her web is a beautiful hope
easily undone, a fabric transient as tears.
She lays it all upon these heady flowers   10
which for her are the world: flushed,
falling, gorgeous and doomed.

3. Consider how much "In the Morning, In the Morning," written in 1895 by A. E. Housman (1859–1936), depends on **implication.** How do we know that the characters are lovers? How are we led to understand what has happened? What lets us know that they are regretful?

In the morning, in the morning,
   In the happy field of hay,
Oh they looked at one another
   By the light of day.

In the blue and silver morning   5
   On the haycock as they lay,
Oh they looked at one another
   And they looked away.

4. After you have read "Read This Poem from the Bottom Up" by Ruth Porritt (p. 25), draw some conclusions about the way layout affects the normal experience of reading verse.

5. Explore the formal decisions the poet made in writing this poem, which presents a dialogue, with interpolated thoughts, between a wife and husband. [Pirouettes are pastries. Earl Grey is a tea.] How does she deploy the poem in a system of indentations? What about the run-on from line 8 to line 9?

Chinese Print: No Translation

PEGGY SHUMAKER (b. 1952)

Without warning, the woman says,
  Our marriage has become a business.
How can you say that, when you know I love you, etc. etc.,
  her husband cries. He serves her pirouettes and Earl Grey
  on porcelain dishes, but it's not enough.   5
What can I give you? What do you want?
  But secretly, so far I'm the only man brave enough
  to take you on, and you know it. Still,
What can I give you? What do you want?
  But if he has to ask, it doesn't count.   10
As in, if he can't swim naked at midnight
  on a deserted beach
  without worrying about phosphorescent plankton
  and our traveler's checks, forget it.
At dawn, she washes up on the beach,   15
  fire-coral dreams searing her thighs.
Brown UPS trucks search for her husband, each one
  delivering what has to be signed for.

6. Choose a poem of your own that you aren't really satisfied with and experiment with its form. Rearrange the sentences into lines either much shorter or much longer than in the original version. Try breaking the poem into stanzas of two, then three lines, and so on. If something *feels right*, you may have found a way to start the poem going again.

7. Look ahead to Shakespeare's Sonnets 30 (p. 204) and 130 (p. 211). What rhythmical balance/imbalance do you find in the lines of each final couplet? How is the feeling or mood of the poems' endings affected? Read them aloud several times before deciding.

8. Write a poem either a) in strictly alternating lines of seven and five *words* in length, or b) in stanzas progressively one line shorter or one line longer than the first one. What difficulties do you find? What opportunities?

POEMS TO CONSIDER

 ### The Woman on the Homecoming Float   *1991*

GILLIAN CONOLEY (b. 1955)

Only once I saw my chance
and broke, hiked up the flatbed, deposed
the queen, the runners-up,
and shot first

the Cadillac rear tires before me   5
front tires of tractor behind,
then the sky over and over
until everyone had to stare
at the brutal truth.

A curiosity more curious than any   10
I poured straight whiskey
all the way down
to the hooded red roses of my heart.

The deputy
his shirt off in the heat   15
smoked one after another
and beseeched why, Ruby why,
long into the twilight
until I heard myself saying
oh why don't we just go to the game   20
and forget it.

It was then he offered me his arm.
In the bleachers I got carried away,
I wanted to throw myself
into the recreations of the dirt   25
and try to hurt a little too
because as everyone said
it was better to die trying
than not to die.

The inky night, the tiara stars   30
were mine.
And I could have been queen.

The Three Poets   1916

EZRA POUND (1885–1972)

Candidia has taken a new lover
And three poets are gone into mourning.
The first has written a long elegy to 'Chloris,'
To 'Chloris chaste and cold,' his 'only Chloris.'
The second has written a sonnet   5
                  upon the mutability of woman,
And the third writes an epigram to Candidia.

Read This Poem from the Bottom Up   1987
RUTH PORRITT (b. 1957)

This simple cathedral of praise.
How you made, from the bottom up,
Is for you to remember
Of Andromeda. What remains

Until you meet the ancient light   5
With your sight you can keep ascending
Its final transformation into space.
And uphold

The horizon's urge to sculpt the sky
Puts into relief   10
Your family's mountain land
Upon the rising air. In the distance

A windward falcon is open high and steady
Far above the tallest tree
Just beyond your height.   15
You see a young pine lifting its green spire

By raising your eyes
Out onto the roof deck.
You pass through sliding glass doors
And up to where the stairway ends.   20

To the top of the penultimate stanza
Past the second story,
But now you're going the other way,
Line by line, to the bottom of the page.

A force that usually pulls you down,   25
Of moving against the gravity of habit,
While trying not to notice the effort
And feel what it's like to climb stairs

Composed upon Westminster Bridge, September 3, 1802
WILLIAM WORDSWORTH (1770–1850)

Earth has not anything to show more fair:
Dull would he be of soul who could pass by

A sight so touching in its majesty:
This City now doth, like a garment, wear
The beauty of the morning; silent, bare,   5
Ships, towers, domes, theatres, and temples lie
Open unto the fields, and to the sky;
All bright and glittering in the smokeless air.
Never did sun more beautifully steep
In his first splendour, valley, rock, or hill;   10
Ne'er saw I, never felt, a calm so deep!
The river glideth at his own sweet will:
Dear God! the very houses seem asleep;
And all that mighty heart is lying still!

 ## The Sacred Cows of Los Angeles   *1982*

GERALD COSTANZO (b. 1945)

As if it had never happened
an old Angeleno will remember
the coming of the word *smog.*

How in 1948 a meteorologist
predicted the end of the past   5
in four letters. How the sacred

cows brought with them traffic
lights and street signs, cross-
walks and the dotted line,

which after a while they began   10
to ignore. Pausing at corners,
they'd drool a pool of oil

and maybe etch a rubber patch,
leaving. They were fed
whatever it took. They were washed   15

and shined. At night they'd idle
through La Cienega or watch
from a lovers' lane over

the cool Pacific. They'd snooze
beneath the flickering face   20
of the Escondido Drive-In

or sleep in garages, nestled
in the waning fumes—safe,
a few hours, from the future, safe

from the sight of the full moon,   25
a pomegranate resting
on the hazy lip of Los Angeles.

Stone   *1971*

CHARLES SIMIC (b. 1938)

Go inside a stone
That would be my way.
Let somebody else become a dove
Or gnash with a tiger's tooth.
I am happy to be a stone.   5

From the outside the stone is a riddle:
No one knows how to answer it.
Yet within, it must be cool and quiet
Even though a cow steps on it full weight,
Even though a child throws it in a river;   10
The stone sinks, slow, unperturbed
To the river bottom
Where the fishes come to knock on it
And listen.

I have seen sparks fly out   15
When two stones are rubbed,
So perhaps it is not dark inside after all;
Perhaps there is a moon shining
From somewhere, as though behind a hill—
Just enough light to make out   20
The strange writings, the star-charts
On the inner walls.

Hamlen Brook   *1982*

RICHARD WILBUR (b. 1921)

    At the alder-darkened brink
      Where the stream slows to a lucid jet
I lean to the water, dinting its top with sweat,
      And see, before I can drink,

      A startled inchling trout   5
        Of spotted near-transparency,
Trawling a shadow solider than he.
      He swerves now, darting out

To where, in a flicked slew
   Of sparks and glittering silt, he weaves
Through stream-bed rocks, disturbing foundered leaves,   10
   And butts then out of view

   Beneath a sliding glass
   Crazed by the skimming of a brace
Of burnished dragon-flies across its face,   15
   In which deep cloudlets pass

   And a white precipice
   Of mirrored birch-trees plunges down
Toward where the azures of the zenith drown.
   How shall I drink all this?   20

   Joy's trick is to supply
   Dry lips with what can cool and slake,
Leaving them dumbstruck also with an ache
   Nothing can satisfy.

Peepers   1992

MARGARET HOLLEY (b. 1944)

One amber inch
of blinking berry-eyed
amphibian,

four fetal fingers
on each hand,   5
a honey and mud-brown

pulse of appetite
surprised into stillness,
folded in a momentary lump

of flying bat-fish   10
ready to jump
full-tilt into anything

—the whole strength
of its struggling length
you can hold in your hand.   15

Its poetry, a raucous
refrain of pleasure
in the April-warm pools

of rain, the insistent
chorus of whistles   20
jingles through night woods,

Females! It's time!
that confident come-on
to a whole wet population

of embraces, eggs, tadpoles   25
—all head and tail,
mind darting in every direction

until the articulating torso,
Ovidian bag of bones,
results in the "mature adult":   30

a rumpled face in the mirror
still sleeping through Basho's°
awakening plop,

re-enchanted daily
by the comforting slop   35
of burgeoning spring woods

and all this sexual chatter,
doing its best to make
the wet and silky season

last forever. Yet   40
as you lie dreaming mid-leap,
splayed in the sheets,

the future as a kind
but relentless scientist
feels around in your flesh   45

for the nerve of surprise;
he just loves
the look of wonder on your face,

the word on your open lips
for the immensity   50
that grips you,

Oh.

32 For Basho's poem, see p. 377.

The Kiss   *1995*

MARTA TOMES *

— a painting by Gustav Klimpt

He knows he is irresistible. No doubt he has
looked in the mirror wearing his stained glass robe

and seen the cropped curls and stately shoulders
of Marc Antony. He cups my head like an infant

and lifts my chin toward him. He thinks I am shy;   5
my eyes are closed, my face turned away. He thinks

that this arm slung about his neck is my embrace,
that I've shrunken my shoulders forward so the dress

slides down my white arms just for him. This swirling
pekoe aura around me, he believes, exudes   10

my great excitement. I am trapped on my knees
on a cliff of flowers, and I've braced myself.

My bare toes tense forward, stiff as triggers.

2

FREE VERSE
Invisible Nets and Trellises

Fluid form has several names, including organic or open form. The familiar name, of course, is **free verse**. Borrowed from the French *vers libre*, the term means verse written without a particular or recognizable meter. Since verse requires some system of measure, some internal signal when a new line should begin, the term *free verse* may seem self-contradictory. Indeed, verse that really is free of any measure often ends up as arbitrary, random, "chopped-up prose." Robert Frost compares such verse to playing tennis without a net—too easy, no fun. W. H. Auden describes the problem:

> The poet who writes "free" verse is like Robinson Crusoe on his desert island: he must do all his cooking, laundry and darning for himself. In a few exceptional cases, this manly independence produces something original and impressive, but more often the result is squalor—dirty sheets on the unmade bed and empty bottles on the unswept floor.

Even Ezra Pound, who championed free verse in 1912, was soon complaining:

> Indeed *vers libre* has become as prolix and as verbose as any of the flaccid varieties that preceded it. It has brought faults of its own. The actual language and phrasing is often as bad as that of our elders without even the excuse that the words are shovelled in to fill a metric pattern or to complete the noise of a rhyme-sound.

He concluded: "Eliot has said the thing very well when he said, No *vers* is *libre* for the man who wants to do a good job."

Despite the danger of slackness, *The Princeton Encyclopedia of Poetry and Poetics* notes that free verse "has become so common as to have some claim to being the characteristic form of the age." Many finely wrought, even formal poems have been written in free verse. That must be the test—the form is good that works.

There is, however, little practical theory of free verse. Poets who have written successfully have done so largely through intuition. A well-tuned ear—a delicate sensitivity to language—finds the right form, right rhythm, which, in Pound's words, "corresponds exactly to the emotion or shade of emotion to be expressed." Poets often do this without being able to explain how, just as readers may respond to such rhythms without knowing, technically, why. The view, passed along by Allen Ginsberg, that length of line is somehow determined by the poet's breath, is purely impressionistic and of no use in practice. (Do poets who write very short lines, for instance, suffer from emphysema?) William Carlos Williams's notion of the "variable foot," suggestive though it is, is also vague. His rhythms and forms may be imitated, but there is no satisfactory account of the principles underlying them.

As a beginning poet, you will have to find tempting models and work experimentally from them in developing your own free verse. Until there is an adequate theory, though, rough distinctions may help. Three basic types of free verse can be distinguished. They may be called end-stopped, run-on, and spatial, though, of course, any given poem may mix these characteristics.

END-STOPPED FREE VERSE

The father of modern end-stopped free verse is Walt Whitman, although there are historical antecedents in the "verse" of the King James Bible of 1611 (especially in Psalms, Ecclesiastes, and chapter 38 of Job), in Christopher Smart's *Rejoice in the Lamb*, and in William Blake's prophetic poems in the eighteenth century. Walt Whitman's "A Noiseless Patient Spider" (p. 12) exemplifies end-stopped free verse, as does the first section of "Song of Myself":

> I celebrate myself, and sing myself,
> And what I assume you shall assume,
> For every atom belonging to me as good belongs to you.
>
> I loaf and invite my soul,
> I lean and loaf at my ease observing a spear of summer grass.   5
>
> My tongue, every atom of my blood, formed from this soil, this air,
> Born here of parents born here from parents the same, and their
>   parents the same,
> I, now thirty-seven years old in perfect health begin,
> Hoping to cease not till death.
>
> Creeds and schools in abeyance,   10
> Retiring back a while sufficed at what they are, but never forgotten,
> I harbor for good or bad, I permit to speak at every hazard,
> Nature without check with original energy.

Line-breaks occur at syntactical or grammatical pauses or intervals; that, simply, identifies end-stopped free verse. Although the lines vary considerably in length, they are generally long and loose, allowing for great variety in rhythm with or without internal pauses (caesuras). They are essentially in prose rhythm, that is, rangy and irregular, but are heightened by recurring phrases, as in line 7, or by recurring parallel structures, as in lines 4–5. Interestingly, the first line is traditional iambic pentameter:

I cĕlĕbráte mўsélf, ănd síng mўsélf.

Whitman seems to imply that his free verse was essentially an opening up of the traditional line of English metrical verse.

End-stopped free verse tends toward long lines because they permit internal pauses and greater internal rhythmic variation. The line-end pauses provide the structure of the verse, with caesural pauses modulating the rhythm. The muscular cadence of end-stopped free verse derives in large part from the tension between these two kinds of pauses.

Short lines of end-stopped free verse diminish the possibility of internal pause and variation. In the logical extreme—where every syntactical unit is given an individual line—the tension disappears and all that remains is chopped prose. Suppose the sixth line of the passage were rearranged:

My tongue,
every atom of my blood,
formed from this soil,
this air. . .

The result merely parallels the phrasal pauses of prose. Beginners often mistakenly divide lines this way, and the impact is about as arresting, in its lack of variety, as a stack of lumber. Line in verse, however one measures or defines it, must somehow *cut across* the natural flow of sentences, at least often enough to allow one to distinguish its rhythm from prose.

End-stopped free verse may, of course, be written in lines shorter than Whitman's. One instance is this droll poem by Jim Daniels (b. 1956):

Short-order Cook

An average joe comes in
and orders thirty cheeseburgers and thirty fries.

I wait for him to pay before I start cooking.
He pays.
He ain't no average joe.   5

The grill is just big enough for ten rows of three.
I slap the burgers down
throw two buckets of fries in the deep frier
and they pop pop spit spit . . .
psss . . .   10
The counter girls laugh.
I concentrate.

It is the crucial point—
they are ready for the cheese:
my fingers shake as I tear off slices   15
toss them on the burgers/fries done/dump/
refill buckets/burgers ready/flip into buns/
beat that melting cheese/wrap burgers in plastic/
into paper bags/fries done/dump/fill thirty bags/
bring them to the counter/wipe sweat on sleeve   20
and smile at the counter girls.
I puff my chest out and bellow:
"Thirty cheeseburgers, thirty fries!"
They look at me funny.
I grab a handful of ice, toss it in my mouth   25
do a little dance and walk back to the grill.
Pressure, responsibility, success,
thirty cheeseburgers, thirty fries.

Stanzas pace the narrative—two, three, and then twenty-three lines, the last recounting the main action and the cook's triumph.

Only lines 1, 8, and 20 are weakly run-on (at the *and*'s of compound sentences). The rest are end-stopped, including lines 7, 15, and 25 where commas would normally set off the distinct clauses. (Their omission perhaps suggests the haste of the action as well as the casualness of the report.) Line 1 establishes what seems to be a norm or base for the poem's rhythm: three accents, "An áverage jóe comes ín," which is answered directly in line 5, "He áin't no áverage jóe," and paralleled in line 7, "I sláp the búrgers dówn," and in lines 11, 13–14. Four longer lines in the first third of the poem have five accents, but with slight caesuras after three accents, as in "and órders thírty cheesebúrgers ‖ and thírty fríes," thus carrying on the rhythmic base of the three-accent lines. Two lines of one accent add emphases, "psss . . ." deftly focusing the *p* and *sp* sounds of line 9, "and they pop pop spit spit . . . /psss . . ." The poem's one other shorter-than-norm line, "I concentrate," also seems expressive.

A striking device at "the crucial point" of the assembly of the burgers and fries is the use of slashes in lines 16–21. With no usual syntactical subordination, the phrases/actions thus isolated seem equal, in an almost cartoonlike speeding up, hasty and also rigid, mechanical. There are slashed lines of three phrases, then three, two, four, and two phrases—a movement that resolves into two lines of three accents:

and smíle at the cóunter gírls.

I púff my chést out and béllow:

Line 24 also repeats the three-accent norm, "They lóok at mé fúnny," and it seems right to see lines 25–26 as an excited *doubling* of the norm; each has, divided by caesuras, two phrases of three accents:

> I gráb a hándful of íce, ‖ tóss it ín my móuth
>
> dó a líttle dánce ‖ and wálk báck to the gríll.

This sort of balance is repeated in the final lines—three words, then two phrases:

> Préssure, ‖ respónsíbílity, ‖ succéss,
>
> thírty cheesebúrgers, ‖ thírty fríes.

We might schematize the accents of lines 25–28 this way:

3	3	
3	3	
1	3	1
	2	2

The near-rhyme of the first and last syllables of line 27—"*Pressure-success*"—emphasizes this feeling of balance. After the relative flexibility of the rest of the poem, this strong balancing of accents and phrases gives closure to the poem's rhythm and may underline the irony in the short-order cook's glory. Though we empathize with him, don't we perhaps also feel that he takes it all a shade too seriously? Such a perspective is invited in the expectation (line 11) and the response of the counter girls: "They look at me funny."

Handled subtly and complexly, the poem's rhythm is at once varied and—notice—*measuring*.

In analyzing and discussing the technical aspect of free verse, it is necessary to follow the poem, that is, to look in it for patterns that may be serving to organize and present—patterns of accent, phrase, repetition, syntax, relative line-length, stanza-shape, and so on. Because the poet is free to use any system at all, or several at once, the critic or inquiring reader may need to be inventive. In "Short-order Cook," a three-accent norm (with variations) modulates into a balancing of phrases. A repeated key phrase is unbalanced in line 2—"and órders thírty cheesebúrgers ‖ and thírty fríes"—but is balanced in lines 23 and 25: "thírty cheesebúrgers, ‖ thírty fríes."

Other poems in end-stopped free verse include Michael Burns's "The First Time" (p. 338), the anonymous "The Frog" (p. 97), Robert Bly's "Waking from Sleep" (p. 209), Whitman's "When I Heard the Learn'd Astronomer" (p. 98). Looking back at Ezra Pound's "The Three Poets" (p. 24), note especially that none of the poem's three sentences lies across the verse lines in the same way, so the pace is varied, lithe and sinewy. Notice, too, that Pound has treated the end of the very long line 5 as a *dropped line* ("upon the mutability of woman"). While the phrase is long enough to have justified a line of its own, observe how wooden the movement would be if it began at the left margin:

> The second has written a sonnet
> Upon the mutability of woman,
> And the third writes an epigram to Candidia.

The dropped line not only adds flexibility and indicates subordination, but also prepares, like a whip whirling backwards, for the rhythmic decisiveness and snap of the last line. Does the shift to present tense—"writes"—perhaps suggest that Pound's speaker *is* the third poet, and this is his epigram to Candidia?

RUN-ON FREE VERSE

Along with others, notably William Carlos Williams and Marianne Moore, Ezra Pound explored and enhanced the possibilities of run-on free verse. The first stanza of his "The Return" exemplifies the form:

> See, they return; ah, see the tentative
> Movements, and the slow feet,
> The trouble in the pace and the uncertain
> Wavering!

The rhythmic character of the passage derives from the very strong run-on lines broken between adjectives and nouns: "the tentative / Movements" and "the uncertain / Wavering!" Both force a slightly abnormal pause, and this extra hesitation rhythmically evokes the tentative, uncertain feeling. Given a line by itself, "Wavering!" unexpectedly ends the stanza's flow, leaving it on an appropriately awkward diminuendo.

Since neither meter nor syntax determines where the lines must end, the choice may at first seem arbitrary in run-on free verse. Line-breaks tend to occur where there is no major grammatical or syntactical pause. Of course, the last line of a poem is inevitably end-stopped, and other lines may be. The texture of run-on free verse may vary, not only with the mixing in of end-stopped lines but also with the differences in *pull* of the various run-ons.

Pull is the force or speed of the line's turn—or, really, the force of the sentence's flow that the line-break ever so slightly interrupts. The eye or voice, reading, tends to pause *and* then hurry on somewhat more than if one were reading the passage as prose. This jog or awareness is the *metrical* element of run-on free verse. Try reading aloud the run-on in

> . . . ah, see the tentative
> Movements,

The wrench or pull is very strong due to the tight grammatical link of adjective to noun. You should feel, first, the slightest *pause* as voice and eye reach the unexpected break in the sentence's flow; then, second, as if to catch up, a slightly muscular *speeding up* as the voice turns the corner. Both the pause and the consequent release of energy give the run-on its rhythmic flavor. (Contrast the effect with a reading of the lines as prose, which is continuous and simply lets "tentative" flow into "movements." No pause, no energy.)

The dual quality of a run-on allows either pause or energy to seem predominant. Here, the effect is a pause, *hesitation*, which seems to imitate the meaning. Similarly, the strong run-ons (between preposition and the rest of the phrase, between adjective and noun) in

> into the pit of
> the empty
> flowerpot

help induce an impression of pause, *slowness*. But another, equally strong run-on may give the impression of speed, as in

> a flight of small
> cheeping birds
> skimming
> bare trees

Many run-ons (including most of those in metered verse) are relatively weak, occurring, for example, between a verb and its adverb or between two prepositional phrases as in Milton's

> thrown by angry Jove
> Sheer o'er the crystal battlements: from morn
> To noon he fell . . .

The pull or imbalance seems only a much slighter dislocation among related *phrases* lying across the line-break.

A simple scale of pull will help: three slashes (///) for strong pull; two (//) for moderate pull; one (/) for weak pull; and zero (0) for end-stopped lines. Here is a good example of run-on free verse:

To Waken an Old Lady

WILLIAM CARLOS WILLIAMS (1883–1963)

Old age is	//	
a flight of small	//	
cheeping birds	/	
skimming	//	
bare trees	/	5
above a snow glaze.	0	
Gaining and failing	/	
they are buffeted	/	
by a dark wind—	0	
But what?	0	10

On harsh weedstalks	/	
the flock has rested,	0	
the snow	/	
is covered with broken	///	
seedhusks	/	15
and the wind tempered	//	
by a shrill	///	
piping of plenty.	0	20

The short, oddly broken lines, with pulls of varying strengths, convey the speed and skittery movement of the small birds.

As always, the criterion is whether the form, free or strict, expresses its content. Of the poem's eighteen lines, thirteen are run-on and only five end-stopped. Seven lines have weak run-ons; four, moderate run-ons; and two, strong run-ons. As to run-ons, the poem has three movements. Lines 1–5 are moderately active (//-//-/-//-/). Lines 6–13 are weakly active (0-/-/-0-0-/-0-/). Lines 14–18 are strongly active (///-/-//-///-0). These movements correspond to the three phases of the poem. In lines 1–6 the birds are mobile, in flight, "skimming." In lines 7–13, they are defeated by the dark wind—the weak run-ons of lines 7–8 suggest their efforts ("Gaining") and their unsuccess ("and failing")—and come to rest on the "harsh weedstalks." The defeat, however, is momentary, for in lines 14–18 the activity is resumed, even increased, as they feed. The strong run-on of line 14—" is covered with broken /// seedhusks"—suggests or imitates the breaking open of the husks; and the strong run-on of line 17, again separating adjective and noun, emphasizes the vivacity of "shrill /// piping of plenty."

The poem's lines range in length from two to six syllables. Lines in the middle, where action slows, are generally longer than those at the beginning or end. Around the stark interrogative at the poem's center ("But what?") are six lines of four or five syllables, while shorter lines are characteristic of the more active parts of the poem. Local effects of the rhythm are also telling. The only two-syllable lines that come together—"skimming // bare trees"—give an impression of the swiftness of the birds' flight.

Another way of measuring what's going on in the rhythm is to scan run-on free verse, that is, mark the accented (´) and unaccented (˘) syllables. We can register the *drag, advance,* or *balance* of each line—how the weight of its syllables is distributed. (Drag has also been called a *falling line*; advance, a *rising line*.) Drag is the backward leaning of a line (accented running to unaccented syllables); it is marked with an arrow pointing left (←). Advance is the forward leaning of a line (unaccented running to accented syllables); the arrow is pointing right (→). And balance is a line whose pattern of accented and unaccented syllables is symmetrical, that is, leaning neither backward nor forward; the arrow points left and right (↔). We mark "To Waken an Old Lady" this way:

Óld áge ĭs   ←

ă flíght ŏf smáll   →

chĕepĭng bírds   ↔

skímmĭng   ←

báre trées   ↔   5

ăbóve ă snów gláze.   →

Gáinĭng ănd fáilĭng   ←

théy arĕ búffĕtĕd   ←

bў ă dárk wínd—   →

But whát?   ↔   10

Ŏn hársh wéedstálks   →

thĕ flóck hăs réstĕd,   ↔

thĕ snów   →

ĭs cóvĕred wĭth brókĕn   ↔

séedhúsks   ↔   15

ănd thĕ wínd témpĕred   →

bў ă shríll   →

pípĭng ŏf pléntў.   ←

Six lines show balance, twelve movement (five drag, seven advance). The poem's three sentences reveal a significant pattern. Sentence 1 (lines 1–6) shows: drag-advance-balance-drag-balance-advance. The mixture seems indeterminate, but ends on advance ("above a snow glaze"). The birds are flying, albeit low and with obstacles. In sentence 2—drag-drag-advance-balance—the rhythm corresponds to the sense: the drag-drag of lines 7–8 suggesting resistance, the difficulty of the birds' making headway against the wind, and ending in balance as they are defeated: "But what?" The first two clauses of sentence 3 repeat this pattern of movement giving way to stasis. In lines 11–12, advance-balance. In lines 13–15, more emphatically, advance-balance-balance. But the third clause (lines 16–18) resolves the pattern in movement: advance-advance-drag. The defeat in flying is replaced by the lively motion of feeding, and the poem ends on a note of muted triumph. The wind, their old adversary, is now tempered by the cheery piping "of plenty."

The similarly short, oddly broken lines of Williams's "Poem" offer an interesting contrast, conveying rather than speed and excitement, a feeling of catlike hesitancy and care.

Poem

As the cat
climbed over
the top of

the jamcloset
first the right   5
forefoot

carefully
then the hind
stepped down

into the pit of   10
the empty
flowerpot

Short lines do not necessarily produce rhythmic speed, any more than long lines necessarily produce slowness or ponderousness (Whitman's spider works rapidly), but in most cases they do. How, then, does Williams achieve the virtual slow motion of "Poem"?

The use of stanzas, though none is end-stopped, clearly slows and tends to accentuate the very deliberate rhythm, as does the fact that the poem is all one fairly long sentence. Moreover, the stronger syllabic norm may contribute. Line-length varies from two to five syllables, but eight of the twelve lines have three syllables. (Only two have two syllables, and only one each has four or five.)

Neither of these explanations seems sufficient, however, to account for the slow-motion rhythm. The marking of run-ons shows that the poem is strongly run-on; only two lines are end-stopped. (The end of the subordinate clause after "jamcloset" counts as end-stopped, though Williams omits the expected comma.) Generally, the run-ons are strongest where the action of the cat is least decisive, most in slow motion; and are weakest in lines 5–8 which describe the cat's actual steps. The strongest run-ons—between preposition and object, or between adjective and noun—occur in lines 2, 3, 5, and 10. Strangely, these seem to produce the effect of the least movement, the reverse of what we might expect.

The explanation becomes clear from a scansion of syllables:

Ăs thĕ cát	/	→
clímbed óvĕr	///	←
thĕ tóp ŏf	///	↔
thĕ jámclósĕt	0	↔
fírst thĕ ríght	///	↔

fórefóot	//	↔
cárefŭllў	/	←
thĕn thĕ hínd	/	↔
stépped dówn	/	↔
ĭntŏ thĕ pít ŏf	///	→
thĕ émptў	//	↔
flówĕrpŏt	0	↔

Only four of the poem's twelve lines show either drag or advance (lines 1, 2, 7, 9). Eight of the lines are balanced. This preponderance of lines in balance, with their symmetrical rhythms, clearly causes a feeling of stasis, which even the momentum of the sentence can scarcely overcome. Perhaps Williams, a doctor, wrote the poem as he wrote so many others, on the back of a sheet from his prescription pad. No doubt he wrote it rapidly, and certainly—the beginning poet will be relieved to know—he didn't write it by conducting any such complicated metrical analysis. Unquestionably, though, he was *listening* to the words and recognizing, as he set them down, the little slow, careful rhythm the poem needed. The secret is listening to the words, and arranging, and listening, and listening again.

Run-on free verse continually plays its line structure against the speech flow of the poem. Other poems in run-on free verse include Gerald Costanzo's "Braille" (p. 381), Sharon Olds's "Sex Without Love" (p. 251), William Greenway's "Pit Pony" (p. 163), Margaret Holley's "The Fireflies" (p. 213). In Gwendolyn Brooks's "We Real Cool" (p. 56), which presents the idealized voice of seven young men at a pool hall called Golden Shovel, the pattern of very strong, identical run-ons produces the effect of rocking counterpoint, an almost mechanical chant. Emphasized by the internal rhymes, this rhythm seems quite deliberately off-balance: "We /// Left school. We /// Lurk late. We /// Strike straight. We /// . . . " The rhythm is resolved only in the last line when, after seven repetitions, the line-ending "We" does not appear.

Just as end-stopped free verse tends to longer lines, run-on free verse characteristically tends to shorter lines. But each free verse poem establishes its own norms. The only rule is that, once a pattern has been established, it is best to keep to it. Lines very much shorter, or longer, than the norm, for instance, stand out and may seem awkward or contrived. A one-word line in "Song of Myself" would seem out of place, as would a very long line in "To Waken an Old Lady."

Many poems mix end-stopped and run-on free verse. The careful modulations in Debra Allbery's "Outings" (p. 117) and Ted Kooser's "Looking for You, Barbara" (p. 59) make them fine examples, as is James Wright's "A Blessing" (p. 326).

Notice in "A Blessing," after the poet has established a norm of generally longer lines (end-stopped or with very weak run-ons), the wonderful surprise conveyed by the strong run-on into the last line, reinforced by the alliterated *b*'s:

> Suddenly I realize
> That if I stepped out of my body I would break
> Into blossom.

VISIBLE FORM

Before the invention of printing in the fifteenth century, poetry was primarily an oral art. It was heard, rather than seen. Songs were sung; epics and narratives were declaimed by traveling bards. Formal meters, clearly accented and countable, allowed a poem's form to be followed by its hearers—just as rhyme, aside from its musical qualities, served to mark the turn from line to line like a typewriter bell. Since the sixteenth century, and especially after the rise of general literacy in the nineteenth century, poetry has come to have an increasingly visual dimension as well, through almost imperceptible evolution. Today we are more accustomed to seeing a poem than to hearing it, and students must be reminded to read poems aloud, particularly older poems, lest they miss the essential music.

The rise of free verse in the twentieth century represents, then, an acceleration of the inclusion in poetry of this visual dimension. With free verse, we *see* the difference from prose; the measure shows on the page, to the eye. The visual of course does not replace the oral (poetry always relies on speech for its vigor) but complements it, opening up new formal possibilities, visual forms, and so enriching the poet's resources.

The poems of William Carlos Williams, unquestionably the American master of run-on free verse, are a virtual library of effects. One of his innovations is the indented pattern of three lines, as in the following passage from "Asphodel, That Greeny Flower." These triads gave him a fixed but flexible medium for longer poems—for varying, for speeding and slowing, the voice.

> My heart rouses
>   thinking to bring you news
>   of something
> that concerns you
>   and concerns many men. Look at   5
>   what passes for the new.
> You will not find it there but in
>   despised poems.
>   It is difficult
> to get the news from poems   10
>   yet men die miserably every day
>   for lack
> of what is found there.
>   Hear me out

         for I too am concerned   15
and every man
         who wants to die at peace in his bed
                  besides.

Another of his significant innovations is free verse in stanzas of the same number of lines, and frequently of the same shape, as in "Poem" (p. 40). Such stanzas provide a regularity in visual form on the page, as well as an additional element of modulation and flow. Stanzaic regularity, reassuringly suggesting order and decisiveness to the eye, complements or counterpoints the freedom of speech inside the form. In the case of one poem, as Williams reports in *I Wanted To Write a Poem*, he changed a stanza of five lines to four to match the poem's other stanza. "See," he said, "how much better it conforms to the page, how much better it looks?"

Stanza patterns in free verse are trellises—a framework of visual regularity on which the morning glory of the new poem fluidly and freely twines. An alliance with form does not imply a loss of freedom. Even though the length or shape of stanzas may seem arbitrary, their use can be organic and expressive of the content and theme, as in Lux's "Tarantulas on the Lifebuoy" (p. 19). (**Theme** is what a poem *as a whole* says, or more often implies, about its subject—that is, the poem's drift, its central meaning.)

In the following poem by Dara Wier (b. 1949), a slight varying of the stanza shape adds an additional characteristic:

Daytrip to Paradox

         Just as you'd expect
my preparations were painstaking
         and exact. I took two

butane lighters and a cooler
         of ice. I knew the route   5
         had been so well-traveled

                  there'd be a store for necessities
and tobacco and liquor and axes.
         And near the Utopian village of Nucla

                  three Golden Eagles watched me   10
from a salt cedar tree. One of them
         held its third talon hard in the eye

of a white Northern Hare. Audubon
         couldn't have pictured it better.
                  Everything was perfect. Naturally   15

         it made me think of Siberia,
the bright inspirational star
         that's handed down the generations,

and the long, terrible nights
    of the pioneers' journey to paradise.   20
  The valley on the way to Paradox

was flat, there would be no choice,
nothing to get me lost.
    Cattleguards, gates and fencing

bordered the open range. Of course   25
  I crossed a narrow bridge
    to get into Paradox proper.

  In the store that doubled
as town hall and post office
    there was an account book for everybody   30

laid square on the counter.
  No one was expected to pay
    hard cold cash in Paradox apparently.

Paradox, of course, isn't a place but a kind of statement, so we recognize at once that the poem's journey is allegorical. A **paradox** is a statement seemingly self-contradictory, which is nonetheless explicable as expressing truth. For example: "For whosoever will save his life shall lose it: and whosoever will lose his life for my sake shall find it" (Matthew 16:25); "Our two souls therefore, which are one" (Donne, "A Valediction: Forbidding Mourning"). A strictly logical paradox reduces itself to absurdity, as with the statement "All generalizations are false." Being itself a generalization, the statement can't be true.

As we might expect, much in Dara Wier's poem makes sense in reference to paradox. The town (category of statements) is small and reached by "a narrow bridge." Given the logical quality of a paradox, the speaker's preparations are "painstaking / and exact." The scenery, which includes a Golden Eagle with its "third talon hard in the eye / of a white Northern Hare," is seemingly perfect, but makes her think of Siberia. The valley is, oddly, flat; and paradoxically "Cattleguards, gates and fencing" define "open range."

The speaker seems properly skeptical. It's only a "daytrip," and her taking along "axes" suggests doubt. Nor is she persuaded by what she finds: "No one was expected to pay / hard cold cash in Paradox apparently." The appearance is no doubt deceiving, as the sound that so firmly joins "*Pa*radox ap*pa*rently" reminds us.

Wier presents the poem in three-line stanzas, but of four differing shapes. The pattern of indentations of stanza 1 is repeated in stanzas 6, 8, 10; that of stanza 2, in stanza 7; that of stanza 3, in stanza 4; and that of stanza 5, in stanzas 9, 11. The appearance is of logical order, exactness, but the differing stanza patterns fall in place more or less randomly. They seem to point now right (stanzas 2, 7), now left (stanzas 3, 4, 6, 8, 10), often both ways or neither (stanzas 1, 5, 9, 11). The shifting pattern is never resolved; and the impression seems finally to be, if logical, of a very jangled sort of logic indeed, going every which way at once—which, perhaps, is the poem's judgment on paradox.

Mechanical patterns other than stanzas can be visually effective; for instance, *centering* all the lines of a poem imposes symmetry on the most uneven material. And there is no reason using a flush *right* margin, rather than a left, won't work for a particular poem, leaving the left side ragged.

Usually subtler, more natural patterns, which show themselves to the poet as a poem develops, work best. Consider this poem by Liz Rosenberg (b. 1955):

The Silence of Women

Old men, as time goes on, grow softer, sweeter,
while their wives get angrier.
You see them hauling the men across the mall
or pushing them down on chairs,
"Sit there! and don't you move!"   5
A lifetime of *yes* has left them
hissing bent as snakes.
It seems even their bones will turn
against them, once the fruitful years are gone.
Something snaps off the houselights,   10
and the cells go dim;
the chicken hatching back into the egg.

Oh lifetime of silence!
words scattered like a sybil's leaves.
Voice thrown into a baritone storm—   15
whose shrilling is a soulful wind
blown through an instrument
that cannot beat time

but must make music
any way it can.   20

The image is less of silence than of being silenced. There are words, a voice, but they are not heard, "scattered," lost in the male cacophony ("baritone storm"), to become a "shrilling" like the stridency of line 5, "a soulful wind," an instrument making "music / any way it can." Not beating time is of course a pun.

This suppression, this diminishing, registers visually in the dwindling of the poem's stanzas—from twelve lines to six, then to two—as well as in the generally shorter lines of stanzas 2 and 3, which after line 15 unrelentingly decrease. The same pattern shows, in miniature, in lines 1–2 and in lines 3–7 and perhaps in lines 9–11. Although it seems casual, the poem's form is both essential and precise.

As you read the Poems to Consider, notice carefully the formal choices the poets have made, like the run-on stanzas of Tess Gallagher's "Kidnaper" (p. 54). Or the edginess implied by the not quite achieved four-line stanza norm of Claudia Rankine's "The Man. His Bowl. His Raspberries." (p. 55). Or the jumpy line-lengths of Toi Derricotte's poem about a light-skinned black "passing" in 1945, "The Weakness" (p. 57). Or the three fairly distinct stanza shapes that register the developing mood of Mary Kinzie's "The Quest" (p. 56). In that poem someone, apparently having watched the morning star fade as full daylight comes, is leaving an old estate, looking back to garden, lawn, and, "as the gate closes," forest, where a few leaves are already changing color with the fall. The tone is one of disappointment, of some enchantment failed or some promised transformation unachieved.

A poem in free verse may be as exact and formally made as a metrical poem. What is important is not the visual forms (they are empty shapes), but the way they may express the inner shape or motion of the poems' subjects and feelings. Any form, any measure, whether free or conventionally metrical—or something else—is only as valuable as the use that is made of it.

SYLLABICS

That something else might be **syllabics**: a formal measure in which only the number of syllables in each line is counted. Strictly speaking, syllabics is not free verse. Since we do not *hear* the count of syllables in English, however, the rhythm is determined *ad hoc*, line by line, as in free verse. For the poet constructing lines by syllable-count, it is only a mechanical trellis like stanza-shapes or measuring by counting the number of *words* per line or, indeed, the number of letters per line or any other nonrhythmical element of the language. Such forms give the poet a fixed pattern on which to deploy, test, and re-deploy the developing sentences in effective ways. Here is a delightful syllabic poem by Marianne Moore (1887–1972):

The Fish

> wade
> through black jade.
>   Of the crow-blue mussel-shells, one keeps
>   adjusting the ash-heaps;
>   opening and shutting itself like   5
>
> an
> injured fan.
>   The barnacles which encrust the side
>   of the wave, cannot hide
>   there for the submerged shafts of the   10
>
> sun
> split like spun
>   glass, move themselves with spotlight swiftness
>   into the crevices—
>   in and out, illuminating   15
>
> the
> turquoise sea
>   of bodies. The water drives a wedge
>   of iron through the iron edge
>   of the cliff; whereupon the stars,   20

    pink
    rice-grains, ink-
        bespattered jelly-fish, crabs like green
        lilies, and submarine
            toadstools, slide each on the other.   25

    All
    external
        marks of abuse are present on this
        defiant edifice—
            all the physical features of   30

    ac-
    cident—lack
        of cornice, dynamite grooves, burns, and
        hatchet strokes, these things stand
            out on it; the chasm-side is   35

    dead.
    Repeated
        evidence has proved that it can live
        on what can not revive
            its youth. The sea grows old in it.   40

Rhyming *a a b b c*, each stanza has lines of one, three, nine, six, and eight syllables. (Moore apparently counts "opening" in line 5 as two syllables—or is simply avoiding what she elsewhere calls "conscious fastidiousness.") The indentations of lines 3–4 and 5 link the rhyme pairs, adding a further impression of fluidity in form to the strongly run-on rhythm—all appropriate to the loosely shifting, watery underseascape of the poem's subject. The effect is reinforced by the surprising lack of rhyme in the last line of each stanza, which may suggest how unsettled is the long war of sea and rock-coast.

The rhyming is extraordinarily inventive, varied. It mingles exact and slant-rhymes, and rhymes on unaccented syllables. It may be as heavy as "wade-jade" in the rhythmically viscous "wade / through black jade," or as light as the merely touched-on "the-sea" of lines 16–17 or the subtle double-rhyme in "swiftness-crevices." Two extremely strong run-ons from monosyllabic lines are startling: "an / injured fan" and "ac- / cident—lack / of cornice." Both seem vividly imitative, like the rhythmic equivalent of extreme close-ups in film. The poem amusingly describes the interface of sea and rock in saying that barnacles "encrust the side / of the *wave*," rather than of the rock, as we might expect. Every detail deftly presents the color and suspense of the struggle which, as the repeating syllabic stanzas imply, is ever-shifting but endless.

For a look at earlier drafts of this poem, see pp. 296-298.

SPATIAL FREE VERSE

A spatial or visual element has been important in a number of the poems already discussed, such as Cummings's "in Just-" (p. 6) and Wier's "Daytrip to Paradox" (p. 43). In a small class of poems, however, the visual may become dominant, making the form primarily spatial or even pictorial, with the elementary structure of line becoming secondary or disappearing. A simple case:

> The
> ball
>   bumps
>   down
>   the
>   steps . . .

Here the lines themselves are clearly secondary to the visual image they create.

Picture poems, which use the shape of an object as their form, are an old tradition. "Easter Wings" by George Herbert (1593–1633), written in meter, is an early example:

Lord, who createdst man in wealth and store,
Though foolishly he lost the same,
Decaying more and more
Till he became
Most poore;
With thee
O let me rise
As larks, harmoniously,
And sing this day thy victories;
Then shall the fall further the flight in me.

My tender age in sorrow did beginne;
And still with sicknesses and shame
Thou didst so punish sinne,
That I became
Most thinne.
With thee
Let me combine,
And feel this day thy victorie;
For if I imp° my wing on thine,
Affliction shall advance the flight in me.

19 *imp:* to graft. Alludes to a term in falconry.

Decreasing and then increasing the lines of each stanza by one foot, Herbert not only makes the poem look like two pairs of angels' wings but also embodies in rhythm its theme of diminution and regrowth. In what is certainly the most delightful and amusing bibliographical scholarship ever published, Randall McLeod of the University of Toronto argues that "Easter Wings" was intended by Herbert as *two—* entirely separate but mirror-image—poems. (Give yourself a treat. See pp. 61–172, *Crisis in Editing: Texts of the English Renaissance,* AMS Press, 1994.)

A colorful poem by William Carlos Williams offers a subtler, contemporary instance of the picture poem:

The Red Wheelbarrow

so much depends
upon

a red wheel
barrow

glazed with rain   5
water

beside the white
chickens

Each stanza is indeed shaped like a wheelbarrow in a side view, with the longer first line suggesting the handle.

Moreover, the little pictures have a startling rhythmic quality as well. Though the couplets are virtually end-stopped, isolating each detail and giving the poem its intense, painterly concentration, the second line of each couplet is reached by a *very* strong run-on. The run-on in stanza 2 even divides, albeit without hyphen, what is a single word: "wheelbarrow" (as the title should remind us). We might illustrate these strong run-ons this way:

If the stanzas are shaped like miniature wheelbarrows, these forcefully turning run-ons rhythmically suggest the wheels! Perhaps the fascination of this famous little poem comes from the way its combined visual and oral form mirrors its subject. The tiny still life catches energy in stasis, a complex vitality only momentarily at rest.

The resonance of shape as meaning also shows in the taut quatrains Williams chose for the following poem:

Complete Destruction

It was an icy day.
We buried the cat,
then took her box
and set match to it

in the back yard.   5
Those fleas that escaped
earth and fire
died by the cold.

Properly, short sentences and terse, end-stopped phrases evoke the bleak scene. In shape, the first quatrain is rigid, boxlike; and the just slightly longer line 6—exactly with the word "escaped"—only for a moment breaks the visual pattern, which lines 7–8 then reestablish decisively.

A poem like this one by Kenneth Patchen (1911–1972) isn't in any normal sense *read*, but perceived:

The Murder of Two Men by a Young Kid Wearing Lemon-Colored Gloves

        Wait.

                                          Wait.

                    Wait.

              Wait. Wait.

    Wait.

                                          Wait.

                    W a i t.

        Wait.

                          Wait.

                                          Wait.

              Wait.

                                    Wait.

   Wait.

                NOW.

Such poems, in which the visual or spatial predominates (or even effectively replaces the oral), comprise the third main type of free verse, along with end-stopped and run-on. Twentieth-century picture poems have been written in the shape of Coca-Cola bottles, traffic cloverleafs with Model T's and Model A's circling them, fireplugs, and umbrellas. John Hollander, in *Types of Shape* (1969), offers poems shaped like a key, a lightbulb, a bell, a heart, New York State, and even a swan and its shadow. So-called **concrete poems** lie between poetry and graphics. On the following page is one of the most famous, by Reinhard Döhl (b. 1934). *Apfel* is German for apple.

Whatever its form, free verse—because it may be invented to suit its occasion or subject—is always changing and fresh. It is not merely poetry written any-old-which-way.

```
     ,pfelApfelApfelApter,
    ,)felApfelApfelApfelApfelA,
   ,felApfelApfelApfelApfelApfe
  ApfelApfelApfelApfelApfelApf,
  pfelApfelApfelApfelApfelApfel,
  [ApfelApfelApfelApfelApfelApfe
  pfelApfelApfelApfelApfelApfelA
  ApfelApfelApfelApfelApfelApfe
  )felApfelApfelApfelApfelApfel/
  \pfelApfelApfelApfelApfelApf
  elApfelApfelApfelWurmAp'
   'elApfelApfelApfelApfel/
    ' ofelApfelApfelApfel/
     ,felApfelApfelA,
      ' ,felAnfel,
```

QUESTIONS AND SUGGESTIONS

---

1. Exchange a poem with someone in the class. Then meet over coffee. What questions might you ask or suggestions might you make?

2. Write a poem in syllabics. Or write a picture poem about an ice cream cone, a tree, a hat, an alarm clock, or other common object. Or write an acrostic, using someone's name or perhaps a short sentence or hidden message. An **acrostic** is a poem in which the first letters of each line have a meaning when read downward:

> **D**azzling
> **a**s the morning sun
> **i**s when your eyes are
> **s**aying
> **y**es to me!

3. How have the following student-poets invented free verse forms for their purposes?

a)   disappearances

SHEILA HEINRICH*

was a man of many disguises
was a man of few words and
one day when they looked where he had been
they found

and no one said   5
so no one ever

b)   *Saviour (Mississippi 1957)*

OMOTEJI ADEYEMON*

Christ was white this morning,
when I went to church
to hear the good news of
his coming and
the resurrection of my soul.   5
Christ was white this morning
and displayed up high.
Then they came and burnt the church down.
Now Christ is black,
with a crown of charcoal thorns.   10
Now Christ is black,
like me,
and lying on the ground.

4. In "Smart" by Bruce Bennett (b. 1940) what *gestures* do you find the poet making in his choice of line-breaks and stanzas? Does Bennett's omission of capitalization and punctuation help his fable?

Smart

like the fox
who grabs a stick
and wades
into the water

deep   5
and deeper
till only his muzzle's
above it
his fleas

leap   10
up and up
onto his head
out onto the stick

which he lets go

off it floats   15
as he swims back
and shakes himself dry

5. Poet Robert D. Sutherland suggests this exercise. To test the integrity and possible effects of lines, try out as many free-versed versions of a prose sentence as you can think of. The sentence he uses: "Bob and Sarah, my friends of many years,

have come back in time for tea." Literally, of course, there are dozens of possibilities. The range is from phrasal units (omitting internal punctuation):

> Bob and Sarah
> my friends of many years
> have come back
> in time for tea.

—to off-the-wall arrangements (mechanically, two words per line):

> Bob and
> Sarah my
> friends of
> many years
> have come
> back in
> time for
> tea.

—or to indented versions, like:

> Bob and Sarah
>   my
>   friends of many
>   years
>   have come back
>   in time for tea.

Play around further with this sentence, or make up an interesting sentence to use. Type the versions, to see how they would look in print. A word processor works well for this exercise. Observe especially how the variations bring out emphases or hidden potential in the sentence. In the indented version above, for instance, the subsentence "years have come back," buried in the original, appears and perhaps suggests some of the meaning of the event to the speaker. Are there other buried subsentences or subphrases?

6. Choose a very short poem in meter (or a stanza from one) and experiment with rearranging it as free verse. What seems gained? lost? (Lines 1–4 of Shakespeare's Sonnet 73 (p. 10), or a passage from Howard Nemerov's "Learning by Doing" (p. 86), would do nicely.)

7. Choose a simple object—a stone, a twig, a leaf, a wristwatch, for example—and study it slowly and carefully with each of your five senses (sight, hearing, smell, taste, touch) in turn. Don't be shy about tasting a watch or listening to a twig! Then write a sentence or two of description for each sense. Comparisons are fine. ("It feels like a flat, closed bowl or box. Heavy. There's a little button on the side that probably opens the lid.")

    Any surprises? Might there be a poem in it? Have a look at Charles Simic's "Stone" (p. 27).

8. **Prose poems,** as they are called, are not verse at all, but perhaps may be best thought of as an extreme variant of free verse. In what ways does this prose poem by Jay Meek (b. 1937) work as poems do, rather than as we expect prose to behave? Test the poet's choice of form by trying to line the poem as verse.

Swimmers

   Coming out of the theater, in the light of the marquee, I can see there is something on my clothing and my hands. When I look back I can see it on the others too, like light off the screen on their faces during the film, or the grey illuminations made at night by summer lightning. It doesn't go away. We are covered with it, like grease, and when by accident we touch each other, we feel it on our bodies. It is not sensual, not exciting. It is slippery, this film over our lives, so that when we come up against one another and slide away, it is as if nothing has happened: we go on, as though swimming the channel at night, lights on the water, hundreds of us rising up on the beach on the far side.

9. Plan a picture poem called "Popsicle," and perhaps try it out on a word processor. What might it say? Do you foresee any technical problem in producing the shape?

POEMS TO CONSIDER

 Kidnaper   1976

TESS GALLAGHER (b. 1943)

He motions me over with a question.
He is lost. I believe him. It seems
he calls my name. I move
closer. He says it again, the name
of someone he loves. I step back pretending   5

not to hear. I suspect
the street he wants
does not exist, but I am glad to point
away from myself. While he turns
I slip off my wristwatch, already laying a trail   10
for those who must find me
tumbled like an abandoned car
into the ravine. I lie

without breath for days among ferns.
Pine needles drift   15
onto my face and breasts
like the tiny hands
of watches. Cars pass.
I imagine it's him
coming back. My death   20
is not needed. The sun climbs again
for everyone. He lifts me
like a bride

and the leaves fall from my shoulders
in twenty-dollar bills.   25
"You must have been cold," he says
covering me with his handkerchief.
"You must have given me up."

The Man. His Bowl. His Raspberries.   *1994*

CLAUDIA RANKINE (b. 1963)

The bowl he starts with
is too large. It will never be filled.

Nonetheless, in the cool dawn,
reaching underneath the leaf, he frees
each raspberry from its stem   5
and white nipples remain suspended.

He is being gentle, so does not think
I must be gentle as he doubles back
through the plants
seeking what he might have missed.   10

At breakfast she will be pleased
to eat the raspberries and put her pleasure
to his lips.

Placing his fingers beneath a leaf
for one he had not seen, he does not idle.   15
He feels for the raspberry. Securing, pulling
gently, taking, he gets what he needs.

The Quest   1982

MARY KINZIE (b. 1944)

for Mary Etta Knapp

Like an old duchessa who has talked all night
whom the Republic's leaders have forgotten,
Venus is guided up the dim cone of rooms,
still glowing through her empty outpost
alone among already vanished stars.   5

The sun increases in her wake.
Putting off his moony Dutch enamel
for direct Baroque, the young retainer
hales up in repeated ormolu
a cold, new wind in the clicking trees.   10

At the corner of the garden
as that surprised vague rash
on a nearly white Bosc°
grows into smiling russet
from far enough away,   15
an adolescent beech
thrusts his pride of bristling opal
from the matted lawn,
blushing when you look back
from the verge.   20

But among that litter of leaf as the gate closes
you have seen, between the bony poplars there, and there,
a few bright charms tied in yellow to the twigs
to tell you in the blowing forest where you should have turned.

13 *Bosc:* pear

 We Real Cool   1959

GWENDOLYN BROOKS (b. 1917)

> *The Pool Players.*
> *Seven at the Golden Shovel.*

We real cool. We
Left School. We

Lurk late. We
Strike straight. We

Sing sin. We   5
Thin gin. We

Jazz June. We
Die soon.

The Weakness   1989

TOI DERRICOTTE (b. 1941)

That time my grandmother dragged me
through the perfume aisles at Saks, she held me up
by my arm, hissing, "Stand up,"
through clenched teeth, her eyes
bright as a dog's   5
cornered in the light.
She said it over and over,
as if she were Jesus,
and I were dead. She had been
solid as a tree,   10
a fur around her neck, a
light-skinned matron whose car was parked, who walked on swirling
marble and passed through
brass openings—in 1945.
There was not even a black   15
elevator operator at Saks.
The saleswoman had brought velvet
leggings to lace me in, and cooed,
as if in the service of all grandmothers.
My grandmother had smiled, but not   20
hungrily, not like my mother
who hated them, but wanted to please,
and they had smiled back, as if
they were wearing wooden collars.
When my legs gave out, my grandmother   25
dragged me up and held me like God
holds saints by the
roots of the hair. I begged her
to believe I couldn't help it. Stumbling,
her face white   30

with sweat, she pushed me through the crowd, rushing
away from those eyes
that saw through
her clothes, under
her skin, all the way down   35
to the transparent
genes confessing.

 The Wrong Street   *1991*

CORNELIUS EADY (b. 1954)

If you could shuck your skin and watch
The action from a safe vantage point,
You might find a weird beauty in this,
An egoless moment, but for
These young white men at your back.   5
Your dilemma is how to stay away from
That three to five second shot
On the evening news of the place
Where you stumble, or they catch
Their second wind, or you run up   10
To the fence, discover that
You are not breeze, or light,
Or a dream that might argue
Itself through the links. Your responsibility
Is not to fall bankrupt, a   15
Chalk-marked silhouette faintly
Replaying its amazement to
The folks tuning in, fist to
Back, bullet to mid-section.
Your car breaks down   20
And gives you up. A friend's
Lazy directions miss
The restaurant by two
Important blocks. All of this
Happened. None of this   25
Happened. Part of this
Happened. (You dream it
After an ordinary day.) Something
Different happened, but now
You run in an   30
Old story, now you learn
Your name.

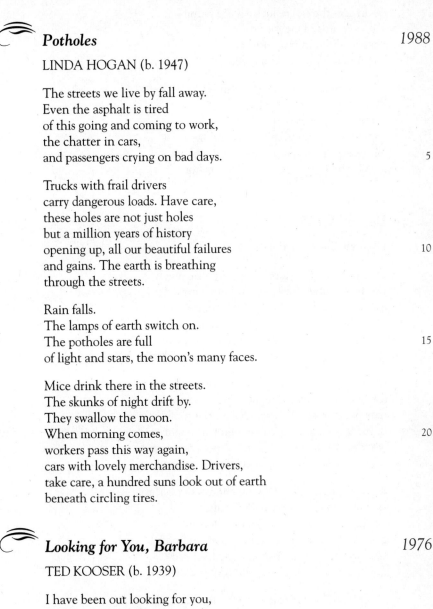

Potholes   *1988*

LINDA HOGAN (b. 1947)

The streets we live by fall away.
Even the asphalt is tired
of this going and coming to work,
the chatter in cars,
and passengers crying on bad days.   5

Trucks with frail drivers
carry dangerous loads. Have care,
these holes are not just holes
but a million years of history
opening up, all our beautiful failures   10
and gains. The earth is breathing
through the streets.

Rain falls.
The lamps of earth switch on.
The potholes are full   15
of light and stars, the moon's many faces.

Mice drink there in the streets.
The skunks of night drift by.
They swallow the moon.
When morning comes,   20
workers pass this way again,
cars with lovely merchandise. Drivers,
take care, a hundred suns look out of earth
beneath circling tires.

Looking for You, Barbara   *1976*

TED KOOSER (b. 1939)

I have been out looking for you,
Barbara, and as I drove around,
the steering wheel turned through my hands
like a clock. The moon
rolled over the rooftops and was gone.   5

I was dead tired; in my arms
they were rolling the tires inside;

in my legs they were locking the pumps.
Yet what was in me for you
flapped as red in my veins   10
as banners strung over a car lot.

Then I came home and got drunk.
Where were you? 2 A.M.
is full of slim manikins
waving their furs from black windows.   15
My bed goes once more around the block,
and my heart keeps on honking its horn.

Barbed Wire   1985

HENRY TAYLOR (b. 1942)

One summer afternoon when nothing much
was happening, they were standing around
a tractor beside the barn while a horse
in the field poked his head between two strands
of the barbed-wire fence to get at the grass   5
along the lane, when it happened—something

they passed around the wood stove late at night
for years, but never could explain—someone
may have dropped a wrench into the toolbox
or made a sudden move, or merely thought   10
what might happen if the horse got scared, and
then he did get scared, jumped sideways and ran

down the fence line, leaving chunks of his throat
skin and hair on every barb for ten feet
before he pulled free and ran a short way   15
into the field, stopped and planted his hoofs
wide apart like a sawhorse, hung his head
down as if to watch his blood running out,

almost as if he were about to speak
to them, who almost thought he could regret   20
that he no longer had the strength to stand,
then shuddered to his knees, fell on his side,
and gave up breathing while the dripping wire
hummed like a bowstring in the splintered air.

3

METER

Spiderwebs and Rabbits in Hats

Solid form includes, along with whole-poem forms (like sonnets), conventional meter, the basic underlying rhythmic pattern of the *line* of verse in English. Although free verse is more formal than its name indicates, meter is happily less formal than it may seem—and less complicated than its thicket of terminology suggests.

Meter means "measure." Some recurring element of the language is used as the unit of line measurement. Languages vary and thus each has its own distinctive basis for meter. Latin verse, for example, used the duration of vowels, long or short, as the measuring element. Chinese, in which all words are monosyllabic, uses syllables. English has always used **accent** as one measuring element. Accent is the emphasis—in loudness, pitch, or duration—with which a syllable is spoken, relative to adjacent syllables. For metrical purposes only two levels of accent (or **stress**) are counted: relatively *heavily* accented syllables (called "accented") and relatively *lightly* accented syllables (called "unaccented").

It may be suggestive to think of meter as underlying the sentence rhythms in the way that the beat in music underlies and makes possible the melody. The bass, thumping along, provides the necessary background to the lilt of the tune. Man took a little wind into his mouth, Frost says, "And then by measure blew it forth."

> By measure. It was word and note,
> The wind the wind had meant to be—
> A little through the lips and throat.
> The aim was song—the wind could see.

ACCENTUAL-SYLLABIC METER

Accentual-syllabic meter has been standard in English since the sixteenth century. It has a rich tradition, as varied as the poets using it: Shakespeare, Donne, Milton, Pope, Wordsworth, Keats, Yeats, Frost, Stevens, Auden, and in recent

61

decades Elizabeth Bishop, Robert Lowell, Richard Wilbur, Howard Nemerov, Philip Larkin, and Mona Van Duyn.

In accentual-syllabic meter, both the number of accents and the number of syllables are counted; the *pattern* of unaccented and accented syllables forms the meter. The elementary pattern or unit is called a **foot**. The basic foot is the *iambic foot*, or **iamb**, which is an unaccented followed by an accented syllable: tĕ TÚM, as in "ăvóid" or "tŏ bréak" or "bў méas|ŭre bléw." Note that, as in the third example, a word may be part of two separate feet. A line of four feet, say, would go like this:

> Hĕ wálked | bĕnéath | thĕ tíme | lĕss trées.

Lines may be composed of any number of feet, though lines of four or five feet (eight or ten syllables) have been the norm. Each line-length has a handy name. **Monometer**, for instance, is a line consisting of one foot: ˘ ´ . In "Upon His Departure Hence" Robert Herrick (1591–1674) provides a rare example of a poem written in monometer:

> Thŭs Í
> Passe by,
> And die:
> As One,
> Unknown,   5
> And gon:
> I'm made
> A shade,
> And laid
> I'th grave . . .   10

Dimeter, also rare, is a line of two feet: ˘ ´ | ˘ ´ . Although it deviates a little from strict iambic dimeter, here is a twentieth century example. (Note: a final unaccented syllable at the end of the line—an extra-syllable or "feminine" ending—is not counted and does not change the meter.)

> Hŏw tíme | rĕvér|sĕs
>
> Thĕ próud | ĭn héart!
>
> Ĭ nów | măke vér|sĕs
>
> Whŏ aímed | ăt árt.

Here is the poem:

For My Contemporaries

J. V. CUNNINGHAM (1911–1985)

How time reverses
The proud in heart!
I now make verses
Who aimed at art.

But I sleep well.   5
Ambitious boys
Whose big lines swell
With spiritual noise,

Despise me not!
And be not queasy   10
To praise somewhat:
Verse is not easy.

But rage who will.
Time that procured me
Good sense and skill   15
Of madness cured me.

Trimeter is a line of three feet: ˘ ´ | ˘ ´ | ˘ ˘ , as in these waltzing lines:

The˘ whis|key˘ ˘(´)on | yŏur bréath

Cŏuld máke | ă smáll | bóy díz|zy̆;

Bŭt Í | hŭng ón | lĭke déath:

Sŭch wáltz|ĭng wás | nŏt éas|y̆.

The poem:

My Papa's Waltz

THEODORE ROETHKE (1908–1963)

The whiskey on your breath
Could make a small boy dizzy;
But I hung on like death:
Such waltzing was not easy.

We romped until the pans   5
Slid from the kitchen shelf;
My mother's countenance
Could not unfrown itself.

The hand that held my wrist
Was battered on one knuckle;   10
At every step you missed
My right ear scraped a buckle.

You beat time on my head
With a palm caked hard by dirt,
Then waltzed me off to bed   15
Still clinging to your shirt.

Tetrameter, very common and serviceable, is a line of four feet: ˘ ´ | ˘ ´ | ˘ ´ | ˘ ´.
(Note: in line 1, "Loveliest" is a dactylic foot substituted for the iamb; and in line
4, the unaccented syllable of the first foot is omitted—its place marked by the
superscript *x*.)

Lóveliĕst | ŏf trées, | thĕ chér|rў nów

Ĭs húng | wĭth blóom | ălóng | thĕ bóugh,

Ănd stánds | ăbóut | thĕ wóod|lănd ríde

ˣWéar|ĭng white | fŏr Éas|tĕrtíde.

The poem:

Loveliest of Trees

A. E. HOUSMAN

Loveliest of trees, the cherry now
Is hung with bloom along the bough,
And stands about the woodland ride
Wearing white for Eastertide.

Now, of my threescore years and ten,   5
Twenty will not come again,
And take from seventy springs a score,
It only leaves me fifty more.

And since to look at things in bloom
Fifty springs are little room,   10
About the woodlands I will go
To see the cherry hung with snow.

Pentameter is a line of five feet: ˘ ´ | ˘ ´ | ˘ ´ | ˘ ´ | ˘ ´. Iambic pentameter has been
the standard line of verse in English from Shakespeare to the present. When it is
unrhymed, it is also called **blank verse,** as in:

Ăll óut|-ŏf-dóors | lóoked dárk|lў ín | ăt hím

Thróugh thĕ | thín fróst | ălmóst | ĭn sép|ărăte stárs,

That găth|ĕrs ŏn | thĕ páne | ĭn émp|tў róoms.

Whăt képt | hĭs éyes | frŏm gív|ĭng báck | thĕ gáze . . .

The poem:

An Old Man's Winter Night

ROBERT FROST

All out-of-doors looked darkly in at him
Through the thin frost almost in separate stars,
That gathers on the pane in empty rooms.
What kept his eyes from giving back the gaze
Was the lamp tilted near them in his hand.   5
What kept him from remembering what it was
That brought him to that creaking room was age.
He stood with barrels round him—at a loss.
And having scared the cellar under him
In clomping here, he scared it once again   10
In clomping off;—and scared the outer night,
Which has its sounds, familiar, like the roar
Of trees and crack of branches, common things,
But nothing so like beating on a box.
A light he was to no one but himself   15
Where now he sat, concerned with he knew what,
A quiet light, and then not even that.
He consigned to the moon, such as she was,
So late-arising, to the broken moon
As better than the sun in any case   20
For such a charge, his snow upon the roof,
His icicles along the wall to keep;
And slept. The log that shifted with a jolt
Once in the stove, disturbed him and he shifted,
And eased his heavy breathing, but still slept.   25
One aged man—one man—can't keep a house,
A farm, a countryside, or if he can,
It's thus he does it of a winter night.

Hexameter (or **Alexandrine**) is a line of six feet: ˘ ´ | ˘ ´ | ˘ ´ | ˘ ´ | ˘ ´ | ˘ ´. Because it tends to be long and sluggish in practice, it is rare. Howard Nemerov (1920–1991) uses it deftly, however, in this epigram:

Power to the People

Whý ăre | thĕ stámps | ădórned | wĭth kíngs | ănd prés|ĭdénts?

Thăt wé | măy líck | thĕir hínd|ĕr párts | ănd thúmp | thĕir héads.

Heptameter, a line of seven feet, is very rare. An example is from "The Book of Thel" by William Blake (1757–1827):

The Lil|ly ŏf | thĕ val|lĕy, breath|ing ĭn | thĕ hum|blĕ grass,

Answ̆ered | thĕ love|lў maid | ănd said: | "Ĭ am | ă wat|'rў weed,

Ănd Ĭ | ăm ver|lў small | ănd love | tŏ dwell | in low|lў vales;

Sŏ weak, | thĕ gild|ĕd but|tĕrflў | scărce perch|es ŏn | mў head."

Over the centuries, tetrameter and pentameter lines have become the norm; they are neither too short and clipped nor too long and clumsy. Monometer or dimeter lines tend to occur only in stanzaic poems of varying line lengths, such as John Donne's "Song" (p. 85), where the two monometer lines give each stanza a con-cluding whirl:

Yet she
Will be
False, ere I come, to two, or three.

If you are inexperienced at meter, this might be a good point to try out the basics. Take a sheet of paper and mark on it, with breve (˘) and ictus (´), blanks for four lines of iambic tetrameter, thus:

˘ ´ ˘ ´ ˘ ´ ˘ ´

˘ ´ ˘ ´ ˘ ´ ˘ ´

˘ ´ ˘ ´ ˘ ´ ˘ ´

˘ ´ ˘ ´ ˘ ´ ˘ ´

Then fit short sentences to the pattern, not worrying much about what they say. Be sure the unaccented and accented syllables are quite obvious. (Your dictionary marks accents if you are in doubt.) Perhaps rhyme lines 2 and 4 for the fun of it. You will get something like:

Thĕ road ĭs going ŭp thĕ hill.

Thĕ road ĭs alsŏ coming down.

Thĕ way ŏne thinks ĭt goes depends.

Thĕ boy ĭs walkĭng home frŏm town.

A variation, when you are that far, is then to make each line *one* foot longer, as "The road is going up the wŏodĕd hill, / The road, ŏf cóurse, is also coming down," et cetera. Harder, but worth a try, is making each line shorter by one foot, as:

> The road goes up the hill.
> It's also coming down.
> The way it goes depends.
> The boy is leaving town.

A further variation might be to make one line run-on, as:

> Going up the hill, the road
> Is also coming down.

Don't be afraid to tinker with your draft. Save it, as we will return to it later.

SUBSTITUTION AND VARIATIONS

The iamb (te TUM) is the basic foot. But, as suggested by anomalies in the scansions already marked, five other feet may be substituted for iambs without changing the metrical pattern. They are:

> **Trochee** (trochaic): accented followed by unaccented syllable: TÚM tĕ.
> ónlў   tótăl   cŏw ănd   the | fárm bĕ|low
>
> **Anapest** (anapestic): two unaccented followed by an accented: tĕ tĕ TÚM.
> ĭntĕrvéne   fŏr ă whíle   lŏv|er ŏf míne
>
> **Dactyl** (dactylic): accented followed by two unaccented: TÚM tĕ tĕ.
> mérrilў   tíme fŏr ă   lóver ŏf | mine
>
> **Spondee** (spondaic): two accented syllables together: TÚM TÚM.
> bréad bóx   in thĕ | swéet lánd   stróng fóot
>
> **Double-iamb:** two unaccented followed by two accented: tĕ tĕ TÚM TÚM.
> ŏf thĕ swéet lánd   in ă gréen sháde

Instead of the double-iamb, many accounts include the **pyrrhic** foot, two unaccented syllables: tĕ tĕ. But since it contains no accent, the pyrrhic is impossible to hear as a unit, and it is almost invariably followed by a spondee. This pattern is so frequent that it seems simpler and more natural to think of it as a double-iamb. A double-iamb, of course, counts as two feet.

Any of these other feet—trochees, anapests, dactyls, spondees, or double-iambs—may be *substituted* for iambs in the norm line. "Slid from" is a trochee substituted as the first foot in the second line of "My Papa's Waltz":

Wĕ rómped ŭntíl thĕ páns

Slíd from | thĕ kítch|ĕn shélf

The slightly unexpected tipping in the rhythm imitates (perhaps) the described action of pans sliding from a shelf. A trochee, an anapest, and a spondee are substituted in lines 13–14:

Yŏu béat | tíme ŏn | mў héad

Wĭth ă pálm | cáked hárd | bў dírt

"Whў áre" is a trochaic substitution in Nemerov's "Whў áre | thĕ stámps | ădórned | with kíngs | ănd prés | ĭdénts?" Note the double-iamb and the anapest substituted in the second line of Frost's "An Old Man's Winter Night":

Thrŏugh thĕ thín fróst, | ălmóst | ĭn sép|ărăte stárs

We said at the outset that accentual-syllabic meter counts both accents and syllables. It does so a good deal less rigorously in practice, you will now recognize, than it perhaps seemed. A pentameter with two substituted spondees will have seven, rather than only five, accented syllables. With two substituted anapests, it will have twelve, rather than ten, syllables—or, with a feminine ending, thirteen total syllables!

Substitution allows an almost infinite rhythmical variety, and it is frequently the means to imitative, expressive effects. Used awkwardly, of course, it can break the flow of the meter. Used deftly, it is the freedom of the formal poem. Meter might best be thought of, not as something that must be rigidly followed, but as something the poet is free to vary.

Meter, it is worth noting, simplifies what we actually hear. In speech we can distinguish a wide and subtle range of accents. In metered verse, however, we count syllables as either **accented** or **unaccented**. That meter is two-valued, for counting, does not of course reduce the variety of accents of natural speech that play over it. Thus, regular meter often sounds much less mechanical than we might expect. Further, the distinction between accented and unaccented syllables is relative; that is, we count a syllable as accented or unaccented *in relation* to the syllables next to it, not by some absolute measurement. The first line of "An Old Man's Winter Night" may be scanned this way:

Ăll óut|-ŏf-dóors | lŏoked dárk|lў ín | ăt hím

We can hear the meter ticking along regularly under the speech rhythm. Although "looked" counts as an unaccented syllable (being next to the more heavily accented "dark-") and although "in" counts as an accented syllable (being next to the still slightly less accented "-ly" and "at"), purely objectively "looked" is more accented than "in."

Thus, a line may be scanned—that is, interpreted or heard—somewhat differently by different readers. A single reader may often be aware of more than one obvious possibility. In the Frost line, for instance, one can also hear "looked dark-" as a spondee; it is the ominous center of the statement and both words might be read as equally heavily accented. Another reader might hear, and mark, the first foot in the line as a spondee, too: "All out-." In scanning, parentheses are often useful to call attention to such other obvious possibilities, so that the rhythmical flexibility of a line won't be lost in the description of it. Similarly, parentheses mark what may be called light or "courtesy" accents: syllables that should be treated as accented even though they barely deserve it, like "in" in "dark|ly in|at him." The parentheses indicate that, although the scanner primarily hears a line in a certain way, he or she is also aware of other ways of hearing it. As the accents of meter are essentially relative, **scansion** should be wisely tentative and undogmatic. In scanning, we do not seek the "correct" answer, but a notation of accents that allows us to perceive and discuss accurately the subtleties of the line.

Two other variations in the system of meter, also considered normal or regular, allow further flexibility. One is **extra-syllable ending** (sometimes called **feminine ending**): a final unaccented syllable at the end of the line, as in Roethke's

Could make | a small | boy diz|zy

or in Frost's

The log | that shift|ed with | a jolt

Once in | the stove, | disturbed | him and | he shift|ed.

Being unaccented, extra-syllable (e-s) endings are regarded metrically as extras and are uncounted; thus, these lines remain iambic trimeter (Roethke) and iambic pentameter (Frost). Extra-syllable endings may, however, be rhythmically useful for expressive or imitative effects. In Frost's lines the lightly accented syllable "with" lets the voice speed toward the abrupt "jolt," and the trochaic substitution "Once in" helps to mimic the loose and jolting motion of the log in the fire. The trochaic substitution that puts two unaccented syllables together—"him and | he shift-"— helps to suggest the old man's restiveness resulting from the fire's disturbing noise. The e-s ending "and | he shift|ed" completes the effect by also suggesting the indecisive quality of the old man's movement as contrasted with the abrupt, finished movement of the log's "jolt" at the regular ending—on an accented syllable—of the preceding line. The e-s ending lets the line end with four syllables, only one of which ("shift-") is accented, giving an effect of slight but unresolved motion. Contrast the effect of the same line with a regular ending: "Once in the stove, disturbed | him and | he stirred."

Another common variation is the omission of the initial unaccented syllable at the beginning of a line. In Housman's "Loveliest of Trees" (p. 64) this occurs three times: in lines 4 ("Wear|ing white | for Eas|tertíde"), 6 ("Twen|ty will | not come | again"), and 10 ("Fif|ty springs | are lit|tle room"). If such monosyllabic feet occurred elsewhere in the line, they would mark a hiatus in the rhythm (see *lame foot*, p. 75); but, occurring innocuously at the beginning of lines, they scarcely disturb the flow. The term for this omission of the initial unaccented syllable is **anacrusis**[*] (Greek: meaning "the striking up of a tune"); and it is marked by a small *x* in scansion, as in these lines from Ben Jonson's "To Celia":

> [x]Come, | my Cel|ia, let | us prove,

> [x]While | we may, | the sports | of love;

> [x]Time | will not | be ours, | for ev|er:

> [x]He, | at length, | our good | will sev|er.

The change in rhythm may be almost imperceptible, especially as in lines 3–4 when an extra-syllable ending in effect re-supplies the missing unaccented syllable of the following line.

Robert Frost remarked that there are really only two meters in English, strict iambic and loose iambic. Strict meter would avoid anapestic or dactylic substitutions, which add syllables to a line. More supple meter might use these substitutions for ease or greater naturalness.

Return now to the draft of your quatrain. Try a few substitutions and perhaps an e-s ending or anacrusis. You will notice now that, in our last version, anacrusis appeared in line 1:

> [x]Go|ing up | the hill, | the road . . .

To make the line shorter by a foot, we might substitute a trochee and what is probably a spondee, thus:

> Going | uphill, | the road . . .

The trimeter has the same four accented syllables as the tetrameter, but counts out as one foot less.

We might combine lines 1–2 into one pentameter line, and then do the same with lines 3–4, producing a couplet:

---

[*]We follow George Saintsbury in *A History of English Prosody*, who allows the term in this sense on occasion (volume I, pp. 64, 78, 170). *Anacrusis* seems preferable to the sometimes-used term *acephalous line*, meaning "headless," or to *decapitation*, as that metaphor inaccurately implies that the variation is major in rhythmical effect. The term *initial truncation* is similarly unpleasant, deriving from a Latin verb that means "to shorten by cutting off, as limbs from trunk or torso; to maim or mutilate."

Gŏing | ŭphíll, | thĕ róad | cŏmes dówn | ăs wéll.

Ĭt góes | thĕ wáy | yŏu gó. | Thăt's hów | tŏ téll.

Or substituting anapests:

Gŏing | ŭphíll, | thĕ róad | ĭs dĕscénd|ĭng ăs wéll.

This version, with only one iamb (and a trochee, a spondee, and two anapests), remains iambic pentameter because it essentially keeps the beat and in a longer passage would seem quite normal. The rhythm may even be expressive as we perhaps feel resistance (as in walking uphill) in the first two feet, and then ease or speed (as in walking downhill) in the longer, quicker strides of the extra syllables of the second part of the line. Or, rather than a couplet, we might arrange it as a quatrain mixing trimeter and dimeter lines:

> Going uphill, the road
>   Is descending as well.
> It goes the way you go.
>   That's how to tell.

For fresh possibilities, write another tetrameter quatrain and play around with substitution, differing line-lengths, et cetera. Or perhaps tinker with the following pentameter quatrain, changing it as much as possible to suit yourself. Scan it first.

> The blazing sun seems like a dandelion.
>
> The silver moon might seem a flower, too.
>
> What then of stars? They might seem whitest clover
>
> In the wide field of darkness over you.

This is an adaptation of a poem that appears on p. 81. After you've had a go, look at the original.

RHYTHM

Meter is a purely mechanical pattern of unaccented and accented syllables: te TUM te TUM te TUM, regular and arbitrary, like the beat in music. An iamb is an iamb, just as an inch is an inch. But something happens when the words of a poem are laid over meter. The result is never precisely regular, is no longer mechanical. The usual stresses of words, their varying importance or placement in the statement, their sounds, as well as the pauses and syntactical connections between them, all work to give the line an individual movement, flavor, weight. This we call rhythm: the play of the words across the rigid metrical pattern.

Meter measures speech, the varied flow of a voice. Rhythm is the result of blending the fixed (meter) with the flexible (speech). The result isn't exactly the te TUM te TUM of meter nor a reproduction of actual speech. A poem is read neither as inflexible meter nor as wholly relaxed speech but always as something between the two.

Although all iambic pentameter lines have exactly the same meter, no two lines have exactly the same rhythm. Variations in rhythm can never be exhausted. The poet, thus, has the freedom of searching out the qualities of rhythm that can make each line unique.

Consider a simple example, the sentence which is part of the first line of a poem by Richard Wilbur ("Juggler"): "A ball will bounce, but less and less." It is as inaccurate to read the line mechanically by the meter ("a BALL will BOUNCE, but LESS and LESS") as it is to read it as one might speak it ("a ball will BOUNCE, but less and less"). In speech, we usually dash off everything but the most emphatic part. In fact, depending on the intention, we might place the primary accent on *any* of the eight words in the sentence. If we are distinguishing a ball from a glass bottle, for instance, we might say, "a BALL will bounce, but less and less." If we are distinguishing a single ball from a box of balls, we might say, "A ball will bounce, but less and less." Similarly, in speech, we might find a perfectly good reason for saying "a ball WILL bounce, but less and less" or "a ball will bounce, BUT less and less," and so on, depending on what we are trying to say in a particular context.

We read this sentence in "Juggler" neither according to the rigid meter nor according to any of those wholly fluid speech emphases. In the poem the meter changes the speech-run a little, giving the sentence a more measured movement; and the speech-run of the sentence loosens the march-step of the meter. The result is distinctive—rhythm. *Speech flowing over meter produces rhythm.*

Normally, the unique qualities of rhythm, especially in its imitative potential, occur where the strength of the speech-run dislodges the meter, that is, where substitution occurs. Such variations in rhythm will often be significant, as in the Frost and Roethke lines discussed. Almost every substitution in the poems cited has some expressive effect. Consider the second stanza of Cunningham's "For My Contemporaries" (p. 63):

But Í sleep well.

Ambitious boys

Whose big lines swell

With spiritual noise,

Line 3, with its four heavy syllables (two spondees), suggests the pompous, proud rhetoric of the poets Cunningham is describing; and the alliterated b's of "Ambitious boys" climax in "big," reinforcing the rhythmical effect. Line 4 is particularly interesting. The anapestic second foot—"-itual noise"—is made rather gummy due to the already elided "-ŭal" of normal pronunciation, though it might be enunciated as "-ŭál." This possibility of four syllables in the foot—"-ítŭăl nóise"—makes us somewhat mouth the line to keep on track. The little muddle is deliberate: it is Cunningham's rhythmic imitation of, and comment on, the muddled intellect he finds in such pompous poetry. The contempt is conveyed by more than the choice of the word "noise."

In Roethke's "My Papa's Waltz" (p. 63) note the probable spondee in line 2— "Cŏuld máke | ă smáll | bŏy díz|zў"—three accents together, which, along with the extra-syllable ending syllable of "díz|zў," might suggest force and the twisting movement that is described. Notice in line 3—"Bŭt Í | hŭng ón | líke deáth"—the imitative "hanging on" of the spondaic "hŭng ón." All three feet in that line might almost be read as spondees: the voice maintains a nearly even pitch throughout the line.

Typically, the unique qualities in rhythm occur where substitutions occur. (One purpose of scansion is to locate such qualities so that they can be discussed accurately.) Even a perfectly regular line, however, may have its own deliciously characteristic rhythm. Consider again Wilbur's "A ball will bounce, but less and less," containing four perfectly regular iambs, te TUM te TUM te TUM te TUM. Within that regularity or, rather, precisely because of it, small differences in stress give the effect of less and less force and so seem to imitate the way a ball slows to a stop in smaller and smaller hops. The first two accents are made fairly forceful by the alliterated *b*'s—"A *b*all will *b*ounce"—while the liquid *l*'s of "*l*ess and *l*ess" are softer and the *s*'s seem to stretch. The second "less" naturally gets less force than the first, but it is the difference in the accents that establishes the line's rhythm. The first iamb is strongest because the contrast between the negligible "A" and the sharp "ball" is very large: "a BALL." Comparatively, the second iamb seems less forceful because the unaccented syllable—"will"—gets some emphasis from its near-rhyme with "ball" and is much less sharply contrasted, in force, with "bounce." The second iamb, "will bounce," is more evenly spread, softer. The same is true of the third iamb, "but less": "but" picks up a little extra emphasis from the already alliterated *b*'s of "ball" and "bounce"; thus the contrast of the unaccented syllable with the accented syllable seems more muted still than in "will bounce." The fourth iamb, "and less," is weaker in both parts. In short, the *difference* between each unaccented syllable and its accented syllable diminishes with each foot. We might show it pictorially, imagining each foot as a piece of string proportionally arranged according to accent:

A ball will bounce, but less and less.

Or we could simply draw the relative rise in each foot:

A ball will bounce, but less and less.

Like a magic trick performed with no props, meter makes possible such rhythmic control because it tunes the ear to careful measurements. "The strength of the genie," Wilbur has said, "comes of being confined in the bottle."

Just as a taut web allows the spider to feel the slightest disturbance, tight metrical structures let us perceive the slightest variation as significant. Tuned to that expectation—te TUM te TUM—we can respond sensitively to the subtleties or counterpoint. Alexander Pope's famous "sound of sense" passage from *An Essay on Criticism* (p. 83) is a treasury of metrical effects. Here, for instance, is the couplet about the Greek hero in the Trojan War, Ajax:

When Ájax strives some rock's vast weight to throw,

The line too labors, and the words move slow

Pope uses several spondaic substitutions to produce the feeling of weight and then of effort. In the second line, in addition to the two spondees—"too lab-" and "move slow"—the third foot is broken by the caesura—"-ors,‖and"—so that the somewhat forced accent on "and" seems itself slow and effortful. In the first line the two spondees (or spondee and near spondee) put five heavy syllables together and so weight the center of the line, as Ajax lifts the boulder he means to hurl. The secret of the line, however, isn't merely a matter of adding a heavier foot or two. The craft lies in the perfectly regular iamb in the fifth foot, "to throw." It is in that small te TUM gesture that we *feel* Ajax's effort. After five nearly even strong syllables, the contrast in weight between "to" and "throw" rhythmically mimics Ajax's gesture:

When Ajax strives some rock's vast weight to throw

Pope's skill is evident in his having varied slightly the normal word order of the sentence. If we move "to throw" back to its normal place, the effect disappears, and Ajax is left standing there with the rock sagging in his hands:

When Ájăx stríves tŏ thrów sŏme róck's văst weíght

Read the two versions of the line aloud. The little fillip of a perfectly regular foot makes us feel the actual attempt to heave the rock. The embodiment of content in form could hardly be more remarkable.

SCANSION

"Excellence" by Robert Francis offers a subtle example of rhythmic sleight of hand. Try scanning it to see what its meter is and how it works. Mark the meter in pencil on this double-spaced version, or on a separate sheet, before you look at the scansion that follows. The poem:

Excellence is millimeters and not miles.

From poor to good is great. From good to best is small.

From almost best to best sometimes not measurable.

The man who leaps the highest leaps perhaps an inch

Above the runner-up. How glorious that inch

And that split-second longer in the air before the fall.

Note: line 1 starts with anacrusis; "^{x}Éx|" is the first foot.
    Go ahead and scan the poem before you read on.
    When such a defective foot occurs *within* a line, however, it is called a **lame foot** and usually suggests disorder or a dramatic break. The first line of W. B. Yeats's "After Long Silence" (p. 309), for instance, may be scanned accurately two ways:

Spéech ăf|tĕr lóng | sílĕnce; | ^{x}ĭt | ĭs ríght,

or:

^{x}Spéech | áftĕr | lóng sí|lĕnce; ĭt | ĭs ríght,

Both scansions suggest the abruptness of beginning to speak after a silence—the first in the trochaic substitution, the second in the normal variation of anacrusis. Both record the halting, jerky rhythm—only two iambic feet in the line. But the second seems less revealing since it suggests iambic smoothness in the last two feet. In the first, the glitch of the lame fourth foot, coinciding with the caesura, suggests not only the abrupt starting of speech, but its starting and stopping . . . and resuming awkwardly, ambiguously (in reading we are uncertain how much emphasis or stress to give "it"). The first scansion is perhaps, therefore, a better record of the line's dramatic rhythm.

In scanning, listen to the poem without imposing a metrical pattern on it. Read each line aloud slowly and more than once. It may also be a good idea to scan several lines tentatively before marking them, to determine what the *norm* of the poem is. Having that norm in mind may help you resolve difficult or ambiguous spots in the rhythm. Since unique qualities most readily appear in variations from the norm, don't *te TUM* so hard that you miss an interesting subtlety. Mark ambiguous syllables (those you can imagine counting two ways) with your preferred interpretation in parentheses. Like substitutions, such feet will often hold a secret of the rhythm. In general, scan to find the lowest common denominator: that is, what is closest to the iambic base, with the fewest variations. The first line of "Loveliest of Trees" (p. 64) could be scanned:

> Lóveli|ĕst ŏf treés, | thĕ chér|rў nów

—thus showing two substitutions (trochee, anapest, iamb, iamb). But the scansion need only show one substitution (dactyl, iamb, iamb, iamb):

> Lóvelĭĕst | ŏf treés, | thĕ chér|rў nów

—which is simpler and reflects the line's generally regular beat.

In discussing rhythm, of course, keep in mind the caesuras and run-ons that give a passage its distinctive flow. In Milton's description of Mulciber's fall (p. 5)—

> Ă súm|mĕr's dáy, ‖ ănd wíth | thĕ sét|tĭng sún
>
> Drópt frŏm | thĕ zén|ĭth, ‖ líke | ă fáll|ĭng stár . . .

the run-on—along with the slight speeding up of the light accents on "with" and "like"—gives the trochaic substitution "Dropt from" its special effectiveness. The substitution brings together two of the couplet's eight real accents—"sun / Dropt"—and creates the anapestlike quickness of "from the zenith." Subliminally, we may also hear the buried sentence, "The setting sun dropt," and feel the merely metaphoric "like a falling star" (a nighttime occurrence) as completing the literal change to evening.

Here, to return to Francis's "Excellence," is our scansion:

> ˣÉx|cĕllénce | ĭs míl|lĭmét|ĕrs ănd | nŏt míles.
>
> Frŏm póor | tŏ góod | ĭs greát. | Frŏm góod | tŏ bést | ĭs smáll.
>
> Frŏm ál|mŏst bést | tŏ bést | sŏmetímes | nŏt méa|sŭráb|lĕ.
>
> Thĕ mán | whŏ leáps | thĕ hígh|ĕst leáps | pĕrháps | ăn ínch
>
> Ăbóve | thĕ rún|nĕr-úp. | Hŏw glór|iŏús | thăt ínch
>
> Ănd thát | split-séc|ŏnd lóng|ĕr ín | thĕ aír | befóre | thĕ fáll.

The norm meter in "Excellence," iambic hexameter, may appear an odd choice for a poem about legerity, the lightness of the high jumper. Perhaps the poet's first line—"Excellence is millimeters and not miles"—gave Francis the meter. Having said that to himself, or written it down, he had at least to consider writing the poem in hexameters, sluggish as they may seem (Pope's "wounded snake"). He might have changed the line to "Excellence is inches and not miles" and had a lighter, pentameter line. Since he uses "inch" later in the poem, it wouldn't have been out of place to make that change. But probably he liked the *feel* of "is millimeters and not miles," with alliterated *m*'s contrasting the tiny and the vast units of measure.

Even if accidental, hexameters were an excellent choice. The poem is less interested in the jumper's lightness or ease than in his difficulty, the extra push or effort that earns excellence, that buys the additional "inch / And that split-second longer in the air." Possibly because hexameter feels as though it goes on a little beyond the pentameter norm of English—seems to have to somehow push its way to its end—it was a perfect choice. Having made that choice, the poet exploits it beautifully, especially in the poem's last line where, after we have become accustomed to lines of six feet, he pushes just a little farther and ends with a heptameter. We don't see that extra length because the words are shorter, but we hear it, even if we don't count the feet. The line itself lasts in the ear just a second longer than the others.

Something subtle, and perhaps not very noticeable to a casual reader, is going on rhythmically in every line of "Excellence." In the first line, the almost spondaic "not miles" provides a rhythmical emphasis on the line's contrast between millimeters and miles, tiny and large, as do the short "i" of "mil-" and the long "i" of "miles." In line 2, the unrelenting monosyllables and the caesural pause may suggest the distance between "poor" and "best," a distance that can be crossed only by such a dogged pace as the line itself has. In line 3 the main effect is in the last foot, where the nearly unaccented secondary accent of the word "meas|ŭr'ăb|lĕ," followed by the unaccented e-s ending, blurs the beat so much that we almost have to force the voice to record it. (We can hardly bring ourselves to say "MÉAS-ŭr-ÁB-lĕ.") And so the line's end perfectly mimes the meaning of "not measurable." This effect is heightened, too, by the temptation to hear an off-rhyme in the last syllable of "measurable" with "miles" and "small," and so to displace the accent falsely onto that last syllable.

Like line 2, line 4 is metrically regular; but the movement is not broken by a caesura. It continues without pause to its end where, after three end-stopped lines, the run-on to line 5 suggests the leap itself. In line 5 a light secondary accent on the last syllable of "glor|ĭŏus" hurries us along to the poem's second run-on. This run-on and the spondee of "split-sec-" in line 6 appropriately hold the voice a bit longer than we expect. The very light accent on "ĭn" perhaps suggests the momentary suspension of the jumper "before the fall."

Scansion has two purposes. One, the simpler, is just to determine (or indicate) a line or passage's metrical norm. The other, more important purpose, is to show those *divergences* from the norm (variations, substitutions, anomalies) that let us begin to describe the line or passage's individual rhythm, its musical qualities, which of course include such other elements as syntax and alliteration. As readers may hear or interpret a passage differently, so their scansions may differ somewhat. The binary nature of meter, which requires that we resolve speech's myriad and complex levels of stress into its two values (accented, unaccented), is at once simplifying and the source of variety of interpretation. Scanning well isn't a matter of being correct or incorrect so much as of learning to hear with fine responsiveness.

METRICAL POTENTIAL

Theories abound that claim meter has psychological effects ranging from simple memory-aiding to the capability of inducing a trance or state of heightened awareness. The poet, though, will be interested primarily in the practical and demonstrable.

Nothing meter does, of course, is more important than its stretching the spiderweb tautly so that every effect may be felt: "subtle variation," as Richard Wilbur notes, "is unrecognizable without the preexistence of a norm." Variations and substitutions, then, may encode in the rhythm the nuance of gesture and feeling. For the reader, rhythm *works* without having to be analyzed. (Did you even notice that Henry Taylor's natural and speechlike "Barbed Wire" (p. 60) is written in iambic pentameter rather than in free verse?) For the poet, creating the perfect rhythm is also usually not a matter of analysis, but of listening patiently for it to appear among the possibilities. Metrical form, as Wilbur adds, "in slowing and complicating the writing process, calls out the poet's full talents."

Once chosen, meter provides the trellis on which tendrils of the sentences unfold. Every phrase, every line, however, cannot be a flower. There will be flat portions—necessary exposition, transition, or preparation for effects to come—and for these, poets will be grateful that the meter, the form, is simply *there*. Its presence allows them, without being particularly brilliant, to keep the poem going, the voice talking, the ball in the air. Often enough, the magic is the unnoticed craft with which the poet gets the rabbit *into* the hat.

Moreover, once the poet launches the form, whether metrical or free verse, it will suggest possibilities for dealing with the subject that might never have occurred to the poet otherwise. This must have happened in the choice of hexameter in Francis's "Excellence" and probably happens in the writing of nearly every good poem. You cannot know the potential until you get there. Rhythmical discoveries result from intuition or trial and error. The poet says something and tests it across the meter; it doesn't feel right so she or he restates it and tries again until the right rhythm just "happens." Persistence makes luck.

As a beginning poet, you may find meter hard to manage at first. As Pope says, however,

> True ease in writing comes from art, not chance,
> As those move easiest who have learned to dance.

With practice, meter becomes second nature. Its rule-of-thumb, simple, binary system bends, through substitution, to fit any purpose. A skillful tennis player no longer has to think about form and so can concentrate on the ball and the game.

Just so, having mastered meter, as a skillful poet you will have your eye on the subject, your mind on the poem.

It isn't mere chance that the finest poets in free verse began and were trained in the practice of meter—Pound and Williams and Moore, or in a more recent generation James Wright, W. S. Merwin, Louis Simpson, Adrienne Rich.

QUESTIONS AND SUGGESTIONS

1. Scan the following poems and consider the significance of rhythmical variations. (For comparison, scansions appear in Appendix II, pp. 382–384).

a)   *Death of the Day*

WALTER SAVAGE LANDOR (1775–1864)

My pictures blacken in their frames

    As night comes on,

And youthful maids and wrinkled dames

    Are now all one.

Death of the day! a sterner Death   5

    Did worse before;

The fairest form, the sweetest breath,

    Away he bore.

b)   *Epitaph*

TIMOTHY STEELE (b. 1948)

Here lies Sir Tact, a diplomatic fellow

Whose silence was not golden, but just yellow.

c)   *Anecdote of the Jar*

WALLACE STEVENS (1879–1955)

I placed a jar in Tennessee,

And round it was, upon a hill.

It made the slovenly wilderness

Surround that hill.

The wilderness rose up to it,   5

And sprawled around, no longer wild.

The jar was round upon the ground

And tall and of a port in air.

It took dominion everywhere.

The jar was gray and bare.   10

It did not give of bird or bush,

Like nothing else in Tennessee.

d) *If I should learn, in some quite casual way*
    EDNA ST. VINCENT MILLAY (1892–1950)

If I should learn, in some quite casual way,

That you were gone, not to return again—

Read from the back-page of a paper, say,

Held by a neighbor in a subway train,

How at the corner of this avenue   5

And such a street (so are the papers filled)

A hurrying man, who happened to be you,

At noon today had happened to be killed—

I should not cry aloud—I could not cry

Aloud, or wring my hands in such a place—   10

I should but watch the station lights rush by

With a more careful interest on my face;

Or raise my eyes and read with greater care

Where to store furs and how to treat the hair.

e) *Delight in Disorder*
ROBERT HERRICK (1591–1674)

A sweet disorder in the dress

Kindles in clothes a wantonness;

A lawn° about the shoulders thrown

Into a fine distraction,

An erring lace, which here and there   5

Enthralls the crimson stomacher,°

A cuff neglectful, and thereby

Ribbands° to flow confusedly,

A winning wave, deserving note,

In the tempestuous petticoat,   10

A careless shoe-string, in whose tie

I see a wild civility,

Do more bewitch me than when art

Is too precise in every part.

3 *lawn*: fine scarf; 6 *stomacher*: bodice; 8 *Ribbands*: ribbons.

f) *In the Field Forever*
ROBERT WALLACE (b. 1932)

Sun's a roaring dandelion, hour by hour.

Sometimes the moon's a scythe, sometimes a silver flower.

But the stars! all night long the stars are clover,

Over, and over, and over!

Other interesting poems to scan include Claude McKay's "The Tropics in New York" (p. 85), Timothy Steele's "Jogging in the Presidio" (p. 86), Robert Hayden's "Those Winter Sundays" (p. 87), W. B. Yeats's "After Long Silence" (p. 309), John Milton's "On His Blindness" (p. 374), Emily Dickinson's "A Bird came down the Walk" (p. 342).

2. Translate the following passage from Lewis Thomas's *The Lives of a Cell* into blank verse (unrhymed iambic pentameter). As much as possible, use the language of the prose. But stretch or compress and, where necessary, add your own touch. For comparison, a version in rhymed couplets is in Appendix II (p. 384.)

> A solitary ant, afield, cannot be considered to have much of anything on his mind: indeed, with only a few neurons strung together by fibers, he can't be imagined to have a mind at all, much less a thought. He is more like a ganglion on legs. Four ants together, or ten, encircling a dead moth on a path, begin to look more like an idea. They fumble and shove, gradually moving the food toward the Hill, but as though by blind chance. It is only when you watch the dense mass of thousands of ants, crowded together around the Hill, blackening the ground, that you begin to see the whole beast, and now you observe it thinking, planning, calculating. It is an intelligence, a kind of live computer, with crawling bits for its wits.

3. When you have scanned Robert Herrick's "Delight in Disorder" (p. 81), consider how the poet also uses syntax and even rhyme, as well as rhythm, to express his theme: that a *little* casualness or spontaneity is more charming than a too-mechanical neatness. How is the poem's long second sentence organized? Are its main subjects (lawn, lace, cuff, ribbands, wave, shoe-string) even properly parallel? How do alliteration and internal rhymes (don't stop looking too soon) help focus the lock-step rigidity of the final couplet?

4. Try making the rhythm and syntax, flow and pauses, of a long *prose* sentence imitate the movement of a skier (mountain climber, bowler, or quarterback fading back to pass). Try the same thing in a few lines of free verse, then in a few lines of iambic tetrameter.

5. Transcribe the lyrics of a popular song you enjoy. What formal devices do you find?

6. How much of the fun of the following poem comes from its meter and rhyme? Experiment by trying a rhymeless, free verse version. (Rearrange, use synonyms like "found" for "discovered.") Invent a character with an amusing name and write a funny quatrain of your own. Or add a quatrain to complete Ewart's little scene: what happens next?

Miss Twye

GAVIN EWART (b. 1916)

Miss Twye was soaping her breasts in her bath
When she heard behind her a meaning laugh

And to her amazement she discovered
A wicked man in the bathroom cupboard.

7. Write an essay comparing the handling of similar themes in Shakespeare's "Song from *Much Ado about Nothing*" and John Donne's "Song" (pp. 84–85), or of similar subjects in Roethke's "My Papa's Waltz" (p. 63) and Hayden's "Those Winter Sundays" (p. 87). Imagine how you might handle a similar poem of your own.

8. The language that we speak, exactly as we use it every day, is heavily iambic: which is what makes meter possible at all. So natural is this, we often do not notice when, in speech or prose, a string of iambs just occurs. So, *speak exclusively in meter for an hour.* And keep it strict, use only iambs. With a trick or two, you'll manage handily. And you will find, we think, not only that it's easy, once you get the hang of it; but further, that, as you relax, the people whom you talk with will not even notice or suspect what you are doing! As, we hope, you haven't noticed that we've written these instructions for this exercise in iambs—nothing but. So scan this, then go out and do the same to anyone you meet. Iambic is a breeze.

POEMS TO CONSIDER

 from *An Essay on Criticism* 1711

ALEXANDER POPE (1688–1744)

　　But most by numbers judge a poet's song;
And smooth or rough, with them, is right or wrong:
In the bright muse though thousand charms conspire,
Her voice is all these tuneful fools admire;
Who haunt Parnassus° but to please their ear,　　　　　　　5
Not mend their minds; as some to church repair,
Not for the doctrine, but the music there.
These equal syllables alone require,
Though oft the ear the open vowels tire;
While expletives their feeble aid do join;　　　　　　　　10
And ten low words oft creep in one dull line:
While they ring round the same unvaried chimes,
With sure returns of still expected rhymes;
Where'er you find "the cooling western breeze,"
In the next line, it "whispers through the trees":　　　　15
If crystal streams "with pleasing murmurs creep,"
The reader's threatened (not in vain) with "sleep":
Then, at the last and only couplet fraught
With some unmeaning thing they call a thought,

5 *Parnassus*: Greek mountain, sacred to the Muses

A needless Alexandrine ends the song,   20
That, like a wounded snake, drags its slow length along.
Leave such to tune their own dull rhymes, and know
What's roundly smooth, or languishingly slow;
And praise the easy vigor of a line,
Where Denham's° strength, and Waller's° sweetness join.   25
True ease in writing comes from art, not chance,
As those move easiest who have learned to dance.
'Tis not enough no harshness gives offense,
The sound must seem an echo to the sense:
Soft is the strain when Zephyr° gently blows,   30
And the smooth stream in smoother numbers flows;
But when loud surges lash the sounding shore,
The hoarse, rough verse should like the torrent roar:
When Ajax° strives some rock's vast weight to throw,
The line too labors, and the words move slow;   35
Not so, when swift Camilla° scours the plain,
Flies o'er th' unbending corn, and skims along the main.

25 *Denham:* poet Sir John Denham (1615–1669); *Waller:* poet Edmund Waller
(1606–1687); 30 *Zephyr:* the west wind; 34 *Ajax:* Greek warrior in *The Iliad;* 36
Camilla: ancient Roman queen, reputed to run so swiftly that she could skim over
a field of grain without bending the stalks, over the sea without wetting her feet.

 ## Song from *Much Ado about Nothing*   1600

WILLIAM SHAKESPEARE (1564–1616)

Sigh no more, ladies, sigh no more;
   Men were deceivers ever;
One foot in sea, and one on shore,
   To one thing constant never:
Then sigh not so, but let them go,   5
   And be you blithe and bonny,
Converting all your sounds of woe
   Into Hey nonny, nonny!

Sing no more ditties, sing no moe°
   Of dumps so dull and heavy;   10
The fraud of men was ever so,
   Since summer first was leavy:
Then sigh not so, but let them go,
   And be you blithe and bonny,
Converting all your sounds of woe   15
   Into Hey nonny, nonny!

9 *moe:* more

Song 1633

JOHN DONNE (1572–1631)

Go and catch a falling star,
  Get with child a mandrake root,°
Tell me where all past years are,
  Or who cleft the Devil's foot,
Teach me to hear mermaids singing,   5
  Or to keep off envy's stinging,
      And find
      What wind
Serves to advance an honest mind.

If thou be'st borne to strange sights,   10
  Things invisible to see,
Ride ten thousand days and nights,
  Till age snow white hairs on thee,
Thou, when thou return'st, wilt tell me
  All strange wonders that befell thee,   15
      And swear
      Nowhere
Lives a woman true, and fair.

If thou findst one, let me know,
  Such a pilgrimage were sweet—   20
Yet do not, I would not go,
  Though at next door we might meet;
Though she were true, when you met her,
  And last, till you write your letter,
      Yet she   25
      Will be
False, ere I come, to two, or three.

2 *mandrake root*: forked root

The Tropics in New York 1920

CLAUDE McKAY (1890–1948)

Bananas ripe and green, and ginger-root,
  Cocoa in pods and alligator pears,
And tangerines and mangoes and grape fruit,
  Fit for the highest prize at parish fairs,

Set in the window, bringing memories 5
   Of fruit-trees laden by low-singing rills,
And dewy dawns, and mystical blue skies
   In benediction over nun-like hills.

My eyes grew dim, and I could no more gaze;
   A wave of longing through my body swept, 10
And, hungry for the old, familiar ways,
   I turned aside and bowed my head and wept.

Jogging in the Presidio 1979

TIMOTHY STEELE (b. 1948)

A laughable and solitary art,
This running. Yet as I head toward the rise,
The snap of gravel underfoot is part
Of loveliness—of wind, Van Ruisdael° skies,

That grove of eucalyptus just passed through, 5
And, here, the mobile shade of fir and pine.
Though wayside skeptics eye me, I pursue
Nothing particular, nothing that's mine,

But merely leaves brought down by a hard rain
Last evening, the clear wind the swallows ride, 10
And the grass over which my shadow bends
Evenly uphill as I hit my stride.

4 *Van Ruisdael:* Dutch painter

Learning by Doing 1967

HOWARD NEMEROV (1920–1991)

They're taking down a tree at the front door,
The power saw is snarling at some nerves,
Whining at others. Now and then it grunts,
And sawdust falls like snow or a drift of seeds.
Rotten, they tell us, at the fork, and one 5
Big wind would bring it down. So what they do
They do, as usual, to do us good.
Whatever cannot carry its own weight
Has got to go, and so on; you expect

To hear them talking next about survival 10
And the values of a free society.
For in the explanations people give
On these occasions there is generally some
Mean-spirited moral point, and everyone
Privately wonders if his neighbors plan 15
To saw him up before he falls on them.

Maybe a hundred years in sun and shower
Dismantled in a morning and let down
Out of itself a finger at a time
And then an arm, and so down to the trunk, 20
Until there's nothing left to hold on to
Or snub the splintery holding rope around,
And where those big green divagations were
So loftily with shadows interleaved
The absent-minded blue rains in on us. 25

Now that they've got it sectioned on the ground
It looks as though somebody made a plain
Error in diagnosis, for the wood
Looks sweet and sound throughout. You couldn't know,
Of course, until you took it down. That's what 30
Experts are for, and these experts stand round
The giant pieces of tree as though expecting
An instruction booklet from the factory
Before they try to put it back together.

Anyhow, there it isn't, on the ground. 35
Next come the tractor and the crowbar crew
To extirpate what's left and fill the grave.
Maybe tomorrow grass seed will be sown.
There's some mean-spirited moral point in that
As well: you learn to bury your mistakes, 40
Though for a while at dusk the darkening air
Will be with many shadows interleaved,
And pierced with a bewilderment of birds.

 ## *Those Winter Sundays* 1966

ROBERT HAYDEN (1913–1980)

Sundays too my father got up early
and put his clothes on in the blueblack cold,

then with cracked hands that ached
from labor in the weekday weather made
banked fires blaze. No one ever thanked him.   5

I'd wake and hear the cold splintering, breaking.
When the rooms were warm, he'd call,
and slowly I would rise and dress,
fearing the chronic angers of that house,

Speaking indifferently to him,   10
who had driven out the cold
and polished my good shoes as well.
What did I know, what did I know
of love's austere and lonely offices?

 ### True or False   1985

JOHN CIARDI (1916–1986)

Real emeralds are worth more than synthetics
but the only way to tell one from the other
is to heat them to a stated temperature,
then tap. When it's done properly
the real one shatters.
                       I have no emeralds.   5
I was told this about them by a woman
who said someone had told her. True or false,
I have held my own palmful of bright breakage
from a truth too late. I know the principle.

Blue Jay   1986

PAUL LAKE (b. 1951)

A sound like a rusty pump beneath our window
Woke us at dawn. Drawing the curtains back,
We saw—through milky light, above the doghouse—
A blue jay lecturing a neighbor's cat
So fiercely that, at first, it seemed to wonder   5
When birds forgot the diplomacy of flight

And met, instead, each charge with a wild swoop,
Metallic cry, and angry thrust of beak.

Later, we found the reason. Near the fence
Among the flowerless stalks of daffodils,   10
A weak piping of feathers. Too late now to go back
To nest again among the sheltering leaves.
And so, harrying the dog, routing the cat,
And taking sole possession of the yard,
The mother swooped all morning.   15

                I found her there
Still fluttering round my head, still scattering
The troops of blackbirds, head cocked toward my car
As if it were some lurid animal,
When I returned from work. Still keeping faith.   20
As if what I had found by afternoon
Silent and still and hidden in tall grass
Might rise again above the fallen world;
As if the dead were not past mothering.

 ## Adam's Curse   *1904*

WILLIAM BUTLER YEATS (1865–1939)

We sat together at one summer's end,
That beautiful mild woman, your close friend,
And you and I, and talked of poetry.
I said: 'A line will take us hours maybe;
Yet if it does not seem a moment's thought,   5
Our stitching and unstitching has been naught.
Better go down upon your marrow-bones
And scrub a kitchen pavement, or break stones
Like an old pauper, in all kinds of weather;
For to articulate sweet sounds together   10
Is to work harder than all these, and yet
Be thought an idler by the noisy set
Of bankers, schoolmasters, and clergymen
The martyrs call the world.'

                And thereupon
That beautiful mild woman for whose sake   15
There's many a one shall find out all heartache

On finding that her voice is sweet and low
Replied: 'To be born woman is to know—
Although they do not talk of it at school—
That we must labour to be beautiful.'   20

I said: 'It's certain there is no fine thing
Since Adam's fall but needs much labouring.
There have been lovers who thought love should be
So much compounded of high courtesy
That they would sigh and quote with learned looks   25
Precedents out of beautiful old books;
Yet now it seems an idle trade enough.'

We sat grown quiet at the name of love;
We saw the last embers of daylight die,
And in the trembling blue-green of the sky   30
A moon, worn as if it had been a shell
Washed by time's waters as they rose and fell
About the stars and broke in days and years.

I had a thought for no one's but your ears:
That you were beautiful, and that I strove   35
To love you in the old high way of love;
That it had all seemed happy, and yet we'd grown
As weary-hearted as that hollow moon.

THE SOUND OF SENSE
Of King Kong or Storm Windows

In the "sound of sense" passage (p. 83) Pope is having fun with the possibilities of language, showing the tricks it can be made to perform. But the fun has a serious side, for smooth "numbers," regularity of meter, is not enough. Nor is avoiding the common faults he mocks. The crux is that "The sound must seem an echo to the sense." The rest of the passage is a library of effects.

When he mentions the gluey effect of open vowels, he provides a line of them: "Though oft the ear the open vowels tire." He illustrates how filler words like "do" make awkward lines: "While expletives their feeble aid do join." Or how monotonously monosyllables can move: "And ten low words oft creep in one dull line." He makes an illustrative hexameter sinuously sluggish:

> A needless Alexandrine ends the song,
> That, like a wounded snake, drags its slow length along.

He contrasts the "roundly smooth" with the "languishingly slow," and shows how quick and easy a line can be: "And praise the easy vigor of a line." He makes sound imitate the difference between a "smooth stream" and "loud surges," or between weight or effort and speed or agility:

> Soft is the strain when Zephyr gently blows,
> And the smooth stream in smoother numbers flows;
> But when loud surges lash the sounding shore,
> The hoarse, rough verse should like the torrent roar.
> When Ajax strives some rock's vast weight to throw,
> The line too labors, and the words move slow;
> Not so, when swift Camilla scours the plain,
> Flies o'er th' unbending corn, and skims along the main.

Like the line showing the hexameter's snakelike slowness, the line showing Camilla's speed is a hexameter! Plainly, it isn't so much the metrical *what* as the rhythmical *how*.

Many things are at work in the sound effects of the passage, and this chapter will look at these cogs in the rhythmical machinery: *diction, syntax, repetition, alliteration and assonance*, and *rhyme*.

DICTION

Precise choice of words is more important than sound. Meaning itself must be overriding—the exact word, not merely something near it. Poetry has no room for *I mean's* and *you know's*. The poet, like his or her best readers, will have keen antennae for the overtones and nuances, the connotations and suggestions that most words carry with them. Connotations are the feelings, the approval or disapproval, that go along with essentially the same denotative information in different words. Consider S. I. Hayakawa's amusing example: the difference between *Finest quality filet mignon* and *first-class piece of dead cow*. Or the difference between *slim* or *slender* (approving), *thin* (approximately neutral), and *skinny* or *scrawny* (disapproving). The language is happily full of words that are near in meaning but differ slightly. When you are stuck for a word, a look in *Roget's New Pocket Thesaurus* can set you off in a fresh direction. But don't trust synonyms blindly—*to chime* (as of a bell) isn't the same as *to peal*. Often the overtones or nuances of a word come from its etymological derivation, as the word "thesaurus" itself comes from a Greek word meaning "treasury."

Under *old*, Roget cites some eighty-seven adjectives, including *aged, elderly, ancient, hoary, antiquated, archaic, antique, timeless, geriatric, senile, timeworn, worm-eaten, old-fashioned, out-of-date, outmoded, passé, stale, veteran, experienced*, and *seasoned*. These words relate to several basic meanings of *old*; some usually apply, for instance, to people (*elderly, senile*), others to things and manners (*archaic, antique, old-fashioned, stale*). Depending on how we felt about him, the same old man might be described as *old-fashioned* or *seasoned* or as *timeless* or *timeworn*. One limitation of a thesaurus, however, is that it won't give us a word like *yellowed* for old. It rarely gives images or metaphors.

As we choose words, we should consider more than meaning and nuance. A word, in general, ought to be of the same level as the other words in the context. A fancy polysyllable, for example, might not fit among more everyday words. We wouldn't say, "Mr. Jones was senectuous"; we would say simply, "old." Sometimes, however, an odd word, from another level or range of meaning, provides exactly the sense and the surprise the poet wants, as with Larkin's "vast unwelcome" in "First Sight" or Cunningham's "spiritual noise." In "My Papa's Waltz," Roethke chooses the less predictable word "countenance" rather than "face":

> My mother's countenance
> Could not unfrown itself

The greater formality and strangeness of "countenance" emphasize the stiffness and the oddness, to the boy, of her expression. Countenance also means precisely the look or appearance of a face as an indication of mood or emotion. Lurking behind the word, too, is its meaning as a verb, to approve or tolerate—which the mother sternly refuses to do. Even the impersonal construction, "Could not unfrown *itself*," contributes to our understanding of the scene.

The surprise of an unexpected word when it turns out to be especially appropriate is exemplified by Robert Herrick's use of "liquefaction" in "Upon Julia's Clothes" (p. 18) or by Robert Hayden's choice of "offices" in "Those Winter Sundays" (p. 87). The primary meaning in "love's austere and lonely offices" is tasks or duties, but the word's overtone of the official reminds us as well of the authority and trust or responsibility that belong to the role of fatherhood. Also, as in "divine offices," the word may suggest a spiritual dimension—duties that are "rites," the carrying out of a ceremony of devotion. Equally, the unexpected word brings imagistic vividness, as when in "Primary Colors" (p. 126) Cathy Song mentions cats' "pincushion paws" or "the clanging colors of crayolas."

Much of our pleasure in a poem like "Enter Dark Stranger" by William Trowbridge (b. 1941) comes from the precision and inventiveness of its diction:

Enter Dark Stranger

In *Shane*, when Jack Palance first appears,
a stray cur takes one look and slinks away
on tiptoes, able, we understand, to recognize
something truly dark. So it seems
when we appear, crunching through the woods.   5
A robin cocks her head, then hops off,
ready to fly like hell and leave us the worm.
A chipmunk, peering out from his hole
beneath a maple root, crash dives
when he hears our step. The alarm spreads in a skittering   10
of squirrels, finches, millipedes. Imagine
a snail picking up the hems of his shell
and hauling ass for cover. He's studied carnivores,
seen the menu, noticed the escargots.

But forget Palance, who would have murdered Alabama   15
just for fun. Think of Karloff's monster,
full of lonely love but too hideous
to bear; or Kong, bereft with Fay Wray
shrieking in his hand: the flies circle our heads
like angry biplanes, and the ants hoist pitchforks   20
to march on our ankles as we watch the burgher's daughter
bob downstream in a ring of daisies.

The poem sets out its sobering theme—that humans, in the eyes of other creatures, are in fact monsters—as a deliciously comic meditation, persuasive yet without moralizing.

Using a stage direction for the title of the poem, Trowbridge draws upon images of three characters from classic movies: first, the nerveless killer played by Jack

Palance in *Shane*, and then Frankenstein's monster (in Boris Karloff's portrayal) and King Kong. Like the dog slinking off at Palance's entrance, the animals in the woods flee us as "something truly dark." The tone is tentative: "So it seems"; and in stanza 2 the speaker modifies the conclusion: "But forget Palance," whose evil is purely wicked and hyperbolically extreme ("would have murdered Alabama / just for fun"). Still tentatively we are invited only to "Think of . . ." If evil, we are perhaps accidentally so, not understanding our own strength or nature; lonely and, for all the horror, driven and pitiable.

Ironically, neither Frankenstein's monster nor Kong is literally human. The attacking ants and flies are drawn from the scenes of peasants with pitchforks pursuing the monster and from the "angry biplanes" circling Kong as he climbs the Empire State Building with the terrified actress in his fist. All this is thematically paradoxical, as the scenes show misguided humans attacking the creatures who at this point in the films have the audience's sympathy.

Notably, too, the animals in stanza 1 are depicted in diction that, once we think of it, suggests movie cartoons. This impression, perhaps hidden in the cur "on tiptoes" and in the colloquial phrase describing the female robin as "ready to fly like hell and leave us the worm," seems clear in the submarine-war image when the chipmunk "crash dives" into his burrow. It is unmistakeable in the snail's "picking up the hems of his shell / and hauling ass for cover." The picture is pure Disney, even to the snail's having "seen the menu, noticed the escargots." The reference recalling a cliché, "the early bird gets the worm," was a signal. In a deeper sense, the poem is about how we choose the images in which we see ourselves.

Generally, **clichés**—stale, timeworn, too familiar words and phrases—are best avoided in favor of freshness. The language of poetry pays attention, and it is the nature of a cliché not to pay attention. Recently a newspaper carried this sentence: "'I think we are enjoying the backlash of the moral decline that peaked in Watergate,' Dr. Weber said." Enjoying a lash of any kind seems unlikely; and the *peak* of a *decline* is language that isn't listening to itself at all.

You can test for a cliché by asking yourself whether the word, phrase, or image you're using is particular or generic. If you say, "She's always there for me," where is *there*? When you need support and companionship, wouldn't you rather have her *here* than *there*? If you're writing about a rainbow, do you see a real rainbow with all its translucence, transience, and tenuousness? No rainbow looks exactly like another. Or do you see the graphic artist's generic sentimental symbol: neat little arches lined up according to the spectrum, violet to blue, flat colors? If you're thinking of the latter, you have a cliché; drop it.

Another test is to ask yourself if you really know what you're talking about when you use the word, phrase, or image. What's a doornail? Is it dumber than a roofing nail? Quieter? Smarter than a finishing nail? A final test: do you get a sensation when you use the phrase, or are you only transmitting general impressions? *Hard as nails* doesn't trigger a feeling of hardness and durability. *Cold as ice* doesn't make you want to shiver. Does *light as a feather* make you feel the ticklish, wispy barbs?

Poetry often generates a kind of cliché all its own, **poetic diction,** which is fancy, pompous, or ornate language that gets used and reused until it becomes simply dull. Words like *o'er* for *over*, *ere* for *before*, or *thou* for *you* are examples. So are such eighteenth-century elegant variations as *finny tribe* for *fish*. Don't use in a poem a word that you wouldn't use in speech—or at least weigh your purpose carefully.

So, roundabout, we come to the sound of words, which is a secondary but important property of diction. In general, the sounds of the words in a passage should be cleanly enunciated, smooth, and easy to say; or, when they are awkward, clogging, hard to say, it should be for a reason related to the sense, as with Pope's deliberately harsh "The hoarse, rough verse should like the torrent roar."

Some words have their own sound effects built in: *hiss*, *buzz*, *snarl*, *snap*, *pop*, *smash*, *whisper*, *murmur*, *hum*, *shout*. Such words are called *onomatopoetic* (noun: **onomatopoeia**). Never mind the Greek name, but keep your ear tuned for words that somehow seem to sound like their meanings. They are more frequent than one might think. Notice the light vowels in *thin*, *skinny*, *slim*, *slender*, and *spindly*. Or the long vowels or clotting consonants in *fat*, *hefty*, *gross*, *huge*, *stout*, *pudgy*, and *thick*. Notice how lightly *delicate* hits its syllables, how heavily *ponderous* does. Feel how your mouth says *pinched*, *tight*, *open*, *round*, *hard*, *soft*, *smooth*.

It isn't that particular sounds, particular vowels or consonants, have meanings as such; *slight* and *threadlike* don't sound much like their meanings. Often, though, there seems to be some at least latent correlation between the meaning and the noise of words that the poet can use. In "Enter Dark Stranger," note especially *crunch*, *hop*, *shriek*, *skitter*, *bob*, and *slink*. Why do so many words beginning *sli-* seem similar: *slice*, *slick*, *slide*, *slight*, *slim*, *slime*, *sling*, *slink*, *slip*, *slit*, *slither*, *sliver*, and perhaps *sly*? The most familiar example of onomatopoeia is Tennyson's

> The moan of doves in immemorial elms
> And murmuring of innumerable bees

"Moan" and "murmur" are onomatopoetic, and the rather slurred, hard-to-count syllables of "innumerable" might also qualify. The hum of the lines, the alliterated *m*'s, *n*'s, and *r*'s that pick up the sounds of "moan" and "murmuring," seems imitative throughout. Such effects should be used sparingly. In the extreme they quickly become silly or obtrusive and overwhelm meaning.

This of course is the fun of the following poem by John Updike (b. 1932):

Player Piano

> My stick fingers click with a snicker
> And, chuckling, they knuckle the keys;
> Light-footed, my steel feelers flicker
> And pluck from these keys melodies.
>
> My paper can caper; abandon   5
> Is broadcast by dint of my din,
> And no man or band has a hand in
> The tones I turn on from within.
>
> At times I'm a jumble of rumbles,
> At others I'm light like the moon,   10

> But never my numb plunker fumbles,
> Misstrums me, or tries a new tune.

Try to tabulate the variety of sound devices by which Updike imitates the tinkly mechanical piano.

SYNTAX

Syntax is the way that words are put together to form phrases, clauses, and sentences. The poet can take advantage of a language's many alternative patterns for formulating or constructing sentences. Placement of modifiers, apposition, series, restrictive or nonrestrictive clauses, active or passive voice, and inversion are obvious formulas. The word *syntax* comes from the Greek *syn* ("together") and *tassein* ("to arrange"): "to arrange together." Also from *tassein* we get the word *tactics*, a military image that may suggest the value of syntax to the poet in deploying forces.

The syntactical qualities of good writing in general—main ideas in main clauses and subordinate ideas in subordinate clauses, for example—apply in poetry. Moreover, poets can often shape meaning expressively by attentive control of syntax. Pope's "some rock's vast weight to throw," for instance, instead of "to throw some rock's vast weight," reenforces the idea by a simple inversion of normal word order. Or note the fussiness implied by the overcarefully inserted "with them" in

> But most by numbers judge a poet's song,
> And smooth or rough, with them, is right or wrong.

The syntax, not the statement itself, communicates the slight contempt, as if Pope were holding the words "with them" away from his nose. Or observe how, in lines 3–7 of "The Fish," Marianne Moore displaces the prepositional phrase, so it comes first, allowing an off-balance, lidlike rhythm to the sentence, and uses a more dislocating semicolon, where a comma would be normal, to emphasize the eccentric movement:

> Of the crow-blue mussel-shells, one keeps
> adjusting the ash-heaps;
>   opening and shutting itself like
>
> an
> injured fan.

Notice, in "Barbed Wire" (p. 60), how Henry Taylor has made all twenty-four lines of the poem into one sentence. Contrast that with Robert Francis's making two sentences of the line in "Excellence"—"From poor to good is great. From good to best is small."—which could have been joined by a comma or semicolon. Review Richard Wilbur's opting, in lines 8–19 of "Hamlen Brook" (p. 27), to make one ongoing sentence of many subsentences. Looking back, what thematic point do you see in Wilbur's choice? As with every aspect of form, the very arrangement of words into clauses and sentences can offer music and meaning.

In these lines from John Donne's "Satire III," the complex and entwined syntax, played skillfully over the line-breaks, rhythmically suggests the difficulty through which "Truth" is approachable.

> On a huge hill,
> Cragged, and steep, Truth stands, and he that will
> Reach her, about must, and about must go;
> And what the hill's suddenness resists, win so

Syntactical displacement and inversions constantly impede the lines' movement. Compare a more normal prose version:

> On a huge, cragged, and steep hill, Truth stands, and he that will reach her must
> go about and about, and in that way win what the hill's suddenness resists.

The effect is supported by the passage's metrical roughness and irregularity throughout, especially by the forced anapest in line 4:

> And what | the hill's sud|denness resists, win so

The voice wants to read "hill's" as accented but must push on to the syllable "sud-" before it finds the line's pattern. This rhythmic drag over "hill's" produces a feeling of the steepness or the abruptness of the slope, which cannot be conquered directly but only by a circling sideward path. Metrical expectation forces an accent on "-ness"; but then, abruptly set off by the caesura, the spondee "win so" brings the line to a halting end. Throughout, the voice seems almost literally to be working against gravity.

In "The Frog" the anonymous poet uses syntactical patterning to produce, in spite of the apparent illiteracy, a very subtle formal structure:

> What a wonderful bird the frog are!
> When he stand he sit almost;
> When he hop he fly almost.
> He ain't got no sense hardly;
> He ain't got no tail hardly either.　　　　　　　　　5
> When he sit, he sit on what he ain't got almost.

Two sets of parallel sentences ("When . . . almost" in lines 2–3 and "He ain't got . . ." in lines 4–5) adroitly set up the last line, which gathers both patterns in its climactic syntax.

Frequently, when someone talks of the speaking "voice" being caught in the words of a poem, it is the syntax that is giving the effect. Robert Frost was a master of coaxing both music and meaning out of syntax. Listen again to the repetitions and emphases of these lines from "An Old Man's Winter Night":

> What kept his eyes from giving back the gaze
> Was the lamp tilted near them in his hand.
> What kept him from remembering what it was

That brought him to that creaking room was age.
He stood with barrels round him—at a loss.   5
And having scared the cellar under him
In clomping here, he scared it once again
In clomping off;—and scared the outer night,
Which has its sounds, familiar, like the roar
Of trees and crack of branches, common things,   10
But nothing so like beating on a box.

Even the four *him*'s in lines 3–6—the first three unaccented—work to a minor climax within the turning and returning syntax that gives a rhythm to the old man's now meaningless movements in the house.

Syntax has been called "the muscle of thought." Its value to a poem's strategy is clear in Whitman's "When I Heard the Learn'd Astronomer":

When I heard the learn'd astronomer,
When the proofs, the figures, were ranged in columns before me,
When I was shown the charts and diagrams, to add, divide, and
    measure them,
When I sitting heard the astronomer where he lectured with much
    applause in the lecture-room,
How soon unaccountable I became tired and sick,   5
Till rising and gliding out I wander'd off by myself,
In the mystical moist night-air, and from time to time,
Look'd up in perfect silence at the stars.

We, too, instantly prefer that "perfect silence" to the astronomer's blab, and the real stars to any talk about them. It is a point, however, the poet can't make by means of adjectives or a metaphor—they are simply "the stars." The closest he comes to being "poetic" is the alliterating phrase in line 7, "the mystical moist night-air," which puns on *mist-mystical.* And we may recall that the verbs for the speaker's actions in line 6, "rising," "gliding," and "wander'd," are proper for describing the motions of heavenly bodies. (Our word *planet* comes from a Greek root meaning "wanderer.")

The poem's force and especially that of the chillingly beautiful last line come from Whitman's manipulation of syntax. Lines 1–4, describing the lecture, have no main clause, and so seem indecisive; and they are long, prosy, choppy, repetitious, clogged with lists and details—in perfect imitation of the lecture. (The device of organizing lines or sentences by repeating the same word or phrase at the beginning of each—as here, with "When . . ." in lines 1–4—is called **anaphora.**) Even the verbs in lines 2–3 are passive. The redundant thump of "where he *lectured* with much applause in the *lecture*-room" seems banal and clumsy. The effect on the listener is also recorded in the syntax. The placement of "sitting"—"I sitting heard"—suggests awkwardness and discomfort. In the contortion of line 5, the adjective "unaccountable" is misplaced; it doesn't really modify the speaker, and should be an adverb: I became unaccountably tired and sick. The suggestion, of course, is that *he*, as a living being, is no more *countable* in figures and columns than the natural stars.

In contrast, everything in lines 6–8 is shorter, simpler, more active. Unlike the dangling and restarting "when" clauses, the balanced prepositional phrases of line 7 give a sense of leisure and space, with "and" easily linking "I wander'd" and "Look'd." Beginning with a verb, line 8 flows with a sense of syntactical resolution. It is also the shortest and (in syntax) most direct line in the poem. This culminating impression of clarity is reenforced by rhythm: line 8 (in a poem of rangy free verse) happens to be perfect iambic pentameter!

Look'd up | in per|fect si|lence at | the stars.

It is not only freedom we feel, but order, unity.

REPETITION

Simply repeating a word or phrase, perhaps with variations, can give a tune to a passage, as in Frost's "having *scared* the cellar under him / In *clomping* here, he *scared* it once again / In *clomping* off;—and *scared* the outer night . . ." In "Learning by Doing" (p. 86) Nemerov speaks in line 24 of the branches "So loftily *with shadows interleaved*" and thus prepares readers for lines 41–43 when at dusk, remembering,

> the darkening air
> Will be *with* many *shadows interleaved*,
> And pierced with a bewilderment of birds.

Syntactical repetition can be almost structural, as in Omoteji Adeyemon's "Saviour (Mississippi 1957)" (p. 56). Line 6 repeats line 1: "Christ was white this morning . . ." and, after the fire, line 13 repeats line 9: "Now Christ is black . . ." This pattern, linking four of the poem's five sentences, balances on the one line devoted to the fire: "Then they came and burnt the church down" (line 8).

Such repetition can serve as a fixed, formal device in the **refrain** of song or songlike poems—the refrain is a line or lines regularly repeated from stanza to stanza, usually at the end—as in Shakespeare's "Sigh no more, ladies, sigh no more" (p. 84), or in this fine lyric by W. B. Yeats (1865–1939):

Mad as the Mist and Snow

Bolt and bar the shutter
For the foul winds blow:
Our minds are at their best this night,
And I seem to know
That everything outside us is   5
Mad as the mist and snow.

Horace there by Homer stands,
Plato stands below,
And here is Tully's open page.

How many years ago   10
Were you and I unlettered lads
Mad as the mist and snow?

You ask what makes me sigh, old friend,
What makes me shudder so?
I shudder and I sigh to think   15
That even Cicero
And many-minded Homer were
Mad as the mist and snow.

The refrain's cumulative force draws upon the phrase's resonating shifts of meaning in each use. In stanza 1, *"Mad as the mist and snow"* refers only to the wildness of literal nature outside the room. In stanza 2, the meaning is extended to include the instinctive wildness of the "unlettered lads" the speaker and his companion once were; and in stanza 3, ominously, to include even the great minds whose books' wisdom now fills the lit room. The poem's opposition of intellect and wild nature implies how frail the former really is.

Repetition also underlies the complex whole-poem forms of sestinas, pantoums, and villanelles. In sestinas (see Appendix I, p. 375) six words repeated in a specified varying order at line-ends determine the form of the poem's stanzas. In pantoums (see p. 376) the entire poem is organized by the rule that two complete lines of each quatrain be repeated in the next quatrain, so that every line in the poem appears twice. In villanelles (see p. 374) lines 1 and 3 of the first triplet are repeated alternately like refrain lines in stanzas 2–5 and then together in stanza 6, and only two rhyme-sounds are used throughout, as in this elegy for his father by Dylan Thomas (1914–1953):

Do Not Go Gentle into That Good Night

Do not go gentle into that good night,
Old age should burn and rave at close of day;
Rage, rage against the dying of the light.

Though wise men at their end know dark is right,
Because their words had forked no lightning they   5
Do not go gentle into that good night.

Good men, the last wave by, crying how bright
Their frail deeds might have danced in a green bay,
Rage, rage against the dying of the light.

Wild men who caught and sang the sun in flight,   10
And learn, too late, they grieved it on its way,
Do not go gentle into that good night.

Grave men, near death, who see with blinding sight
Blind eyes could blaze like meteors and be gay,
Rage, rage against the dying of the light.   15

And you, my father, there on the sad height,
Curse, bless, me now with your fierce tears, I pray.
Do not go gentle into that good night.
Rage, rage against the dying of the light.

ALLITERATION AND ASSONANCE

Alliteration is the repetition of consonant sounds in several words in a passage; **assonance,** the repetition of vowel sounds. The *b*'s in these lines of "An Old Man's Winter Night" are alliteration:

> . . . like the roar
> Of trees and crack of *b*ranches, common things,
> But nothing so like *b*eating on a *b*ox.

Also alliterated, less emphatically, are the *r*'s, the hard *c*'s (including of course "box"—"bocks"), and the *n*'s. Assonance appears in the similar vowels of "cr*a*ck" and "br*a*nches," of "c*o*mmon" and "b*o*x." The *b*'s are clearly onomatopoetic, suggesting the sounds of the old man's clomping about. The *r*'s may suggest the storm, much as in Pope's "But when loud surges lash the sounding shore, / The hoarse, rough verse should like the torrent roar." The assonance of "common" and "box," along with the climaxing of the string of *b*'s and hard *c*'s in "box," gives the word something very near the emphatic finality of rhyme. Every element of "box" repeats sounds heard earlier in the lines.

Given the limited number of common sounds in English, alliteration and assonance would be hard to avoid. Using them is more discovering, or taking advantage of, than imposing them. Their main value, often more subliminal than obvious, is the linking of sounds to thread lines together so that they are tight and harmonious. In Milton's "Men called him Mulciber; and how he fell / From Heaven they fabled" (p. 5), the alliterated *m*'s and then *h*'s and *f*'s, and *l*'s throughout, give the clauses a musical unity. The assonance of "Men" and "fell" helps to frame the line. Similarly, four *b*'s in the last two quatrains of Roethke's "My Papa's Waltz" (p. 63)—"battered," "buckle," "beat," and "bed"—thread the poem's climaxing music. The *s*'s frame the poem's last line—"Still clinging to your shirt"—and the short *i*'s and internal rhyme of "St*i*ll cl*i*nging" are onomatopoetic.

Alliteration and assonance also serve to emphasize or pair related words or phrases. The *s*'s in Pope's "The sound must seem an echo to the sense" unify and also sharply emphasize the central meaning. Such emphatic pairing underlines comparison or contrast, as in Francis's "Excellence is *m*illimeters and not *m*iles" or in Nemerov's "That we may lick their *h*inder parts and thump their *h*eads." How potent such alliteration may be can be seen by comparing the last two lines of this stanza of Poe's "To Helen"—

> On desperate seas long wont to roam,
>   Thy hyacinth hair, thy classic face,
> Thy Naiad airs have brought me home

> To the glory that was Greece
> And the grandeur that was Rome.

—to an earlier version of the same lines, which are flat and insipid:

> To the beauty of fair Greece
> And the grandeur of old Rome.

Look back to "Mad as the Mist and Snow" and "Do Not Go Gentle into That Good Night," and notice the alliteration and assonance. You won't miss the *b*'s in stanza 1 of the first, nor the *h*'s and *l*'s in stanza 2, nor the *m*'s in stanza 3. Assonance is harder—don't overlook "mi*nd*s" and "ni*ght*" in line 3, or "*is*" and "m*is*t" in lines 5–6. "Do Not Go Gentle into That Good Night" is musically richer. Notice how the long *o* of "go" is picked up in stanzas 1 and 2 by "Old," "close," "Though," "know," "no," and "go" again. Sharpen your pencil if you really want to see how densely Thomas has woven the sound-colors!

RHYME

By definition, **rhyme** is an identity in two or more words of vowel sound and of any following consonants. Exact rhymes: *gate-late*; *own-bone*; *aware-hair*; *applause-gauze*; *go-throw*. Rhymes normally fall on accented syllables. Double (or extra-syllable) rhymes normally fall on an accented and unaccented syllable: *going-throwing*; *merry-cherry*; *army-harm me*; but they may fall on two accented syllables, as in *ping-pong*, *sing-song* or *breadbox-dread locks*. Triple rhymes are *merrily-warily*; *admonish you-astonish you*; *head you off-instead you scoff*. There are a few natural four-syllable rhymes, like *criticism-witticism*.

English is not an easy language to rhyme. Many familiar words have no natural rhymes, like "circle" or "month." For some words there is only one natural rhyme: "strength-length," "fountain-mountain." A word as much used as "love" offers only meager possibilities: *above, dove, glove, shove, of*. Despite a poet's best contortions, it is hard to make such rhymes fresh; consequently, *unrhymed* verse is equally standard, as the much-used blank verse of Shakespeare's plays and many of Frost's dramatic monologues. Other properties of sound, like alliteration and assonance, can make unrhymed verse as musical or effective as need be.

The difficulty of rhyme in English has opened up a wide variety of inexact rhyme—**off-** or **slant-rhymes**—that the poet may use with considerable freshness. One device is terminal alliteration, as in *love-move, bone-gone, what-bat*, or "*chill-full*." Another is **consonance** (identity of consonants with different main vowels), as in *bad-bed, full-fool, fine-faun*, or *summer-simmer*; or near consonance as in *firm-room, past-pressed*, or *shadow-meadow*. There is assonance, of course, as in *bean-sweet* or *how-cloud*; and Emily Dickinson has even made length of vowel work, as in "*be-fly*" or the fainter "*day-eternity*."

Rhyming accented with unaccented (or secondarily accented) syllables is also a common method of off-rhyme, as in "*see-pretty*," "*though-fellow*," "*full-eagle*," "*fish-polish*," "*them-solemn*," "*under-stir*." There is no need to be systematic about the varieties of off-rhyme. Anything will do—recall Marianne Moore's "The Fish"

(p. 46). In this World War I poem by Wilfred Owen (1893–1918), off-rhyme becomes nearly as formal as exact rhyme. The persistent refusal to rhyme gives the poem an off-key sound in keeping with its ironic theme.

Arms and the Boy

Let the boy try along this bayonet-blade
How cold steel is, and keen with hunger of blood;
Blue with all malice, like a madman's flash;
And thinly drawn with famishing for flesh.

Lend him to stroke these blind, blunt bullet-leads   5
Which long to nuzzle in the hearts of lads,
Or give him cartridges of fine zinc teeth,
Sharp with the sharpness of grief and death.

For his teeth seem for laughing round an apple.
There lurk no claws behind his fingers supple;   10
And God will grow no talons at his heels,
Nor antlers through the thickness of his curls.

Rhyme works in a number of ways. It may serve simply as a formal device: musically pleasurable, part of the poem's tune. It may be charming and graceful, or grand and sonorous, or abrasive. Its precision may close a poem's box up tight, as in this epigram by Emily Otis (b. 1906):

Mother-in-Law

It stops me in a sudden spot
like unsuspected chewing gum—
the sticky thought that I am what,
he fears, she will become.

Or, like alliteration, rhyme may emphasize comparison or contrast, as "chance-dance" almost sums up the thematic opposition in Pope's

True ease in writing comes from art, not chance,
As those move easiest who have learned to dance.

Nor need rhyme always fit a rigid pattern. In Robert Frost's "After Apple-Picking," the line-length varies; so does the occurrence of the rhymes:

After Apple-Picking

My long two-pointed ladder's sticking through a tree
Toward heaven still,
And there's a barrel that I didn't fill
Beside it, and there may be two or three
Apples I didn't pick upon some bough.   5

But I am done with apple-picking now.
Essence of winter sleep is on the night,
The scent of apples: I am drowsing off.
I cannot rub the strangeness from my sight
I got from looking through a pane of glass   10
I skimmed this morning from the drinking trough
And held against the world of hoary grass.
It melted, and I let it fall and break.
But I was well
Upon my way to sleep before it fell,   15
And I could tell
What form my dreaming was about to take.
Magnified apples appear and disappear,
Stem end and blossom end,
And every fleck of russet showing clear.   20
My instep arch not only keeps the ache,
It keeps the pressure of a ladder-round.
I feel the ladder sway as the boughs bend.
And I keep hearing from the cellar bin
The rumbling sound   25
Of load on load of apples coming in.
For I have had too much
Of apple-picking: I am overtired
Of the great harvest I myself desired.
There were ten thousand thousand fruit to touch,   30
Cherish in hand, lift down, and not let fall.
For all
That struck the earth,
No matter if not bruised or spiked with stubble,
Went surely to the cider-apple heap   35
As of no worth.
One can see what will trouble
This sleep of mine, whatever sleep it is.
Were he not gone,
The woodchuck could say whether it's like his   40
Long sleep, as I describe its coming on,
Or just some human sleep.

Sometimes rhymes are in adjacent lines, but they may be separated by as many as three other lines, as are "break-take" in lines 13–17 and "end-bend" in lines 19–23. The triple-rhyme "well-fell-tell" in the quickly turning lines 14–16 appropriately helps to convey the indefinable transition from waking to dreaming. Near the end of the poem, in a masterful touch, "heap" in line 35 doesn't find its line-end rhyme until, after seven lines, "sleep" appears in line 42, although the word teasingly occurs three times *within* intervening lines.

This is a good example of **internal rhyme.** Unlike end-rhyme, which occurs at line-ends as part of the formal organization of a poem, internal rhyme may occur anywhere within lines and is musically "accidental," though it may be wonderfully expressive:

> And I keep hearing from the cellar bin
> The rumbling sound
> Of load on load of apples coming in.

Internal rhyme may be as overt and corny as in the popular song's "the lazy, hazy, crazy days of summer," or as casual as it appears in Nemerov's "Learning by Doing" (p. 86) where along with alliteration and assonance it almost secretly laces the poem:

> Maybe a hundred years in sun and shower
> Dismantled in a morning and let down
> Out of itself a finger at a time
> And then an arm . . .

These lines of Richard Wilbur's "Year's End" show masterly control:

> I've known the wind by water banks to shake
> The late leaves down, which frozen where they fell
> And held in ice as dancers in a spell
> Fluttered all winter long into a lake . . .

The lovely whirling sound within the "which" clause is mainly the result of the internal rhyme of "held," which attaches to the end-rhyme "fell" and unexpectedly spins the voice toward the end-rhyme "spell." The quick movement is intensified by the only technically accented "in" of "ăs dáncĕrs in ă spéll," with three essentially unaccented syllables speeding the line. Although hardly noticeable, the "rhyme" of two *in*'s—one unaccented, the other technically accented, "ĭn ice ăs dáncĕrs ĭn ă spéll"—also contributes to the magical feeling of whirling, as does the light, hidden rhyme in "And" and "dancers."

Part of the effect, too, comes from syntactical suspension. We wait a line and a half for the clause's subject, "which," to find its verb, "Fluttered." This suspension mirrors the suspended motion of the leaves (dancers) as, in ice, they *seem* to be still turning but are not. The alliterated *f*'s of "frozen," "fell," and "Fluttered" help mark off this suspension within the continuing *l*'s that begin with "late leaves" in line 2 and culminate with "long into a lake" in line 4. The trochaic substitution "Flúttĕred" signals the resumption of reality. Motion in stasis—leaves in ice, dancers in a spell.

Playing with rhymes to see what they can do is fun, as with Richard Armour's "bottle-lot'll." The more outrageous, the better. In *Don Juan* Lord Byron (1788–1824) offered up such rhymes as "fellows-jealous" or "the loss of her—philosopher." The twentieth-century master of outlandish rhyme was Ogden Nash (1902–1971), who reported that kids eat spinach "inach by inach," who advised "if called by a panther / Don't anther," and who remarked that a man who teases a cobra will soon be "a sadder he, and sobra." Gerard Manley Hopkins rhymed "Saviour-gave you a" in a serious sonnet, "Hurrahing in Harvest"; but such contrived rhymes are best saved for poems that intend to be funny.

Too much rhyme is like too much lipstick. Robert Frost's test for rhymes was to see if he could detect which had occurred to the poet first. Both rhyme words had to seem equally natural, equally called for by what was being said. If one or the other seemed dragged in more for rhyme than sense, the rhyming was a failure. This is a good test, but a difficult one as well. If you sometimes have to settle for a slightly weak rhyme, put the weaker of the pair *first*; then, when the rhyme-bell sounds in the ear with the second, it will be calling attention to the more suitable and natural word.

TEXTURE

Diction, syntax, repetition, alliteration and assonance, and rhyme function together, along with rhythm, to give a poem its **texture.** As cloth gets its texture or character from the quality of the interwoven strands, so a poem has a texture or "feel" that comes from the interweaving of its technical elements and its meanings. Consider how these elements mingle in this poem by Conrad Hilberry (b. 1928):

Storm Window

At the top of the ladder, a gust catches the glass
and he is falling. He and the window topple
backwards like a piece of deception slowly
coming undone. After the instant of terror,
he feels easy, as though he were a boy   5
falling back on his own bed. For years,
he has clamped his hands to railings, balanced
against the pitch of balconies and cliffs
and fire towers. For years, he has feared falling.
At last, he falls. Still holding the frame,   10
he sees the sky and trees come clear
in the wavering glass. In another second
the pane will shatter over his whole length,
but now, he lies back on air, falling.

The narrative focuses on two moments only, an "instant of terror" at the beginning of the fall and a momentary sense of suspension that follows, as the character accepts the inevitability of what is occurring. The outcome, though foreseen in line 13—"the pane will shatter over his whole length"—is not yet. Eight of the poem's fourteen lines are run-on and, moreover, seven have extra-syllable (e-s) endings. Six of the eight sentences open at caesuras, mid-line, so a rhythmic sense of continuity and descent is strong. In fact, the rest of the poem only repeats the action stated in the first line and a half:

At the top of the ladder, a gust catches the glass
and he is falling.

Everything else is instant-replay or elaboration, giving the effect of stasis or slow-motion. ". . . falling" in line 2 is picked up by "falling" at the end of line 9 and by "falling" at the end of the last line. The action is no further along at the end of the poem than in line 2.

Crucially, lines 9 and 14, ending with the present participle, are the only two end-stopped lines in the poem that complete sentences. In a way they define the poem's structure, organizing it as lines 1–9 and 10–14. Albeit unrhymed, a poem of fourteen lines in iambic pentameter suggests the sonnet-form, and this division corresponds

Here is a scansion with metrical substitutions or variations (anacrusis, extra-syllable ending) underlined; some repetitions, alliteration, assonance, and rhyme are italicized:

At the tóp of the *lád* der, ‖ a gúst cátch es the *gláss*

and he is *fáll ing*. ‖ He and the wín *dŏw* tóp plĕ

x*báck* wărds lĭke ă píece ŏf dĕcép tion slów lў

cóm ĭng ŭndóne. ‖ Áftĕr thăt ín stănt ŏf tér rŏr,

hĕ féels éasў, ‖ ăs thóugh hĕ wére ă bóy   5

x*fáll* ĭng báck ŏn hĭs ówn béd. ‖ Fŏr yéars,

hĕ hăs clámped hĭs hánds tŏ ráil ĭngs, bál ănced

ăgáinst thĕ pítch ŏf bál cŏníes ănd clíffs

ănd fíre tówĕrs. ‖ Fŏr yéars, ‖ hĕ hăs *féared fáll* ĭng.

Ăt lást, hĕ fálls. ‖ Stíll hóld ĭng thĕ *fráme*,   10

hĕ *sées* thĕ ský ănd trées cŏme cléar

ĭn thĕ wáv ĕrĭng gláss. ‖ *Ĭn* ănóth ĕr séc ŏnd

thĕ páne wĭll shát tĕr ó vĕr hĭs whóle léngth,

bŭt nów, ‖ hĕ líes báck ŏn *áir*, ‖ *fáll* ĭng .

roughly to the octave/sestet of the sonnet, with the "turn" coming (after the flashback of lines 7–9) with line 10's return to the narrative, "At last, he falls." Another verbal repetition links the first instant, "topple / *backwards*," to the second ("easy"): "falling *back* on his own bed," and appears again in line 14 as "lies *back* on air." The repeated "For years" in lines 6 and 9 gives the generalized flashback a feeling of stasis.

Though never obtrusive, the metrical orchestration is deft. Six of the poem's eleven anapests occur in the lively action of lines 1–4, three of them in line 1—a line, remarkably, with no regular iambic foot. Only the second accented syllable of the double-iamb "-dĕr, ă gúst cátch-" interrupts what would be an entirely quick, rising, anapestic rhythm—and marks the instant when the wind irretrievably catches the saillike expanse of window. Alliterating, "*ladder*" and "*gust*" and "*catch*" join in the sound and expressive force of the word "*glass*" at line's end.

Two very strong run-ons, from line 2 and to line 4, give line 3, which lacks a caesura, its sense of undramatic but unstoppable, and unbalanced, movement. Anacrusis, a light accent, an anapest, the e-s ending, and the trochee starting line 4, all contribute; as do the alliterating *d*'s of "win*d*ow," "*d*eception," and "un*d*one," as well as the lightly hidden rhymes in "*undone*" and in "win*dow*" and "slo*wly*." But it is the momentum of the run-ons and the lack of a distinct pause in line 3 that assure the effect. The very vagueness of the image—"like *a piece of deception* slowly / coming undone"—allows no sensory or explanatory detail to fix the inexorable movement of the meaning.

The lack of a distinct caesura gives line 8 a similar inexorability, flowing from the unbalanced caesura very near the end of line 7 and to line 9's uncertainly pronounced "and fire towers" (and fi-ur tow'rs? and fire tow'rs?). Railings and balconies are common but, for a suburban householder, cliffs and fire towers? The character's unease or disorientation shows in the odd usage of "*clamped* his hands *to*." (We'd say clamped hands *on*, or clamped some third thing *to*.) The word "pitch" also seems strangely ambiguous. Meaning angle or slant, it might refer to "cliffs" (to which its short *i* links it in sound) but hardly to "balconies." After "railings," the image might be the pitch, the alternate dip and rise, of a ship's bow and stern, suggesting dizziness. The unease perhaps also shows in the almost compulsive succession of short *a*'s: h*a*s, cl*a*mped, h*a*nds, b*a*lanced, and b*a*lconies.

The poem's sentences run mostly across three (and once four) lines. Only two are less than a line and they come together at the "turn," where the slow-motion fall resumes:

> For years, he has feared falling.
> At last, he falls. Still holding the frame,
> he sees the sky and trees come clear
> in the wavering glass.

After the rather abstract sensations of "topple / backwards" and "he feels easy," the visual image in line 11—and the perspective, on his back in the air, looking up through the falling window—vividly brings that second moment of the fall into sharp focus. It is the poem's only monosyllabic line. The emphatic assonance of line 5, "h*e* feels *ea*sy," echoes now in the exact rhymes: "he s*ees* the sky and tr*ees* come clear." Along with the monosyllables, what gives the starkness, the illusion of precision, is the line's being *tetrameter*. Indeed, the poem began to shift from pentameters in line 7; and lines 10–12 and 14 are tetrameters. Disguised by the substitutions and variations' adding syllables, the change is only fully felt in this line, the poem's third without a caesura. The iambic plainness gives way to polysyllabic agitation in line 12—three anapests again, enough syllables for a pentameter. Emphasizing length, line 13 is again a pentameter, and lacks a caesura. Perhaps starting with "frame" in line 10, long *a*'s appear in "w*a*vering" and "p*a*ne"; and a little ripple of *r*-words—"clea*r*," "wave*r*ing," "anothe*r*," "shatte*r*," and "ove*r*"—climaxes in "*air*" in line 14. But it is the almost unnoticeable transformation into tetrameters that gives the poem's second half a subliminal feeling of suspended motion.

Two lines in the poem have two caesuras, lines 9 and 14. Comparing them will help clarify the unusual line 14, which somehow combines impressions of resolution/irresolution (or stability/instability). Caesuras near line-ends tend to be unbalancing, but here, symmetrically placed, they also suggest balance. The centered clause seems almost parenthetical, floating:

> but now [he lies back on air] falling.

The comma after "now," isn't really needed and so serves mainly as a rhythm-marker. Metrically, the first half of the line is entirely regular: two iambs; the second half entirely irregular: trochee, spondee, e-s ending. Consider this simpler alternative which fails to preserve the delicate balance of meaning:

> but now, falling, he lies back on air.

Every formal element in "Storm Window" bends to support Hilberry's microscopically precise narrative, which locates that second moment along the spectrum of feeling between resignation and acceptance. Long feared yet anticipated, the sensation includes a paradoxical relief that it is finally happening. Even incidentals, like the word-play in "At the *top* . . . *top*ple," are thematically meaningful in the poem's texture—reminding us, for instance, that etymologically *topple* means to fall (or cause to fall) from a high place. Perhaps one piece of self-deception that must come undone is that we never fall. In line 14, is "lies" conceivably a pun?

There is nothing showy about Hilberry's skillful management of every detail of rhythm and sound and meaning. Everything serves vividly, exactly, to present the poem's subject. "*Ars celare artem,*" as Horace's famous dictum says. The art is to hide the art.

QUESTIONS AND SUGGESTIONS

---

1. One adjective has been omitted in A. E. Housman's "Bredon Hill," in line 8. Housman himself tried out a number of words before he found the one he wanted to characterize the English countryside. What possibilities would you suggest? (Housman's successive notions appear in Appendix II, p. 385.)

Bredon Hill

In summertime on Bredon
   The bells they sound so clear;
Round both the shires they ring them
   In steeples far and near,
   A happy noise to hear.   5

Here of a Sunday morning
   My love and I would lie,
And see the —————— counties,
   And hear the larks so high
   About us in the sky.   10

The bells would ring to call her
   In valleys miles away:
"Come all to church, good people;
   Good people, come and pray."
   But here my love would stay.   15

And I would turn and answer
Among the springing thyme,
"Oh, peal upon our wedding,
And we will hear the chime,
And come to church in time."   20

But when the snows at Christmas
On Bredon top were strown,
My love rose up so early
And stole out unbeknown
And went to church alone.   25

They tolled the one bell only,
Groom there was none to see,
The mourners followed after,
And so to church went she,
And would not wait for me.   30

The bells they sound on Bredon,
And still the steeples hum.
"Come all to church, good people,"—
Oh, noisy bells, be dumb;
I hear you, I will come.   35

2. Think up comic rhymes for these hard-to-rhyme words. How might the best pairs be worked into a funny poem? Check the possibilities in Appendix II, p. 385.

circle	*rhinoceros*	*broccoli*	*umbrella*
stop-sign	*evergreen*	*pelican*	

3. Try your hand at a villanelle, of which Dylan Thomas's "Do Not Go Gentle into That Good Night" (p. 100) is a classic example. A description of the form is in Appendix I, p. 374. Start by working up several possibilities for the two repeated lines. Which seem likeliest to reappear naturally as the poem goes along?

4. Here is a paraphrase of a poem called "The Fourth of July." Following its general sense as closely as possible, but choosing your own form, lineation, diction, syntax, images, and elaborations, *write* the poem. Compare your version with the poem by Howard Nemerov, which may be found in Appendix II, p. 385.

Having happened to drink too much tonight, I see from a hill the town's fireworks at a distance, fine rockets exploding slowly and very colorfully over the harbor. I also happen to be crying, because I remember the various fireworks we could purchase during my boyhood and use by ourselves— dangerously no doubt. Now there are laws of course, by means of which we are prevented from the harms and abuses that former freedom sometimes caused. And now the town's government can put on an entirely safe display, which can be far more grand than any single person could afford then (small pinwheels, a few firecrackers—one of which might have got tied to a dog's tail—and the like). In fact, this public display is gorgeous: giant rockets bursting in the sky like flowers, or showers and fountains of precious or semiprecious stones, with huge booms resounding long afterward. Tears of happiness fill my eyes. On such a night I fervently hope that God will bless this country of ours and that He will also bless the town's responsible and well-paid authorities who are in charge of this celebration of our independence.

5. Consider the structure of the ever-branching sentence of the first twelve lines of this poem by Richmond Lattimore (1906–1983). What is the effect? Also, what is the effect of the stanzas? of the single last line? (If line 13 were prose, wouldn't we expect a comma after "station"?)

Catania to Rome

The later the train was at every station,
the more people were waiting to get on,
and the fuller the train got, the more time it lost,

and the slower it went, all night, station to station,
the more people were on it, and the more people
were on it, the more people wanted to get on it,

waiting at every twilight midnight and half-daylight
station, crouched like runners, with a big suitcase
in each hand, and the corridor was all elbows armpits

knees and hams, permessos and per favores, and a suitcase
always blocking half the corridor, and the next station
nobody got off but a great many came aboard.

When we came to our station we had to fight to get off.

6. Using as rhyme words *box-side-locks-wide*, write a reasonably coherent quatrain (*a b a b*). Then, reordering, rhyme: *box-locks-side-wide* (*a a b b*). Can you also do *wide-locks-side-box* and so on? (See Appendix II, p. 386, for comparison.)

7. As you write your next poem, listen for possible alliterations, assonances, and internal rhymes (even in free verse). Check a thesaurus often to see whether there is a more exact (and perhaps alliterating or rhyming) word you may be overlooking. Listen to the sound of your poem by reading it aloud.

8. "To Autumn" is the most charming and perhaps the most perfect of Keats's great odes. Search it carefully, in detail, for its texturing of diction, syntax, sound, and indentation. The effects are often subtle, so don't settle for a hasty look. For instance, what do you make of the phrase "full-grown lambs"? What word does Keats avoid? How does this choice help to set the tone of the ending?

To Autumn

JOHN KEATS (1795–1821)

Season of mists and mellow fruitfulness,
    Close bosom-friend of the maturing sun;
Conspiring with him how to load and bless
    With fruit the vines that round the thatch-eves run;
To bend with apples the moss'd cottage-trees,
    And fill all fruit with ripeness to the core;
        To swell the gourd, and plump the hazel shells

With a sweet kernel; to set budding more,
And still more, later flowers for the bees,
Until they think warm days will never cease,   10
    For summer has o'er-brimm'd their clammy cells.

Who hath not seen thee oft amid thy store?
   Sometimes whoever seeks abroad may find
Thee sitting careless on a granary floor,
   Thy hair soft-lifted by the winnowing wind;   15
Or on a half-reap'd furrow sound asleep,
   Drows'd with the fume of poppies, while thy hook
    Spares the next swath and all its twined flowers:
And sometimes like a gleaner thou dost keep
   Steady thy laden head across a brook;   20
   Or by a cyder-press, with patient look,
    Thou watchest the last oozings hours by hours.

Where are the songs of spring? Ay, where are they?
   Think not of them, thou hast thy music too,—
While barred clouds bloom the soft-dying day,   25
   And touch the stubble-plains with rosy hue;
Then in a wailful choir the small gnats mourn
   Among the river sallows, borne aloft
    Or sinking as the light wind lives or dies;
And full-grown lambs loud bleat from hilly bourn;   30
   Hedge-crickets sing; and now with treble soft
   The red-breast whistles from a garden-croft;
    And gathering swallows twitter in the skies.

POEMS TO CONSIDER

The Plain Style   1991

DAVID BAKER (b. 1954)

Many of us carried what we could—not much.
Stars pointed out the pitiful, few clouds
as blear or ashen absences in our sky.
We strained through the ruined evening
until breath tore burning from our throats.   5
Sometimes disaster speaks most convincingly
in a lowered voice, his whole hand strangling

my arm, his *hurry hurry* more hiss than command.
Then the trees were in flames. Then cinders.
We could only watch the gutters run thick   10

with pitch and tarpaper on fire before it fell.
What had we saved? Some few clothes and pans,
pictures of elders stiff among children,
one lamp, old durable pains. Enough to summon

a plain living again though rain   15
would not soothe us for weeks—too late
to dampen the horror or save the spring fields.
I will never forget his huge, singed face.
Sometimes disaster sees most clearly with open
eyes raised to the sky, as in a desperate prayer,   20
or the most serious, irreversible curse.

Grief   *1844*

ELIZABETH BARRETT BROWNING (1806–1861)

I tell you, hopeless grief is passionless;
That only men incredulous of despair,
Half-taught in anguish, through the midnight air
Beat upward to God's throne in loud access
Of shrieking and reproach. Full desertness,   5
In souls as countries, lieth silent-bare
Under the blanching, vertical eye-glare
Of the absolute Heavens. Deep-hearted man, express
Grief for thy Dead in silence like to death:—
Most like a monumental statue set   10
In everlasting watch and moveless woe
Till itself crumble to the dust beneath.
Touch it; the marble eyelids are not wet;
If it could weep, it could arise and go.

Eagle. Tiger. Whale.   *1992*

GERALD BARRAX (b. 1933)

I'm old enough to stand,
a boy looking at himself
in the long mirror of a chifforobe,
Black child with sandy hair
tightly curled, hazel eyes.   5
I haven't learned the words,
I photograph everything into my cells:
my little yellow dress with puffed pleated shoulders

and my little pearl buttons;
my little high-topped white shoes and yellow socks;   10
my little blue ribbon somewhere.
The room behind me is dark,
nothing in the mirror but me
as in a spotlight, yet I feel her presence,
my seventeen-year-old mother, beautiful,   15
leaning somewhere behind me.
       No one can explain what I've seen, a slim Black
woman lying on her back, red geyser pumping from
her open mouth, she stares into the ceiling's yellow
eye. I see her from her right, the foot of the brass bed,   20
my head three feet high. Someone screams "Lord God
Lord God he done shot the woman" while the soft
splash, splash. I stand so calm, seeing, until somebody
yells "Git that chile outta here." Who knows who
knows how I got there from next door, visiting Aunt   25
Annie over in Gadsden, for neither mother nor father
is there to tell me "Forget it."
                    dont tell dont
tell James Albert's sister whispers in the dim coal shed.
She has hair everywhere,   30
the only subject, verb, object, adverb
I can put together.
It's my birthday, I come to her yard
to pick figs from their tree. James Albert's
daddy said I can, I pull a fig,   35
she whispers "don't tell, don't tell,"
I feel my hand disappear into the hot full-noon mouth
of Alabama's summer solstice,
lips, lips, tongue curling around, probing
the fruit from my paralyzed fist.   40
She changes my hands from left to right,
leaves me partially ambidextrous and stuttering
to describe it.
       Now that I've read a lot,
I've learned boxes of "reflection," "homicide," "initiation"   45
to put visions into,
just as we have done with *eagle tiger whale god*
with handles and edges to finger,
inert and seamless,
no desire to break in, not letting anything out.   50
But there is that boy who can still do this:
In the Zaire rain forest a snow leopard like a ghost leaps

and with its perfect knives
slices open this box I've made.

Balance

1990

MARILYN NELSON WANIEK (b. 1946)

He watch her like a coonhound watch a tree.
What might explain the metamorphosis
he underwent when she paraded by
with tea-cakes, in her fresh and shabby dress?
(As one would carry water from a well—   5
straight-backed, high-headed, like a diadem,
with careful grace so that no drop will spill—
she balanced, almost brimming, her one name.)

She think she something, stuck-up island bitch.
Chopping wood, hanging laundry on the line,   10
and tantalizingly within his reach,
she honed his body's yearning to a keen,
sharp point. And on that point she balanced life.
That hoe Diverne think she Marse Tyler's wife.

The Question Answered

1793

WILLIAM BLAKE (1757–1827)

What is it men in women do require?
The lineaments of gratified desire.
What is it women do in men require?
The lineaments of gratified desire.

As She Has Been Taught

1983

MEKEEL McBRIDE (b. 1950)

The building, a tall one, is on fire again.
On the twenty-first floor, she,
dressed in smoky silks,

settles in to watch.
Below, she can see enameled firetrucks   5
roaring down streets
no wider than the ruler on her desk.

She wonders how they think they'll stop the fire
with their tiny hoses
and matchstick ladders.   10
Watching her building shadowed on the next
she sees the roof's on fire,
the silhouette of it
fanned into flames
that almost look   15
like dancers
twining topsy-turvy in a dark field.
She feels safe, feels warm
in the celluloid flames that are,
after all, only the red silks   20
her sleeping mind has wrapped around her.

But the rescue squad
of volunteer pharmacists,
and paper-pale priests
kicks down the door, helps her   25
through the iridescent halls
into blackened streets
where she is blanketed
by the ladies auxiliary.

Even though the alarm   30
has been silenced, they slip her
into the colorless cradle of amnesia
while her lover, his arms scalded
by a great bouquet of crimson roses,
wanders dully   35
through the water-ruined rooms.

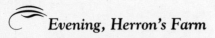

Evening, Herron's Farm   1986

CHASE TWICHELL (b. 1950)

Lit by kerosene,
the windows of the milking barn
recall the dearly departed light.

The basket of early apples
will be heavy by nightfall,   5
empty again by dawn.

Aligned in the cool apparatus,
the black-and-white bodies shift
and lean, their hooves and udders
shell and ivory   10
in a realm of little color.
Milk spurts
into the glass globes overhead.

In the old graveyard
the stones have long since   .15
tipped into the lengthening grass.

The animals bide in dusky quarters,
drowsing over the coarse
molasses of fodder.

I can almost penetrate   20
their remote intelligence,
bedding down in twilight
under the broken music.

Watercress trembles in the brook,
bitter as the wish to come home   25
to this place,
where all my sufferings
would be imaginable.

 Outings   *1991*

DEBRA ALLBERY (b. 1957)

I remember asking *Why go*
for a ride just for a ride? Why walk
through cemeteries reading the stones?
I was five. We had driven out past their old farm,
then left our cars along the main road—   5
my aunt, uncle, grandfather, cousins,
my parents. We chewed sassafras roots
my grandfather pulled up and peeled
as we shuffled the hot chalk of the road.
Then we came to two private gardens   10

of graves, mowed, shaded. Our parents
nodded at some of the names
while we children murmured how pretty
the marble, how long ago the years,
as we edged between where the bodies were buried.   15

I found my own name and age, a girl
dead in the spring of 1860.
Read her marker aloud in my new-reader voice:
Deborah, 5 years, She hath done what she could.

When I got older I would stay   20
in the car on our visits to Greenlawn,
where an uncle and cousin had since been taken.
Winter, my sister would sit in my lap.
I remember her asking *Why*
do we have to go to this place?   25
I said *Because*, our breaths frosting the windows.
And when we drove away she and I drew pictures
on the glass. With gloved fingers
we wrote our autographs and watched
what was passing beyond the spaces   30
our names had cleared.

CONTENT

The Essential Something

5

SUBJECT MATTER
Nightingales and Fried Shoes

Content, the other half of the indivisible equation, is harder to describe systematically than form. In the past, certain subjects were deemed "poetic" and others were not. Today almost nothing is off-limits to the poet. If someone says that one can't start a poem with "fried shoes," a poet will almost certainly accept the challenge. (Gregory Corso said it, and John Hollander wrote the poem.)

Even today, however, any of several assumptions can blind the beginning poet to the freedom of subject matter: the assumption that poems should be about certain traditional subjects, for instance: the seasons, love (especially a lost love), "the meaning of life"; or the assumption that poems should be, somehow, *grand*—high flown, solving all the world's problems at once, full of important pronouncements; or the corollary assumption that the ordinary, everyday things that we experience—things close to the nose, as Williams says—aren't proper subjects.

Writing under these assumptions, one might feel compelled to write about "poetic" subjects, like the nightingale—that familiar figure of British poetry—without realizing that the nightingale isn't indigenous to the Americas and that few Americans have seen the bird, much less heard its song. The common sparrows in the backyard, a construction site at night, a seldom seen neighbor, or a cat stepping carefully into and out of a pot will more likely offer fruitful subjects. Pay attention to the everyday world we usually ignore, and you will find ripe subjects for poems.

Equally blinding for the beginning poet is the assumption that poetry is mainly direct self-expression: what happened to *me*, what *I saw*, what *I feel*. Poets risk psycho-babble—endlessly reporting their own feelings, their own experience (only because it's their experience), unaware that they are boring a listener. This unrelenting looking inward, of course, also keeps such poets from looking outward. If they notice the cat, the construction site, or the neighbor, it is only to rush on to how such things affect them individually. The poem that begins, "I see the ugly machines," will surely end with an over-blown pronouncement about "the world as I see it." Such poems put the poet's feelings at the center rather than the potentially evocative elements of the construction site. This poet won't likely notice how the streetlight makes the cement mixer glow like a moon, won't wonder about the ladder of the cranes, or the alien alphabet left by truck tires.

We're all tempted to write poems that spill out our feelings. And poets, of course, do express themselves, though rarely as directly as it may seem.

In the following poem, notice how William Matthews (b. 1942) begins by deflecting attention away from himself, thereby taking in the scene's deeper significance:

Men at My Father's Funeral

The ones his age who shook my hand
on their way out sent fear along
my arm like heroin. These weren't
men mute about their feelings,
or what's a body language for?   5

And I, the glib one, who'd stood
with my back to my father's body
and praised the heart that attacked him?
I'd made my stab at elegy,
the flesh made word: the very spit   10

in my mouth was sour with ruth
and eloquence. What could be worse?
Silence, the anthem of my father's
new country. And thus this babble,
like a dial tone, from our bodies.   15

By decentering the son's grief (which nevertheless lies at the heart of this poem), Matthews can foreground the small gestures that reveal the mourners' hidden feelings: a mixture of generosity and selfishness. The dead father's peers lament the loss of their friend, and at the same time they fear for their own lives. Naturally the men wouldn't admit or acknowledge, perhaps even to themselves, that they have such feelings, but their fear is palpable. The awkward handshake between them and the son jolts his arm "like heroin"—powerful, strange, dangerous, forbidden. Whereas the unobservant might see only the son standing before his father's coffin to eulogize him, this poet says he stood with his *back* to his father's body, suggesting that he, too, wanted to shun the dead, perhaps because his father reminded him of his own life's precariousness. The son, "the glib one," speaks the appropriate words of praise for his father, though they turn sour in his mouth for all that remains unsaid. All this noise—body language and spoken language, a babble meaningless as a "dial tone"—speaks of the survivors' desire to drown out the silence they feel hovering behind them. Matthews shows how small commonplace actions speak more powerfully than grand pronouncements.

The point is that *poems must be interesting*. Whether they elucidate one of the great human truths or not, they had better be interesting—or we are likely to leave them half-read and turn the page. Poems compete with everything else in the world for our attention. As E. E. Cummings says, "It is with roses and locomotives (not to mention acrobats Spring electricity Coney Island the 4th of July the eyes of mice and Niagara Falls) that my 'poems' are competing. They are also competing with each other, with elephants, and with El Greco."

Poems must be interesting. And there is nothing like *subject matter* to do the job. Subject matter is up front, obvious, and able to draw a reader into a poem, like a story that begins, "As she faced the firing squad . . ." Or a poem that opens, "How do they do it? The ones who make love / without love?" (Sharon Olds, "Sex Without Love," p. 251). Subject matter helps differentiate one poem from another. Especially for the beginning poet, an arresting subject, interesting, fresh, and specific, can make up for any number of technical blunders.

New poets sometimes despair that everything has already been written, that there's nothing new to write about. Love, loss, death, birth—the great universal themes of humanity have been written many times over. But the poets of each succeeding age must write them anew, explore them from their unique perspective in their own idiom and voice. In many ways the world is much the same place it has always been. We have wars and famine, peace and bounty; we are brave and noble, selfish and narrow. We love, we work, we try to make sense of life. But we experience all these things in a way often very different from other ages. Our relationship with the natural world, for instance, has changed since we get most of our food and clothing from grocery stores and shopping malls rather than from hunting or harvesting. And slightly changed are the relationships between men, women, children, parents, and the haves and have-nots. We live with day care centers, car phones, oil spills, heart transplants, twelve-step groups, suburban blight, and megasupermarkets selling lemongrass and c.d.s.

We each participate in this contemporary world in our own way. We each discover our own subject matter. Find what is close to your nose. Explore what makes you unique, your particular upbringing, your heritage, your point of view. Venture into parts of your neighborhood you have always passed up. Step into the bingo hall or feed store or pawn shop. Hang out in the barber shop and listen to the banter, or start up a conversation at a yard sale.

A good subject needn't be grand. It may be something actually seen (a bluejay defending its nest, someone rollerblading at 5 a.m.) or something imagined (the moonlit interior of Simic's stone, p. 27). It may be something impersonal, like fireflies, or something personal, recalled, as in Matthews's poem. Family stories may open out into vivid landscapes as they did for Rita Dove (b. 1952) in her Pulitzer-Prize-winning sequence about her grandparents, *Thomas and Beulah* (1986).

Dove began with a story her grandmother told about her grandfather "when he was young, coming up on a riverboat to Akron, Ohio, my hometown." And the fascination led, poem by poem, to a wonderful re-creation of their lives, an imaginative document of the African-American experience in the industrial Midwest. "Because I ran out of real fact, in order to keep going, I made up facts . . ." Like old

photographs coming to life, poems such as this show the potential of a good subject. Notice how the Depression of the 1930s provides background:

A Hill of Beans

One spring the circus gave
free passes and there was music,
the screens unlatched
to let in starlight. At the well,
a monkey tipped her his fine red hat   5
and drank from a china cup.
By mid-morning her cobblers
were cooling on the sill.
Then the tents folded and the grass

grew back with a path   10
torn waist-high to the railroad
where the hoboes jumped the slow curve
just outside Union Station.
She fed them while they talked,
easy in their rags. *Any two points*   15
make a line, they'd say,
and we're gonna ride them all.

Cat hairs
came up with the dipper;
Thomas tossed on his pillow   20
as if at sea. When money failed
for peaches, she pulled
rhubarb at the edge of the field.
Then another man showed up
in her kitchen and she smelled   25
fear in his grimy overalls,
the pale eyes bright as salt.

There wasn't even pork
for the navy beans. But he ate
straight down to the blue   30
bottom of the pot and rested
there a moment, hardly breathing.
That night she made Thomas
board up the well.
Beyond the tracks, the city blazed   35
as if looks were everything.

In this quiet poem Dove gives us people who ask for little else than the chance to
make do. When they can't afford peaches for cobblers, the wife pulls rhubarb at the
edge of the field. They enjoy the brief wonder of the circus, then return to their
routines of eking out a living and helping out those worse off than themselves.

Someone always is. Unlike the hoboes Beulah feeds—who at least take pleasure in their freedom—the man who eats the entire pot of unseasoned beans without stopping reeks of fear, suggesting he's on the run, hunted. She doesn't pry into his secret. His presence reminds Beulah that hidden danger lurks beyond the boundaries of their neighborhood, that the well may be poisoned, and that looks aren't everything.

Occasionally a poet will stumble upon a lucky subject, as Miller Williams did for "The Curator" (p. 152). In 1991, visiting the great museum in St. Petersburg, the Hermitage, he heard the story the poem tells from the curator himself, then a man in his eighties. The story concerned events fifty years earlier when the city, then Leningrad, was under siege by the Germans in World War II. Unable to use a tape recorder or take notes, Williams rushed back to the bus and jotted down three or four pages of vivid recollections. The poem, he remarks, though it went through many revisions, "is as literally true as told to me as any other poem I ever wrote."

Stories imagined out of real events can also prove to be vital subjects. In 1965 Philip Levine made his first visit to Orihuela, Spain, the village that had been home to the poet Miguel Hernandez. Like many other artists and intellectuals in the Spanish Civil War of the 1930s, Hernandez sympathized with the Republican forces that opposed the fascist Francisco Franco, and like many others he paid the consequences of his beliefs. Following the defeat of the Republicans, Hernandez tried to escape into Portugal but was imprisoned and, owing in part to the prison's deplorable conditions, died in 1942 at the age of 31. When Levine first visited the region of Hernandez's birth, Hernandez's wife and son were still living there. Levine reports he never forgot that first visit, and some thirty years later he wrote the following poem. In it, Levine says, he imagines how Hernandez would feel coming home from exile "had exile been possible," returning to that world Levine saw on his first visit. The poem explores the question, What if . . . ?

The Return: Orihuela, 1965

for Miguel Hernandez

You come over a slight rise
in the narrow winding road
and the white village broods
in the valley below. A breeze
silvers the cold leaves   5
of the olives, just as you knew
it would or as you saw
it in dreams. How many days
have you waited for this day?
Soon you must face a son grown   10
to manhood, a wife to old age,
the tiny, sealed house of memory.
A lone crow flies into the sun,
the fields whisper their courage.

Anything can become a good subject, if seen with new and lively insight. As William Matthews says in his essay "Dull Subjects" (*Curiosities*, University of Michigan Press, 1989), "It is not, of course, the subject that is or isn't dull, but the quality of attention that we do or do not pay to it . . . . Dull subjects are those we have failed." Given the right attention, a good subject may come from anything: a news item or photograph, something in a biography the poet is reading, a story overheard from older relatives. It may grow out of watching a small town parade (Gillian Conoley, "The Woman on the Homecoming Float," p. 23), old couples at the mall (Liz Rosenberg, "The Silence of Women," p. 45) or young mothers taking their babies out in strollers:

Primary Colors

CATHY SONG (b. 1955)

They come out in warm weather
like termites
crawling out of the woodwork.
The young mothers chauffeuring
these bright bundles in toy carriages.   5
Bundles shaped like pumpkin seeds.

All last winter,
the world was grown up,
gray figures hurrying along
as lean as umbrellas;   10
empty of infants,
though I heard them at night
whimpering through a succession
of rooms and walls;
felt the tired, awakened hand   15
grope out from the dark
to clamp over the cries.

For a while, even the animals vanished,
the cats stayed close to the kitchens.
Their pincushion paws left padded tracks   20
around the perimeters of houses
locked in heat.
Yet, there were hints of children
hiding somewhere,
threatening to break loose.   25
Displaced tricycles and pubescent dolls
with flaxen hair and limbs askew
were abandoned dangerously on sidewalks.
The difficult walk of pregnant mothers.
Basketfuls of plastic eggs   30
nestled in cellophane grass

appeared one day at the grocer's
above the lettuce and the carrot bins.

When the first crocuses
pushed their purple tongues   35
through the skin of the earth,
it was the striking of a match.
The grass lit up, quickly,
spreading the fire.
The flowers yelled out   40
yellow, red, and green.
All the clanging colors of crayolas
lined like candles in a box.
Then the babies stormed the streets,
sailing by in their runaway carriages,   45
having yanked the wind
out from under their mothers.
Diapers drooped on laundry lines.
The petals of their tiny lungs
burgeoning with reinvented air.   50

The penultimate word, "reinvented," cues us in to the poem's strategy; it reinvents the familiar. Putting aside what we take for granted—that people and animals kept indoors by cold weather come outside to enjoy the first warm days of spring—Song turns inside out a commonplace subject and makes it extraordinary. Images normally suggestive of fruitfulness and hope take on a menacing attitude. Babies, young mothers, spring flowers, the sudden growth of grass—the speaker turns a keen eye to these ordinary sights of spring and connects them with termites, clanging crayons, and fire, suggesting that behind the most familiar world lurks something powerful, even threatening. The poem's speaker seems alien to, even repulsed by, the scene and so is able to notice what we typically ignore. For instance, she says, "plastic eggs / nestled in cellophane grass / appeared one day at the grocer's" as if she had never seen Easter decorations before. The hidden children of stanza 3 were "*threatening* to break loose"; in stanza 4 the "flowers *yelled out* / yellow, red, and green"; "the babies *stormed* the streets." Such sharp observations create an insidious undercurrent in the poem that suggests the speaker feels a mixture of repulsion and attraction to children and to spring.

Discovering a good subject may be partly luck, but luck comes to poets who are alert, who keep their antennae out, who make new combinations, who truly *see*. In the words of that accidental wit Yogi Berra, "You can observe a lot just by watching." As other poets' poems remind us, the subjects for poetry are boundless, especially when one allows poems to bloom from the ordinary, a noticed detail, a stray connection, something forgotten. Try to see everything with a cleansed eye. Look at things. Study a slice of bread, for instance; really see it and then write about what you notice. Free yourself of assumptions about the staff of life and shimmering fields of golden grain. Look at the bread. Like the purloined letter in Poe's story, the secret is hidden in the open. Look. Notice.

It is easy to see what everybody else sees, notice only what everybody does. The result is clichés—not only clichés of language, but clichés of observation, of thought, and even of feeling. We all fall victim to them and the result is a dead subject.

When a poem merely describes a scene or recounts an event we know all too well, it has a dead subject. Retelling the story of Romeo and Juliet or the assassination of JFK, if the poem only reports what we already know, won't interest a reader. The poem must see the subject from a unique perspective. What about Juliet's mother at a niece's wedding? What about the autoshop in Dallas that towed the blood-stained car?

The vision to see something anew, singularly, is at the center of making good poems. Insights don't have to be large. Indeed, most of the original ones are small. In "Primary Colors" Cathy Song describes the bundled babies as "shaped like pumpkin seeds" and presents cats with "pincushion paws." In "Icicles" (p. 211) Mark Irwin describes them as "slender beards of light" and one as a "clear carrot." Rita Dove gives us "pale eyes bright as salt." Shakespeare calls leafless trees "bare ruined choirs" in Sonnet 73 (p. 10). These small insights are triumphs of observation. The term **image** (or imagery) is sometimes used to refer to such visual detail and the mental pictures it evokes, even if simply literal ("The white diagonal lines in the empty parking lot . . . "). But the term is also used for metaphors (". . . lie like fishbones on a gray plate") which reenforce such visual perceptions.

Accurate perception is not just an aesthetic choice; we have a moral obligation to see what is truly there, not just what we would like to see. The speaker of this poem by Adrienne Rich (b. 1929) makes clear this responsibility:

The Slides

Three dozen squares of light-inflicted glass
lie in a quarter-century's dust
under the skylight. I can show you this:
also a sprung couch spewing
dessicated mouse-havens, a revolving bookstand   5
rusted on its pivot, leaning
with books of an era: *Roosevelt vs Recovery*
The Mystery & Lure of Perfume   My Brother Was Mozart
I've had this attic in mind for years
                        Now you   10
who keep a lookout for
places like this, make your living
off things like this: You see, the books are rotting,
sunbleached, unfashionable
the furniture neglected past waste   15
but the lantern-slides—their story
could be sold, they could be a prize
                  I want to see
your face when you start to sort them. You want

> cloched hats of the Thirties, engagement portraits   20
> with marcelled hair, maillots daring the waves,
> my family album:
>   This is the razing of the spinal cord
> by the polio virus
> this, the lung-tissue kissed by the tubercle bacillus   25
> this with the hooked shape is
> the cell that leaks anemia to the next generation
> Enlarged on a screen
> they won't be quaint; they go on working; they still kill.

The antique dealer whom the speaker addresses yearns for images of the mythic good old days: charming young ladies sporting fanciful clothes and hairstyles. Such a view of the past is romantic, even sentimental. Most of us succumb to it now and then. But among the musty books and ruined furniture, the dealer will find images of the past we often overlook. Instead of romance the person Rich addresses will find the physician's medical slides. Polio, tuberculosis, sickle-cell anemia: "they won't be quaint; they go on working; they still kill." The point is not that we must always look on the dark side of existence, but that we mustn't ignore the complete picture, we mustn't blind ourselves with cliché perspectives, cliché images.

Though *image* usually refers to visual sensations, the term includes the nonvisual senses of sound, touch, smell, and taste. Rich's images of "a quarter-century's dust" and "rotting books" prompt our senses of smell and touch. Our noses crinkle. We want to recoil. In Roethke's "My Papa's Waltz" (p. 63) notice how many kinds of images come into play. We see the pans slide from the shelves and hear them bang on the floor. We feel the rollicking dance of the father, hear and feel him beating time. We even smell the whisky on his breath. Poems that excite many of our senses draw us in and convince us. We can live inside them.

PRESENTING

Emotions, in themselves, are not subject matter. Being in love, or sad, or lonely, or feeling good because it is spring, are common experiences. Poems that merely say these things, *state* these emotions, won't be very interesting. We respect such statements, but we can't be moved by them.

The *circumstances* of the emotion, the scene or events out of which it comes, however, are subject matter. Don't tell the emotion. Tell the causes of it, the circumstances. Presented vividly, they will not only convince us of its truth but will also make us dramatically *feel* it. Theodore Roethke doesn't state his feeling about his father in "My Papa's Waltz" (p. 63). He lets us feel it for ourselves by presenting us with the particular scene out of which the feeling came. In "A Hill of Beans," Dove doesn't tell us the circus felt magical. She says "the screens unlatched / to let in starlight." In "The Slides," Rich presents her theme—romanticizing the past—by counterpointing the "marcelled hair" with the hook-shaped cell "that leaks anemia." Frequently, presenting the facts, showing the scene, will be the only way of adequately making your point or describing the emotion. What word or list of words that describes the emotions of love, fear, pain, mischief, panic, delight, and helplessness could begin to sum up what the boy (and the grown man) feel in (and about) the little scene in "My Papa's Waltz"?

The key is **presenting**; not to *tell* about, but to *show*. Put the spring day with mothers and their children in strollers *into* the poem. Put the circus monkey *into* the poem. Put the handshake between mourners *into* the poem.

Chapters 1–4 look at some of the ways in which imitative elements of form (shape, sound, rhythm) help in *presenting*. Chapter 7 considers metaphor. For now, let's examine the management of subject matter, some of the ways in which a poet may handle it in a poem to make it effective.

Subject matter should be presented accurately. Accuracy of information, of detail, of terminology tends to make the presentation convincing. Whether writing about antiques, rocking chairs, leopards, Denver, black holes in space, or the physiology of the grasshopper, the poet should know enough, or find out enough, to be reasonably authoritative. Tulips don't bloom in July. Whales are mammals, not fish. Jackie Joyner-Kersee won gold medals for the heptathalon *and* the long jump in 1988. Common knowledge and plain observation are usually enough. Good reference books and field guides help too. Margaret Holley in "The Fireflies" (p. 213) asserts her authority by describing the "larva whose labor is to eat, molt, // and feverishly expand / before the newly secreted / chitin hardens into another shell." Rich knows the cell shape of sickle-cell anemia. The entire premise of "Tarantulas on the Lifebuoy" (p. 19) stems from Thomas Lux's information that in semitropical regions those "scary arachnids" often drown in swimming pools. Sometimes poets will come upon a subject that sends them to the library and requires becoming something of a specialist.

In presenting subject matter, *particulars* offer overtones of thought and emotion to a poem, giving it depth and substance. We don't need (or want) *every* detail to make a poem vivid and moving. We need details that are significant and resonant. A poem will bore us with inconsequence if it places us at 51° latitude and 4° longitude on January 17th at 2:28 p.m. beside a 118-year-old willow near a farm pond owned by Mr. John Johnson. The right detail in the right place moves us. Thomas Hardy (1840–1928) deftly handles details to create an atmosphere of loss:

Neutral Tones

We stood by a pond that winter day,
And the sun was white, as though chidden of God,
And a few leaves lay on the starving sod;
    —They had fallen from an ash, and were gray.

Your eyes on me were as eyes that rove   5
Over tedious riddles of years ago;
And some words played between us to and fro
    On which lost the more by our love.

The smile on your mouth was the deadest thing
Alive enough to have strength to die;   10
And a grin of bitterness swept thereby
    Like an ominous bird a-wing. . . .

Since then, keen lessons that love deceives,
And wrings with wrong, have shaped to me
Your face, and the God-curst sun, and a tree,   15
    And a pond edged with grayish leaves.

The white sun, the ash tree, the unspecified words that "played" between the lovers, the grayish leaves—Hardy's discrimination, his careful selection of which details to include and which to ignore, presents the bleak memory, the neutral tones of the last moment of a love affair. Consider the difference between saying "a pale sky" and saying "the sun was white," between saying "tree" and saying "ash." Or "oak," "blossoming pear," "hemlock." Suppose in "The Slides" Adrienne Rich hadn't given us the titles of the books (*Roosevelt vs Recovery*, *The Mystery & Lure of Perfume*, *My Brother Was Mozart*). The poem would lose more than a sense of vividness and accuracy; it would lose the ironic contrast set up between the titles and the diseases "that go on working." The concerns of the books may be dated, even silly; illness isn't. In Roethke's "My Papa's Waltz" the detail about the "pans" sliding from the "kitchen shelf" does more than indicate the rowdiness of the drunken father's dancing. It tells us something about the middle-class or lower-middle-class family—a kitchen neither large nor elegant. More important, it sets the scene in the kitchen. Suggestions abound. The father, who works with his hands ("a palm caked hard by dirt"), has come home late from work, having stopped off for his whiskey. He has come in by the back door, into the kitchen. Dinner is over and the pans back on the shelf, but the boy and his mother are still in the kitchen. That they have not waited dinner, or waited it longer, measures the mother's stored-up anger, as does the word "countenance," which suggests how formidably she has prepared herself. The incongruity of the father's merriment is all the stronger because the waltzing begins, so inappropriately, in the kitchen.

This poem by William Stafford (1914–1993) shows a fine articulation of details:

Traveling Through the Dark

Traveling through the dark I found a deer
dead on the edge of the Wilson River road.
It is usually best to roll them into the canyon:
that road is narrow; to swerve might make more dead.

By glow of the tail-light I stumbled back of the car   5
and stood by the heap, a doe, a recent killing;
she had stiffened already, almost cold.
I dragged her off; she was large in the belly.

My fingers touching her side brought me the reason—
her side was warm; her fawn lay there waiting,   10

alive, still, never to be born.
Beside that mountain road I hesitated.

The car aimed ahead its lowered parking lights;
under the hood purred the steady engine.
I stood in the glare of the warm exhaust turning red;   15
around our group I could hear the wilderness listen.

I thought hard for us all—my only swerving—,
then pushed her over the edge into the river.

Some of the details, like "the Wilson River road," attest to the reality of the incident. The speaker has seen dead deer along the road before and is not sentimental
("It is usually best to roll them into the canyon"). The most effective detail, perhaps, is the "glow of the tail-light," which bathes the whole scene an eerie red.
Everything about the car is made to participate. The glow is red, like blood. The
parking lights are "lowered," as if in respect or recognition of the tragedy. The
engine "purred" like an animal, and the exhaust is "warm." The doomed warmth
and life of the fawn could not be more ironically emphasized. Stafford has not
added these details to the grim tableau—they are all naturally a part of it—but he
uses them superbly to illuminate the event.

Absent specifics, left-out particulars all too often result in missed opportunities.
Take, for example, this sonnet, once submitted in a writing workshop.

To One Who Shed Tears at a Play

Because I hold that fleeting moment dear
I prison it within each shining word
As fragile as the flight of startled bird,
Yet strong as iron bands. I still can hear
The actors speak their lines. The climax near,   5
They find frustration, sorrow, and they gird
Themselves for bitter loss. And you who heard
Pay them the priceless tribute of a tear.

O, gentle heart! May that day never come,
When you are heedless of the sight of grief,   10
Though only grief that mimics. For the sum
Of your vicarious sharing brings relief.
The callous heart is like a broken drum,
A bitter fruit, a sere and withered leaf.

Apart from the rather archaic rhyme-word "gird" and the padded "For the sum / Of
your vicarious sharing" instead of simply "For your vicarious sharing," the poem's
central problems lie in its curious abstractness about the subject, someone who
cries at a play.

Consider the missing particulars, the missed opportunities. We know nothing
about the person who cries: not age, nor sex, nor any other detail, although such

information might considerably affect our responses. Nor do we get a strong sense of the speaker's relationship to this person. Was it a stranger who happened to be in the next seat? a friend? a relative? perhaps a son or daughter? Why did that person's sympathetic reaction strike the speaker as valuable? We don't even know what the play was, though that detail might have been useful. We are strangely barred from the very event that is supposed to move us. Its color and convincingness are left out.

DESCRIPTIVE IMPLICATION

Particulars may give a poem its richly colored surface, evoking vividly for the reader the subject or the setting in which an action occurs. They may also, implicitly, provide a sort of running commentary on the subject or action—and on the speaker's attitude about either. Consider the selection of detail in this poem by Elizabeth Bishop (1911–1979):

First Death in Nova Scotia

In the cold, cold parlor
my mother laid out Arthur
beneath the chromographs:
Edward, Prince of Wales,
with Princess Alexandra,   5
and King George with Queen Mary.
Below them on the table
stood a stuffed loon
shot and stuffed by Uncle
Arthur, Arthur's father.   10

Since Uncle Arthur fired
a bullet into him,
he hadn't said a word.
He kept his own counsel
on his white, frozen lake,   15
the marble-topped table.
His breast was deep and white,
cold and caressable;
his eyes were red glass,
much to be desired.   20

"Come," said my mother,
"Come and say good-bye
to your little cousin Arthur."
I was lifted up and given
one lily of the valley   25
to put in Arthur's hand.
Arthur's coffin was

a little frosted cake,
and the red-eyed loon eyed it
from his white, frozen lake.   30

Arthur was very small.
He was all white, like a doll
that hadn't been painted yet.
Jack Frost had started to paint him
the way he always painted   35
the Maple Leaf (Forever).
He had just begun on his hair,
a few red strokes, and then
Jack Frost had dropped the brush
and left him white, forever.   40

The gracious royal couples
were warm in red and ermine;
their feet were well wrapped up
in the ladies' ermine trains.
They invited Arthur to be   45
the smallest page at court.
But how could Arthur go,
clutching his tiny lily,
with his eyes shut up so tight
and the roads deep in snow?   50

The poem very selectively presents a child's view of death. The speaker mentions
almost nothing outside the "cold, cold parlor," nor anything before or after the
one event, seeing little Arthur in his coffin. The poem refers to only two details of
the parlor, the color lithographs of the royal family and the stuffed loon on its
marble-topped table. Although no other furnishings appear in the poem, these
two are sufficient to suggest the ornate and rather formal nature of the room, as
well as something about the household (its patriotism, its family loyalty, its pro-
priety). We accept the poem as autobiographical and assume the speaker to be a
little girl.

The loon and the chromographs of the royal family share several aspects. Like
Arthur himself and his coffin ("a little frosted cake"), both are studies in white and
red. The loon's breast and "frozen lake" of marble-topped table are white, and his
glass eyes are red. "The gracious royal couples" are "warm in red and ermine" (a
white, thick fur)—the only colors noted. Arthur is "white, forever," except for the
"few red strokes" of his hair. Very likely it is the red and white of the loon and the
chromographs that make the little girl notice them and associate them with her
dead cousin. And both are connected with death. "Uncle Arthur, Arthur's father"
had killed the loon and had it stuffed. And the ermine of the royal family similarly
comes from animals that have been killed to provide decorative fur. These particulars give the poem its icy, rich unity: red and white; warm (royal family) and cold
(loon). The funeral reminds the little girl of a birthday, the "little frosted cake" of
the coffin.

The particulars suggest beautifully the little girl's incomprehension of what she is witnessing. The loon is not so much dead as silent: "Since Uncle Arthur fired / a bullet into him, / he hadn't said a word." "He kept his own counsel" and only "eyed" little Arthur's coffin. The girl's fantasy that the royal family had "invited Arthur to be / the smallest page at court" is the only way that she can translate her cousin's death into her experience. ("Jack Frost" suggests the dimensions of her experience.) Her mother's well-meaning but too careful " 'Come and say good-bye / to your little cousin Arthur' " invites the fantasy. Although the girl doesn't understand, she is nonetheless aware that the confusion between life (red) and death (white) will resolve itself ominously. "But how could Arthur go, / clutching his tiny lily, / with his eyes shut up so tight / and the roads deep in snow?" (Lily and snow are yet more white.) That question, with which the poem ends, shows how fragile is her defense against the grim truth.

Bishop's handling of the details of "First Death in Nova Scotia" quietly gathers up nuances until they become symbolic. The poem does not *state* its evaluation of the child's experience, but *implies* it in the choice of particulars. The literal reds and whites of loon and royal family symbolize the confusion about life and death in her feelings. Like most effective details, they function in more than one way, on more than one level. As Pound says, "the natural object is always the adequate symbol."

The choice and ordering of the details help reveal the way the narrator feels about the narrative. This is **tone**: the poet's or the speaker's attitude toward the material. Tone may be, for instance, approving, disapproving, pitying, admiring, doubting, ironic. Every element in a poem, including diction, imagery, and rhythm, will contribute to its tone, establishing a mood, conveying the poet's or the speaker's sense of the subject. Thomas Hardy's tone in "Neutral Tones" might be described as bitter. Thomas Lux's "Tarantula's on the Lifebuoy" (p. 19) mingles the whimsical and the philosophical. William Olsen in "The Dead Monkey" (p. 148) balances the pathos of the scene with dark irony ("We toasted with him to stupidity because / there's not always enough stupidity around to celebrate").

In Bishop's poem, the voice is the little girl's. (Behind it we also sense the poet's voice, selecting, controlling.) The tone is uncomprehending and, finally, questioning. Her uncertainty is suggested by the displacement of her attention from Arthur's corpse to the familiar and so comforting loon and chromographs. The mother must beckon her forward: " 'Come,' said my mother, / 'Come and say good-bye / to your little cousin Arthur.' " In the final lines, the shift from the close-up view of Arthur, eyes shut, "clutching his tiny lily," to the wide-shot of "the roads deep in snow" outside, lets us see her incomprehension from a pitying distance.

CAMERA WORK

One useful way of thinking of **visual detail** is as cinematography: camera angle or location, close-up or distant shot, fade-in or fade-out, panning, montage, and so on. Working with only the black squiggles of words on a page, the poet somehow controls what readers see with the mind's eye. Bishop first makes us see a white, frozen lake and then the marble-topped table when she says that the stuffed loon

> kept his own counsel
> on his white, frozen lake,
> the marble-topped table.

The two, in effect, become one; lake turns into table. It is, of course, a simple enough comparison and, in reading, happens so fast that we scarcely notice. But we have for a moment had a glimpse of an iced-over lake, something like a superimposition of two shots in a film. The poet no doubt manages such things intuitively, absorbed by the scene in the inner eye, but nonetheless picking angle, distance, and focus. Look at Roethke's "My Papa's Waltz" again (p. 63), and note how cinematographically it is done. We never glimpse the father's face. We see his *hand* twice, however: close-ups of the hand on the boy's wrist, the battered knuckle; and of the "palm caked hard by dirt." We are also given a close-up of the buckle and the shirt. The camera is *at the boy's eye-level*, sees what he sees; and the man now speaking sees again what he saw as a boy. Note, incidentally, that he says "My right ear scraped a buckle," not the expected reverse: "A buckle scraped my right ear." How perfectly we see that he cannot blame the father for anything!

As another instance of camera work, consider again Shakespeare's quatrain:

> That time of year thou mayst in me behold
> When yellow leaves, or none, or few, do hang
> Upon those boughs which shake against the cold,
> Bare ruined choirs, where late the sweet birds sang.

Line 2 shows us first the yellow leaves of fall, then the later absence of leaves. It is a distant shot; we don't see a particular tree, simply yellow leaves in the aggregate. But notice how, as the camera seems to pan from "yellow leaves" to "none," it suddenly stops and moves in for a close-up shot: "or few." So close are we to a few leaves, we are probably seeing a single tree. The sense of loss is intensified, and the desolation of the few surviving leaves is greater than that produced by "none." "Boughs" in line 3 seems a close-up still, but we are now looking *up* into the branches. In line 4 the branches are compared to "Bare ruined choirs"; that is, choir lofts of a ruined and roofless church. For a moment we have the impression of standing inside such a church, looking upward through its buttresses (like the branches) at the sky. The film word for the effect might be a "dissolve." It is only momentary, however; and in the last half of line 4 we are looking at the early winter boughs again, but this time with a superimposed shot of the same boughs in summer, with birds in them. The musical association between the songbirds and the choir lofts supports the shift. Good description is not only a matter of choosing effective details but also of visualizing them effectively, from the right angle and the right distance.

Telling a story always involves the projection of scenes into the reader's or hearer's mind. The poet's narrative methods, as in the thirteenth-century Scottish ballad "Sir Patrick Spence," often approximate the film techniques of dissolve, jumpcut, or superimposition. Notice how the anonymous poet, especially in the syntactical leap of lines 11–12, dissolves one scene into another. What the poet chooses to show—or *not* to show—is illuminating.

Sir Patrick Spence

The king sits in Dumferling toune,
    Drinking the blude-reid wine:
"O whar will I get guid sailor
    To sail this ship of mine?"

Up and spak an eldern knicht°,   5
    Sat at the kings richt kne:
"Sir Patrick Spence is the best sailor
    That sails upon the se."

The king has written a braid° letter,
    And signed it wi' his hand,   10
And sent it to Sir Patrick Spence,
    Was walking on the sand.

The first line that Sir Patrick red,
    A loud lauch lauchèd° he;
The next line that Sir Patrick red,   15
    The teir° blinded his ee.

"O wha° is this has don this deid,
    This ill deid don to me,
To send me out this time o' the yeir,
    To sail upon the se!   20

"Mak haste, mak haste, my mirry men all,
    Our guid schip sails the morne."
"O say na sae°, my master deir,
    For I feir a deadlie storme.

"Late late yestreen I saw the new moone,   25
    Wi' the auld° moone in hir arme,
And I feir, I feir, my deir master,
    That we will cum to harme."

O our Scots nobles wer richt laith°
    To weet° their cork-heild schoone°;   30
Bot lang owre a'° the play wer playd,
    Their hats they swam aboone°.

O lang, lang may their ladies sit,
    Wi' their fans into their hand,
Or ere° they se Sir Patrick Spence   35
    Cum sailing to the land.

---

5 *knicht:* knight; 9 *braid:* broad forthright; 14 *lauched:* laugh, laughed; 16 *teir:* tear;
17 *wha:* who; 23 *na sae:* not so; 26 *auld:* old; 29 *laith:* loath; 30 *weet:* wet; 30 *schoone:*
shoes; 31 *Bot lang owre a:* But long before all; 32 *aboone:* above them; 35 *ere:* before;

O lang, lang may the ladies stand,
  Wi' their gold kems° in their hair,
Waiting for their ain° deir lords,
  For they'll se thame na mair.   40

Haf owre°, haf owre to Aberdour,
  It's fiftie fadom° deip,
And thair lies guid Sir Patrick Spence,
  Wi' the Scots lords at his feit.

---

38 *kems:* combs; 39 *ain:* own; 41 *haf owre:* halfway over; 42 *fadom:* fathom.

The sparks that kindle poems are their particulars. A list of things we see in "Sir Patrick Spence"—blood-red wine / king's right knee / letter signed with his hand / sand / a tear blinding an eye / new moon with the old moon in her arm / cork-heeled shoes / hats swimming / sitting ladies with fans / standing ladies with combs in their hair—provides a curiously moving visual synopsis of the story.

That it is the king's *right* knee attests to the scene's unquestionable reality. That the letter is signed with his *hand* explains why Sir Patrick, though he knows the peril, has no choice but to obey. His contempt for the nobles is suggested by their being loath (far too strong an emotion?) to wet their fancy shoes, perhaps as they went aboard the ship. And their fancy hats swimming above them reminds us both of the nobles' vanity and of their tragedy which is nonetheless moving. The ladies' sitting, then standing, tells the distress occasioned by the wreck . . . which is yet (fans, combs) pitifully inadequate. Focusing on the nobles' deaths (it's *their* hats we see) leaves unmarked and unimagined the doubtless courageous deaths of Sir Patrick and his loyal crew. The last two lines

And thair lies guid Sir Patrick Spence,
  Wi' the Scots lords at his feit.

strangely treat Sir Patrick, not as he must be (fifty fathoms deep), but as if he were formally laid out for burial, with the lords—arranged like the dog at the knight's feet in the copper plaque on a tomb—at his feet. The poet needn't explain to us, he has simply shown us, what true nobility is.

Visual details—description—are the touches of color that make a scene vivid and convincing, like the nobles' floating hats. These details can be psychological or dramatic symbols, like Bishop's loon. Notice, however, that none, if any, of the poems we have been discussing is wholly or mainly descriptive. Purely descriptive poems, though we are tempted to write them, are likely to be boring, like slides of someone's trip to the Grand Canyon. Description needs some dramatic or thematic thrust to carry it. Philip Levine in "The Return" renders the village of Orihuela through the eyes of a political exile who has longed for home; the description does emotional work; it doesn't decorate.

While the right detail can convince a reader, careless use of abstractions can undermine the reader's confidence in the poet. In the work of many beginning poets words like *love*, *hate*, *peace*, *happiness*, *innocence*, and *evil* ring as hollow and sound as pretentious as political speeches. Trust William Carlos Williams's famous dictum, "No ideas but in things." He does not mean *no* ideas, but rather ideas arrived at through particulars. Not the one nor the other, but the inductive relationship of the two. How would one sort out the gestures of the mourners from the ideas about loss and fear in William Matthews's "Men at My Father's Funeral" without robbing both of their significance? Or Elizabeth Bishop's understanding of the child's experience in "First Death in Nova Scotia" from the objects that exemplify the girl's confusion?

The difference between statement and implication is crucial. Abstractions *state* a meaning, whereas particulars may *imply* a meaning. Abstractions fail when they draw conclusions unwarranted by example. Abstractions that are earned, distilled from details, convince readers. The details of Hardy's scene in "Neutral Tones" prepare us for the haunting paradox in the middle of the poem: "The smile on your mouth was the deadest thing / Alive enough to have strength to die." The speaker arrives at the "keen lessons" about love after he has presented the particulars of the lovers' last moments together. Emily Dickinson persuades us of the effects of "great pain" (p. 267) through her scrupulous precision:

> After great pain, a formal feeling comes—
> The Nerves sit ceremonious, like Tombs—

In this poem, Stephen Dobyns (b. 1941) grounds his conclusions in a particular set of circumstances:

Bleeder

> By now I bet he's dead which suits me fine,
> but twenty-five years ago when we were both
> fifteen and he was camper and I counselor
> in a straightlaced Pennsylvania summer camp
> for crippled and retarded kids, I'd watch   5
>
> him sit all day by himself on a hill. No trees
> or sharp stones: he wasn't safe to be around.
> The slightest bruise and all his blood would simply
> drain away. It drove us crazy—first
> to protect him, then to see it happen. I   10
>
> would hang around him, picturing a knife
> or pointed stick, wondering how small a cut
> you'd have to make, then see the expectant face
> of another boy watching me, and we each knew
> how much the other would like to see him bleed.   15
>
> He made us want to hurt him so much we hurt
> ourselves instead: sliced fingers in craft class,
> busted noses in baseball, then joined at last

into mass wrestling matches beneath his hill,
a tangle of crutches and braces, hammering at   20

each other to keep from harming him. I'd look up
from slamming a kid in the gut and see him watching
with the empty blue eyes of children in sentimental
paintings, and hope to see him frown or grin,
but there was nothing: as if he had already died.   25

Then, after a week, they sent him home. Too much
responsibility, the director said.
Hell, I bet the kid had skin like leather.
Even so, I'd lie in bed at night and think
of busting into his room with a sharp stick, lash   30

and break the space around his rose-petal flesh,
while campers in bunks around me tossed and dreamt
of poking and bashing the bleeder until he
was left as flat as a punctured water balloon,
which is why the director sent him home. For what   35

is virtue but the lack of strong temptation;
better to leave us with our lie of being good.
Did he know this? Sitting on his private hill,
watching us smash each other with crutches and canes,
was this his pleasure; to make us cringe beneath   40

our wish to do him damage? But then who cared?
We were the living children, he the ghost
and what he gave us was a sense of being bad
together. He took us from our private spite
and offered our bullying a common cause: 45

which is why we missed him, even though we wished
him harm. When he went, we lost our shared meanness
and each of us was left to snarl his way
into a separate future, eager to discover
some new loser to link us in frailty again.   50

Unquestionably, this is a grisly subject: boys on crutches beating each other up because they really want to beat up a hemophiliac. The particulars are grotesque, but Dobyns does not include them just to appall us with the boys' cruelty, boys—we might have hoped—who would have treated the hemophiliac with more understanding and patience. He recounts their maliciousness to explore its causes, the paradoxical transition from wanting too much "to protect him" to wanting some accident to happen to him. The camp director knew the campers wouldn't long resist the urge to harm the hemophilic boy, so he sent him home, "too much responsibility." The director didn't want to be held accountable for what the boys were bound to do: "For what // is virtue but the lack of strong temptation." He assumes the boys are innately brutal. His only recourse: remove the object of their temptation, "better to leave us with our lie of being good" than try to change human nature.

Dobyns presents the poem as a recollection. After twenty-five years, that summer—and what it showed him about himself—still troubles the speaker. He wants to make sense of it. In remembering he decides that the hemophiliac's frailty gave the boys "a common cause." A common victim bound the boys together, even if in a community of cruelty. Without him they were separate, alone, waiting for another scapegoat to appear and redeem them from their isolation. Dobyns doesn't press his case, but by the time the reader comes to the end of the poem, it suggests wider applications for the actions of the group. The boys might also suggest gang behavior, the psychology of persecutors and torturers: why the stronger group bullies the weaker. Dobyns doesn't make these larger claims, he allows us to make them ourselves. Often the universal themes in a poem remain muted, lying beneath the surface for sensitive readers to discover on their own.

CLARITY, OBSCURITY, AND AMBIGUITY

Nobody really champions **obscurity**. Robert Francis puts it succinctly: "It is not difficult to be difficult." If what you are saying is worth saying, nothing can be gained (and everything can be lost) by obscuring it. If what you are saying is not worth saying, no reader will find you more interesting for making that fact hard to discover. Don't confuse clarity with the undeveloped, the simplistic, the unexamined. Poems that handle complex issues may be demanding: all the more reason for you to be as clear as possible. To film the mysteries of a coral reef, the diver needs a camera with a sharp lens.

Nor is obscurity the same as **ambiguity**, which permits more than one reading of a poem simultaneously. The connotations of its words, the rhythm of its sentences, the implications of its images and metaphors, the weight of its symbols, its use of allusion, its shape and sounds—every aspect of a poem can yield ambiguity. Ambiguity enriches poetry; it creates its depth and resonance so that we return to a poem again and again, drawing more from it each time. How clear Bishop is in telling us the loon is "cold and caressable," yet how ambiguous the phrase is, juxtaposing hard and soft sensations, discomfort and pleasure, connecting both with the initial hard "c" sound. Even the oddness of the word "caressable" itself is suggestive, as if no more familiar word, like "touchable," might do; does the speaker herself long for a caress, to be given special attention, to be loved? And the tiny coffin is "a little frosted cake"; does the image suggest a submerged attraction to death—mixed with a repugnance, since the cake is *frosted*, cold? All the readings may be relevant at once, like concentric circles; they are complementary, reenforcing one another, adding more dimensions to a highly complex situation, the speaker's memory of her first experience with death.

The beginning poet will find that being clear can be difficult, for what may seem obvious to the poet may be anything but obvious to the reader. We have often watched student poets writhe as class discussion about their poems came to ludicrous conclusions about what they meant. The fault lies sometimes with readers who don't pay close enough attention and so miss a signal. But often the poet, in a state of ingenious solitude, has so tangled and hidden the signals in the underbrush that no one can spot them; see Robert Francis's little essay "The Indecifer- able Poem" (p. 356). When readings of a poem contradict each other—or just point in totally different directions—the result is obscurity. Given several mutually exclusive choices, a reader is like the proverbial ass between two piles of hay. It couldn't make up its mind and so starved to death. Sometimes the obscurity is an accident, a confusing sentence fragment or an infelicity of wording that escaped editing and proofreading—for example, a pronoun that doesn't refer to what the poet thinks it does.

Theories of interpretation we will leave to theorists. Don't "analyze" your own work; you can't spin around the dance floor if you're staring at your feet. What's crucial for the beginning poet to remember is that readers may read in a poem things which the poet did not intend, as well as read it in ways the poet did intend. That's the nature of ambiguity. A poem of multiple layers will lend itself to multiple readings. Responsible readers try to make sure that their reading of a poem accounts for, or at least does not contradict, each of the poem's features. It's unfair to ignore signals in a poem about how it should be read in order to make another reading work. We would be irresponsible, for instance, to ignore the *tone* of Bishop's poem so as to argue that it is about a greedy little girl who cares more about cake than about her cousin.

With any poem that works in a personal way, a reader's response will inevitably call up personal experiences, associations, and feelings. These will never be exactly like the poet's, just as one person can never hope to convey to another person the *exact* mental picture of a particular place. (Even pointing out a particular star to someone is hard.) So long as the reader's "poem" doesn't violate or undermine the clues to the poet's "poem," the transaction is fitting. Indeed, it is what any poet hopes for: that readers will make the poem truly their own.

QUESTIONS AND SUGGESTIONS

1. After studying a pine cone or a sliced-open orange (or some other common object) for twenty minutes or so, write a description of it. Concentrate on what you see, but include smell, touch, taste, and sound if you can.

2. Write a poem about one of the following, or a similarly odd or unique subject. Include a lot of particulars.

a courthouse wedding	the backstroke	climbing a phone pole
parchesi	avocado skin	hammers
mitosis	carousel horses	amethysts

3. Write a poem in which someone encounters a creature or creatures, and through the encounter arrives at some evocative/moving/troublesome—but in any case interesting—conclusions. You might want to read or re-read these poems as models: William Stafford, "Traveling through the Dark," (p. 131), Enid Shomer, "Among the Cows" (p. 164), Thomas Lux, "Tarantulas on the Lifebuoy"

(p. 19), James Wright, "A Blessing" (p. 326), Michael Heffernan, "Slugs" (p. 309), and C. Lynn Shaffer, "A Butterfly Lands on the Grave of My Friend" (p. 350).

4. Here is a poem that has been rewritten so that abstractions and clichés replace imagery, detail, and implication. Freely revise it, inventing images and details you feel might be evocative. Compare your poem with those by others in your writing group (and with the original in Appendix II, p. 386). How similar do the poems seem?

Eavesdropping

We overheard a woman tell our mother
that if she couldn't afford to keep us
she should send us away.
That summer my brothers and sisters
and I planned to run away from home.   5
We thought about places we could go
but we were too scared to think straight
and too young to have a lot of ideas.
All our talk really shook up
our baby sister who was afraid   10
to be left alone one second.
She would get in bed with me at night
and hang on for dear life.
I was cold-hearted and made her go back
to her own bed even though I felt guilty   15
because we hadn't considered
she was afraid we'd abandon her too.

5. Among the pleasures of this sonnet by David Wojahn (b. 1953) are its topicality, its contemporary subject matter, and its adaptation of the sonnet form. How does the precision of Wojahn's details help create the poem's irony?

The Assassination of John Lennon as Depicted by the Madame Tussaud Wax Museum, Niagara Falls, Ontario, 1987

Smuggled human hair from Mexico
Falls radiant around the waxy O

Of her scream. Shades on, leather coat and pants, Yoko
On her knees—like the famous Kent State photo

Where the girl can't shriek her boyfriend alive, her arms   5
Windmilling Ohio sky.

       A pump in John's chest heaves

To mimic death-throes. The blood is made of latex.
His glasses: broken on the plastic sidewalk.

A scowling David Chapman, his arms outstretched,
His pistol barrel spiraling fake smoke   10

In a siren's red wash, completes the composition,
And somewhere background music plays *Imagine*

Before the tableau darkens. We push a button
To renew the scream.
                      The chest starts up again.

6. Suppose you were writing a description of the sunken hulk of the luxurious
passenger liner *Titanic*, which went down in 1912 after hitting an iceberg in the
North Atlantic. What visual details would you focus on or invent? For each,
imagine the placement or movement of the camera. Close-up, middle, or distant
shots, for example? In what sequence? Carefully arrange a sentence or several
sentences to duplicate this effect.

7. In this poem by James Dickey (b. 1923), how are scene and detail used to help
interpret the episode? What do the comparisons of Doris to a mouse and of the
speaker to a black snake imply about the relationship? Is the love-making really
successful? (Listen for the overtones in lines 85–97.)

Cherrylog Road

Off Highway 106
At Cherrylog Road I entered
The '34 Ford without wheels,
Smothered in kudzu,
With a seat pulled out to run   5
Corn whiskey down from the hills,

And then from the other side
Crept into an Essex
With a rumble seat of red leather
And then out again, aboard   10
A blue Chevrolet, releasing
The rust from its other color,

Reared up on three building blocks.
None had the same body heat;
I changed with them inward, toward   15
The weedy heart of the junkyard,
For I knew that Doris Holbrook
Would escape from her father at noon

And would come from the farm
To seek parts owned by the sun   20

Among the abandoned chassis,
Sitting in each in turn
As I did, leaning forward
As in a wild stock-car race

In the parking lot of the dead.   25
Time after time, I climbed in
And out the other side, like
An envoy or movie star
Met at the station by crickets.
A radiator cap raised its head,   30

Become a real toad or a kingsnake
As I neared the hub of the yard,
Passing through many states,
Many lives, to reach
Some grandmother's long Pierce-Arrow   35
Sending platters of blindness forth

From its nickel hubcaps
And spilling its tender upholstery
On sleepy roaches,
The glass panel in between   40
Lady and colored driver
Not all the way broken out,

The back-seat phone
Still on its hook.
I got in as though to exclaim,   45
"Let us go to the orphan asylum,
John; I have some old toys
For children who say their prayers."

I popped with sweat as I thought
I heard Doris Holbrook scrape   50
Like a mouse in the southern-state sun
That was eating the paint in blisters
From a hundred car tops and hoods.
She was tapping like code,

Loosening the screws,   55
Carrying off headlights,
Sparkplugs, bumpers,
Cracked mirrors and gear-knobs,
Getting ready, already,
To go back with something to show   60

Other than her lips' new trembling
I would hold to me soon, soon,
Where I sat in the ripped back seat
Talking over the interphone,

Praying for Doris Holbrook   65
To come from her father's farm

And to get back there
With no trace of me on her face
To be seen by her red-haired father
Who would change, in the squalling barn,   70
Her back's pale skin with a strop,
Then lay for me

In a bootlegger's roasting car
With a string-triggered 12-gauge shotgun
To blast the breath from the air.   75
Not cut by the jagged windshields,
Through the acres of wrecks she came
With a wrench in her hand,

Through dust where the blacksnake dies
Of boredom, and the beetle knows   80
The compost has no more life.
Someone outside would have seen
The oldest car's door inexplicably
Close from within:

I held her and held her and held her,   85
Convoyed at terrific speed
By the stalled, dreaming traffic around us,
So the blacksnake, stiff
With inaction, curved back
Into life, and hunted the mouse   90

With deadly overexcitement,
The beetles reclaimed their field
As we clung, glued together,
With the hooks of the seat springs
Working through to catch us red-handed   95
Amidst the gray breathless batting

That burst from the seat at our backs.
We left by separate doors
Into the changed, other bodies
Of cars, she down Cherrylog Road   100
And I to my motorcycle
Parked like the soul of the junkyard

Restored, a bicycle fleshed
With power, and tore off
Up Highway 106, continually   105
Drunk on the wind in my mouth,
Wringing the handlebar for speed,
Wild to be wreckage forever.

POEMS TO CONSIDER

The Study of Genius   *1994*

SANDRA McPHERSON (b. 1943)

> *Laurel and Hardy Convention, Las Vegas, 1992*

I am passing behind one of five Ringling
Brothers clowns, the one with green hair
and white piping on billowing outline,
as he stands at the back of the convention
and watches the film.   5

He is sensing
the staircasing in his body,
the coiling within the standstill,
while two shadow-and-light gentlemen
goof with all the hopeful grandeur   10

of one's double-fat face, his tasty pique—
his partner's pencil elementariness
and high-pitched sniffling
bringing the spat to a damp, shy close.
Green Hair follows every movement   15

for the years it takes
to bone this costume out as a human *if*.
The act feels so new, of these old two,
that he lives to know what makes it so.
While, to his right, the transvestite,   20

modeling his attention,
wears his study of the wives,
his Forties Schiaparelli suit,
fox stole, wartime entire costume change
of earrings, brooch, and hat,   25

his lingerie blouse complementing
the gray slender silhouette
of rationed jersey (square shoulders
mostly his own). And plastic shoes.
And those of us who dress up as ourselves   30

seem the slackest students, ready-to-wear,
unscripted as chit-chat, our gestures flat,

our timing countable by neither chimes nor jewels.
We can only revere
the elderly child actors on the dais,   35

tracking the other definition of genius,
that guardian spirit of earlier place and time,
watching reels of their creator-child,
re-running around, that scrappy, indefatigable guide
to the unrecoverable self.   40

 ## The Dead Monkey   1988

WILLIAM OLSEN (b. 1954)

A face framed in a pink lace baby's hood was youth and age
collapsed to a wizened black walnut. It had no idea
that we were there, New Orleans, 1981, or that we were
growing envious of its owner, an unshaven but rich-looking Mexican
who hoisted it from the ground, not altogether modest   5
about the attention he and it were getting from all of us,
eating our beignets, watching this binary configuration,
man and monkey, kiss, kiss again, patching up
some make-believe quarrel between lovers.
Suddenly it leapt up a trellis of morning glory vines,   10
swung from a brass chandelier over the human circus of breakfasters
and scrambled across the street into a moving bus,
arms and legs toppling one over the other
as it tried to keep up with its death.
The man walked out to the ridiculous end to his happiness,   15
stealing the delight from us, like surreptitious newlyweds,
poor enough in spirit to be amazed by fact.
Taking it in his arms, crying to make himself alone,
this Mexican was living proof that suffering
is not all that crazy about company.   20
When the crowd dispersed, he seemed relieved,
as if too much had already been suffered
without us adding our thimbleful.
That night we saw the Mexican without his monkey in a bar,
buying everyone drinks and laughing hysterically   25
about the whole thing, saying *death is my life.*
If that sounds a bit dramatic, blame it
on sweet bourbon, this is just what he said,
being just lucid enough to mix up life and death

and stupid enough to want to share in their confusion.   30
We toasted with him to stupidity because
there's not always enough stupidity around to celebrate,
and when we were good and drunk we turned ourselves out into the night,
between more bars we saw more bars,
windows like photographs fleshed out with   35
bodies that destroyed their secrets,
we took the journey across the dangerous street,
entranced by the idea of getting somewhere,
sick for everything but home.

 ### Shopping in Tuckahoe   1988

JANE FLANDERS (b. 1940)

One could spend years in this parking lot
waiting for a daughter to find just the right
pair of jeans. From time to time I slip the meter
its nickel fix. Across the street in Epstein's
basement, shoppers pick their way through bins   5
of clothes made tempting by the words "marked down."
We have replaced making things with looking for them.

My mood is such I almost miss what's happening next door,
where a weedy lot is conducting its own
January clearance with giveaways galore—   10
millions of seeds, husks, vines, bare sepals
glinting like cruisewear in the cold sun.
"Come in," says the wind. "We love your pale hair
and skin, the fine lines on your brow."

The shades of choice are bone and dust, everything   15
starched, rustling like taffeta, brushing against me
with offers of free samples—thorns, burrs, fluff,
twigs stripped of fussy flowers.
Greedy as any bargain hunter, I gather them in,
till my arms are filled with the residue of plenty.   20

By the time my daughter reappears, trailing her scarves
of pink and green, she will be old enough
to drive home alone. I have left the keys for her.
She'll never spot me standing here like a winter bouquet
with my straw shield, my helmet of seeds and sparrows.   25

My Father's Rage   1992

ANDREW HUDGINS (b. 1951)

As I kicked through the swinging door,
the turkey shifted on the platter.
I juggled, lost it, clipped the bird
with the platter's edge, and the hot meat
slid, skittered—greasy—on the floor,   5
and smacked the polished army boots
of Sergeant Turner, our Thanksgiving guest.
My Daddy grabbed me by the throat
and slammed me up against the wall,
which boomed. My mother gasped. I lost   10
my breath and couldn't get it back.
"You stupid idiot!" my father screamed.
Then Sergeant Turner touched Dad's arm.
"Lon," he said, "we've eaten worse—
when we were growing up." Dad sighed,   15
and then, reluctantly, he let me drop.
But now his crazy rage is gone
to whole days watching teevee, watching
golf, football, news. His rage gone to whole days
watching the fucking weather station.   20
And I, goddamn his eyes, I want it back.

 ## Names of Horses   1977

DONALD HALL (b. 1928)

All winter your brute shoulders strained against collars, padding
and steerhide over the ash hames, to haul
sledges of cordwood for drying through spring and summer,
for the Glenwood stove next winter, and for the simmering range.

In April you pulled cartloads of manure to spread on the fields,   5
dark manure of Holsteins, and knobs of your own clustered with oats.
All summer you mowed the grass in meadow and hayfield, the mowing
     machine
clacketing beside you, while the sun walked high in the morning;

and after noon's heat, you pulled a clawed rake through the same acres,
gathering stacks, and dragged the wagon from stack to stack,   10

and the built hayrack back, uphill to the chaffy barn,
three loads of hay a day from standing grass in the morning.

Sundays you trotted the two miles to church with the light load
of a leather quartertop buggy, and grazed in the sound of hymns.
Generation on generation, your neck rubbed the windowsill   15
of the stall, smoothing the wood as the sea smooths glass.

When you were old and lame, when your shoulders hurt bending to graze,
one October the man, who fed you and kept you, and harnessed you every
    morning,
led you through corn stubble to sandy ground above Eagle Pond,
and dug a hole beside you where you stood shuddering in your skin,   20

and lay the shotgun's muzzle in the boneless hollow behind your ear,
and fired the slug into your brain, and felled you into your grave,
shoveling sand to cover you, setting goldenrod upright above you,
where by next summer a dent in the ground made your monument.

For a hundred and fifty years, in the pasture of dead horses,   25
roots of pine trees pushed through the pale curves of your ribs,
yellow blossoms flourished above you in autumn, and in winter
frost heaved your bones in the ground—old toilers, soil makers:

O Roger, Mackerel, Riley, Ned, Nellie, Chester, Lady Ghost.

 ## Aunt Sue's Stories   *1921*

LANGSTON HUGHES (1902–1967)

Aunt Sue has a head full of stories.
Aunt Sue has a whole heart full of stories.
Summer nights on the front porch
Aunt Sue cuddles a brown-faced child to her bosom
And tells him stories.   5

Black slaves
Working in the hot sun,
And black slaves
Walking in the dewy night,
And black slaves   10
Singing sorrow songs on the banks of a mighty river
Mingle themselves softly
In the flow of old Aunt Sue's voice,
Mingle themselves softly

In the dark shadows that cross and recross   15
Aunt Sue's stories.

And the dark-faced child, listening,
Knows that Aunt Sue's stories are real stories.
He knows that Aunt Sue never got her stories
Out of any book at all,   20
But that they came
Right out of her own life.

The dark-faced child is quiet
Of a summer night
Listening to Aunt Sue's stories.   25

The Curator   1992

MILLER WILLIAMS (b. 1930)

We thought it would come, we thought the Germans would come,
were almost certain they would. I was thirty-two,
the youngest assistant curator in the country.
I had some good ideas in those days.

Well, what we did was this. We had boxes   5
precisely built to every size of canvas.
We put the boxes in the basement and waited.

When word came that the Germans were coming in,
we got each painting put in the proper box
and out of Leningrad in less than a week.   10
They were stored somewhere in southern Russia.

But what we did, you see, besides the boxes
waiting in the basement, which was fine,
a grand idea, you'll agree, and it saved the art—
but what we did was leave the frames hanging,   15
so after the war it would be a simple thing
to put the paintings back where they belonged.

Nothing will seem surprised or sad again
compared to those imperious, vacant frames.

Well, the staff stayed on to clean the rubble   20
after the daily bombardments. We didn't dream—
You know it lasted nine hundred days.
Much of the roof was lost and snow would lie

sometimes a foot deep on this very floor,
but the walls stood firm and hardly a frame fell.　　25

Here is the story, now, that I want to tell you.
Early one day, a dark December morning,
we came on three young soldiers waiting outside,
pacing and swinging their arms against the cold.
They told us this: in three homes far from here　　30
all dreamed of one day coming to Leningrad
to see the Hermitage, as they supposed
every Soviet citizen dreamed of doing.
Now they had been sent to defend the city,
a turn of fortune the three could hardly believe.　　35

I had to tell them there was nothing to see
but hundreds and hundreds of frames where the paintings had hung.

"Please, sir," one of them said, "let us see them."

And so we did. It didn't seem any stranger
than all of us being here in the first place,　　40
inside such a building, strolling in snow.

We led them around most of the major rooms,
what they could take the time for, wall by wall.
Now and then we stopped and tried to tell them
part of what they would see if they saw the paintings.　　45
I told them how those colors would come together,
described a brushstroke here, a dollop there,
mentioned a model and why she seemed to pout
and why this painter got the roses wrong.

The next day a dozen waited for us,　　50
then thirty or more, gathered in twos and threes.
Each of us took a group in a different direction:
Castagno, Caravaggio, Brueghel, Cezanne, Matisse,
Orozco, Manet, DaVinci, Goya, Vermeer,
Picasso, Uccello, your Whistler, Wood, and Gropper.　　55
We pointed to more details about the paintings,
I venture to say, than if we had had them there,
some unexpected use of line or light,
balance or movement, facing the cluster of faces
the same way we'd done it every morning　　60
before the war, but then we didn't pay
so much attention to what we talked about.
People could see for themselves. As a matter of fact

we'd sometimes said our lines as if they were learned
out of a book, with hardly a look at the paintings.   65

But now the guide and the listeners paid attention
to everything—the simple differences
between the first and post impressionists,
romantic and heroic, shade and shadow.

Maybe this was a way to forget the war   70
a little while. Maybe more than that.
Whatever it was, the people continued to come.
It came to be called The Unseen Collection.

Here. Here is the story I want to tell you.

Slowly, blind people began to come.   75
A few at first then more of them every morning,
some led and some alone, some swaying a little.
They leaned and listened hard, they screwed their faces,
they seemed to shift their eyes, those that had them,
to see better what was being said.   80
And a cock of the head. My God, they paid attention.

After the siege was lifted and the Germans left
and the roof was fixed and the paintings were in their places,
the blind never came again. Not like before.
This seems strange, but what I think it was,   85
they couldn't see the paintings anymore.
They could still have listened, but the lectures became
a little matter-of-fact. What can I say?
Confluences come when they will and they go away.

6

A CAST OF CHARACTERS
Duke, Drunk, Pig, and Lily

In every poem there is a voice, a **speaker**—someone who *says* whatever it is. Usually the speaker is the poet. Often, however, it is not. In Emily Dickinson's "I heard a Fly buzz—when I died—" (p. 168), the speaker describing her own death can't be the poet. The Victorian Englishman Robert Browning was not the Renaissance Italian duke who speaks in "My Last Duchess" (p. 166); nor, obviously, is Philip Levine the brave pig that speaks in "Animals Are Passing from Our Lives" (p. 186). These speakers are **dramatic characters,** or *personae* (singular: **persona**), and the poems in which they appear are **dramatic monologues.**

The poet's freedom to invent or imagine, to create fictional characters and scenes, is of course as great as the novelist or playwright's. The truth of *Othello* or *Jane Eyre* is not less for their being imaginative constructs. It is always our own experience of deception and jealousy, of hypocrisy and kinship, of pride or valor or love, that makes such works possible for us as writers and certifies them for us as readers when they are true.

Every poem is a dramatic monologue in a sense, an utterance with an "utterer," a speaker, and an at least implicit circumstance in which the utterance is uttered. For readers who don't know the poet personally, any poem involves the perception of a presented character, real or otherwise. Thus, even the poet writing or trying to write in his or her own voice, is always creating a self, in tone, stance, and theme. As in life we show different faces to different people or in different situations (at the beach, in church), so in writing, often without realizing it, we change or adjust the voice we use, presenting ourselves differently; we quite naturally adopt somewhat different *personae*. This process, when the issues are serious, may even amount to exploring one's identity, ethnicity, gender, or heritage; that is, to self-discovery.

In this sense of voice or character, writing often leads to working through our own experiences in ways that may surprise us. Motives, re-examined, may seem more complicated; incidents that seemed straightforward may turn out to be ambiguous or revealing. This same complexity will appear in characters we invent or borrow from life. The heroic is truer when it is not seen as perfect. Cordelia's unswerving love is in some measure balanced by the unswerving pride of her refusal to speak, a pride similar to that of her demanding father, Lear. Villainy is often balanced in some way, by wit or vitality we must admire. There is something to be said even for Browning's awful Duke. Such figures of immense power and fine taste, greedy but also generous as patrons, whatever else we may think of them, made possible the art of the Renaissance. We are awed by more than his evil.

Perhaps drama arises out of this richness—or mixture—of character. In Rita Dove's "The House Slave" (p. 208), for instance, it is the speaker's relative privilege and comfort—after all, she is free to fall asleep again—that gives poignancy to her perspective. The poet has chosen this perspective because the point is not simply guilt of masters and suffering of slaves. The dramatic focus is more complex and the theme of wider relevance.

Since, as Elizabeth Bowen says, "Nothing can happen nowhere," the place of a poem often reveals character tellingly, as in Dickey's "Cherrylog Road" (p. 144); and the occasion of a poem certainly does, as in W. D. Snodgrass's "Leaving the Motel" (p. 170) or in Jane Flanders's "Shopping in Tuckahoe" (p. 149). We might of course be shown Flanders's speaker anywhere, at a party the Saturday night before or mowing her lawn, but the moment "in this parking lot," waiting for a daughter who is shopping for jeans, shows how she has drifted to the edge of her own life.

The poem, then, creates its own stage, scenery, and actor. And the speaker's range of diction, familiarity or formality, choice of images, and so on, help create the speaker's character for the reader, as when Flanders has the woman describe an adjacent weedy lot as "conducting its own / January clearance with giveaways galore— / millions of seeds, husks, vines, bare sepals / glinting like cruisewear in the cold sun." Because people are interesting, putting people into poems is an easy way of making poems interesting.

Consider this local "character" in a poem by X. J. Kennedy (b. 1929). The first and last stanzas describe her and recount the action, but she speaks for herself in the main portion of the poem.

In a Prominent Bar in Secaucus One Day

To the tune of "The Old Orange Flute"
or the tune of "Sweet Betsy from Pike"

In a prominent bar in Secaucus° one day
Rose a lady in skunk with a topheavy sway,
Raised a knobby red finger—all turned from their beer—
While with eyes bright as snowcrust she sang high and clear:

1 *Secaucus*: town in the industrial marsh of New Jersey, near New York City

"Now who of you'd think from an eyeload of me   5
That I once was a lady as proud as could be?
Oh I'd never sit down by a tumbledown drunk
If it wasn't, my dears, for the high cost of junk.

"All the gents used to swear that the white of my calf
Beat the down of the swan by a length and a half.   10
In the kerchief of linen I caught to my nose
Ah, there never fell snot, but a little gold rose.

"I had seven gold teeth and a toothpick of gold,
My Virginia cheroot was a leaf of it rolled
And I'd light it each time with a thousand in cash—   15
Why the bums used to fight if I flicked them an ash.

"Once the toast of the Biltmore°, the belle of the Taft°,
I would drink bottle beer at the Drake°, never draft,
And dine at the Astor° on Salisbury steak
With a clean tablecloth for each bite I did take.   20

"In a car like the Roxy° I'd roll to the track,
A steel-guitar trio, a bar in the back,
And the wheels made no noise, they turned over so fast,
Still it took you ten minutes to see me go past.

"When the horses bowed down to me that I might choose,   25
I bet on them all, for I hated to lose.
Now I'm saddled each night for my butter and eggs
And the broken threads race down the backs of my legs.

"Let you hold in mind, girls, that your beauty must pass
Like a lovely white clover that rusts with its grass.   30
Keep your bottoms off barstools and marry you young
Or be left—an old barrel with many a bung.

"For when time takes you out for a spin in his car
You'll be hard-pressed to stop him from going too far
And be left by the roadside, for all your good deeds,   35
Two toadstools for tits and a face full of weeds."

All the house raised a cheer, but the man at the bar
Made a phonecall and up pulled a red patrol car
And she blew us a kiss as they copped her away
From that prominent bar in Secaucus, N.J.   40

17, 18, 19, *Biltmore, Taft, Drake, Astor*: once fashionable hotels in New York;   21 *Roxy*:
a movie palace.

Part of the fun (and of the pathos) in this portrait comes of our recognizing that,
however much truth is mingled with her exaggeration, she was never quite so
much a lady as she believes. Her language tells us about her world: "All the *gents*
used to swear that the white of my calf / *Beat* the down of a swan *by a length and a
half.*" Her ideas of elegance fall painfully short: bottle beer in preference to draft

and, as an instance of fine dining, the humdrum Salisbury steak. In this way the poet communicates *around* what she is saying so that we perceive her as Kennedy wants us to, not as she perceives herself. We end up admiring her less for the reason she gives (that she was once a grand lady) than for her blarney and her bravery of spirit. Like Chaucer's Wife of Bath, she is indomitably human.

The range of possible characters, of course, extends beyond persons you actually know or might encounter. A celebrity, or mythical or historical character such as Eve in this poem by Linda Pastan (b. 1932), may become freshly exciting if the poet discovers an aspect no one has thought of.

Mother Eve

Of course she never was a child herself,
waking as she did one morning
full grown and perfect,
with only Adam, another innocent,
to love her and instruct.   5
There was no learning, step by step,
to walk, no bruised elbows or knees—
no small transgressions.
There was only the round, white mound
of the moon rising,   10
which could neither be suckled
nor leaned against.
And perhaps the serpent spoke
in a woman's voice, mothering.
Oh, who can blame her?   15

When she held her own child
in her arms, what did she make
of that new animal? Did she love Cain
too little or too much, looking down
at her now flawed body as if her rib,   20
like Adam's, might be gone?
In the litany of naming that continued
for children instead of plants,
no daughter is mentioned.
But generations later there was Rachel°,   25
all mother herself, who knew
that bringing forth a child in pain
is only the start. It is losing them
(and Benjamin so young)
that is the punishment.   30

25 *Rachel:* One of the Jewish matriarchs; wife of Jacob and mother of Joseph and Benjamin. Genesis, esp. chapters 29–30, 35.

NARRATIVE

Many poems, far more than one might guess offhand, are in fact **narratives**: they tell (or imply) a story. Robert Browning's crime-thriller *The Ring and the Book* (1868–1869) or Vikram Seth's *The Golden Gate* (1986), for instance, are novel-length. From Chaucer's tales to Keats's "The Eve of St. Agnes" to Frost's "The Witch of Coös," poets have written what are in effect short stories. Louis Simpson is the contemporary master.

The compression and sharper focus of verse make it ideal for short narrative. We can readily imagine the material of this poem by Fleda Brown Jackson (b. 1944), say, presented as prose fiction.

Kitten

She is thirteen. Her cat, Sneakers,
has just had another litter of kittens
to be chloroformed by her father
in the large cooking pot. "Keep whichever
you want," he says, "mother or kitten,   5
just one." She is sitting on her bed
petting the male kitten with thick
tan fur. She sits close to her Silvertone
radio, moves her mouth to the music.
A rifle cracks in the back yard,   10
then a scuffle like a rat
under the house. Sneakers has gotten
away, not quite dead, is crouched
in a far corner wailing a low
steady wail. She watches the square   15
knob on her dresser, lit with sun,
the back hairs of her kitten ablaze
in the sunlight like little spines.
Under her is the live crawlspace.
She holds the little paws of her kitten,   20
pushes her thumbs gently into the center
of the pads with almost divine
tenderness, watches the claws extend
involuntarily, translucent little hooks.
She has a vision of pushing until they fly   25
outward like darts, or rays of sun,
leaving the kitten with buff-
colored buttons of feet. She names it
Buffy, imagines buffing the DeSoto
with the kitten, rubbing him flat   30
as her grandmother's fox stole,
popping in little marbles for eyes
that would catch the light,

hard. Her father is calling kitty, here
kitty, his flashlight in the cat's   35
eyes. It is Jungle-Cat, leaping out
of a 3-D screen among arrows, flying
at the audience. She stretches out on
the bed and brushes her face across
her smooth animal. A dark creature passes   40
through the back chambers of her thought
like a shadow, enters a kingdom
of shadows, stirring and stirring.

The prose story, conventionally, would be much longer. It would certainly add details and dialogue to develop and color the first scene of the girl's conversation with her father, which the poem sums up in lines 1–5 and then abandons with a jump-cut as sudden as those in "Sir Patrick Spence" (p. 137). The story would no doubt use exposition to present the family situation, which the poem trusts to implication (house with an open crawlspace under it, the DeSoto, the grandmother's fox stole). But the poem seizes the narrative gist in its vivid main scene: the girl, petting the male kitten, hears her father beneath the floor trying to kill Sneakers.

She suffers the father's authoritarian hardness without protest or tears and apparently, since she has chosen the kitten, with little particular feeling for the mother-cat. This wasn't Sneakers's first litter, so the girl had faced a similar choice at least once before; and she has, it seems, learned more than a little of the father's hardness. Nor is it quite affection for the kitten she feels as, pressing "with almost divine / tenderness," she "watches the claws extend / involuntarily, translucent little hooks," or as she cruelly fantasizes buffing the DeSoto with him.

The girl's possessiveness is unsettling—Sneakers, "Her cat" in line 1, is only "the cat" in line 35, wailing in pain and terror. It is "her Silvertone / radio," to whose popular songs she mouths the words, her bed, her dresser; and "the male kitten" of line 7 has become "her kitten" in line 17 and by line 40, as stretched out on the bed she brushes her face across his fur, "her smooth animal." Her possessiveness is jarring, but her repressed anger is ferocious. The imagery of "spines," "hooks," "darts," "Jungle-Cat, leaping out / of a 3-D screen among arrows," as her father creeps forward for the kill, takes on a deeper resonance. A kitten herself, thirteen, she begins to understand how to make herself dangerous.

A dark creature passes
through the back chambers of her thought
like a shadow, enters a kingdom
of shadows, stirring and stirring.

One senses what form her implacable rebellion is about to take.

All the fundamentals of good narrative may be useful to the poet—starting the action as near the dramatic climax as possible, for instance, or the choice between summary narration or full scenic presentation for a particular part of the story. If you look back to poems like Gillian Conoley's "The Woman on the Homecoming Float" (p. 23), Claudia Rankine's "The Man. His Bowl. His Raspberries." (p. 55), Henry Taylor's "Barbed Wire" (p. 60), Rita Dove's "A Hill of Beans" (p. 124), or Miller Williams's "The Curator" (p. 152), you may observe similar skills in deploying narrative.

One technical element of narrative, usually more closely associated with fiction, should be mentioned: **point of view**. Who speaks? Or, more exactly, who *reports* the action?

Stories normally are told either in *first person* ("I") or in *third person* point of view. In first person, a *character* speaks. It may be a central character, like the young woman in Tess Gallagher's "Kidnaper" (p. 54) or the young man in James Dickey's "Cherrylog Road" (p. 144), or a minor character, like the anonymous patron who reports the goings-on in X. J. Kennedy's "In a Prominent Bar in Secaucus One Day." Advantages of first person include immediacy and sympathy. A restriction, of course, is that the character can only report what he or she knows or sees or believes, so that the view of the action must be limited to that one perspective. In "Cherrylog Road," for example, we can know about Doris Holbrook only what the young man observes or believes. A minor character as narrator is useful in lending credibility, especially when the action is unusual, or in providing a voice for commentary, as the nephew does in T. S. Eliot's "Aunt Helen" (p. 171).

Narration in *second person* is possible, but rare. As in Cornelius Eady's "The Wrong Street" (p. 58), it is invariably idealizing or typicalizing. We encounter it often in directions ("To get to the American Legion Hall you go down Smith Street . . . ").

Using third person ("he, she"), the narrator may be either *omniscient*, reporting even the thoughts of several characters, or *limited* to a single sympathetic character (and that character's awareness). Third person limited point of view, exemplified in Fleda Brown Jackson's "Kitten" or Rita Dove's "A Hill of Beans" (p. 124), is similar to first person, with perhaps a shade more objectivity. Often, one can substitute for the other. In "A Hill of Beans," shifting to first person—"That night *I* made Thomas / board up the well"—makes only a minor difference, as would shifting to third person in "Cherrylog Road": "*They* left by separate doors / Into the changed, other bodies / Of cars, she down Cherrylog Road / And *he* to *his* motorcycle . . ." Switching first for third person in this way (or vice versa) is a handy test that may suggest a more effective strategy for a poem. Notice, however, the switch would not work well in "Kitten." Why not?

Third person omniscient narration allows for shifting of interest from one character to another, or even, as in "Sir Patrick Spence" (p. 137), for reporting actions occurring simultaneously in different geographical locations. In Frost's "Home Burial" (p. 177), about another troubled domestic situation, the speaker, the narrative "voice," is reporting an event *no one* other than the couple is present to observe. (The lonely action in "An Old Man's Winter Night," p. 65, is also recorded omnisciently.) Further, notice that this omniscient speaker can report the angles, thoughts, feelings of *both* characters, switching back and forth to control the interpretation. In "He saw her from the bottom of the stairs" (line 1), we are in the husband's point of view; he sees her "starting down, / Looking back over her shoulder at some fear." "Some fear," we understand, is *his* guess or interpretation of her look. "He said *to gain time*" (line 6) presents his reason. However, "She let him look, *sure that he wouldn't see*" (line 15) presents *her* thinking.

The power of Frost's intense psychological drama comes from the poet's management of the point of view, so that we feel from both sides this intolerable confrontation between husband and wife. Every gesture is loaded with threat or menace. Any poet interested in narrative will find fascinating Randall Jarrell's essay on the poem (in *The Third Book of Criticism*), which shows line by line, word by word, how Frost has packed the scene with dramatic significance.

As camera-location is to description, so point of view is key to narrative.

The short poem usually compresses its narrative into a single key scene, implying or summarizing everything else. But it may also employ brief flashbacks as "Kitten" does in lines 1–6, or as you will observe Robert Browning doing in "My Last Duchess" (p. 166) or Robert Frost doing in "Home Burial" (p. 177), when the characters refer to or recall earlier events. Claudia Rankine's remarkable "Out of Many, One" (p. 180), however, presents its story in a number of vivid, quickly realized scenes, which form a sequence of discrete subpoems that seem to cover events of some weeks or even months. Written, as the poet notes, "in modified Jamaican Creole where slight changes are made to suggest a Creole voice," the poem offers a moving narrative of immigrant experience.

NEGATIVE CAPABILITY

Underlying the poet's ability to imagine and project characters is what John Keats called "negative capability." (He used the phrase in a letter to his brothers George and Thomas, 21 December 1817.) A "quality . . . which Shakespeare possessed so enormously," it is essentially the capability "of remaining content with half-knowledge" and "annulling self," and so being able to enter other identities. In another letter (to Richard Woodhouse, 27 October 1818), Keats speaks of "the chameleon poet." "A poet," he says, "is the most unpoetical of anything in existence, because he has no Identity—he is continually in for and filling some other body." The empathy includes men and women, of course, but also "The Sun,—the Moon,—the Sea . . ." Negative capability comes to a sort of emptying of the self, suspending judgments, so as to imagine others and even the natural from the inside: "if a sparrow come before my window, I take part in its existence and pick about the gravel" (letter to Benjamin Bailey, 22 November 1817). In conversation, according to Woodhouse, Keats even "affirmed that he can conceive of a billiard Ball that it may have a sense of delight from its own roundness, smoothness volubility & the rapidity of its motion"!

The force of empathy shows clearly in this poem by William Greenway (b. 1947). The occasion is a tour of a no longer worked coal mine in Wales. The experience is described vividly, especially in the image of the condensing breath coming out as "a soul up / into my helmet's lantern / beam."

Pit Pony

There are only a few left, he says,
kept by old Welsh miners, souvenirs, like
gallstones or gold teeth, torn
from this "pit," so cold and wet my
breath comes out a soul up   5
into my helmet's lantern
beam, anthracite walls running,
gleaming, and the floors iron-rutted
with tram tracks, the almost pure
rust that grows and waves like   10
orange moss in the gutters of water
that used to rise and drown.
He makes us turn all lights off, almost
a mile down. While children scream
I try to see anything, my hand touching   15
my nose, my wife beside me—darkness palpable,
velvet sack over our heads, even the glow
of watches left behind. This is where
they were born, into this nothing, felt
first with their cold noses for the shaggy   20
side and warm bag of black
milk, pulled their trams for twenty
years through pitch, past birds
that didn't sing, through doors
opened by five-year-olds who sat   25
in the cheap, complete blackness listening
for steps, a knock. And they
died down here, generation after
generation. The last one, when it
dies in the hills, not quite blind, the mines   30
closed forever, will it die strangely? Will it
wonder dimly why it was exiled from the rest
of its race, from the dark flanks of the soft
mother, what these timbers are that hold up
nothing but blue? If this is the beginning   35
of death, this wind, these stars?

The guide's mention of the pit ponies, none of which is even there, focuses the speaker's imagination on their strange, lightless lives spent entirely underground in the times when the mine was being worked. Even pity for the five-year-olds working as doorkeepers "in the cheap, complete blackness" can't compete with the strangeness of these animals' lives. The final lines evoke, empathetically *participate* in, the oddness felt in the few surviving ponies' misapprehension of the open-air world of wind and stars. Perhaps only the word "cheap" in line 26 implies (and indicts) the economic cruelty of the now-abandoned system, but that awfulness is made unforgettable.

We are all familiar with the talking animals of Aesop's fables and the Saturday morning cartoons, which are flimsily anthropomorphic at best. But our fellow creatures *do* think and feel—dream, remember, plan, communicate, believe. How the world appears to them, though, remains largely unexplored. As Donald R. Griffin of the Museum of Comparative Zoology at Harvard argues (in *Animal Minds*, 1992), "Cognitive ethology presents us with one of the supreme scientific challenges of our times." He notes: "Whatever thoughts and feelings nonhuman animals experience may be quite different from ours, and presumably much simpler." This is a frontier across which poems like Greenway's venture, careful to avoid the tritely anthropomorphic, engaging imaginatively the strangeness and difference. The translation, inevitably into human terms, nonetheless must seem precise.

In this poem Enid Shomer (b. 1944) purposely experiments with such empathy as a spiritual exercise:

Among the Cows

Advised to breathe with the Holsteins
    as a form of meditation,
I open a window in my
    mind and let their vast humid breath,
sticky flanks, the mantric switching   5
    of their tails drift through. I lie down
with them while they crop the weedy
    mansions, my breasts muffled like the
snouts of foxes run to ground. I
    need to comfort the cows, the way   10
heart patients stroke cats and the grief
    of childhood is shed for dogs. I
offer them fans of grass under
    a sky whose grey may be the hide
of some huge browser with sun and   15
    moon for wayward eyes. It begins

to rain. How they sway, their heavy
    necks lift and strain. Then, like patches
of night glimpsed through a bank of clouds,
    they move toward four o'clock, the dark   20
fragrant stalls where dawn will break first
    as the curved pink rim of their lips.
I want to believe I could live
    this close to the earth, could move with
a languor so resolute it   25
    passes for will, my heart riding
low in my body, not this flag

in my chest snapped by the lightest
breeze. Now my breath escapes with theirs
          like doused flames or a prayer made   30
visible: May our gender bear
          us gracefully through in these cumbrous frames.

Observation—"their vast humid breath, / sticky flanks, the mantric switching / of their tails"—leads to metaphor, and so to a delicately comic intuition: the grey of the sky "may be the hide / of some huge browser with sun and / moon for wayward eyes." The cosmos, for them, is like themselves. They move without moving, "like patches / of night glimpsed through a bank of clouds," because of course it is the clouds that move. The dawn, when it comes, will come "first / as the curved pink rim of their lips." Paradox seems natural. Languor can be "so resolute it / passes for will." Aware of what joins her to these magnificent beasts, the speaker finds that breath itself, in the simple act of breathing, becomes a prayer that she is praying, too. "May our gender bear / us gracefully through in these cumbrous frames."

Or consider the startling empathy in this poem by Louise Glück, (b. 1943):

The Gold Lily

As I perceive
I am dying now, and know
I will not speak again, will not
survive the earth, be summoned
out of it again, not   5
a flower yet, a spine only, raw dirt
catching my ribs, I call you
father and master: all around,
my companions are failing, thinking
you do not see. How   10
can they know you see
unless you save us?
In the summer twilight, are you
close enough to hear
your child's terror? Or   15
are you not my father,
you who raised me?

The flower speaks. At full blossom, aware of dying, it prays for itself and its "companions," perhaps to the sun, "you who raised me," hoping yet to be saved. Using questions to soften the quality of positive assertion, as Greenway does in "Pit Pony," Glück registers the experience in our language: "dying," "speak," "terror," "child," "father." Recalling its beginning, the lily refers to being "not / a flower yet, [but] a spine only, raw dirt / catching my ribs" as it emerged from the earth. The dramatic chill of the poem comes from the speaker's seeming exceptional. The others, "failing," already believe that "you do not see," but for the speaker there is the glimmer of this last appeal.

Negative capability lets poets get convincingly inside the skin of other people, whose situations may be quite different from our own. Even the mad make sense to themselves. Equally, none of us, having come somewhat differently to where we are, will be entirely the same. So the dramatic characters in poems involve sensitivity to quirk as well as to quiddity, even when the character is like or even is the poet. Putting aside defensiveness, suspending judgments, we may need negative capability most when we write about ourselves.

IRONY

Irony is saying one thing but meaning another, as when you drop a pile of dishes and someone says, "Beautiful!" More generally, irony refers to any discrepancy between the literal meaning of a statement and what the speaker intends *or* what a hearer will understand. With good reason, the term has come up in discussing a number of the poems in this chapter. In poems with a dramatic speaker, irony (in one or another of its various forms) is the poet's way of communicating with the reader *around* what the speaker is saying. Irony may deepen and enrich by making the reader aware of things (or aware of them in ways) the speaker doesn't see. It may even contradict the drift of what the speaker is saying. Notice how Robert Browning (1812–1889), who never says a word in his own voice, uses unintentional irony to characterize the villainous Duke of Ferrara (who speaks the whole poem):

My Last Duchess

That's my last duchess painted on the wall,
Looking as if she were alive. I call
That piece a wonder, now: Frà Pandolf's hands
Worked busily a day, and there she stands.
Will't please you sit and look at her? I said   5
"Frà Pandolf" by design, for never read
Strangers like you that pictured countenance,
The depth and passion of its earnest glance,
But to myself they turned (since none puts by
The curtain I have drawn for you, but I)   10
And seemed as they would ask me, if they durst,
How such a glance came there; so, not the first
Are you to turn and ask thus. Sir, 'twas not
Her husband's presence only, called that spot
Of joy into the Duchess' cheek: perhaps   15
Frà Pandolf chanced to say "Her mantle laps
Over my lady's wrist too much," or "Paint
Must never hope to reproduce the faint
Half-flush that dies along her throat": such stuff
Was courtesy, she thought, and cause enough   20
For calling up that spot of joy. She had
A heart—how shall I say?—too soon made glad,
Too easily impressed; she liked whate'er

She looked on, and her looks went everywhere.
Sir, 'twas all one! My favor at her breast,   25
The dropping of the daylight in the West,
The bough of cherries some officious fool
Broke in the orchard for her, the white mule
She rode with round the terrace—all and each
Would draw from her alike the approving speech,   30
Or blush, at least. She thanked men—good! but thanked
Somehow—I know not how—as if she ranked
My gift of a nine-hundred-years-old name
With anybody's gift. Who'd stoop to blame
This sort of trifling? Even had you skill   35
In speech—which I have not—to make your will
Quite clear to such an one, and say, "Just this
Or that in you disgusts me; here you miss,
Or there exceed the mark"—and if she let
Herself be lessoned so, nor plainly set   40
Her wits to yours, forsooth, and made excuse,
—E'en then would be some stooping; and I choose
Never to stoop. Oh sir, she smiled, no doubt,
Whene'er I passed her; but who passed without
Much the same smile? This grew; I gave commands;   45
Then all smiles stopped together. There she stands
As if alive. Will't please you rise? We'll meet
The company below, then. I repeat,
The Count your master's known munificence
Is ample warrant that no just pretense   50
Of mine for dowry will be disallowed;
Though his fair daughter's self, as I avowed
At starting, is my object. Nay, we'll go
Together down, sir. Notice Neptune, though,
Taming a sea-horse, thought a rarity,   55
Which Claus of Innsbruck cast in bronze for me!

The Duke is addressing the agent of a Count, whose daughter he wants to marry and make his next Duchess. He is on his best behavior. Nonetheless, we quickly see his domineering ("since none puts by / The curtain I have drawn for you, but I" or "if they durst"); his pride ("My gift of a nine-hundred-years-old name"); his arrogance ("and I choose / Never to stoop"); his greed ("no just pretense / Of mine for dowry"); and, of course, the falseness of his jealousy, for in fact he can say nothing that does not suggest that his last Duchess was innocent as well as young and charming. The agent is not his equal, but the Duke declines precedence—"Nay, we'll go / Together down, sir"—in a gesture that is meant to appear democratic and in fact appears calculated and false. He unintentionally sums up his unpleasant purpose: "his fair daughter's self, as I avowed / At starting, is my object." An *object*. Like the painting, like the little Neptune "cast in bronze for me!" The pun is Browning's, of course, tipping us off, since the Duke means only "my aim, my objective."

Another monologue in which the reader is led to perceive more, or differently, than the speaker is "I heard a Fly buzz" by Emily Dickinson (1830–1886):

> I heard a Fly buzz—when I died—
> The Stillness in the Room
> Was like the Stillness in the Air—
> Between the Heaves of Storm—
>
> The Eyes around—had wrung them dry—   5
> And Breaths were gathering firm
> For that last Onset—when the King
> Be witnessed—in the Room—
>
> I willed my Keepsakes—Signed away
> What portion of me be   10
> Assignable—and then it was
> There interposed a Fly—
>
> With Blue—uncertain stumbling Buzz—
> Between the light—and me—
> And then the Windows failed—and then   15
> I could not see to see—

The first three stanzas present a typical deathbed scene. The room is quiet with the ominous silence that sometimes falls between the "Heaves of Storm," an image that suggests the interrupted agonies of the dying speaker. The dashes and the emphatic capital letters give an impression of breathless portentousness, and there is already a curious abstractness about the speaker's perceptions. The relatives and perhaps friends in the room are mentioned impersonally only as "Eyes around" and "Breaths." They and the speaker alike await the moment of death, "when the King / Be witnessed—in the Room." Whether the "King" is God or simply death, the expectation is a large and dramatic one: "King." But no majestic event occurs: only a fly appears, that unpleasant insect drawn to carrion.

The confusion of the speaker's senses is suggested by her application of visual qualities to a sound: "With Blue—uncertain stumbling Buzz." (This is **synesthesia**: the perception, or description, of one sense modality in terms of another, as when we describe a voice as velvety or sweet.) Impossibly for so small a creature, the fly seems to "interpose" "Between the light—and me." In line 15 the speaker, still trying to account for her loss of sight outside herself, blames the "Windows," reporting oddly that they "failed." The final line records the still flickering consciousness inside the already senseless body before it, too, goes out like the speck of afterlight on a television screen: "I could not see to see—" The final dash suggests the simple tailing off of awareness, without resolution. The grand expectation of "the King" has been ironically foreclosed by the merely physical, naturalistic collapse of sense and consciousness. The dying speaker never understood.

Irony comes in as many flavors as ice cream. **Verbal irony** involves a discrepancy between what is *said* and what is *meant*. To say "Lovely day!" when the weather is awful, for instance. Irony of this sort may range from poking fun to sarcasm. In this poem by Henri Coulette (1927–1988), irony releases bursts of pent-up bitterness:

The Sickness of Friends

Do I give off in the wee,
small hours a phosphorescent
glow, perhaps, like rotting wood?

Am I in the Yellow Pages?
I am sick of the sickness   5
within me that so lures them

to their phones when the night stops
in a dead calm: "H'llo." It's Dick,
who can't bear to be alone;

or Jane, who needs a father;   10
or Spot, who leads a dog's life.
Even the operator

has twin raw scars on her wrists,
but I'm fine, unmarked, floating
in the bath of their self-love.   15

The calls come, we infer, "in the wee, / small hours." Hence, the speaker's sardonic question about glowing "like rotting wood," and thus attracting the calls, as well as about being "in the Yellow Pages." The friends' sickness is not physical; Dick just "can't bear to be alone," Jane "needs a father." With "Spot, who leads a dog's life," the bitterness burns through again. Dick, Jane, and Spot, we recall, are characters in first-grade readers. The operator's scars (from a recent suicide attempt) are only resentful exaggeration, like Spot—*everybody* wants his sympathy—and we understand, translating his irony, that he is *not* fine. The calls are a "bath" of the friends' *self*-love: not what he longs for, expressions of their love for *him*. The "sickness / within me that so lures them" is apparently his yet greater loneliness, which forces him to submit to their demands for attention rather than assert his own need.

Instances of irony may also be distinguished by whether it is deliberate or accidental. As in the last example, the speaker may be quite conscious of it. Or, as in "My Last Duchess" or "I heard a Fly buzz," the speaker may be unconscious of the irony. The term **dramatic irony** is used when the speaker or character acts in a certain way because the character is unaware of something the reader or audience knows. Hamlet does not kill the King when he is at prayer, lest the King, repentant and thus in a state of grace, go straight to heaven. Hamlet does not know what the audience has been shown: that the King, burdened with guilt because he cannot regret his crime, is unable to pray.

When the speaker within the poem is aware of the irony, it can be excruciatingly painful. Notice, in this poem by W. D. Snodgrass (b. 1926), how the speaker's double awareness colors everything. When he says of the kids in lines 1–2 that "they'll stay the night," he is comparing: *we won't.*

Leaving the Motel

Outside, the last kids holler
Near the pool: they'll stay the night.
Pick up the towels; fold your collar
Out of sight.

Check: is the second bed   5
Unrumpled, as agreed?
Landlords have to think ahead
In case of need,

Too. Keep things straight: don't take
The matches, the wrong keyrings—   10
We've nowhere we could keep a keepsake—
Ashtrays, combs, things

That sooner or later others
Would accidentally find.
Check: take nothing of one another's   15
And leave behind

Your license number only,
Which they won't care to trace;
We've paid. Still, should such things get lonely,
Leave in their vase   20

An aspirin to preserve
Our lilacs, the wayside flowers
We've gathered and must leave to serve
A few more hours;

That's all. We can't tell when   25
We'll come back, can't press claims;
We would no doubt have other rooms then,
Or other names.

He isn't speaking to the other lover so much as musing to himself, checking things
to attend to ("is the second bed / Unrumpled, as agreed?")—or perhaps speaking
for both of them, in the single isolation they ironically share: "Our lilacs." The dismal possibilities for keepsakes, "Ashtrays, combs," measure the situation; and even
these, like the motel matches, are off-limits. The flowers will last only "A few more
hours," and the putting an aspirin in their water to preserve them a bit, "should
such things get lonely," is a sad domestic gesture, more sorrowing than hopeful.
These are, we understand, casual lovers, without plans or "claims." The self-
directed irony of the last line is savage. Should they come back, he has said in line
27, "We would no doubt have other rooms then." He adds: "Or other names." The
very abruptness is a whiplash that tells us he doesn't mean merely that they would
sign in under a different false name. They might well be with different lovers.

Life itself is often ironic; things turn out in unexpected ways, or surprise us by the discrepancy between appearance and reality. Such **situational irony** is exemplified in this poem by T. S. Eliot (1888–1965):

Aunt Helen

Miss Helen Slingsby was my maiden aunt,
And lived in a small house near a fashionable square
Cared for by servants to the number of four.
Now when she died there was silence in heaven
And silence at her end of the street.   5
The shutters were drawn and the undertaker wiped his feet—
He was aware that this sort of thing had occurred before.
The dogs were handsomely provided for,
But shortly afterwards the parrot died too.
The Dresden clock continued ticking on the mantel-piece,   10
And the footman sat upon the dining-table
Holding the second housemaid on his knees—
Who had always been so careful while her mistress lived.

Though kin, the speaker remains aloof, and it is clear that the aunt's character was defined by her concern for the proprieties. These now seem merely empty, whether observed (by the undertaker, who "wiped his feet") or flouted (by the footman and second housemaid).

Robert Frost's "Home Burial" (p. 177) is rich in ironies. In the largest sense, it is ironic that husband and wife, despite mutual need, are unable to understand or to reach out to one another. Divided by their natures, she cannot comprehend the practicality with which he expresses his grief in the necessary digging of the grave, and he cannot fathom the guilt out of which comes the unreasonableness of both her grief and her blaming him (and herself). His accidentally ironic comment on the "little graveyard" where their dead child is buried, "Not so much larger than a bedroom, is it?" and something in her fascination with watching him dig—

"I thought, Who is that man? I didn't know you.
And I crept down the stairs and up the stairs
To look again, and still your spade kept lifting . . . "

—lead to the inexplicable sexuality at the heart of their quarrel. We sense this symbolism even in phrases like "Mounting until she cowered under him."

SYMBOLS

A **symbol** is something that stands for or represents something else, like the x in an algebraic equation or the stars and stripes in the flag. In literature a symbol stands for or represents something, usually thematic and intangible, beyond the literal.

Symbols may be fairly minor and local to a particular poem, like the reds and whites of loon and royal family in "First Death in Nova Scotia" or the short-lived flowers in "Leaving the Motel," which symbolize the relationship. Symbols may also be general and open-ended, as the wheelbarrow in "The Red Wheelbarrow" perhaps symbolizes labor, fertility, or even the importance of seeing the world in a certain way. Some things, from frequent use, carry predictable symbolic associations. The rose, for instance, is a traditional symbol for beauty and transience, as in Robert Herrick's "To the Virgins, to Make Much of Time" ("Gather ye rosebuds while ye may . . . ").

The poet will find symbols aplenty in the material at hand—cork-heeled shoes and gold combs in "Sir Patrick Spence" (p. 137), blacksnake and mouse in "Cherrylog Road" (p. 144), and the menace of cats to express the girl's rage in "Kitten." There is usually no need to invent or import symbols, which may ring false. Things already in the scene will do, and will naturally tend to become symbolic. The value of symbols lies in their resonance. Because a meaning is not stated, it can spread out like circles in water; or, like a beam of light, can illuminate anything that lies in its path, at whatever distance, thus applying to any number of situations or actions of a similar kind.

Some poems are deliberately, primarily symbolic, like this one by Robert Frost:

The Road Not Taken

Two roads diverged in a yellow wood,
And sorry I could not travel both
And be one traveler, long I stood
And looked down one as far as I could
To where it bent in the undergrowth;   5

Then took the other, as just as fair,
And having perhaps the better claim,
Because it was grassy and wanted wear;
Though as for that the passing there
Had worn them really about the same,   10

And both that morning equally lay
In leaves no step had trodden black.
Oh, I kept the first for another day!
Yet knowing how way leads on to way,
I doubted if I should ever come back.   15

I shall be telling this with a sigh
Somewhere ages and ages hence:
Two roads diverged in a wood, and I—
I took the one less traveled by,
And that has made all the difference.   20

The difference between two paths in a real wood, we understand, isn't likely to be very important. Certainly it would not have the significance claimed: "And that has made all the difference." Paths in a wood are pretty much alike, and it is usually possible to return another day and find little changed.

So we sense at once that "The Road Not Taken" is primarily symbolic. It is about the nature of choice, and "all the difference" implies that the poem concerns some life-choice. The difference comes, the speaker claims, from his having taken "the one less traveled by." The poem seems a simple and proud affirmation of nonconformity.

But Frost is rarely as simple as he seems. Despite the assertion "I took the one less traveled by," the two roads (as lines 6–12 make clear) were virtually indistinguishable: "just as fair," "perhaps the better claim," "really about the same," "equally lay / In leaves no step had trodden black." It certainly wasn't a case of choosing between good and bad: "sorry I could not travel both." A reader may also wonder, since "way leads on to way" in life, how the speaker can know what lay down that other road, or know what difference (if any) his choice made. Why doesn't he, speaking in the present, not just assert the claim of the last two lines, rather than *predicting* that he will do so at a distant future time, "ages and ages hence"? Why that "sigh"? Above all, if the point is the pleasure and advantage of the road taken, why is the poem called "The Road *Not* Taken"? The symbolism is more complicated and interesting than a reader might at first perceive.

In such poems symbols arise naturally from literal, presented circumstances. A walk in a wood becomes a paradigm of the psychological process of choice, and perhaps of the way we rationalize experience after the fact. In Elizabeth Barrett Browning's "Grief" (p. 113) the "monumental statue" initially appears as a comparison in a simile. Or the symbol may be simply asserted, as in Wallace Stevens's "Anecdote of the Jar" (p. 79) or, here, in "We Wear the Mask" by Paul Laurence Dunbar (1872–1906). We may infer, *outside* the poem, that it is about the African-American experience, but the symbol, of a suffering group's masking its pain, is universal.

> We wear the mask that grins and lies,
> It hides our cheeks and shades our eyes,
> This debt we pay to human guile;
> With torn and bleeding hearts we smile,
> And mouth with myriad subtleties. 5
> Why should the world be overwise,
> In counting all our tears and sighs?
> Nay, let them only see us, while
> > We wear the mask.
>
> We smile, but, O great Christ, our cries 10
> To thee from tortured souls arise.
> We sing, but oh the clay is vile
> Beneath our feet, and long the mile;
> But let the world dream otherwise,
> > We wear the mask! 15

QUESTIONS AND SUGGESTIONS

1. Consider the dramatic situation in this poem by Nancy Eimers (b. 1954). Who is the speaker? What implications might a reader be aware of? Is there irony?

Training Films, Nevada, 1953

When the pigs squealed away from the noise,
which was everywhere, and the blast,
which was down in the ground and high in the air,
and the heat, which was tearing around
inside them, we were looking down   5
from the helicopter and trying to hold
the camera steady. All along we'd been worried
about the younger kids—that, trying to see,
they'd stick their necks out of the trenches
and get a red-hot eyeful, or get scared and run   10
before it was safe to be out and running.
The sergeant had *ahemed* and written three words
on the blackboard, *noise, heat, blast,*
and said, boys, if you're close enough to be risking
blindness or sterility, you'll be killed anyway   15
by the heat or the flying glass. And I saw
these two kids sneak a look at each other,
not as innocent now. I thought of the little Bikini Islanders
chanting a native version of "You Are My Sunshine"
in the training films. The pig we called Control   20
was safe and sound in his little pit,
but the others were running everywhere,
bumping into each other, making that awful sound
that I think is only terror, pure, unmixed with embarrassment.
We didn't know the sound would follow us   25
long after we'd pulled away into the air.
Later that day, when things were quiet again,
they threw the pigs in the back of a truck.
A few were still moving around and moaning,
so I took the butt of my rifle to one,   30
having been taught not to pity
an animal being slaughtered,
or it will die hard.

2. Try writing a poem using the voice of one of the following:

    a surgical nurse on the late shift

    a turtle turned on its back by kids

    a major league outfielder

a widow

George Eliot on her wedding night in Venice

a boy who is proud of a pocket knife he has stolen

Michael Jackson, Tonya Harding, or Lisa Marie Presley

a weed

What might you need to know or find out, or imagine, in order to make the poem convincing and interesting?

3. Each of these poems presents a woman in her own voice. Consider the differences in character and presentation.

a) *Woman's Work*

JILL FRESHLEY*

From the west window
I can see the men
gathered around the calf,
strung up for the butchering
like the crucified Christ.   5
Their breath hangs, like hickory smoke,
in the air for a moment,
and I'm glad to be in my kitchen,
warm and smelling of bread.
They make the first cut   10
down his white belly
and warm their hands
in the steam belching out
as the snow beneath them flushes
a sudden and angry red.   15

I turn my head away,
recalling the many chilly mornings
I'd fed that calf, stroked its muzzle
and called it by name.
I take the loaves from the oven   20
and set them to cool,
then sit down to my knitting again.
I remember the year on my birthday
when we went up in the airplane
and I thought how from there   25
the plowed fields resembled an afghan,
all golden like harvested corn,
like the brown when it's planted
and the green when it's grown.

b)   *Letter to the Cracker Company*

J. ALLYN ROSSER (b. 1957)

Forgive my clumsy writing, but
I am old. My fingers, and
I used to take pride
but hope you can read this.

I don't eat much, the cat even   5
ran away. You could see
in her eyes when she looked up
when there wasn't enough.

But I still buy them still
three blocks away, not far   10
but when you are old
it is a long way to go

to return crackers
when they are crumbled
when I open the package   15
already all crumbled

and my table is small
so a lot spills on the floor
and now even the cat.
I know it's not your fault   20

sometimes crushed on delivery
trucks or the shelf but my table
is small and I am too old
to take anything back.

c)   *Those Men at Redbones°*

THYLIAS MOSS (b. 1954)

Those men at Redbones who call me Mama don't
want milk.

They are lucky. A drop of mine
is like a bullet. You can tell
when a boy has been raised on ammunition,   5
his head sprouts wire. All
those barbed afros.

Those men at Redbones who call me Mama want
to repossess.

One after the other they try   10
to go back where they came from.
Only the snake
has not outgrown the garden.

°*Redbones*: a bar and poolroom

4. "I can't put toothbrushes in a poem, I really can't" (Sylvia Plath). Give it a try.

5. Write a poem about either your father or your mother, using an anecdote (real or imagined) that occurred before you were born. Maybe an old photograph will help.

6. Read a biography of a celebrity or historical figure who interests you, looking for an incident that might make a poem. Even if you don't write the poem, plan how you might handle it.

7. Write a poem about a person whom you disapprove of or dislike. Imagine an incident that will reveal his or her character.

POEMS TO CONSIDER

 Home Burial   *1914*

ROBERT FROST (1874–1963)

He saw her from the bottom of the stairs
Before she saw him. She was starting down,
Looking back over her shoulder at some fear.
She took a doubtful step and then undid it
To raise herself and look again. He spoke   5
Advancing toward her: 'What is it you see
From up there always—for I want to know.'
She turned and sank upon her skirts at that,
And her face changed from terrified to dull.
He said to gain time: 'What is it you see,'   10
Mounting until she cowered under him.
'I will find out now—you must tell me, dear.'
She, in her place, refused him any help
With the least stiffening of her neck and silence.
She let him look, sure that he wouldn't see,   15
Blind creature; and awhile he didn't see.
But at last he murmured. 'Oh,' and again, 'Oh.'

'What is it—what?' she said.

                          'Just that I see.'

'You don't,' she challenged. 'Tell me what it is.'

'The wonder is I didn't see at once.   20
I never noticed it from here before.
I must be wonted to it—that's the reason.
The little graveyard where my people are!
So small the window frames the whole of it.

Not so much larger than a bedroom, is it?   25
There are three stones of slate and one of marble,
Broad-shouldered little slabs there in the sunlight
On the sidehill. We haven't to mind *those*.
But I understand: it is not the stones,
But the child's mound—'

         'Don't, don't, don't, don't,' she cried.   30

She withdrew shrinking from beneath his arm
That rested on the bannister, and slid downstairs;
And turned on him with such a daunting look,
He said twice over before he knew himself:
'Can't a man speak of his own child he's lost?'   35

'Not you! Oh, where's my hat? Oh, I don't need it!
I must get out of here. I must get air.
I don't know rightly whether any man can.'

'Amy! Don't go to someone else this time.
Listen to me. I won't come down the stairs.'   40
He sat and fixed his chin between his fists.
'There's something I should like to ask you, dear.'

'You don't know how to ask it.'

         'Help me, then.'

Her fingers moved the latch for all reply.

'My words are nearly always an offense.   45
I don't know how to speak of anything
So as to please you. But I might be taught
I should suppose. I can't say I see how.
A man must partly give up being a man
With women-folk. We could have some arrangement   50
By which I'd bind myself to keep hands off
Anything special you're a-mind to name.
Though I don't like such things 'twixt those that love.
Two that don't love can't live together without them.
But two that do can't live together with them.'   55
She moved the latch a little. 'Don't—don't go.
Don't carry it to someone else this time.
Tell me about it if it's something human.
Let me into your grief. I'm not so much
Unlike other folks as your standing there   60
Apart would make me out. Give me my chance.

I do think, though, you overdo it a little.
What was it brought you up to think it the thing
To take your mother-loss of a first child
So inconsolably—in the face of love.   65
You'd think his memory might be satisfied—'

'There you go sneering now!'

                     'I'm not, I'm not!
You make me angry. I'll come down to you.
God, what a woman! And it's come to this,
A man can't speak of his own child that's dead.'   70

'You can't because you don't know how to speak.
If you had any feelings, you that dug
With your own hand—how could you?—his little grave;
I saw you from that very window there,
Making the gravel leap and leap in air,   75
Leap up, like that, like that, and land so lightly
And roll back down the mound beside the hole.
I thought, Who is that man? I didn't know you.
And I crept down the stairs and up the stairs
To look again, and still your spade kept lifting.   80
Then you came in. I heard your rumbling voice
Out in the kitchen, and I don't know why,
But I went near to see with my own eyes.
You could sit there with the stains on your shoes
Of the fresh earth from your own baby's grave   85
And talk about your everyday concerns.
You had stood the spade up against the wall
Outside there in the entry, for I saw it.'

'I shall laugh the worst laugh I ever laughed.
I'm cursed. God, if I don't believe I'm cursed.'   90

'I can repeat the very words you were saying.
"Three foggy mornings and one rainy day
Will rot the best birch fence a man can build."
Think of it, talk like that at such a time!
What had how long it takes a birch to rot   95
To do with what was in the darkened parlor.
You *couldn't* care! The nearest friends can go
With anyone to death, comes so far short
They might as well not try to go at all.
No, from the time when one is sick to death,   100
One is alone, and he dies more alone.
Friends make pretense of following to the grave,

But before one is in it, their minds are turned
And making the best of their way back to life
And living people, and things they understand.   105
But the world's evil. I won't have grief so
If I can change it. Oh, I won't, I won't!'

'There, you have said it all and you feel better.
You won't go now. You're crying. Close the door.
The heart's gone out of it: why keep it up?   110
Amy! There's someone coming down the road!'

'You—oh, you think the talk is all. I must go—
Somewhere out of this house. How can I make you—'

'If—you—do!' She was opening the door wider.
'Where do you mean to go? First tell me that.   115
I'll follow and bring you back by force. I *will!*—'

Out of Many, One   *1994*

CLAUDIA RANKINE (b. 1963)

Man called Country

Early morning him take
Windward Road to the beach,
drifting down far end

toward the fishermen
bent forward, them backbone   5
set against them flesh,

all of them muscle
gone tight
as the fish-filled net

be dragged from the sea.   10
Them two snapper, just there,
will do, Country say,

as him dimple pierce
him right cheek when him think,
already, though the day   15

barely start, them tired for true.

Back-a-yard

Thirsty, hot, odor
of sweat at him nostrils,
Country harvest greens

from back field, haul   20
flats filled with mud-caked
yams to the river

where water, mirroring
an blue-washed sky,
run brown along him arm.   25

Squinting against
glare, him speak to the heat:
Lord it hot.

And rotting mangoes drain
to roots of trees, them sugar   30
soaking the earth, attracting

flies and him one goat,
while the sun, a red tongue,
smolder in the sky.

From where she stand,   35
she see Country
working the field

as she stir oxtail,
crushing dried herbs
between she palms, rubbing   40

she hands clean
above the pot. Green flakes
spice the bubbling liquid.

All day hot steam rising.
Flesh pull back from the bone.   45
Red coals collapse to ash.

Jubilee Market

Stalls along the road
sell merchandise in from Florida:
dungarees, Palmolive, Root Beer

and Cherry Coke;   50
and from a tape player set down
in a wagon of pineapples

carnival's latest hit:
Agony.
Agony. Agony.   55

How him fret
as him walk beside she
for him hear men say, *She*

a beautiful woman.
Yes Mister. Desire flatten   60
out she floral print back

and hyacinths,
bougainvillea cut
on the bias, sway

in the sweetest breeze.   65
Into the gutter water run
to greater wetness, salt.

Interior

Naked as the day him born,
where mangrove trees
drop branches mid-trunk   70

him ford Black River,
dreaming in words: *Me waan*
fi- me woman. Me waan.

Red Hills Road

Roots protrude
like joints from earth   75
woven with vines

and chicory, and
sweating green leaf
press into leaf

on climbing stems   80
as Country drag him foot
on the path of red earth

leading to them ragged,
water-marked, wood
fence—him go enter   85

the house just now,
but him taking a minute,
for what him want

to say to she,
is him got to go: America.   90
Land fill of opportunity

if you willing
to work. And him,
him wanting to work.

Hellshire Beach

In atmosphere   95
turn blue with dusk
as frondlike

clouds tease
the moon into pieces,
while the sea   100

sucks in debris
at water's edge,
winds embrace them

with firmness
so unyielding   105
she turn and look toward it.

America go kill you,
but I tell you already,
if you feel you must,

go'long, go'long.   110

The Dark

Night John Crows glide
above the roof, them crescent wings
reaching in blackest sky,

as the outside bear up
the latched door. Over him   115
long, slumbering body

she draw a sheet, tuck
him in with prayers, kneel
on the wooden floor.

West Harbour

Blue and white pansies   120
cover the green of she dress
and she, too far to hear,

hear Country foot drop
as a throbbing sound
when him board the ship deck.   125

Him see she on the landing,
snapshot, blue mahoe tree.
Light of late afternoon

slipping through leaves
as him ship cut   130
clean lines in blue water.

At the ship's rear, the sea
heal itself. The sky
streak yellow and orange,

open into swelling dusk.   135

Tuesday Morning, Loading Pigs   *1984*

DAVID LEE (b. 1944)

The worse goddam job of all
sez John pushing a thick slat
in front of the posts
behind the sow in the loading chute
so when she balked and backed up   5
she couldn't turn and get away
I never seen a sow or a hog load easy
some boars will
mebbe it's because they got balls
or something I don't know   10

but I seen them do it
that Brown feller the FFA
he's got this boar he just opens the trailer door
he comes and gets in
course he mebbe knows what   15
he's being loaded up for

it was this Ivie boy back home
the best I ever seen for loading
he wasn't scared of nothing
he'd get right in and shove them up   20
he put sixteen top hogs
in the back of a Studebaker pickup
by hisself I seen it
when he was a boy he opened up
the tank on the tractor   25
smelling gas
made his brains go soft they sed
he failed fifth grade
but it wasn't his fault
he could load up hogs   30

I always had to at home
cause I was the youngest
I sed then it was two things
I wouldn't do when I grown up
warsh no dishes or load up hogs   35
by god they can set in the sink
a month before I'll warsh them
a man's got to have a principle
he can live by is what I say
now you grab her ears and pull   40
I'll push from back here
we'll get that sonofabitch in the truck

The Rural Carrier Discovers That Love   1982
Is Everywhere

T. R. HUMMER (b. 1950)

A registered letter for the Jensens. I walk down their drive
Through the gate of their thick-hedged yard, and by God there they are,
On a blanket in the grass, asleep, buck-naked, honeymooners
Not married a month. I smile, turn to leave,

But can't help looking back. Lord, they're a pretty sight,   5
Both of them, tangled up in each other, easy in their skin—
It's their own front yard, after all, perfectly closed in
By privet hedge and country. Maybe they were here all night.

I want to believe they'd do that, not thinking of me
Or anyone but themselves, alone in the world   10
Of the yard with its clipped grass and fresh-picked fruit trees.
Whatever this letter says can wait. To hell with the mail.
I slip through the gate, silent as I came, and leave them
Alone. There's no one they need to hear from.

   ### *Animals Are Passing from Our Lives*   1968

PHILIP LEVINE (b. 1928)

It's wonderful how I jog
on four honed-down ivory toes
my massive buttocks slipping
like oiled parts with each light step.

I'm to market. I can smell   5
the sour, grooved block, I can smell
the blade that opens the hole
and the pudgy white fingers

that shake out the intestines
like a hankie. In my dreams   10
the snouts drool on the marble,
suffering children, suffering flies,

suffering the consumers
who won't meet their steady eyes
for fear they could see. The boy   15
who drives me along believes

that any moment I'll fall
on my side and drum my toes
like a typewriter or squeal
and shit like a new housewife   20

discovering television,
or that I'll turn like a beast
cleverly to hook his teeth
with my teeth. No. Not this pig.

American Classic   *1981*

LOUIS SIMPSON (b. 1923)

It's a classic American scene—
a car stopped off the road
and a man trying to repair it.

The woman who stays in the car
in the classic American scene   5
stares back at the freeway traffic.

They look surprised, and ashamed
to be so helpless . . .
let down in the middle of the road!

To think that their car would do this!   10
They look like mountain people
whose son has gone against the law.

But every night they set out food
and the robber goes skulking back to the trees.
That's how it is with the car . . .   15

it's theirs, they're stuck with it.
Now they know what it's like to sit
and see the world go whizzing by.

In the fume of carbon monoxide and dust
they are not such good Americans   20
as they thought they were.

The feeling of being left out
through no fault of your own, is common.
That's why I say, an American classic.

 In the Mirror   *1995*

TRICIA STUCKEY*

Come here,
he said
reaching an arm out
across the rusty-colored
red vinyl of the long bench seat.   5

Come here,
sit next to me.
Sliding over,
she watched him
watch the road.   10
Come closer,
he said
and the crazy grin spread
across his tanned face.
The teeth of his smile   15
shone in the sunlight
and his hair
sprung from his head
like a mane.
Closer,   20
he said,
and slung an arm
around her shoulder
pulling her to his side.
The dust flew up   25
from the road
and the big red truck
bounced and flung itself
down the old dirt road.
Look here,   30
he said
glancing toward the glare
of the side-view mirror.
She sang along, off key,
not knowing the words,   35
and leaned in closer still.
There,
he said,
in the mirror.
She tilted her head   40
and caught a glimpse
of her face next to his,
slightly sunburned,
eyes bright, teeth shining
from a crazy grin,   45
hair twisted into ropes
by the wind.
Look closely,
he said.
This is the way   50
I will always think of you.

7

METAPHOR

Telling It "Like" It Is

Metaphor is the ever-fresh, magical spring of poetry. Aristotle declared that "the greatest thing by far is to be a master of metaphor. It is the one thing that cannot be learned from others; and it is also a sign of genius, since a good metaphor implies an intuitive perception of the similarity in dissimilars." Inextricably entwined both with the ways in which we think and with the origin and nature of language itself, metaphor seems inexhaustibly complex in theory. Fortunately, just as we needn't know much about human musculature to run, we needn't have a theory of metaphor to use it.

Robert Frost's definition suffices: "*saying one thing in terms of another.*" **Metaphor** means (literally, from the Greek) *transference*: we transfer the qualities of one thing to another, something normally not considered related to the first thing, as in "The sun hangs like a bauble in the trees." Qualities of a bauble transfer to the sun. The center of our solar system, our source of heat, light, food has been dethroned, has become weak, trivial, gaudy, and, perhaps, silly. Notice how much the particular choice of words contributes. An earring is also a bauble, but a sun that is an earring touches a very different emotional register.

Conventionally the subject, the thing that undergoes transference, is the **tenor** (sun); the source of transferred qualities is the **vehicle** (bauble). When the transference is explicit, or stated, it is called **simile**, syntactically announced by *like* or *as* (or *as though, as if, the way that*). Simile shows *similarity* between tenor and vehicle as in "The sun hangs *like* a bauble." The italicized phrases in the following lines are similes.

> The wild tulip, at the end of its tube, blows out its great red bell
> *Like a thin clear bubble of blood*

> Robert Browning

> She dreamed of melons *as a traveller sees*
> *False waves in desert drouth*
>
> Christina Rossetti

> It is *as if I float on a still pond,*
> *drowsing in the bottom of a rowboat,*
> *curled like a leaf into myself.*
>
> Elizabeth Spires

>   their bedroom door halved
> The dresser mirror *like a moon*
> *Held prisoner in the house*
>
> Yusef Komunyakaa

> I eat men *like air.*
>
> Sylvia Plath

Tom Andrews (b. 1961) makes lively use of similes in this poem as he plays with a great Victorian poet's struggle to discover one thing in terms of another. What is Andrews suggesting about the resemblances (or lack of them) between language and film, between artist and audience?

Cinema Vérité: The Death of Alfred, Lord Tennyson

The camera pans a gorgeous snow-filled landscape: rolling hills, large black trees, a frozen river. The snow falls and falls. The camera stops to find Tennyson, in an armchair, in the middle of a snowy field.

Tennyson:
> It's snowing. The snow is like . . . the snow is like crushed aspirin,
> like bits of paper . . . no, it's like gauze bandages, clean teeth, shoelaces,
>   headlights . . . no,
> I'm getting too old for this, it's like a huge T-shirt that's been chewed
>   on by a dog,
> it's like semen, confetti, chalk, sea shells, woodsmoke, ash, soap,
>   trillium, solitude, daydreaming . . . Oh hell,
> you can see for yourself! That's what I hate about film!

He dies.

When the transference is implicit, we use the term **metaphor.** A metaphor so compresses its elements that we *identify* the tenor with the vehicle. "The sun *is a* *bauble* hung in the trees." "The gun *barked*." "The ship *ploughs* the sea." Often we can untangle the compression into a looser form and pinpoint each element. "The gun made a noise like a dog's bark." "The ship cuts the water as sharply as a plough cuts the soil." As you work on your poems, strive for the intensity that metaphoric compression creates, so that "Filled with elation, I quickly left the house" might become "I fandangoed across the doormat."

Through careful handling of metaphor Sylvia Plath (1932–1963) in her "Nick and the Candlestick" shifts a mood of despair to one of hope. The poem opens with a speaker, a young mother, who, alone at night with her infant son, feels overwhelmed by the harshness and uncertainty of her circumstances. Then she notices how a sputtering candle "Gulps and recovers its small altitude, / Its yellows hearten." By implicitly comparing the candle to a person who apparently swallows her fear, stands up straight and takes heart, the speaker seems to find some solace. Associations and connotations abound in the poem. The candle's *"small* altitude" might imply a limited recovery; "recover" has medical overtones, suggesting perhaps clinical depression: next time the candle might sputter and go out.

The tones and overtones of metaphor give it its power. Metaphor eludes exact translation; through its dense evocativeness, it not only compresses and compacts but also expresses the inexpressible—it tells it "like" it is. Metaphors are italicized in the following fragments.

The silver *snarling* trumpets

John Keats

The *dust* of snow

Robert Frost

When the first crocuses
pushed their purple *tongues*
through the *skin* of the earth,
it was the striking of a match.

Cathy Song

Life's *but a walking shadow, a poor player*
That struts and frets his hour upon the stage
And then is heard no more. It is a tale
Told by an idiot, full of sound and fury,
Signifying nothing.

William Shakespeare

The hedge-clipper's bicycle, *a pair of spectacles* at this distance,
Leans against some *reticent* shrubs.

Vickie Karp

Here is a whole poem, by Peter Wild (b. 1940):

Natural Gas

When you push the lever up
the warm gases *leap* through the house.

All night I lie awake
as beside me you lie *buried* in the dark,
listening to the thermostat click on and off,   5

the ghosts of the *fierce creatures*
starting, stopping, puzzled in the pipes
all the way from Texas.

Metaphors and similes are often more generally referred to as *figures of speech*, by some as *figures of thought*, and also as *tropes*. Classical rhetoricians list scores of such tropes which we needn't concern ourselves with here. However, two common figures are worth mentioning in particular; they both involve substitution, **metonymy** and **synecdoche**. In metonymy we *substitute* one thing for something associated with it: "He lives through the bottle." "The school bus drags her from her bed." "The tuxedos sniff at the beggar." In synecdoche we *substitute* a part for the whole or a whole for the part: "Eight hands raised the barn." "I drove my mother's wheels to the beach." "A thousand sails docked in the harbor."

Metaphor often surprises us into seeing things afresh, as if with new eyes. Qualities in the metaphor focus, in the subject, qualities we might not have noticed or noticed so vividly. The English poet Craig Raine (b. 1944) is a master of metaphor. Rain, he says, "scores a bull's-eye every time." A beetle on its back struggles "like an orchestra / with Beethoven." Scissors go "through the material / like a swimmer doing crawl." A city seen from the air is "a radio / with its back ripped off." Of a light bulb: "light ripens / the electric pear." A rose grows "on a shark-infested stem." Metaphor, thus, increases the colorful particularity of a poem. Notice how much more pictorial than the mere word "icicles" are Mark Irwin's images: "Slender *beards of light* / hang from the railing" or "touching the *clear carrot* / cold to his lips" (p. 211).

The distance between the tenor and vehicle, between their connotations, gives metaphor its resonance. In the best metaphors the meeting of tenor and vehicle, like a small chemical reaction, creates a flash of recognition. Tenor and vehicle too closely related (the sun *is a star*) won't flash; metaphors too unrelated (the sun *is a tow truck*) may dazzle with their strangeness only to leave a reader in the dark. A metaphor must do more than flash and dazzle. It establishes a commitment that what follows the metaphor will be somehow connected with it. If the bauble metaphor continued, "The sun hung like a bauble stuck in the trees, its broken rockets / slippery as banana peels of the gods," the reader would begin to suspect the poet was only showing off: Mere dazzle grows wearisome.

When a subject is abstract, such as the emotion in Emily Dickinson's "After great pain, a formal feeling comes" (p. 267), metaphor allows the poet to express in particular terms what would otherwise remain vague and generalized:

This is the Hour of Lead—
Remembered, if outlived,
As Freezing persons, recollect the Snow—
First—Chill—then Stupor—then the letting go—

Metaphor and its attendant vivid imagery can sweep us into a world of such intense emotion that readers scarcely bother to ask how the emotion originated, as in the rollicking invective of this poem by Pamela Alexander (b. 1948):

Look Here

Next time you walk by my place
in your bearcoat and mooseboots,
your hair all sticks and leaves
like an osprey's nest on a piling,
next time you walk across my shadow   5
with those swamp-stumping galoshes
below that grizzly coat and your own whiskers
that look rumpled as if something's
been in them already this morning
mussing and growling and kissing—   10
next time you pole the raft of you downriver
down River Street past my place
you could say *hello*, you canoe-footed fur-faced
musk ox, pockets full of cheese and acorns
and live fish and four-headed winds and sky, *hello*   15
is what human beings say when they meet each other
—if you can't say hello like a human don't
come down this street again and when you do don't
bring that she-bear, and if you do I'll know
even if I'm not on the steps putting my shadow   20
down like a welcome mat, I'll know.

What a ride this poem gives us. Is it "about" a woman who has been rejected by a man for another woman ("a she-bear") and now is delivering a tirade against him, calling him inhuman for his oafishness and boorishness? Such a reading is legitimate but limiting; it doesn't begin to account for all the pleasure the poem gives us, seeing this "you" with hair like an osprey's nest, a stinking "musk ox" with "pockets full of cheese" and "live fish." Such inventiveness seems soothing almost, as if the power of metaphor can redeem the angry speaker. Though she may be incensed by this man, she hasn't lost her sense of humor.

THE METAPHORICAL LINK

Language itself is deeply metaphorical. We speak of the *eye* of a needle, the *spine* of a book, the *head* and *mouth* of a river (which are oddly at opposite ends), a flower *bed*, of *plunging* into a relationship, of *bouncing* a check, or of *going haywire*, without thinking of the buried metaphors—of faces, bodies, sleeping, swimming, or the tangly wire used for bailing hay. Dead metaphors (which include the clichés discussed in Chapters 4 and 9) show a primary way language changes to accommodate new situations. Confronted with something new, for which there is no word, we thriftily adapt an old word as a comparison, and soon the new meaning seems perfectly literal. The part of a car that covers the engine, for instance, is a *hood*. On early cars, it was in fact rounded and looked very like a hood; but the word survives, although now hoods are flat and look nothing like hoods. (They still cover the engines' *heads*.) Sometimes the perfectly literal becomes metaphorical. Actual trunks were strapped to the back of early automobiles, and the word survives, although now the trunks are built-in and we may forget their likeness to trunks in an attic. Such metaphors continue to be useful even after their sense has evaporated. We say someone is "mad as a hatter" although there aren't many hatters around and although the chemical which, in fact, often made them crazy is no longer used.

Without us, the world is wordless. Adam's naming the animals of Eden is an archetype of one of humanity's greatest concerns: naming things so we can talk about them. We're not finished with our naming—and never will be. We still have no common words for many things, relationships, feelings, activities: a single filament of a spider's web, unmarried couples living together, the strange green light of a tornado, or the many appearances of the sea's surface. Reportedly, Eskimos have more than twenty words for snow; yet we make do with barely two or three. Translators often find no precise equivalent for the ways different languages notice and name the parts of the world.

Feelings are especially inarticulate and require metaphor to be understood; through metaphor Dickinson expresses the feeling of deadness that follows "great pain." We get frustrated with the general words for emotions—*love, hate, envy, awe, respect, rage*—because they don't express our particular feeling, and it is precisely their particularity that makes emotions important to us. In our desire to say what we feel, we turn to metaphor, borrowing the vocabulary of other things—in Dickinson's case ceremonious tombs and freezing to death—to say what there are no exact words for. The classical Roman orator Quintillian praised metaphor for performing the supremely difficult task of "providing a name for everything." The more complex the issue, the more we need something else to explain it, as the double helix helps us understand DNA and the mobius strip relativity.

Within their context words fall somewhere on a scale between the purely literal and the purely figurative. If you say, "I cross the street up here," you are speaking on the literal level. If you say, "She carries a heavy cross," you are speaking on the figurative level where the vehicle becomes a symbol and has little relationship to the literal—a listener doesn't actually see someone hoisting a large wooden object. Poems that are wholly literal or wholly symbolic are usually tedious. Even in highly symbolic poems like Frost's "The Road Not Taken" (p. 172) and Glück's "The Gold Lily" (p. 165) the images let us see in the first case a leafy path in fall and in the second a gold lily unfurling toward the light.

Metaphors work in an amazing variety of ways (no catalog could be complete) and do an amazing variety of jobs, sometimes so complexly that no analysis can explain them. They may illustrate or explain (the heart is like a pump); emphasize; heighten; communicate information or ideas; or carry a tone, feeling, or attitude. They may even work—Hart Crane's phrase is the "logic of metaphor"—as a mode of discourse, a sort of language of associations, as they do in "Sir, Say No More" by Trumbull Stickney (1874–1904):

> Sir, say no more,
> Within me 'tis as if
> The green and climbing eyesight of a cat
> Crawled near my mind's poor birds.

The eerie sensation communicates perfectly, though a critic might work all day to untangle the threads the image knots up so simply.

Though a metaphorical leap may seem inexplicable and arbitrary, the metaphor may communicate clearly, as in "Loan" by Warren Nelson:

> Moon, I am clumsy in these boots.
> Loan me a small bird's feet.

Why the speaker addresses the moon (perhaps the poem's real subject is love?) or why he elects to ask for "a small bird's feet" we do not know. But in the image itself (this is the whole poem) we hear a plaintive human desire that we understand.

So accustomed are we to metaphor that we rarely appreciate how fully it serves. In Shakespeare's sonnet "That time of year thou mayst in me behold" (p. 10), for instance, metaphors provide almost the whole effect of the poem, translating emotions into vivid and dramatic particulars about winter trees, choirlofts, twilight, and embers. The metaphors virtually stand for or present the emotion. Like literal particulars, metaphors enrich the texture and color of a poem, as well as evoke a poem's complex of emotion.

For practical purposes distinguishing between simile and metaphor is far less important than recognizing their similarities. Because they are explicit, similes may seem simpler, closer to the straightforward, logical uses of language. But the evocative quality of any metaphor or simile depends on context. The oddly popular notion that metaphor is stronger than simile, more forceful or evocative, is not really true.

Look again at Browning's lines:

> The wild tulip, at the end of its tube, blows out its great red bell
> Like a thin clear bubble of blood

Unquestionably, the simile "Like a thin clear bubble of blood" is more startling, more evocative, than either of the metaphors, "tube" for the stem and "great red bell" for the flower. It clearly carries the main, somewhat unpleasant tone of the passage (the speaker is comparing the city and the country to the disadvantage of the latter). The vaguely clinical "tube" (and "bell," which has laboratory overtones) beautifully set up the grimly lovely "Like a thin clear bubble of blood."

Consider this poem by Hart Crane (1899–1932).

My Grandmother's Love Letters

There are no stars tonight
But those of memory.
Yet how much room for memory there is
In the loose girdle° of soft rain.

There is even room enough   5
For the letters of my mother's mother,
Elizabeth,
That have been pressed so long
Into a corner of the roof
That they are brown and soft,   10
And liable to melt as snow.

Over the greatness of such space
Steps must be gentle.
It is all hung by an invisible white hair.
It trembles as birch limbs webbing the air.   15

And I ask myself:

"Are your fingers long enough to play
Old keys that are but echoes:
Is the silence strong enough
To carry back the music to its source   20
And back to you again
As though to her?"

Yet I would lead my grandmother by the hand
Through much of what she would not understand;
And so I stumble. And the rain continues on the roof   25
With such a sound of gently pitying laughter.

4 *girdle:* a sash or belt

On a rainy night in an attic the speaker has come upon his grandmother's love letters. In how many ways—through similes, metaphors, images, connotations—
Crane echoes what is tenuous, delicate, and precarious. The speaker's tone, his
doubt about how he can cross the distance between his grandmother's intimate life
and his own life, registers this delicacy.

The opening stanza creates a parallel between the stars that exist only in memory (for it is a rainy night) and the grandmother who lives on in the speaker's
memory and in the love letters. Stars, of course, even on a clear night are themselves echoes, light that has traveled billions of light-years from its source; we
never know the actual star, only what has reached us across great time and space.

Stanza 2 focuses the more general ruminations about memory to the care that entering the past requires. The closing phrase "liable to melt as snow," (line 11) makes the letters so frail that even touching them (body heat quickly melts snow) could destroy them, much less opening them up and reading them. "Frail," "delicate," "flimsy," "friable"—none of these adjectives satisfies as the simile does. Notice how much we lose if the line were to rely on the metaphor alone: "and liable to melt."

Picking up on the "room for memory" in the "loose girdle of soft rain" (rain also melts snow) of stanza 1 and linking it with the fragile letters of stanza 2, stanza 3 leads to the realization that "Over the greatness of such space / Steps must be gentle." These "steps" offer multiple resonances: they suggest the *stairs* to the attic; the speaker's foot*steps* in the quiet echoing space on top of the house, preparing for his *stumbling* in the last stanza; the *stages* in the process of remembering; and the tones and semitones—the steps—of the piano *keys* of stanza 5 (which, in turn, suggest *keys* that lock and unlock private spaces). The letters, themselves, serve as *keys* to the grandmother's intimate life.

Piano keys are also white, and images of whiteness underlie the poem, tying together its multiple strains. Starlight, of course, is white, and the comparison of the soft brown letters to snow evokes their original state as well—the *white* papers the grandmother once held in her hands. The "invisible white hair" that "trembles as birch limbs webbing the air" (lines 14–15) associates the delicacy of memory and the letters with the attic's fragile cobwebs, with birch branches (perhaps glimpsed outside the window), with the quiet sounds in the attic, with the piano's remembered sounds (an "air" is also a tune), and with the color of the grandmother's hair—invisible now, except in memory. Through metaphor Crane connects strength and delicacy, time and space, light and sound, distance and intimacy in a poem that itself subtly explores the nature of interconnections.

Metaphor says more in an instant than pages of explication can delineate. Instantly, intuitively, the reader apprehends the pertinent elements and ignores the irrelevant. Our analysis of "My Grandmother's Love Letters" follows where intuition leads and enumerates the relevant qualities that Crane's metaphors suggest. But for any poem the sum of the parts, however illuminating, rarely equals the effect of the metaphors as a whole.

In Sylvia Plath's famous simile "I eat men like air," we understand at once what the speaker, "Lady Lazarus," is claiming, but what goes into our understanding? Eating something suggests we have power over it, and perhaps that we have killed it (or will when we eat it). Eating something "like air" further reduces it, making it inconsequential, common, negligible. Air, as Plath uses it, takes on a different tone than "air" as Dickinson uses it in this stanza of "After great pain" (p. 267).

> The Feet, mechanical, go round—
> Of Ground, or Air, or Ought—
> A Wooden way
> Regardless grown,
> A Quartz contentment, like a stone—

The speaker's indecisiveness or indifference in settling on one metaphor—"Ground, or Air, or Ought— / A Wooden way"—dramatizes how "Regardless" intense pain makes its victim. Plath's speaker exudes boundless energy; Dickinson's is down for the count; her feet are earth or air or wood or obligation or nothing ("ought" is a variation of "aught")—she doesn't seem to know or care. Crane's phrase "webbing the air" can allude to music since he has woven musical metaphors into the poem's texture. In each occurrence of "air" we screen out qualities that might undermine the metaphor. We don't consider how eating air might make Lady Lazarus hiccup, or that Dickinson's "Mechanical feet" might be musical (except as a dirge!), or that air—the space of the attic air—is unimportant or negligible.

In a poem called "Exeunt," Richard Wilbur mentions a cricket that "like a dwindled hearse / Crawls from the dry grass." Cricket and "dwindled hearse" are both long, dark or black, and shiny. The insect's slow movement ("Crawls") and the solemn speed of a hearse (which might be described as moving at a crawl) correspond. The adjective "dwindled" makes sure that we see the hearse at such a distance or in such reduction that the cricket isn't overshadowed by its mass. Miniaturization suggests fragility. The hearse's associations with death appropriately color the late-summer slow pace of the cricket, whose normal sprightliness and agility are past, and imply its impending death with the coming of cold weather. Differences are muted (size, by "dwindled") or ignored (legs or wheels, for example). Compared to the hearse, the cricket symbolizes and suggestively pictures the "death" of the summer.

As Crane's poem indicates, the tone or suggestiveness of metaphors, though essential to a poem's power, often act subliminally, creating a hidden network that holds a poem together. We see such threads in this poem by Dave Smith (b. 1942):

Parkersburg, W. Va.

Along the river tin roofs
the color of blood
release little rivulets
of greasy smoke,

longjohns hang in the wind   5
like loose-jointed ghosts.
I can see the current
herringbone

against the blue slate rocks.
I am told my grandfather   10
used to come here.
I toss someone's whiskey bottle

to see it spread out like stars.
No one notices this.
I wonder if anyone remembers   15
the day he fell.

The images—"tin roofs / the color of *blood*," "*rivulets* of smoke," longjohns "*like loose-jointed ghosts*," "I see the current / *herringbone*," the breaking bottle that spreads out "*like stars*"—all function separately in meaning, but subliminal connections link them. That the scene literally includes the river makes the "rivulets" of smoke appropriate. The sense of linear connection of river and rivulets with the color of the also liquid "blood" points subtly toward the speaker's felt interest in his grandfather—who used to come to Parkersburg, where the speaker now finds himself. The grandfather's belonging to an earlier time somehow faintly links him to the present old-fashioned longjohns on the laundry lines; and of course he is the particular "ghost" that haunts the speaker's awareness as he now views the place. The cloth of longjohns and the "herringbone" pattern of the river's current seem related. And the *falling* whiskey bottle seems mysteriously to connect with the time the grandfather "fell" (line 16). The word "fell" itself may be either literal or metaphorical: perhaps literal in the sense of "fell down" (part of some undisclosed anecdote?), perhaps metaphorical in the sense of "fell in death." Thematic importance makes the latter seem likelier, given the poem's elegaic mood; and if so, the grandfather's dissolution in death and into eternity is picked up by, gives the emotional significance to, the bottle crashing "like stars." We may not be wrong if we go as far as to think of the grandfather as a man who wore longjohns and drank a drop in his day. These links or resonances among the metaphors give the poem its haunting unity. The speaker's feeling is equally unprovable, unresolved; the poem ends with questioning: "I wonder if anyone remembers . . . "

PATTERN AND MOTIF

Often metaphors function locally; that is, they have no particular connection to other metaphors or other parts of the poem, as in X. J. Kennedy's "In a Prominent Bar in Secaucus One Day,"

> In the kerchief of linen I caught to my nose
> Ah, there never fell snot, but *a little gold rose*.

Or, later,

> Now I'm *saddled* each night for my butter and eggs
> And *the broken threads race* down the backs of my legs.

"Gold rose," "saddled," and "broken threads" are essentially separate images. Metaphors often, however, work in patterns or interactions, as with Browning's "tube" and "thin clear bubble of blood" or Hart Crane's snow, cobwebs, white hair, and birch branches. In Kennedy's poem, for example, the snot/"little gold rose" image does form a secondary pattern with other flower/plant images:

> Let you hold in mind, girls, that your beauty must pass
> *Like a lovely white clover that rusts with its grass*

and

> And be left by the roadside, for all your good deeds,
> *Two toadstools* for tits and a face *full of weeds*.

The sequence—gold rose, rusting clover, toadstools, weeds—parallels the poem's theme of decline and decay, providing a **motif:** a pattern of recurrent, unifying images or phrases. Similarly, the various racing references (a vocabulary the speaker relishes) compose a motif or subtext that tells us about her experiences and character.

Such unifying links, patterns, or motifs between and among the metaphors in a poem must, in part, be conscious effects on the poet's part. But it is probably a matter more of recognizing and developing possibilities than of cold-bloodedly inventing or imposing them. Often the poet need only perceive the potential pattern in the material, and as the poem develops, explore its possibilities. In this way metaphor can help a poet think. In her poem "Sex Without Love," (p. 251) Sharon Olds imbues those who "make love / without love" with qualities of athletes and priests, helping her explore answers to the question, "How do they do it?"

In this poem by Alicia Ostriker (b. 1937) two main metaphors guide the development of the ideas.

Dissolve in Slow Motion

When you watch a marriage	
Dissolve, in slow motion,	
Like a film, there is a point	
Early on when the astute	
Observer understands nothing	5
Can prevent the undesired	
End, not shrinks, or friends,	
Or how-to-love books,	
Or the decency or the will	
Of the two protagonists	10
Who struggle gamely like lab	
Mice dropped in a jar	
Of something viscous: the	
Observer would rather snap	
The marriage like a twig,	15
Speed the suffering up, but	
The rules of the lab forbid.	
Other rules govern decay	
From within; so she just watches.	
The little paws claw	20
Then cease, the furred	

Bubbles of lungs stop.
The creatures get rigid.
Has something been measured?
It all gets thrown away.   25

The first key metaphor, given in the title and elaborated by the simile "Like a film" in lines 1–3, puts to work the language of film to examine how a marriage comes apart. The comparison is double: the marriage breaks up, dissolving, vanishing as in the slow fading out of a film image (a "dissolve") *and* does so with the abnormal slowness of action projected at a slower-than-real speed ("in slow motion"). The metaphors, more abstract than visual, operate primarily as idea, implying both the painful slowness and the inevitability ("nothing / Can prevent") of the marital breakup.

The second main metaphor enters as a simile in lines 11–13: "like lab / Mice dropped in a jar / Of something viscous." The sense of inevitability and slowness continues in the details of the "viscous" substance and the mice's helplessness: beyond their control they are "dropped." The ideas have now developed into a sharp picture. (The main metaphors may be linked in the secondary sense of "dissolve" as a chemical process.)

A third image appears in lines 14–15, the contrasting preference that the marriage might "rather snap / . . . like a twig"; but the second main image resumes in lines 15–16: "but / The rules of the lab forbid." Lines 17–18 are essentially parenthetical; as the lab metaphor portrays the suffering as imposed entirely from without, these lines establish the corollary of internal breakup and fault—the "decay / From within"—that is necessary to the accuracy of the theme. But the second main metaphor, after the emphasis of the stanza-break, continues and brings the feeling to its climax in the vivid picture of the mice's death. A fourth metaphor— "the furred / *Bubbles* of lungs"—carries laboratory or chemical overtones, but primarily emphasizes the frailty of the mice's (and the marriage's) hold on life. (The omission of the comma we might expect after "The little paws claw" also suggests the simplicity with which the end comes and resistance stops.) The poem's final lines complete the second main metaphor, implying that though some truth may be reached (was "measured"), the loss is ironically total nonetheless. Throughout the poem Ostriker's use of passive voice and technical language—first of film, then of the laboratory—creates a cool tone which makes the breakup all the more poignant.

When metaphors dominate or organize a passage or even a whole poem, we call them **extended metaphors** or **conceits.** Secondary metaphors spring from the first, controlling metaphor, as do metaphors of the humble and commonplace in Christopher Buckley's "Sparrows" (p. 210) or the whole scene of a harbor at dawn in Robert Bly's "Waking from Sleep" (p. 209). In this poem by Mary Oliver (b. 1935) the extended metaphor controlling the whole poem identifies music with a brother "Who has arrived from a long journey," whose reassuring presence makes the flux and danger of the world—"the maelstrom / Lashing"—seem, for the moment, tamed.

Music at Night

Especially at night
It is the best kind of company—

A brother whose dark happiness fills the room,
Who has arrived from a long journey,

Who stands with his back to the windows   5
Beyond which the branches full of leaves

Are not trees only, but the maelstrom
Lashing, attentive and held in thrall

By the brawn in the rippling octaves,
And the teeth in the smile of the strings.   10

So compelling is the fantasy of the metaphor that it is impossible to say whether the trees outside the windows are part of the metaphorical description of the brother or part of the literal scene. The real and the imagined weave into one picture.

John Donne, in "A Valediction: Forbidding Mourning" (p. 215), presents the calm parting of true lovers (one of whom is going on a journey) in terms of metaphors from religion, geology, astronomy, and metallurgy. He compares their parting to the peaceful deaths of virtuous men, to the unharmful movements of the heavens ("trepidation of the spheres") in contrast to earthquakes, and to the fineness of gold leaf which, though hammered to "airy thinness," never breaks. The poem's final image is yet more startling: the lovers are likened to a pair of drawing compasses! The whole world seems ransacked and brought to bear, to center, on these lovers, whose parting comes to seem as momentous as the metaphors that express it.

Emily Dickinson's poem "A Route of Evanescence" similarly delights us when we realize what it is about and how evocative its comparisons are. In the first four lines we see something moving rapidly—a wheel, colors (cochineal is a brilliant red dye)—but it is so fast ("Rush") that we cannot identify it.

A Route of Evanescence
With a revolving Wheel—
A Resonance of Emerald—
A Rush of Cochineal—
And every Blossom on the Bush   5
Adjusts its tumbled Head—
The mail from Tunis°, probably,
An easy Morning's Ride—

7 *Tunis:* North African city

The mystery clears in lines 5–6 when we gather that, whatever it is, it has to do with disturbing the flowers on a bush—a hummingbird! The mere glimpse of its colors and fan-shape in lines 1–4 evokes the bird's quick and jerky flight ("Resonance,"

"Rush"). The personification of the blossoms as "tumbled heads" prepares for the metaphorical guess in lines 7–8: "The mail from Tunis, probably." The exaggeration, "An easy Morning's Ride," offhandedly insists on the hummingbird's speed in flight and celebrates the exotic quality of an ordinary back yard that enjoys such colors as emerald and cochineal. If we remember that many of our bird neighbors winter in Florida or South America (if not North Africa), the metaphor hardly seems far-fetched. If we also remember that the hummingbird picks up and delivers pollen from flower to flower—that population of "tumbled Head[s]"—the comparison with the "mail" seems less than outrageous. Even the pun mail/male may not be irrelevant, so we may guess why the news so "tumble[s] Head[s]"! The poem's dazzling metaphors lead not only to a vivid action picture of the hummingbird but also to a fresh experience of how strange and colorful the merely everyday truly is.

MIXED METAPHOR

Metaphors may go wrong in several ways; when this happens, they are usually called **mixed metaphors.** The trouble sometimes comes from not shielding the comparison from qualities that are irrelevant or unintentionally off-key. "Your eyes are lakes, along whose edge a velvet green of scum sparkles with insects like a jeweler's tray," for instance, is a blunder. Too many things are happening at once; and though the jeweler's tray is a lively image, the reader is all too likely to be misdirected into responding to the scum around the eyes. Or the trouble comes when elements of a metaphor are not congruent with one another, as in "The feather of smoke above the cabin slowly flapped its wings and disappeared across the winter sky." A feather doesn't have wings, and we can't imagine the flapping of what does not exist. Eliminating the individual feather and making the first part of the image less distinct, however, might make it work: "The feathery smoke above the cabin slowly flapped and disappeared across the winter sky."

   In "It Dropped so low—in my Regard" Emily Dickinson insists on having a metaphor two ways and very nearly spoils a poem:

> It dropped so low—in my Regard—
> I heard it hit the Ground—
> And go to pieces on the Stones
> At bottom of my Mind—
>
> Yet blamed the Fate that flung it—*less*   5
> Than I denounced Myself,
> For entertaining Plated Wares
> Upon my Silver Shelf—

"It" is apparently some idea, illusion, or bit of wishful thinking, which turns out to be false. Stanza 1 identifies it with something fragile, breakable, like china: "And go to pieces on the Stones." But stanza 2 identifies it with merely "Plated Wares": silver plate rather than sterling silver. Such metal can't fall and break, "go to pieces"; rather, it bends or dents. The poem's metaphors divide it against itself.

Metaphor ranges from the sharp and colorful, through a variety of less distinct impressions, to essentially nonimages—muted echoes and vague, shadowy partial shots, soft superimposition, or momentary flashes to a different scene. Consider Shakespeare's Sonnet 30:

> When to the sessions of sweet silent thought
> I summon up remembrance of things past,
> I sigh the lack of many a thing I sought,
> And with old woes new wail my dear time's waste:
> Then can I drown an eye, unused to flow,   5
> For precious friends hid in death's dateless night,
> And weep afresh love's long since cancelled woe,
> And moan the expense of many a vanished sight:
> Then can I grieve at grievances foregone,
> And heavily from woe to woe tell o'er   10
> The sad account of fore-bemoaned moan,
> Which I new pay as if not paid before.
>   But if the while I think on thee, dear friend,
>   All losses are restored and sorrows end.

Through connotation the main pattern of images presents a series of legal and quasi-legal terms: "sessions," "summon," "dateless," "cancelled," "expense," "grievances," "account," "pay," "losses," and "restored," which together suggest a court proceeding over some financial matter. The implicit metaphors make for a complex tone: a certain judicial solemnity, an irrecoverable loss, some technical injustice, which the miraculous appearance of the "dear friend" overturns. This shadowy story exists more as a quality of the sonnet's diction than as metaphor, and yet accrues through a number of passing comparisons. We see no courtroom and, so delicately is it written, are hardly aware of the source of the metaphors.

METAPHORICAL IMPLICATION

Even simple metaphors may work with an almost inexhaustible subtlety and often do much more than either poet or reader may be aware. Consider two poems, two girls (a "lass" and a "maid"), and two pairs of metaphors in "A Red, Red Rose" by Robert Burns (1759–1796) and "She Dwelt Among the Untrodden Ways" by William Wordsworth. First, the Burns:

> O, my luve's like a red, red rose
> That's newly sprung in June.
> O, my luve's like the melodie
> That's sweetly played in tune.
>
> As fair art thou, my bonnie lass,   5
> So deep in luve am I;
> And I will luve thee still, my dear,
> Till a'° the seas gang° dry.

8 *a'*: all; *gang*: go

Till a' the seas gang dry, my dear,
And the rocks melt wi' the sun;   10
And I will luve thee still, my dear,
While the sands o' life shall run.

And fare thee weel, my only luve,
And fare thee weel a while!
And I will come again, my luve,   15
Though it were ten thousand mile!

Focus on the two metaphors in the first stanza. Read the four lines over and over until you can say them with your eyes shut. Relax. Let the associations be visual. Experience them instead of thinking about them.

The metaphors—rose, melody—tell us more about the speaker's affection for the girl and more about the girl herself than we realize. How might the speaker see the girl he loves as a "newly sprung" red rose? Qualities we associate with roses that he might be transferring to the girl could include beautiful, fresh, natural, and might go on to fragrant, happy (we find roses at joyful occasions), healthy, lively, and maybe passionate since the emphatic "red, red" suggests strong feeling.

The metaphor of the "melodie" in lines 3–4 might reenforce some of these and incline us to add having a musical voice or being in harmony with herself and her environment. Let's ask some questions about her, however, which may at first seem silly. Don't try to answer them by thinking, but just see what answer comes to you. If one doesn't, don't worry about it. Go from question to question slowly and don't bear down on any of them. Look for what you see just beyond the edge of your field of vision, for what you know just beyond the edge of your knowledge.

Is the girl a city girl or a country girl?

Is she an indoor girl or an outdoor girl?

Is she an introvert or an extrovert? quiet or fun-loving? shy or fond of company?

What is her complexion? the color of her hair? Is she slight or robust?

Does she like dancing?

Where is the melody played? indoors or outdoors? by whom? with what instruments?

Every reader's responses will differ a little because we are going beyond what is really demonstrable to the deep resonances of the images. Most readers, though, will agree on many of the responses. Hard to define though it may be, we arrive at something like a consensus. Having visualized the rose outdoors, we may well imagine the melody as played outdoors. The word "melodie" itself suggests a simple tune, hardly chamber music. That the melody is "played in tune" (no accomplishment for professionals) suggests amateur musicians. The vitality of "newly sprung in June" suggests natural growth and may shield out the impression

of a very formal garden. "Sweetly" and "newly sprung" imply youth and innocence, and they somewhat temper the passion that "red, red rose" may imply, so
we register an impression of the girl's sexuality but do not make much of it. The
pun in "sprung" suggests perhaps physicality, vigor, and liveliness. "Red, red" may
evoke a bright complexion; she is used to the outdoors, sunshine, and exercise.
The music implies other people, a gathering, doubtless a happy one; and one at
which the girl, like the melody, is not far from the center of attention. We may
end up with the impression, then, that she is gregarious, active, popular, at ease
with company and in the outdoors. Since Burns was a rural Scot poet (known, by
the way, for his many romantic entanglements) our reading fits with what we
know about him.

Music outdoors, amateur musicians, a fiddle perhaps. Roses. A sociable occasion. A lively, beautiful girl, a "bonnie lass," fond of company. A *country dance?*

Such are the resonances of Burns's metaphors. The "rightness" he probably felt
when he wrote these lines (like the "rightness" we feel when we read them) almost
certainly derives from a quick, intuitive apprehension of just such accumulating
associations and nearly undetectable nuances.

Turn now to Wordsworth's poem: another country girl, another pair of images.

> She dwelt among the untrodden ways
>   Beside the springs of Dove,
> A maid whom there were none to praise
>   And very few to love:
>
> A violet by a mossy stone   5
>   Half hidden from the eye!
> —Fair as a star, when only one
>   Is shining in the sky.
>
> She lived unknown, and few could know
>   When Lucy ceased to be;   10
> But she is in her grave, and, oh,
>   The difference to me!

Wordsworth tells us, apart from the two metaphors in stanza 2, a good deal more
about Lucy than Burns tells about his lass. But the resonance of the metaphors is no
less fascinating. Lucy's beauty is of a very different kind. In contrast to a rose, the violet offers other qualities: pale, delicate, quiet, shy, very young, fragile, and, in context,
sickly. The moss implies shade, trees, moisture, perhaps a moist spot not far from a
stream. We don't see these things, of course, but have a sense of them outside the
frame of the picture. The camera moves in for a close-up shot, for we see the violet
clearly. The moss also implies that the stone is imbedded, not movable. The stone's
mass and hardness emphasize, by contrast, the violet's smallness and fragility. Its
immobility and mossy age emphasize the violet's sensitivity; its permanence, the violet's youth and transience. The stone is very like (and it would not be irrelevant if we
are reminded of) a gravestone. ("Her grave" is in fact mentioned in stanza 3.) The
stone also, doubtless, symbolizes the harsh, isolating, and indifferent circumstances of

her life. The syntax is ambiguous; we can't conclude whether the violet hides itself or the stone hides it. If she is shy and withdrawn, it is perhaps not altogether by choice.

Another ambiguity links the images of violet and star. Is the violet "Fair as a star"? or is it Lucy, directly, who is "Fair as a star"? It matters little since the comparison necessarily involves all three, but the ambiguity has the effect of relating violet and star more directly than the images in Burns's first stanza are related. The star is presumably the evening star, at twilight, when it is for a brief time the "only one" before the gathering dark lets other stars be seen. The soft, dusk color of the sky may be pale and violet. And both violet and star are shapes radiating from a center. The fragility of the evening's first star, as it first becomes visible, parallels the delicacy and half-hiddenness of the violet. The transition from violet to star is flawless.

The star adds other qualities to the emotional portrayal of Lucy in these metaphors. Bright, sharp, fine, its beauty is permanent and enduring, though it will soon be "lost" among the many bright stars of the night sky. It is also, as the violet was not, publicly visible. The transition from violet to star, from close-up to long shot, is itself an image of Lucy's death, her disappearance from earth and reappearance in heaven. So, the poem implies, Lucy's unknown beauty in life was transformed in death to a kind of perfection and permanence. The two couplets seem irreversible, as are Burns's couplets. (Try it.)

Here, at its subtlest, the natural object becomes symbolic. Things become meanings. Naming creates a world. As John Crowe Ransom noted: "The image cannot be dispossessed of a primordial freshness, which idea can never claim. An idea is derivative and tamed. The image is in the natural or wild state, and it has to be discovered there, not put there, obeying its own law and none of ours."

QUESTIONS AND SUGGESTIONS

1. Make up as many metaphors or similes as you can for a common object (street light, fire plug, telephone pole, dandelion leaves, floor lamp, shoe, cat's eyes, end of a leaf's stem where it connects to its twig, stars, or others). Use the best one in a poem.

2. A metaphor or simile has been omitted from these passages. What comparisons would you choose? (The originals are in Appendix II, p. 387.)

    a) Raspberries _____, redly in their leaves   [verb]

    b) [of a country funeral procession going up a hill road]

        Four cars like _____
        behind the hearse, old Chevies and a Ford,
        they fluttered up where the land rose out of view

    c) A black fly flew slowly up,
        droning, _____-ing the halves of the air

d) In a week or two, forsythia
   will shower its peaceful _____
   all over the towns.

e) The clarinet, a dark tube
   _____ in silver

f) Big as _____,
   two white launches between water and sky
   march down the bay.

g) The green creek whirled by a boat's wash
   into _____

h) Dreams are the soul's _____

3. Study the qualities that link tenor and vehicle in this famous poem by Ezra Pound. Then relax and try to respond to the metaphorical implications. Can you decide whether it is day or night outside the subway station? Clear or rainy? What is the season? What are the people in the station wearing?

In a Station of the Metro

The apparition of these faces in the crowd;
Petals on a wet, black bough.

4. In this poem by Rita Dove (b. 1952), notice the similes and metaphors. How are they suitable for the presumably historical speaker? In what ways do they shade the poem's literal details?

The House Slave

The first horn lifts its arm over the dew-lit grass
and in the slave quarters there is a rustling—
children are bundled into aprons, cornbread

and water gourds grabbed, a salt pork breakfast taken.
I watch them driven into the vague before-dawn   5
while their mistress sleeps like an ivory toothpick

and Massa dreams of asses, rum and slave-funk.
I cannot fall asleep again. At the second horn,
the whip curls across the backs of the laggards—

sometimes my sister's voice, unmistaken, among them.   10
"Oh! pray," she cries. "Oh! pray!" Those days
I lie on my cot, shivering in the early heat,

and as the fields unfold to whiteness,
and they spill like bees among the fat flowers,
I weep. It is not yet daylight.   15

5. Each of these poems grows from its metaphors. As far as possible, identify the elements brought into the transference. Don't quit too soon!

a) *Oread*

H.D. (1886–1961)

Whirl up, sea—
whirl your pointed pines,
splash your great pines
on our rocks,
hurl your green over us,   5
cover us with your pools of fir.

b) *On Being Served Apples*

BONNIE JACOBSON*

Apples in a deep blue dish
          are the shadows of nuns
Apples in a basket
          are warm red moons on Indian women
Apples in a white bowl   5
          are virgins waiting in snow
Beware of apples on an orange plate:
          they are the anger of wives

c) *Watermelons*

CHARLES SIMIC (b. 1938)

Green Buddhas
On the fruit stand.
We eat the smile
And spit out the teeth.

d) *Waking from Sleep*

ROBERT BLY

Inside the veins there are navies setting forth,
Tiny explosions at the water lines,
And seagulls weaving in the wind of the salty blood.

It is the morning. The country has slept the whole winter.
Window seats were covered with fur skins, the yard was full   5
Of stiff dogs, and hands that clumsily held heavy books.

Now we wake, and rise from bed, and eat breakfast!—
Shouts rise from the harbor of the blood,
Mist, and masts rising, the knock of wooden tackle in the sunlight.

Now we sing, and do tiny dances on the kitchen floor.   10
Our whole body is like a harbor at dawn;
We know that our master has left us for the day.

e)   *Sparrows*

CHRISTOPHER BUCKLEY (b. 1948)

Like the poor, they are with us always . . .
what they lack in beauty is theirs
in good cheer—tails like pump handles
lifting them first among songsters, chiding
citylight or roadside to evening's praise.   5
Gristmills, hardy gleaners, but for them
the weeds and thorns would find us wanting.
Ragmen to the wind, Sophists of the twig,
they pause to bathe in the ample dust
and accept the insect as relish to the seed.   10
So it is becoming to not be too fastidious
when you are rapidly inheriting the earth.

6. As a group or on your own, list about twenty concrete but common nouns in one column and about twenty active, present tense verbs in another. For example: ladle, saunter, seed corn, crank, swim, cop, glaze, chain, truck tire, bloom, moon, hail, belittle, petunia, snare, flit, cup, trunk, score, swing, sewing machine, towel, clover. (Notice how many words can be either nouns or verbs.) Now, almost arbitrarily, draw lines to connect them, so that the petunia belittles the . . . , or the moon glazes the . . . , or hail blooms. What kind of metaphors can you make? "Hail blooms like clover"? Try exploring the richest through a poem.

7. In this poem by Robert Francis, how is the comparison of the woman to "an old apple" visually accurate? Tonally suggestive? See if you can decide whether line 8 is literal or metaphorical. Given the poem's subject, what is the effect of the *a a a a* rhyme scheme?

Cadence

Puckered like an old apple she lies abed,
Saying nothing and hearing nothing said,
Not seeing the birthday flowers by her head
To comfort her. She is not comforted.

The room is warm, too warm, but there is chill   5
Over her eyes and over her tired will.
Her hair is frost in the valley, snow on the hill.
Night is falling and the wind is still.

8. Underline all the similes and metaphors in Cathy Song's "Primary Colors" (p. 126). Explore their metaphorical links and implications.

POEMS TO CONSIDER

 Sonnet 130 1609

WILLIAM SHAKESPEARE (1564–1616)

My mistress' eyes are nothing like the sun;
Coral is far more red than her lips' red;
If snow be white, why then her breasts are dun;
If hairs be wires, black wires grow on her head.
I have seen roses damasked, red and white,   5
But no such roses see I in her cheeks;
And in some perfumes is there more delight
Than in the breath that from my mistress reeks.
I love to hear her speak, yet well I know
That music hath a far more pleasing sound;   10
I grant I never saw a goddess go;
My mistress, when she walks, treads on the ground:
    And yet, by heaven, I think my love as rare
    As any she belied with false compare.

 Icicles 1978

MARK IRWIN*

Slender beards of light
hang from the railing.

My son shows me
their array of sizes:

one oddly shaped,   5
its queer curve,

a clear walrus tooth,
illumined, tinseled.

We watch crystal cones
against blue sky;   10

suddenly some break loose:
an echo of piano notes.

The sun argues
ice to liquid.

Tiny buds of water,   15
pendent on dropper tips,

push to pear shapes:
prisms that shiver silver

in a slight wind
before falling.   20

Look, he says laughing,
a pinocchio nose,

and grabs one
in his tiny hand,

touching the clear carrot,   25
cold to his lips.

The Orthodox Waltz   *1990*

ALICE FULTON (b. 1952)

Courtship, the seamless mesh
under taffeta havocs
of hoopskirt, smoke

hoops from his Lucky Strikes
her words jumped through.   5
Women dancing had the harder part,

she'd heard, because they must
dance backward.
He kept his ear pressed

like a safecracker's   10
stethoscope against
her head, kept his

recombinant endearments
tumbling toward a click.
The lachrymose music,   15

his clasp and lust-
spiel, displaced her
mother's proverbs. How nimble

they were, those girls
gliding by on dollies.   20
What had her mother said

that sounded wise? Was it
"Women dancing must be agile
as refugees with jewels

tied to their thighs"?   25

 **One Summer Hurricane Lynn Spawns Tornados
as Far West as Ely**   *1992*

LYNN EMANUEL (b. 1948)

The storm with my name dragged one
heavy foot over the roads of the county.
It was a bulge in a black raincoat, pointed
and hard as the spike in a railroad tie;
it dipped like a dowser's rod and screamed   5
like the express at the bend at Elko.
It made the night feverish and the sky
burn with the cold blue fire of a motel sign.
Oh that small hell of mine nipped at the town,
turned the roads to mud, lingered at the horizon,   10
a long clog, a sump. All sigh and lamentation,
the whole city of grief rose up to face that black
boot that waited to kick us open like a clay pot.

The Fireflies   *1992*

MARGARET HOLLEY (b. 1944)

Sparks from a bonfire,
bits blown from a furnace,
they drift over the black meadow,

the pulsing shrimps
with their candles flaring,   5
each comma carrying its own lantern.

You remain indoors
reading by lamplight, glowworm,
larva whose labor is to eat, molt,

and feverishly expand   10
before the newly secreted
chitin hardens into another shell.

Out here it is a time of fire
between the first awareness
of desire   15

and its denouement,
a time of craving unfulfilled,
the bright transparency

of the verb "to want"
in all its conjugations.   20
For now, your cocoon of pages

keeps you as quiet
as the pupa, the doll,
that seems to just hang around

doing nothing,   25
while under the exoskeleton
a major transformation occurs.

What can I say to you,
except that out here sometimes
the body becomes an intermittent torch   30

finally consenting to burn,
consenting to know what it is
one wants

and may or may not have,
to walk in the dark by one's own light,   35
ablaze, transparent,

and as transient
as these, their minute lamps
making a silent firework of praise.

A Valediction: Forbidding Mourning   *1633*

JOHN DONNE (1572–1631)

As virtuous men pass mildly away,
    And whisper to their souls to go,
Whilst some of their sad friends do say
    The breath goes now, and some say, No;

So let us melt, and make no noise,   5
    No tear-floods, nor sigh-tempests move,
'Twere profanation of our joys
    To tell the laity our love.

Moving of th' earth° brings harms and fears,
    Men reckon what it did and meant;   10
But trepidation of the spheres°,
    Though greater far, is innocent.

Dull sublunary° lovers' love
    (Whose soul is sense) cannot admit
Absence, because it doth remove   15
    Those things which elemented° it.

But we by a love so much refined
    That our selves know not what it is,
Inter-assured of the mind,
    Care less, eyes, lips, and hands to miss.   20

Our two souls therefore, which are one,
    Though I must go, endure not yet
A breach, but an expansion,
    Like gold to airy thinness beat.

If they be two, they are two so   25
    As stiff twin compasses are two;
Thy soul, the fixed foot, makes no show
    To move, but doth, if th' other do.

And though it in the center sit,
    Yet when the other far doth roam,   30
It leans and hearkens after it,
    And grows erect, as that comes home.

9 *Moving of th' earth*: earthquakes; 11 *trepidation of the spheres*: irregular movements in
the heavens; 13 *sublunary*: below the moon; hence, subject to change; 16 *elemented*:
composed.

Such wilt thou be to me, who must
    Like th' other foot, obliquely run;
Thy firmness makes my circle just,   35
    And makes me end where I begun.

Getting Dressed in the Dark   1988

VICKIE KARP (b. 1953)

June, yet the roses are still asleep in their black dormitory,
Illusions of grandeur dissolving mid-air like sugar in weak tea.

Soon, they will hoist themselves out of their despair,
Muscling in on the atmosphere with their fragrant animosity.

The hedge-clipper's bicycle, a pair of spectacles at this distance,   5
Leans against some reticent shrubs.

For blocks, the lawns are strewn with tattered burlap.
Brown, stained with the sweat of dew, it could be clothing

Tossed from your dreams, the entire wardrobe
Of your dread unconscious pitched out   10

As your body, the quivering pelt, slept on
Clad only in bracelets of air.

In the bedroom, surrounded by four-legged non-creatures
—Table, chair, dresser, bed—

The body rises, shifting its inner tropic from swamp to tree,   15
Pats the floor for its shoes, places a thumb

On each side of a sock—the mugging grin of a boy
About to stick out his tongue—

And slowly, as if dipping a foot into cold water,
Rolls the puddle up over each ankle.   20

Upright now, wrapped in a drape by the window, see the bit of cloth
With flaps like arms that lies chest down on the neighbor's lilacs?

A pale shirt? A smoking victim from that night you thought
You were Deianira° in a world without a doting Heracles?

Soon, the red velvet she might have found to enchant him   25
Without killing him will hang at the top of every ladder of thorns.

24 *Deianira:* wife who inadvertently caused the death of her unfaithful husband Heracles
by the gift of a poisoned tunic.

The Crow   1991

RENÉE ASHLEY (b. 1949)

At dusk, the flat lake, blacker
than a crow's wing, is still.
It bargains with the hills

for the last blue hour. Our pines
harbor three invisible birds; their voices   5
are the voices of the half-night.

There is no impasse at dark, only
the slow change to some other thing,
some other time when the currency

of light is valueless and gem-eyed   10
mammals scour the hedges for food.
At midnight, the long-eared owl will call

from the pitch pine, call plainly
for what he knows is his. The whisper of tree
and wing and fur is fate.   15

We have not the eyes for darkness
and our ears are poor cousins
to those who measure the night. We

are the pale ones, the sleeping ones,
who, when the black crow cries   20
his alarum, rise feebly and face the light.

Children of Sacaton   1992

GREG PAPE (b. 1947)

I came to Sacaton to teach the children
metaphor—look at the clock, a moon
nailed to the wall, a madman's eye.
What I said was good for a laugh,
a puzzled look, or a *so what*.   5
I learned many ways to call the roll.
I fell in love with many faces.
Because I was a kind stranger
they told me their secrets, their fears,

their fathers. They showed me   10
the sleeping chief in the mountains.
See? There's his head, and there's his feet.
They explained Mul-Cha-Tha, the place
of happenings. Their mothers
made baskets, sang the old songs,   15
worked in Phoenix, or drank beer all day.
They already knew metaphor. They said
the wind is the long hair of the horse
I ride in the mountains. They said
the saguaros are the old people dancing.   20
If the sun gets hungry, one of them said,
you better look out.

8

BEYOND THE RATIONAL
Lightning Bolts and Burglars

All the arts, poetry among them, are magical. Something essential to their power always remains elusive, beyond craft. Labor at it as the artist may, the best usually just comes, like the gushing up of Kubla Khan's sacred river.

The Greeks explained the magic through the **Muses,** nine goddesses who aid and inspire writers and musicians. The frustrations of writing and composing, of getting it right, led artists to consider these muses fickle, difficult to please—they had to be courted and seduced. The Christian and Renaissance explanation of this magic was similar: **inspiration** (from Latin, "to be breathed into"). The divine wind blows where it will. The Romantic explanation was **genius,** some freak of nature or of the soul. Followers of Freud explain the magic through the **subconscious,** a bubbling up from hidden parts of the mind. The Spanish poet Federico García Lorca calls the magic *the Duende,* a word common in his native Andalusia, but impossible to translate into English. Duende "furnishes us with whatever is sustaining in art." It comes to the artist, an old musician told Lorca, not from the artist's conscious control or native talents but "from inside, up from the very soles of the feet." Researchers into creativity have figured out that people who tend toward the arts free-associate more easily than those in science and technology, but these psychologists have still not figured out what qualities of the mind, or the brain, engender this ability.

The creative person, C. G. Jung says, "is a riddle that we may try to answer in various ways, but always in vain." The power remains unexpected and mysterious, even frightening. Randall Jarrell likens the magic of poetry to being struck by lightning. The poet may stand on high ground in a thunderstorm, but nothing guarantees the poet will be struck.

In their origins the arts were primitive and no doubt occult. Julian Jaynes, in *The Origin of Consciousness in the Breakdown of the Bicameral Mind* (1976), argues that poetry was originally the "divine knowledge" or "divine hallucinations" of primitive peoples. "The god-side of our ancient mentality . . . usually, or perhaps always, spoke in verse . . . . Poetry then," he adds, "was the language of the gods."

WORD MAGIC

On the walls of their caves Stone-age people drew the beasts they hunted and the plants they harvested as if to gain some mysterious, ceremonial mastery over them. The oldest poems we have are the charms, prayers, spells, curses, and incantations that accompanied the magical rites of ancient cultures. For almost any human experience—from the sacred to the mundane—we can find a corresponding chant, dirge, prayer, or ditty. These poems bless apple trees or warriors' weapons, clear up a boil, cast out demons, and drive off a swarm of bees. There are poems to sanctify the newlyweds' first bed, celebrate a birth, curse the rich and powerful, strengthen medicinal herbs, or send the dead safely to the next life.

Like the best poems, magic poems are precise. Cut from the particular world of the speaker, they fit the speaker's specific needs and longings. This chant, a shaman's address to the spirits, comes from Siberia; the original is in Yukaghir, a language of which only a few hundred speakers are left.

> You, owners of the green and trees, help me,
> Sea mother, who has as cover seven snow mounds,
> As bed, eight ice layers,
> As collar, black foxes,
> As foam, arctic foxes,   5
> As waves, cub foxes.
> Help me, sea-mother-owner.

Far removed from the Yakut region, we still find the chant vivid. It begins by invoking the spirits of "the green and trees," then turns to a specific power, the sea mother, honoring her by calling up images of the white north and the hibernal creatures she rules. We, too, respond to the bitter but alluring cold, imagining the foxes scurrying through forests. The chant's repetition and parallelism, probably memory aids, register its rising urgency, leading to the simple plea, "Help me."

The following literary example of a magic spell, from A *Midsummer-Night's Dream*, also conjures up a magic world. After a quarrel, the fairy king, Oberon, enchants his sleeping queen, Titania, so that she will fall for the first oaf she spots after waking.

> What thou seest when thou dost wake,
> Do it for thy true-love take;
> Love and languish for his sake.
> Be it ounce° or cat or bear,
> Pard°, or boar with bristled hair   5
> In thy eye that shall appear
> When thou wak'st, it is thy dear.
> Wake when some vile thing is near.

4 *ounce*: lynx; 5 *Pard*: leopard.

Oberon's spell prompts us to anticipate, to our great delight, what isn't on the stage, but will be shortly, in the person of Bottom, wearing the head of an ass. Though Oberon normally speaks in blank verse, befitting the dignity of his noble position, when he casts the spell, he speaks in rhyme. The resonance of repeated sounds heightens the magic as with the words of the witches Macbeth encounters:

> Eye of newt, and toe of frog,
> Wool of bat, and tongue of dog,
> Adder's fork, and blindworm's sting,
> Lizard's leg, and howlet's wing—
> For a charm of pow'rful trouble.
> Like a hell-broth boil and bubble.
> Double, double, toil and trouble,
> Fire burn and cauldron bubble.

The word "*spell*" itself suggests how powerful words are. As part of the curative, ancient peoples often literally spelled out the charm—something like a physician's prescription. An old charm in England against rabies called for writing down the spell on a piece of paper and feeding it to the mad dog. Evoking the essential power of language, of the ABC's, the occult word "abracadabra" was often spelled out in a triangle as part of a magic formula.

As with all kinds of magic, the first criterion of word magic is that those who wield it and those likely to be helped or harmed must believe in its power. On plantations in the antebellum South, according to John W. Blassingame in *The Slave Community* (1972), overseers and masters dealt very cautiously with slaves they believed possessed magical powers. Shrewd men and women who convinced the masters of their power might avoid getting sold or whipped, or intercede for others threatened with punishment. Against the conjurer's magic even the strength of the oppressor could seem feeble.

In the 1930s the Federal Writers' Project, collecting narratives of former slaves, recorded this love-spell:

> Little pinch o' pepper,
> Little bunch o' wool.
>
> Mumbledy—mumbledy.
>
> Two, three Pammy Christy beans,
> Little piece o' rusty iron.   5
>
> Mumbledy—mumbledy.
>
> Wrop it in a rag and tie it with hair,
> Two from a hoss and one from a mare.
>
> Mumbledy, mumbledy, mumbledy.
>
> Wet it in whiskey   10
> Boughten with silver;
> That make you wash so hard your sweat pop out,
> And he come to pass, sure!

Apparently a former slave helped sustain himself during the lean times after the Civil War by selling such spells. Whites and blacks, women and men, handed over the two bits he charged in hopes of winning the hearts of those they loved. Oddly, the charm's ending seems off-rhythm, suggesting perhaps either an error in transcription or in memory, or maybe that the man deliberately gave the transcriber the wrong verse.

We resort to magic and prayer when science and human effort fail us. We have better treatment now for rabies, but are at as much a loss as any one who lived in Reconstruction Tennessee or Elizabethan England to understand why someone falls in love with one person instead of another, and so we may still count off on the petals of a daisy, *loves me, loves me not.* Rational and sophisticated as we like to consider ourselves, at our most intense and puzzling moments—moments at the heart of poetry—words often remain our greatest solace.

Our most familiar believers in word magic are children. From the toddler chirping out "Pat-a-cake," to the older parodist sneering at authority, "Glory, glory, hallelujah, Teacher hit me with a ruler," children love language. From generation to generation, songs and charms are passed along because children believe in their power. Children govern their groups with rhyme ("One potato, two potato, three potato, four"); wish with it ("Star light, star bright, first star I see tonight"); threaten with it ("See this finger, see this thumb? / See this fist, you better run"); and accuse with it ("Liar, liar, pants on fire"). And when cornered, they make their defense, "I'm rubber, you're glue / What you say bounces off me and sticks to you." Like all preliterate peoples, children delight in words, find them powerful, fear and respect them.

Though most don't like to admit it, adults aren't much different. Certain words remain taboo, and though we all know them, we avoid them in public, and they can't be printed in this paragraph. We use magical words in church, in court, and when we quarrel. With pledges, oaths, and vows people become wives and husbands, nuns, physicians, presidents, witnesses, and citizens. In uttering the words we cross a threshold; we are not exactly the same person as before we pronounced them.

Good poems recognize the potency of words and draw upon it. Read again and again over the years, the best poems seem magically fresh. Passing centuries often do not dim this mysteriously self-renewing energy. Such poetry comes from, and keeps us in touch with, a fundamental power deep within the human psyche, where dark rivers from time-beyond-memory carve the stone. One source of this power is sound, "the musical qualities of verse," what T. S. Eliot (1888–1965) calls the **"auditory imagination."** It is, he says,

> the feeling for syllable and rhythm, penetrating far below the conscious levels of thought and feeling, invigorating every word; sinking to the most primitive and forgotten, returning to the origin and bringing something back, seeking the beginning and the end. It works through meanings, certainly, or not without meanings in the ordinary sense, and fuses the old and obliterated and the trite, the current, and the new and surprising, the most ancient and the most civilised mentality.

The age-old forms of language itself, its glacial mass and electrical suddenness, give shape to every new thought and discovery in our consciousness.

Like sound, images tap into this power. They can reach beyond the rational to some magical apprehension deep in our personal and collective memories. Freudian symbols and Jungian archetypes, magic talismans, superstitions, and dreams seem outcroppings of this subterranean granite of human experience. So, too, is metaphor, with its inexplicable leaps, uncanny logic, and magical rightness. In "The Red Ant," transcribed about 1873 from the Paiute in Arizona, the anonymous poet's whole world-view crystallizes in seeing the ant, with its one sting, as an exceptionally brave warrior:

> The little red ant
>> Descended the hill
> With one arrow only.

Metaphors are often nonrational, though the best make a superior kind of sense; operating through *analogical* rather than through *logical* processes, they give us a way beyond linear thinking to apprehend.

Poets need not, perhaps should not, concern themselves too directly with the sources of poetry's magic. It is enough to know that when writing well we may tap into this energy as we flip on a light without considering how trees and animals eons ago drew energy from the sun, then dissolved into the black lakes and the frozen black rivers, which we now drill and mine, and from which, through dynamos and copper wires, ancient light arrives in the lamp on our desk.

THE SENSE OF "NONSENSE"

At times we may get so bogged down in pondering the imponderabilities of language that we forget what any nursery rhyme, like this one, reminds us.

> Bat, bat,
>> Come under my hat,
> And I'll give you a slice of bacon;
>> And when I bake,
>> I'll give you a cake
> If I am not mistaken.

Nonsense is fun. Part of the magic of words is how often and easily they give us pleasure without asking us to pay dues. A killjoy might ask *why* such incongruous images as "bat" and "bacon" appear in this verse. We're not irresponsible if we answer simply: because the words sound good together. What a delight to be led along by the string of *bat-hat-bacon-bake-cake-mistaken*. All the more fun *because* the elements are incongruous. In a post-Freudian, post-Marxist era, theorists might reckon some hidden political and sexual agenda in phrases such as "the cow jumped over the moon" and "the dish ran away with the spoon." To such talk we feel inclined to say, "Fiddle-de-dee." Here is a famous example of nonsense poetry by Lewis Carroll (1832–1898).

Jabberwocky

'Twas brillig, and the slithy toves
    Did gyre and gimble in the wabe;
All mimsy were the borogoves,
    And the mome raths outgrabe.

"Beware the Jabberwock, my son!   5
    The jaws that bite, the claws that catch!
Beware the Jubjub bird, and shun
    The frumious Bandersnatch!"

He took his vorpal sword in hand:
    Long time the manxome foe he sought—   10
So rested he by the Tumtum tree,
    And stood awhile in thought.

And as in uffish thought he stood,
    The Jabberwock, with eyes of flame,
Came whiffling through the tulgey wood,   15
    And burbled as it came!

One, two! One, two! And through and through
    The vorpal blade went snicker-snack!
He left it dead, and with its head
    He went galumphing back.   20

"And hast thou slain the Jabberwock?
    Come to my arms, my beamish boy!
O frabjous day! Callooh! Callay!"
    He chortled in his joy.

'Twas brillig, and the slithy toves   25
    Did gyre and gimble in the wabe;
All mimsy were the borogoves,
    And the mome raths outgrabe.

In *Through the Looking Glass* Humpty Dumpty tells Alice that "'slithy' means 'lithe and slimy'. . . there are two meanings packed up in one word." He explains "mimsy" as another "portmanteau" (or suitcase) word that packs up "flimsy and miserable." And "toves" are "something like badgers . . . something like lizards—and . . . something like corkscrews" that "make their nests under sundials" and "live on cheese." These definitions only heighten the absurdity.

Yet the story of "Jabberwocky" is clear enough: a boy quests after the dreaded Jabberwock, slays it with his sword, and is hailed for his deeds. The story is *archetypal*, like the story of David and Goliath. (**Archetype:** a general or universal story, setting, character-type, or symbol that recurs in many cultures and eras.) Because the pattern comes across, we don't much concern ourselves with who the "beamish boy" is or that the Jubjub bird and "frumious Bandersnatch" are still lurking out there. The reader recognizes the poem as a joyous celebration of, among other things, language: its inventiveness, its whimsical sounds, its Jabberwock that "came whiffling" and "burbled as it came."

Nursery rhymes and poems like "Jabberwocky" are related to riddles, jokes, and other word games, reminding us of the deep roots that join poetry—and all of the arts—to *play*. After all, the more common word for a dramatic composition is a *play*; we *play* musical instruments, and literary devices like metaphors and puns *play* on words. The play of language allows the juxtaposition of all sorts of things from the palpably untrue to the delectably outrageous. The impossible happens. Grammatically, one noun can substitute for another so that "The cow jumps over the fence" becomes "The cow jumps over the moon." The cow can also "jump to conclusions," or "jump a jogger in the park." And if we're so inclined, the cow might "jump ship in Argentina on a silvery mission to choke the articulated artichokes of criminal post(age) stamps." The syntax of a sentence may seem to be clear while its meaning remains murky; the linguist Noam Chomsky once offered this example, "Colorless green ideas sleep furiously." Nonsense can undermine our confidence in language, and many other patterns we normally take for granted, and help us appreciate its inventiveness and mystery.

While creating art certainly requires work and we speak of the finished product as a *work* of art, we must also keep in mind that art grows out of play—goofing around, free-associating, seeing what happens next and next. If we read the following poem by James Tate (b. 1943) as a kind of game, we can avoid troubling ourselves so much about what it means and appreciate what it does, how it plays with patterns of words and phrases, shuffling them to create new patterns.

A Guide to the Stone Age

for Charles Simic

A heart that resembles a cave,
a throat of shavings,
an arm with no end and no beginning:

How about the telephone?
—Not yet.   5

The cave in your skull,
a throat with a crack in it,
a heart that still resembles a cave:

How about the knife?
—Later.   10

The fire in the cave of your skull,
a beast who died shaving,
a cave with no end and no beginning:

A big ship!
—Shut up.   15

Instructions which ask you to burn other instructions,
a circle with a crack in it,
a stone with an arm:

A hat?
—Not the hat.   20

A ship with a knife in it,
a telephone with a hat over it,
a cave with a heart:

The Stone Age?
—There is no end to it.   25

Notice, despite the strangeness of the poem, how shrewdly Tate manages its surface: twenty-five lines of alternating three- and two-line stanzas. Each stanza type
serves a different function. The tercets offer a kind of list; the couplets a question
and an answer. Each element in the first stanza reappears at least once in combinations with new items in the following tercets; for instance the parts of line 1, "A
heart that resembles a cave," reappear in "The cave in your skull" (line 6), "a heart
that still resembles a cave" (line 8), "The fire in the cave of your skull" (line 11),
and then in the final tercet stanza, "a cave with a heart" (line 23). The last line
reverses the order of the first line.

A colon closes each tercet and introduces the couplet which apparently proposes some item to be included (e.g., line 4: "How about the telephone?"); at first,
each possibility (telephone, knife, ship, hat) is rejected; then in the final tercet all
the rejected items are included in the first two lines while its last line rearranges
the items of line 1. This stanza, unlike the others, uses only one method of creating
the noun phrase: *Noun + with + noun + preposition + noun* in the first two lines, and
in the last line, a simplification, *noun + with + noun.*

In the final couplet, the first line echoes the title, and the last line seems to
comment on the poem: "There is no end to it" implies—among other things—that
the process of combining and recombining could go on endlessly. This ending, of
course, is part of the poem's playfulness, for the poem *does* end just at the point
where it claims, "There is no end to it."

Throughout the poem, Tate takes care that we sense the poem's jocularity. The
Abbott and Costello bantering in the couplets seems to come to a head with the
central couplet (lines 14–15). "A big ship!" the interjector proposes. And the
respondent, as if out of exasperation, rejoins, with a half-rhyme, "Shut up!" The
deflation of the tone alerts us that we are not meant to take the whole poem seriously, despite its often grim imagery of warfare and brutality.

Perhaps besides word games Tate has intended other games. The poem also contains five three-line and five two-line stanzas; 5 is the sum of 3 + 2. The twenty-
five lines of the poem is the product of 5 times 5, five fives, each five lines can be
read as a separate group. Five lines end with the word "it." The numbers 2, 3, and 5
form a sequence of prime numbers; the list of which is infinite.

The poem's meaning may be unclear but Tate's intentions aren't. The poem is a
game. When a poem indicates we should approach it primarily as a puzzle, we

begin to ask ourselves where the game begins and ends, if our sense of its rules are really its rules. Tate questions rules themselves. The "Guide" doesn't so much guide us as jab at the efficacy of any guide (much less one to a pre-linguistic era). The poem seems to be an instance of "Instructions which ask you to burn other instructions," an unending cycle. By dedicating the poem to the poet Charles Simic, a surrealist realist or realistic surrealist, Tate ups the ante of the game.

In poems such as Tate's, words, phrases, images, whole passages are used as objects, for their tone and color, rather than for their representation, for their "meaning." They are analogous to abstract art where, for instance, a streak of red seems to confront a field of green paint. Such paintings aren't about the realistic rendering of reality but about form, shape, color, perception, and paint itself. The poet John Ashbery (b. 1927), a proponent of experimental poetry, looks to music for an analogy of his purposes:

> I feel I could express myself best in music. What I like about music is its ability of being convincing, of carrying an argument through successfully to the finish, though the terms of this argument remain unknown quantities. What remains is the structure, the architecture of the argument, scene or story. I would like to do this in poetry.

Elsewhere in a poem called "What Is Poetry," Ashbery speaks of "Trying to avoid / Ideas, as in this poem." Just as we can string together a perfectly regular syntactic sequence with nonsense parts ("the cow crawled to conclusions"), so, too, poets like Tate and Ashbery can use the framework of argument without its logical components. As Paul Carroll suggests in an essay on Ashbery, "multiple combinations of words and images (islands of significance) continually form, dissolve, and reform." Since meaning is not fixed, such poems invite the reader to take center stage, to help create the poem.

Since the nineteenth century the avant-garde has constantly scrutinized notions of "meaning" and "reality." One wave of experimentation has followed another, challenging the notions of some generations, adopting and adapting techniques of others to create their own innovations. (Some of the movements in poetry include Symbolism, Imagism, Modernism, Surrealism, Dadaism, Futurism, Objectivism, Projectivism, Post-Modernism, Beat poetry, the New York School, Language poetry.) By tapping into the potential of language, poets can suppress the ordinary conscious workings of the mind and allow the profound, subliminal effects of sound, images, and metaphor to confront the reader directly—without a concern for a poem's explicit "meaning." Eliot describes the assumptions behind such poems:

> The chief use of the "meaning" of a poem, in the ordinary sense, may be (for here . . . I am speaking of some kinds of poetry and not all) to satisfy one habit of the reader, to keep his mind diverted and quiet, while the poem does its work upon him: much as the imaginary burglar is always provided with a bit of nice meat for the house-dog. This is a normal situation of which I approve. But the minds of all poets do not work that way; some of them, assuming that there are other minds like their own, become impatient of this "meaning" which seems superfluous, and perceive possibilities of intensity through its elimination.

Eliot's *The Waste Land* is an early example of experimental poetry; it challenges meaning by suppressing the "habits" of narrative and logical argument in favor of a succession of characters, voices, scenes, fragments of scenes, images, quotations, allusions, and snippets; it is as much about itself as an object as about some other "subject."

METAPHORS OF EXPERIENCE

Among its more ordinary—even traditional—functions, the nonrational in literature breaks down the barriers we usually erect between the normal and abnormal so as to present highly charged experiences: what is baffling, contradictory, vital, passionate. The outrageous duke of Browning's "My Last Duchess" (p. 166) is an abnormal personality. His detachment toward executing his last wife appalls us: he considers people pawns, disposable if they displease him. Such fastidiousness and cool cruelty fascinate us.

The worlds of the evil, the eccentric, the mad, and the supernatural have long appealed to poets not because as poets we are necessarily obsessed with violence, cruelty, insanity, and mysticism but because in dramatizing such extremes, poets can cast in relief complex human emotions and experiences. In this poem by Norman Dubie (b. 1945) the mad speaker effectively dramatizes the fierce grief felt over a child's death:

A Blue Hog

I didn't have to buy the acid.
I found it in an old battery in the barn
Where the cows make sea noises
And the cobwebs are plated gold.
There were packets of birdseed, white floats   5
Of cork, turpentine, and an old black fishline
Which shouldn't have worked but did.
All of it a sin for the taking—
I chose the acid for its smoke
And the fishline to tie around my toe   10
To remind me of the smoke.
I threw the rotten apples into the yard
And the blue hog charged.
He was unpardonable, having
Killed my sister's child. John couldn't   15
Butcher him—*to eat that hog*
Would be to eat the child.
I poured the acid into pink Christmas bulbs
And sewed them into the hollowed apples.
I put them out into the sun to soften.   20
The hog swallowed them whole like smoke.

By the time he looked under himself
He was already broke. My long dress shook.
He stopped to give me a look,
And then ran straight at the barn.   25
His head and shoulders passed through the boards.
The horse inside
Had a hissing fit over him. Nobody
Has ridden that horse since
Except for the devil   30
Who's said to still be in the district.

The speaker's quirky images set against her matter-of-fact tone signal that we are in the province of the bizarre, where emotions run amuck and reality is off-kilter. The details this poem presents are extraordinary, even gruesome—a child killed by a *blue* hog, poison apples apparently fashioned from Christmas ornaments and battery acid, a spooked horse ridden by the devil.

The poem's metaphors, which become odder as the poem continues, play a central role in creating the speaker's peculiar reality. The first metaphor, "Where the cows make sea noises," leads us into this realm. The lowing of cows, the swishing of their tails may sound like the moan and splash of the sea. Yet her associating these thoroughly land-bound animals with the ocean tends to blur the distinction we normally make and begins to establish a speaker who cannot discern the real world from the world her mind invents.

Our impression that the speaker's sense of reality is skewed grows with each line. Nothing is quite what it seems. She misidentifies seed packets as "birdseed." She tells us that the fishing line "shouldn't have worked but did," though she doesn't use the line even to tie something up. She wants it to do the work of a symbol, "to remind me of the smoke," perhaps of the battery acid burning out the hog's internal organs. She views the odds and ends she scrounges in the barn as monumental, " *a sin* for the taking" instead of, in the usual phrase, "ripe for the taking." She pronounces the hog "unpardonable," and since no one else seems able to destroy the animal, she takes the necessary guilt upon herself.

Her reasoning unsettles the reader. She can make plans, predict their results, and carry them out, yet her methods and rationale are out of proportion, and violent. Instead of killing the hog directly, she devises the elaborate scheme. A car battery, bulbs, apples—by themselves negligible, benign—taken together become her instrument of death.

Clearly the speaker's reaction to the child's death is abnormal, and she was likely unhinged before the hog killed the child. But the ferocity of her response casts in relief the complex of emotions that follows losing a child: the anger, vindictiveness, anguish, and guilt. We can share in the poem's emotions because we, too, have felt grief. Dubie's speaker is irrational, but her emotions aren't, for emotions aren't reasonable; they're either appropriate or inappropriate, and often a messy mixture of both. The excesses of the mad farm woman's behavior manifest the inscrutable muddle of emotions we feel in times of crisis.

Dubie's speaker offers an extreme example of the use of the strange; in the following poem by Susan Prospere (b. 1946) we see a more normal use.

Ministering Angels

When I saw the pony in June, she was dressed
for a different climate—something nearer
her ancestral beginnings (she was Welsh)—
for she had rounded the great climacteric turn
that left her hormones delicately imbalanced   5
and her eyes were misted over
as if the Atlantic Ocean had raised its tide
over the Welsh coast until it took her.
She would drink from the porcelain bathtub
in the pasture long drafts of invisible water,   10
then would stand for hours in the kudzu,
enveloped in its dark contagion,
while the horseflies drilled,
until they were dizzy, after her.

All one day I worked to remove the coat   15
she no longer discarded in the ardent weather.
I sheared her, lacking shears, with scissors,
operating them with blistered fingers
until they moved automatically, flashing
over her body like bright, clacking stars.   20
The tufts of hair falling around her
accumulated into a dark, furred shadow
that repeated her strange predicament
and would stay on the ground to remind us,
when she left, of the way   25
we collapse downward before rising.

So I willed her alive,
at least for one more evening,
the ministering angels walking all night
beside her through the orchard,   30
explaining the lie of the next strata,
while occasionally pulling down for her,
from the trees, the phosphorescent pears.
Before morning, having earned their rest honestly
through good works, they draw a bath   35
in the outdoor tub and bathe in the open,
relishing the high, post-Victorian moment,
having stayed on earth long enough to remember.

Prospere reports that the angels appeared in her poem not because she believes in the actual existence of these supernatural beings; rather, they grew out of the poem's metaphoric matrix—metaphors of the incongruous. The angels are as out of place as the bathtub (an image of the domestic and private) which serves for a drinking trough in the pasture, and as out of place as the aging Welsh pony, no longer able to shed her heavy coat, living out her last days on the family farm in sweltering Mississippi. As she was writing the poem, Prospere says, she asked herself what would "bathe in the open" in such a bathtub, and concluded angels would. Such angels seem fitting ministers to the aging pony whose furred shadow recalls "the way / we collapse downward before rising."

The grandeur of Prospere's language allows this celestial visitation to seem possible. Phrases like "the great climacteric turn," "dark contagion," and "the high, post-Victorian moment" support an attitude of ceremony and solemnity that underlies the poem. Metaphors that liken the pony's cataracted eyes to the Atlantic "raising its tide / over the Welsh coast" and the scissors to "clacking stars" help create a universe in the poem where massive forces can be played out on the local level of the farm, where a minor creature might be attended by angelic ministers.

The angels themselves act like "metaphors" for the speaker's feelings; they figure her desire for a kind of heaven-on-earth for the aging pony: she wills the pony alive "at least for one more evening," when the ministering angels will feed her the also-dying "phosphorescent pears" dropping from the orchard.

MIND DREAMS AND BODY DREAMS

Our most everyday—or "everynight"—experience of the nonrational is dreams. In dreaming we seem to translate our conscious experiences and obsessions into a host of symbols and situations. While immersed in a dream, we find these symbols highly charged, but when we wake and our conscious mind tries to sort through them, we often are baffled by them even as we *feel* their deep importance. The simple acts of falling asleep or waking up remind us that at times we exist simultaneously on more than one plane of consciousness. Look back to Frost's "After Apple-Picking" (p. 103) and notice how in "drowsing off" the speaker loses the distinction between the day-world of the fruit harvest and the coming dream-world where the "magnified apples" loom in his mind; reality becomes dreamy and the dream becomes real.

Charles Simic (b. 1938) sets the following poem in that peculiar region between waking and sleeping. While napping with a woman he loves, the speaker forms the raw materials of his unconscious into an imaginary prisoner who is imagining the napping couple.

The Prisoner

He is thinking of us.
These leaves, their lazy rustle
That made us sleepy after lunch
So we had to lie down.

He considers my hand on her breast,   5
Her closed eyelids, her moist lips
Against my forehead, and the shadows of trees
Hovering on the ceiling.

It's been so long. He has trouble
Deciding what else is there.   10
And all along the suspicion
That we do not exist.

The prisoner apparently represents conflicting aspects of the dozy speaker's awareness. On one hand the speaker feels lucky—for lunch, summery trees, his lover,
which to a prisoner would be paradise. On the other hand, the speaker cannot be
wholly content. He senses the precariousness of such happiness. In stanza 1 the
lovers are "us," "we," inclusive pronouns. But in stanza 2, possibly as she has drifted
off to sleep, he says "my hand on her breast," not on "your breast," suggesting the
lovers have drifted apart into their separate selves. In his uneasiness and isolation,
the half-awake speaker responds to his immediate experience from a distance, from
the perspective of an imagined prisoner: "He considers . . . ."

With stanza 3 the speaker almost becomes the prisoner: "It's been so long"
implies the prisoner's awareness, duplicating in some way the speaker's distrust of
his good fortune. As he slips toward sleep, the speaker's fading sense of his sur-
roundings becomes the prisoner's difficulty in imagining "what else is there" in his
fantasy room. As the speaker's distrust deepens, it becomes the prisoner's doubts
about the existence of his imaginary lovers. The communal "we" reappears in the
last line only to negate its truth: "That we do not exist."

Isolated in his own consciousness and in his own history, the speaker is "The Prisoner" of the title. Somehow, we come to understand, the speaker has projected the
prisoner out of his own misgivings. In the dim, unguarded moments between wakeful-
ness and sleep, his self-doubt will not let him accept his real experience for what it is.

Normally we use our senses to test whether what we are experiencing is really
happening. "Pinch me," we say when something seems too marvelous to believe. But
our senses don't always tell the truth. Optical illusions prove that. In our dreams we
can experience the sensations of waking life without any of them occurring in reality. A dream experience can be so vivid and a waking experience so strange that we
might ask, as Keats does in the end of "Ode to a Nightingale," "Do I wake or sleep?"

In this passage from his 1855 *Leaves of Grass*, Whitman captures the frantic
energy and the wild confusion of dreams where the divisions between the real and
unreal break down, and weird, often erotic, images erupt in our heads:

O hotcheeked and blushing! O foolish hectic!
O for pity's sake, no one must see me now! . . . . my clothes were
    stolen while I was abed,
Now I am thrust forth, where shall I run?

Pier that I saw dimly last night when I looked from the windows,
Pier out from the main, let me catch myself with you and stay
    . . . . I will not chafe you;   5

I feel ashamed to go naked about the world,
And am curious to know where my feet stand . . . . and what is
   this flooding me, childhood or manhood . . . . and the hunger
   that crosses the bridge between.

The cloth laps a first sweet eating and drinking,
Laps life-swelling yolks . . . . laps ear of rose-corn, milky and just
   ripened:
The white teeth stay, and the boss-tooth advances in darkness,   10
And liquor is spilled on lips and bosoms by touching glasses, and
   the best liquor afterward.

When we are asleep and dreaming we hardly question our fantastic experiences. Images and events blend seamlessly into one another. Poems like Whitman's operate through such a self-breeding series of **associations:** one image suggests another and the images in their sequence replace rational and discursive ways of saying something. When the method fails and the poet has not arranged the images so that a reader's responses follow them naturally, impenetrable obscurity results. When association succeeds, it produces poems of great compressive power.

We would be foolish to approach Whitman's dream-vision with only our rational minds, to look simply for its "meaning," for its meaning lies beyond interpretation; it lies within our response to the sensual, frenetic images piling atop one another and within the frenzied pace of its sentences. It recalls to us our own befuddling, even embarrassing, dreams where each element harbors a powerful significance, often a significance beyond our powers to define it. The force of Whitman's images seems primitive. The landscape is biological, perhaps even bio-"logical"; the self is alone, thrust out naked (how many of us have had similar dreams?) to contend with the mysterious pier, with slippery footing, and with the orgiastic imagery of yolks, milky rose-corn, teeth, and liquor.

In both our waking and dreaming lives our bodies act and react without our conscious control; this is perfectly normal. Our lungs expand and contract, our heart beats, our blood circulates, and our synapses fire. We're not aware of these autonomic responses until something out of the ordinary happens, and even then our bodies do most of their work outside our consciousness. After narrowly avoiding a head-on collision, you pull the car over to compose yourself: you realize your heart is pounding, your lungs are straining, your skin is sticky with sweat. However, you still aren't aware of the minute explosions at your nerve endings, for instance, or how your pancreas is operating. This immense nonconscious activity of our bodies—which constitutes what "being alive" literally means—forms the basis of this poem by Nina Cassian (b. 1924):

Ordeal

I promise to make you more alive than you've ever been.
For the first time you'll see your pores opening
like the gills of fish and you'll hear
the noise of blood in galleries
and feel light gliding on your corneas   5

like the dragging of a dress across the floor.
For the first time, you'll note gravity's prick
like a thorn in your heel,
and your shoulder blades will hurt from the imperative of wings.
I promise to make you so alive that   10
the fall of dust on furniture will deafen you,
and you'll feel your eyebrows like two wounds forming
and your memories will seem to begin
with the creation of the world.

—Translated from the Romanian by Michael Impey and Brian Swann

This poem's eerie power recalls that of primitive spells. On one level the poem
seems to address some particular other, for the intimacy of the tone implies that
the speaker—whoever she is—in some way knows the person she addresses. The
speaker promises to "make you more alive than you have ever been." Such a
promise suggests the expansive claims a lover makes. On another level, of course,
the poem addresses us.

Through metaphor and a form of synesthesia, Cassian creates the ordeal, carrying us into a world so minute that the senses seem to merge, and we arrive at our
very creation, as individuals and as a species. The speaker promises that the "you"
will be able to *see* pores opening "like the gills of fish," *hear* the noise of blood, and
feel—not see—the light as it glides across the cornea "like the dragging of a dress
across the floor." By magnifying autonomic responses, the speaker seems to imply
that the "you" will not only become acutely aware of the microscopic processes of
the body but also feel a latent spirituality and realize that within our bodies we harbor the processes of creation itself. Line 9, ". . . your shoulder blades will hurt from
the imperative of wings," implies that the aching is caused by one's need to be
more than human, to be perhaps a celestial creature.

SURREALITY

Influenced by psychology, twentieth-century poetry has often used the dream as an
analogy for the nonrational. **Surrealism,** a movement that began in France in the
1920s, gave us a word that sums up the artistic application of the unconscious:
surreal. The unconscious, free-associative, nonrational modes of thought (intuition, feeling, fantasy, imagination) put us in touch with a *surreality*, literally, a
super reality. Surrealistic poetry merges the inner and the outer world, dream and
reality, the flux of sensations or feelings and the hard, daylight facts of experience.

Surrealism has often been misunderstood as poetry and art where anything goes;
one just puts down whatever pops into one's head. A careful look at the work of
the great French Surrealists like André Breton and Paul Éluard tells us otherwise.
Paul Auster notes that poems which stick to surrealism's ostensible principle of
"pure psychic automatism" rarely resonate. Even poems like Breton's, which
employ the most radical shifts and oddest associations, use "an undercurrent of
consistent rhetoric that makes the poems cohere as densely reasoned objects of

thought."* In this poem notice how Paul Éluard (1895–1952) creates a nonrational poem that nevertheless employs familiar modes of logical argument. The first stanza poses a question, and the rest of the poem sets out to answer it.

The Deaf and Blind

Do we reach the sea with clocks
In our pockets, with the noise of the sea
In the sea, or are we the carriers
Of a purer and more silent water?

The water rubbing against our hands sharpens knives.   5
The warriors have found their weapons in the waves
And the sound of their blows is like
The rocks that smash the boats at night.

It is the storm and the thunder. Why not the silence
Of the flood, for we have dreamt within us   10
Space for the greatest silence and we breathe
Like the wind over terrible seas, like the wind

That creeps slowly over every horizon.

—Translated from the French by Paul Auster

The phrase which Auster translates as "with clocks / In our pockets" (lines 1–2) in the original poem is "*avec des cloches / Dans nos poches*," literally: "with bells in our pockets." "*Cloche*" means the large bell found, for instance, in a belfry; the French words for smaller bells are *clochette* and *sonnette*. We derived our English word *clock*, from *cloche*; the earliest clocks—often placed on the townhall—rang out the hour. Sailors still use "bells" to measure time, and when we're "saved by the bell," we're saved by time running out (itself a phrase from the hourglass and its sands).

In trying to keep the sense, spirit, and sound of an original, translators of poetry must weigh literal meanings against considerations of connotation, idiom, form, sound, and rhythm. Auster's choice of "clocks" is shrewd. To the surrealists a poem's sounds often matter more than one particular meaning. "Clocks" permits an internal rhyme with "pockets," registering Éluard's internal rhyme ("cloches," "poches"), while retaining the absurdity and lucidity of Éluard's first image. Our pockets can't hold something as huge as a town bell (or a clock—we carry *watches* in our pockets), but on a metaphoric level we might carry along to the sea the weight of regulation and social order, which both town bells and clocks imply. The French have a phrase for parochialism which makes this point: *esprit de clocher*, literally, spirit of the bell tower. Part of the surrealist agenda is to strip away the layers of received social attitudes to create a fresh realization of language, self, and reality.

Éluard's poem doesn't so much dismiss the rational as transcend or absorb it. The question-answer structure suggests a rational approach toward understanding

The Random House Book of Twentieth Century French Poetry, 1982.

while the terms of Éluard's argument shift and change. For instance, the sea, the exterior and interior silences, and the flood seem simultaneously to refer to reality and to act as metaphors for our complex experience of that reality. In effect, Éluard makes us question the divisions between our rational and nonrational experiences of reality, and between the reality that exists independently of our senses and the reality we know through our senses. The title helps posit these questions. We know the sea primarily through sight and sound, but how do the deaf and blind experience the sea? Isn't the sea to them different from the sea known by the sighted and hearing? When they touch it and feel its sharpness and coldness, might they think of knives? Yet, no matter who observes it, the sea is still itself; it exists apart.

The poem also suggests that we may be deaf and blind in a metaphoric sense—blinded and deafened by *a priori* knowledge, by preconceptions. Simultaneously the poem may imply a parallel, though inverse, reading: is the knowledge we carry in ourselves "purer and more silent," perhaps more "real" than the reality we experience around us?

Our experience of reading the poem imitates what it seems to be about: the multiplicity, fluidity, and ultimate mysteriousness of physical and metaphysical existence.

Since the origination of surrealism in France, poets have widely adapted its strategies, allowing them to break free of the literal and rational so as to handle experience in fresh and surprising ways. Consider this metaphorical fantasy by Susan Mitchell (b. 1944):

Blackbirds

Because it is windy, a woman
finds her clothesline bare, and without rancor
unpins the light, folding it into her basket.
The light is still wet. So she irons it.
The iron hisses and hums. It knows how to make the best of things.   5
The woman's hands smell clean. When she shakes them out,
they are voluminous, white.

All night my hands weep in gratitude
for little things. That feet are not shoes.
That blackbirds are eating the raspberries. That parsley   10
does not taste like bread.

From now on I want to live
only by grace. In other words, not to deserve things.
Without rancor, the light dives down
among the turnips. I eat it with my stew.   15

Today the woman's hands smell like roots. When she
shakes them out, they are voluminous, green.
All day they shade me
from the sun. The blackbirds have come to sit in them.
Since this morning, the wind has been enough.   20

Instead of finding nothing on the clothesline, the woman discovers the something that does remain: the sunlight that dries laundry. "Without rancor" she seems to decide to accept this light in terms of the laundry; she unpins it, folds it, feels its dampness, irons it—all literally impossible, but metaphorically her actions suggest acquiescence and the kind of truths we find in parables.

The speaker, in telling the story of the woman (who perhaps represents a version of herself), also comes to a decision: "to live / only by grace. In other words, not to deserve things." Through juxtaposition, she likens this state of grace to the light that generously does its work, "dives down / among the turnips," gives us food, without resenting that it gets nothing in return. In the final stanza Mitchell extends the metaphors to offer a picture of peaceful acceptance: the woman's hands become the sheltering shade trees, resting places for the birds.

By blurring the lines between reality and the imagination, the nonrational poem can register that edge of consciousness where the mind creates its own truth. Devils ride horses and angels draw baths. Eyebrows are wounds and hands weep. Looking at an iris, the poet sees the dark curve of the anther as tracks, as a train driving "deep into the damp heart of its stem." And he may then recall a train journey he took as a boy with his grandmother and (perhaps from a film or who knows where) the image of a boy on a French railway platform holding an iris and "waving goodbye to a grandmother"—until reality is lost in the connections the mind makes (David St. John, "Iris, " p. 243). Imagining what it must be like inside a stone, "cool and quiet / Even though a cow steps on it full weight," the poet remembers that "sparks fly out / When two stones are rubbed" and thinks that "perhaps it is not dark inside after all; / Perhaps there is a moon shining" (Charles Simic, "Stone," p. 27). Experience may seem to double and loop around on itself as when, after the disastrous fact, we try to evaluate the force of premonition (Marie Howe, "The Good Reason for Our Forgetting," p. 246). Like talking to ourselves, fantasy may express the deepest and most serious feeling; we reveal ourselves in daydreams no less than in sleeping dreams.

From the hypnotic power of magic spells and the enigmatic playfulness of nursery rhymes and experimental poems like Tate's "A Guide to the Stone Age" to the mysterious reasoning of "Blackbirds," poetry has always cast its buckets deep into the human imagination, below the strata of rationality and logic. The subliminal powers of rhythm, image, metaphor, and structure remain as ancient as language itself; the poet-shaman, the bard, is an ancient figure who still lives among us. Though we live in a world of digital clocks, slipped discs, and blackeyed peas, we still live in the woods of the fantastic and the Himalayas of dream. Poems that bare themselves to the magic of the mind help us re-see the ordinary work-a-day world we live in as the extraordinary place it is.

QUESTIONS AND SUGGESTIONS

1. Imagine that you are a blade of grass, a dandelion in a parking lot, a sewing machine, a brick in a chimney, a mountain, a basketball, or another inanimate

object that occurs to you. What might you *feel* as that thing (specific sensations like the touch of air, ground, a hand)? What have been your experiences? What might you be aware of? Write a poem in the first person, speaking as that object.

2. Try your hand at a prayer, a curse, a blessing, a chant, or a magic spell. Use concrete imagery and lively rhythms.

3. What is the speaker objecting to about the Muse in the following poem? Who are the "they" and the "black ties" in the third stanza? How do the contrasting river scenes signify the differences between the kinds of poems from which the notion of a Muse seems to originate and the kinds of poems the speaker wants to write? Compare the attitude toward the Muse in this poem with that in "La Muerte, Patron Saint of Writers" by Clarissa Pinkola Estés (p. 244).

Against the Muse

MICHELLE BOISSEAU (b. 1955)

Go down to the stream and dip your rosebud
      fingernails among the fish flickering
          like earrings in a roomful
of dancers, go down to that stream,
those neoclassical waters   5
              where the humming of houseboys
    beating laundry with willow sticks
        frames you like a really good haircut,
go down to that stream, take your gold
sandals with you and leave my rivers alone.   10

              I don't know what these slumped roofs
along the banks are,
        just the way I like it,
     so discouraged-looking at first I can't tell
if they're abandoned barns or apartment houses,   15
the yellow kitchen clock, the strip of garden
          with a view of the 5:08 and the 10:40
        that hardly come around anymore,
and the barges unbraiding the muddy water
        rattle with coal raked out of my head.   20

I'm tired of them always inviting you
        as soon as a basket appears
    without a load of apricots
or canaries. Even if they slapped you together
        with creek mud instead of blue foam   25
           and took some plastic drinking straws
           instead of reeds to blow you up,
     they'd still dress you in wafting stuff

> so all the black ties and the bartender
> out on the terrace would turn to see the wonder. 30
> A little breeze comes up and your frock
> laps about you, fine feathers
> though no bones to speak of,
> wren, sparrow,
>
> and hardly the nerve 35
> to move out of earshot, turn your back
> on the great house,
> window dazzle, banked blossoms,
> Euclidean inclinations
> and come down here where the moss 40
> can give you a good soaking and,
> if you hear them coming for you,
> fill you with its messages.

4. (*For a group*) Each person take a piece of paper and write down a noun or verb—something concrete, sensual, resonant: like "plummet" or "biscuit." Pass your word on to the next person who writes down a word that rhymes or half-rhymes with the word, for instance "plunder" with "plummet" and "fist" with "biscuit." Next, fold the paper down so only the second word shows, and pass the paper on to the next person who writes a rhyme or half-rhyme for it, folds the paper, and passes it on. Continue until every person has written on every piece of paper. Now, using the words on one of the pieces of paper, each of you write a poem. Don't try to make sense, but make it sound good. Read over your poem. Does it have anything to do with whatever else you've had on your mind? Take turns reading the poems aloud. Do they seem to make sense?

5. In this poem the speaker makes statements that seem at first to be enigmatic but turn out to have a reasonably clear symbolic meaning. Does the comparison to "the size of a very small boy" suggest an interpretation? Using this poem as a model, create a speaker for whom an activity provides the basis for rich metaphoric possibilities.

The Trapper

PETER KLAPPERT (b. 1942)

I am digging a pit
deeper than I will need.

Already
on the other side of this mountain
something is crying in a small hoarse voice. 5

It is breaking its teeth on my teeth.

Some shy animal is taking its paw
apart in the darkness.
Some poor animal is looking through its bones.

When I grab at my lungs they contract   10
like an old leather bellows.

Something the size of a very small boy
is kicking against that trap.

6. For several nights try recording your dreams. Write down as much as you
remember, paying particular attention to the imagery, but without questioning it.
Now in a sonnet or a sonnetlike poem (of roughly fourteen lines which includes a
turn somewhere past the midpoint), work the images into a poem in which you are
going about your normal life, walking through the supermarket, perhaps, or
swimming laps at the pool.

7. Study the ways these poems use details of insomnia and grief to create
"metaphors of experience." How might you account for the "you" in Judith Root's
poem conversing with insomnia? How does Etheridge Knight's use of color signal
the emotion of the poem?

Insomnia

JUDITH ROOT (b. 1944)

After years of sleeping
like a rock, you wake up
one night with an itch.
Bored with the moon's slow arc
moving light squares along the wall,   5
you trade quips with your insomnia.
How much you have in common.
You meet secretly, until you depend
on its visits, wait for it
with cognac and English ovals.   10

But it comes and goes at odd hours
with lipstick on its collar
and a hollow stare when you say
Sarah, Melissa or Sue.
Fans of mascara stain your pillow   15
and you beg sleep, your old lover,
to take you back.

Too late. Insomnia's burrowed
like hundreds of tiny organisms
under your skin. To them   20
you are the earth. They divide
into tribes and roam your body

searching for the right spot
to settle down. The itch means
they've just discovered fire.   25

A Poem of Attrition

ETHERIDGE KNIGHT (1931–1991)

I do not know if the color of the day
Was blue, pink, green, or August red.
I only know it was summer, a Thursday,
And the trestle above our heads
Sliced the sun into black and gold bars   5
That fell across our shiny backs
And shimmered like flat snakes on the water,
Worried by the swans, shrieks, jackknives,
And timid gainers—made bolder
As the day grew older.   10
Then Pooky Dee, naked chieftain, poised,
Feet gripping the black ribs of wood,
Knees bent, butt out, long arms
Looping the air, challenged
The great "two 'n' a half" gainer . . .   15
I have forgotten the sound of his capped
Skull as it struck the block . . .
The plop of a book dropped? The tear of a sheer blouse?
I do not know if the color of the day
Was blue, pink, green, or August red.   20
I only know the blood slithered, and
Our silence rolled like oil
Across the wide green water.

8. Write a wild nonsense poem. Coin a few words, and see if a reader can guess
what they mean.

POEMS TO CONSIDER

 ## from *A Midsummer-Night's Dream (V, i)*   *1600*

WILLIAM SHAKESPEARE (1564–1616)

Lovers and madmen have such seething brains,
Such shaping fantasies, that apprehend
More than cool reason ever comprehends.

The lunatic, the lover, and the poet
Are of imagination all compact.   5
One sees more devils than vast hell can hold;
That is, the madman. The lover, all as frantic,
Sees Helen's beauty in a brow of Egypt.
The poet's eye, in a fine frenzy rolling,
Doth glance from heaven to earth, from earth to heaven;   10
And as imagination bodies forth
The forms of things unknown, the poet's pen
Turns them to shapes and gives to airy nothing
A local habitation and a name.
Such tricks hath strong imagination,   15
That, if it would but apprehend some joy,
It comprehends some bringer of that joy;
Or in the night, imagining some fear,
How easy is a bush supposed a bear!

 Song of the Stars   *transcribed 1902*

ANONYMOUS, Passamaquoddy

We are the stars which sing.
We sing with our light.
We are the birds of fire.
We fly across the heaven,
Our light is a star.   5
We make a road for Spirits,
A road for the Great Spirit.
Among us are three hunters
Who chase a bear:
There never was a time   10
When they were not hunting;
We look down on the mountains.
This is the Song of the Mountains.

 The Earthquake   *transcribed 1873*

ANONYMOUS, Paiute

In that land, in that land,
    In that glittering land;
Far away, far away,
    The mountain was shaken with pain.

Iris

1976

DAVID ST. JOHN (b. 1949)

There is a train inside this iris:

You think I'm crazy, & like to say boyish
& outrageous things. No, there is

A train inside this iris.

It's a child's finger bearded in black banners.   5
A single window like a child's nail,

A darkened porthole lit by the white, angular face

Of an old woman, or perhaps the boy beside her in the stuffy,
Hot compartment. Her hair is silver, & sweeps

Back off her forehead, onto her cold & bruised shoulders.   10

The prairies fail along Chicago. Past the five
Lakes. Into the black woods of her New York; & as I bend

Close above the iris, I see the train

Drive deep into the damp heart of its stem, & the gravel
Of the garden path   15

Cracks under my feet as I walk this long corridor

Of elms, arched
Like the ceiling of a French railway pier where a boy

With pale curls holding

A fresh iris is waving goodbye to a grandmother, gazing   20
A long time

Into the flower, as if he were looking some great

Distance, or down an empty garden path & he believes a man
Is walking toward him, working

Dull shears in one hand; & now believe me: The train   25

Is gone. The old woman is dead, & the boy. The iris curls,
On its stalk, in the shade

Of those elms: Where something like the icy & bitter fragrance

In the wake of a woman who's just swept past you on her way
Home   30

& you remain.

 La Muerte, Patron Saint of Writers   1993

CLARISSA PINKOLA ESTÉS

Here buses rattle like buckets
of bolts; brake drums made stronger
by prayers to Santiago. The paint of these buses
regalo blue, cielo red, tierra y sanguine.
Up front Old Virgin Mother rides lookout,   5
and it is the law: all bus tires must be square,
all drivers must be certifiably blind,
all riders must have springs in their necks
and their ass cheeks.
The men wear their hats extra jammed on.   10
The women tie the live chickens together loosely
on purpose, just to make trouble. And the old
toothless one sags next to me. She has always
just eaten a tub of garlic, she has always just rubbed
her armpits and genitals with vinegar and goat cheese.   15
She is always leaning toward me, never away.
And I am always her seat mate, or that of her older sister
or her aged father. Always I am sitting thigh to thigh
with La Muerte. Now this La Muerte, this old one, laughs
maniacally at absolutely nothing, and over and over,   20
and always right in my face. Her breath fogs my vision, wilts
my hat brim, makes my nose cry. I work hard to stay by her,
to love her, love her cackle, love her odor, to love the pain
that I feel. If I can love her, if I can stand this pain,
of being near what others flee,   25
I will be able to write tonight,
and maybe for as long as a month.

Ah La Muerte, patron of las chupatintas, the pen-pushers,
you who only travel by bursting bus or teeming train or
broken car or bombed-out lorry, you who run   30

all over my page, screeching, "Catch me if you can,"
you who hide between the lines as though they are hedges,
peering over like some old baby in a macabre peek-a-boo.
Ah La Muerte, my love, my lover, pray for us, your writer children.
Give us all those acrid, sour, dour, and sickeningly sweet   35
smirks and smells, exactly the ones we need to write right.
Please, I beg you in all my authorial insanity, sit beside us
now and forever, fertilize our writing for ever and always
with the holy compost of your smiles.

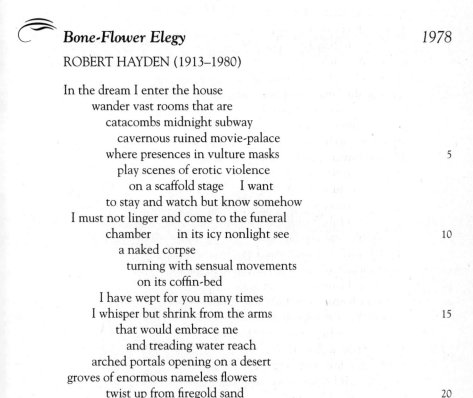

Bone-Flower Elegy   *1978*

ROBERT HAYDEN (1913–1980)

In the dream I enter the house
    wander vast rooms that are
      catacombs midnight subway
        cavernous ruined movie-palace
      where presences in vulture masks   5
        play scenes of erotic violence
          on a scaffold stage   I want
to stay and watch but know somehow
I must not linger and come to the funeral
    chamber   in its icy nonlight see   10
      a naked corpse
        turning with sensual movements
        on its coffin-bed
    I have wept for you many times
    I whisper but shrink from the arms   15
      that would embrace me
      and treading water reach
    arched portals opening on a desert
groves of enormous nameless flowers
      twist up from firegold sand   20
    skull flowers flowers of sawtooth bone
      their leaves and petals interlock
        caging me for you beastangel
        raging toward me
      angelbeast shining come   25
        to rend me and redeem

The Good Reason for Our Forgetting   1988

MARIE HOWE (b. 1950)

Who would have the day back you saw coming in dreams
long before the actual stood like a flower

gone bad in the jar? The dreamed drunken driving,
steering from the back seat, or the garden of mazes

and he forever turning as you felt your way along   5
the broken bushes. Even the street of barking dogs

you finally walked through, empty-handed, pointed
to one thing. Who would have it back?

After the fact, you throw the stinking water out,
scrub the sink and turn into the new life   10

as if dreaming, knowing it is no dream, knowing
better. Although, some nights, you smelled it,

didn't you? A certain dissembling deep in his eyes
you could never reach, not with love

not with fearfulness. You smelled, you were almost   15
sure of it, something like flowers,

the beast too long neglected. But that was before,
and long before you heard the story of the boy

and his father, how left alone for three days
they played cowboys, and how the father fell   20

on the first day, fell down and stayed there, playing
dead, the boy thought, and how he tried

to lift his father's head, tried to feed him
to make him stop, feed him breakfast, and how

he didn't stop, not for one minute, not once.   25
Who would have the day back when it happened to him?

Or the day before the day when he imagined himself
a boy, and deservedly happy?

Like the night, when the light from your lamp fell
on your face with what seemed an affectionate look.   30

Famous   *1982*

NAOMI SHIHAB NYE (b. 1952)

The river is famous to the fish.

The loud voice is famous to silence,
which knew it would inherit the earth
before anybody said so.

The cat sleeping on the fence is famous to the birds   5
watching him from the birdhouse.

The tear is famous, briefly, to the cheek.

The idea you carry close to your bosom
is famous to your bosom.

The boot is famous to the earth,   10
more famous than the dress shoe,
which is famous only to floors.

The bent photograph is famous to the one who carries it
and not at all famous to the one who is pictured.

I want to be famous to shuffling men   15
who smile while crossing streets,
sticky children in grocery lines,
famous as the one who smiled back.

I want to be famous in the way a pulley is famous,
or a buttonhole, not because it did anything spectacular,   20
but because it never forgot what it could do.

PROCESS
Making the Poem Happen

9

FINDING THE POEM
Headwaters

How do you start a poem? Where does it come from? Like the confluence of streams into the headwaters of a river, many sources come together to create a poem. Often these sources are hidden, subterranean, difficult to trace. Step into a river and try to name where the water washing against your knees originated. Clearly, the impulses of both form and content come together to begin a poem and create a common momentum. Writing a poem requires finding something to say, and also finding a way to say it.

Many beginning poets start a poem out of a burning desire to say something in particular, to express some emotion or idea, to write about hot love's sudden coolness or the numbing dreariness of winter rain or the disappearance of the ozone layer. The urge to write *about* something often gives the poet the first impulse. But poetry isn't primarily "about" something. If it were, a mere prose summary could fire us up as much as the poem. Though some subjects may seem worthier of a poem than others, it's not so much the *subject* that makes a poem a poem; it's the way the poet uses *language* and *form* to express the subject. Yes, it feels great to get off our chests what we truly care about. But to make someone else care, a poem has to move others through language. We might, for instance, get people to nod in agreement by declaring that people who sleep together without love are essentially cold. That won't surprise an audience, however, as Sharon Olds (b. 1942) does:

Sex Without Love

How do they do it, the ones who make love
without love? Beautiful as dancers,
gliding over each other like ice-skaters

over the ice, fingers hooked
inside each other's bodies, faces   5
red as steak, wine, wet as the
children at birth whose mothers are going to
give them away. How do they come to the
come to the come to the   God come to the
still waters, and not love   10
the one who came there with them, light
rising slowly as steam off their joined
skin? These are the true religious,
the purists, the pros, the ones who will not
accept a false Messiah, love the   15
priest instead of the God. They do not
mistake the lover for their own pleasure,
they are like great runners: they know they are alone
with the road surface, the cold, the wind,
the fit of their shoes, their over-all cardio-   20
vascular health—just factors, like the partner
in the bed, and not the truth, which is the
single body alone in the universe
against its own best time.

Olds weaves together positive and negative imagery to disturb and arrest us. The lovers are "beautiful as dancers," but they *hook* their fingers in each other. Their faces are the color of meat, or wine, *and* wet as the faces of babies—not babies who will be loved, but babies who will be *given away*, as one gives away old clothes or sundry household junk. We all respect the cool dedication of an athlete in training, but a *lover* in training? The positive and negative imagery reflects the poem's mixture of admiration and aversion, a sense of wonder and an ironic sense of wondering why. Olds begins with a question rich in suggestion, "How do they do it?": What is the way they do it? How can they tolerate doing it? How is it they don't need love like the rest of us? Isn't it lonely? Her second question, which begins on line 8 with "How can they come to the," registers a hesitation, a struggle to find the right words to complete the phrase, while at the same time suggesting, through its rhythm and its repetition, sexual excitement. The poem tries out answers to these questions, not easy ones, and probably not the first that Olds thought of as she worked on the poem.

By leaving herself open to many possible answers, she allows the poem to argue with itself; the poem suggests the processes a thoughtful person goes through to understand a problem: Is this the reason? What about that possibility? No, I'm forgetting *this*. Yeats wrote, "We make out of the quarrel with others, rhetoric, but of the quarrel with ourselves, poetry." In making speeches or debating others, we take one position and stick with it. When writing poems, however, we hold the many sides of a question, turning them over in our minds. We're not sure where our ruminations will lead us. As poets, Yeats said, we "sing amid our uncertainty."

Just as the painter works in paint or the sculptor in marble (lucky us, we don't have to shell out all our cash at the art supply store), the poet works with words, shaping them into a whole.

So while the first impulse toward a poem may be to write *about* something important to you, the writing of the poem starts with language, with feeling your way into the poem word by word, groping for the right sentence, and then the next—step by step, wading into the stream. But how do we get into language to begin a poem?

IMITATION, MENTORS, MODELS, AND SO FORTH

The best advice to a beginning poet is unquestionably: READ. No matter how much you've read, you probably haven't read enough. Often, most of the poems beginning poets have read are the tame ones that passed muster with school boards, or the jingles of greeting cards, or the lyrics of pop music—mostly thin stuff without the driving rhythms of drums, guitars, and keyboards. But poetry isn't predictable or easy. Poetry is what disturbs, what disturbs through language. Not necessarily a wild disturbance; it may be like a wind that comes up over a pond and sends ripples into the cattails.

Part of your work as a poet is to know how other poets have used language, and reading their works shows you new ways to use it. Nothing that anyone knows or can tell you about poetry will be as useful as what you discover, first-hand, for yourself. We want to write a poem in the first place because we have read a poem that captivates us. The poem we write will inevitably be (or at least try to be) like that poem. What else can it be? The poet's notions of what poetry is, or what poems can do, come from the poems she or he knows and admires. The more you know, the more you'll feel poetry's sources and potential. There is, after all, no disgrace in having learned something from somebody. Why reinvent the wheel? The undisguised confidence of "I can do that" is the seed from which poets and poems sprout and grow.

Get under your skin poems of all kinds, old and new, fashionable and unfashionable. Read Shakespeare, Keats, and Dickinson. Read poems published this week. As a poet writing at the end of the twentieth century, be intimate with the voices of poets in your own generation and the generations just before yours. Living poets, poets experiencing the same world you do—with its interstates, yellow bell peppers, tattoos, and nuclear plants—are just as essential as poets in the literary canon. Don't read *just* what everyone else is reading. Search out poems of other ages and cultures too. Try the hidden corners and odd nooks. Browse. Sniff out.

What you are looking for are the poems—the poets—that really speak to you, the poems and poets that, as Emily Dickinson said, make you feel physically as if the top of your head were taken off. Find one poet you love, find another. Look their books up in the library, the bookstore, in *Books in Print*. Take your lunch money to buy their books. *Memorize* their poems, learn them *by heart*—with all the phrase's connotations. Make them part of your inner being, and you will gain what Robert Pinsky calls the "pleasure of possession—possession of and possession by"— another poet's words. These poems will be your models, after which you'll fashion your own poems. All poets' secrets are hidden in the open, in the poems, and it isn't necessary to clean her brushes or tune his strings to apprentice yourself to the best poets writing.

"Imitation, conscious imitation," advises Theodore Roethke, "is one of the great methods, perhaps *the* method of learning to write." Rather than being a problem, **imitation** is the inescapable route toward becoming a poet. College basketball players study the reverse lay-ups of the pros. Medical residents stand at the elbows of surgeons making their rounds. Architecture students crane their necks to take in the cornices and I-beams of the buildings around them. Apprentice poets read. As a student, you may write Dickinson poems, Yeats poems, Frost poems, Bishop poems, any number of other poets' poems. Every role you like, you will try out, not always consciously. As you discover and absorb admiration after admiration, the influences begin to neutralize each other and naturally disappear. The poems you write will begin to be in your own voice, not in Ginsberg's or Plath's or Wilbur's. Don't worry about finding your own voice. Like puberty, it will just happen. The greater danger is not in being too much influenced but in being too little influenced—fixing early or fanatically on a single mentor and clinging to that one voice, or finding the whole truth in one theory or another. Beware especially of theories: it is *poems* you want.

Sometimes a new poem springs from a particular poem by another poet as, here, Donald Justice (b. 1925) takes off from "Piedra Negra sobre una Piedra Blanca" by the Peruvian poet César Vallejo (1892–1938).

Variations on a Text by Vallejo

Me moriré en Paris con aguacero . . .

I will die in Miami in the sun,
On a day when the sun is very bright,
A day like the days I remember, a day like other days,
A day that nobody knows or remembers yet,
And the sun will be bright then on the dark glasses of strangers   5
And in the eyes of a few friends from my childhood
And of the surviving cousins by the graveside,
While the diggers, standing apart, in the still shade of the palms,
Rest on their shovels, and smoke,
Speaking in Spanish softly, out of respect.   10

I think it will be on a Sunday like today,
Except that the sun will be out, the rain will have stopped,
And the wind that today made all the little shrubs kneel down;
And I think it will be a Sunday because today,
When I took out this paper and began to write,   15
Never before had anything looked so blank,
My life, these words, the paper, the gray Sunday;
And my dog, quivering under a table because of the storm,
Looked up at me, not understanding,
And my son read on without speaking, and my wife slept.   20

Donald Justice is dead. One Sunday the sun came out,
It shone on the bay, it shone on the white buildings,
The cars moved down the street slowly as always, so many,

Some with their headlights on in spite of the sun,
And after a while the diggers with their shovels   25
Walked back to the graveside through the sunlight,
And one of them put his blade into the earth
To lift a few clods of dirt, the black marl of Miami,
And scattered the dirt, and spat,
Turning away abruptly, out of respect.   30

If imitation is the sincerest praise, Justice pays his deepest respects to his inspiration. Not only does he play variations on Vallejo's composition—repeating phrases, syntax, images, and words—but the grave diggers, who wait for the funeral party to be on its way, speak the tongue of the Peruvian poet. It's as if Vallejo's spirit presided over the creation of the poem. Justice's variations, his use of repetitions, give the poem the tone of an incantation—apropos for someone imagining his own, albeit sun-drenched, funeral.

You might want to glance at Vallejo's poem (p. 274.) and compare it to Justice's. You don't need much Spanish to see how the poems are related. Vallejo's is a spare sonnet-length poem of two four-line and two three-line stanzas. Justice's is longer, richer in detail—three ten-line stanzas. Justice and Vallejo may not have written their poems all on a stormy day (or in Justice's case with his dog quivering under his feet), but it sounds as though they both came to a revelation about the day they would die after looking at a blank page. Both poems begin with the future tense and shift to the past tense about two-thirds into the poems, after the phrases, "César Vallejo ha muerto" and "Donald Justice is dead." Both poems repeat phrases that include the anticipated death day ("jueves" means "Thursday,") and the words *day* and *today* ("día" and "hoy").

Justice takes his epigraph from Vallejo's first line, which can be translated, "I will die in Paris in a downpour," then adapts it to open with a similar declaration, but one that fits his own experience: "I will die in Miami in the sun, . . . A day like the days I remember." Justice grew up in Miami where most days are "sun-days." He imagines his death will be a returning home to where the sun shines "on the bay" and "on the white buildings" whereas Vallejo imagines his death will be far from his native land; he will die a stranger. These differences account in part for the contrast in tone. Vallejo speaks of isolation and desolation. (In fact, he did die in Paris on a rainy day.) Justice, however, seems reconciled to his fate, contented enough that he can linger with the diggers and the dirt, "the black marl," his home ground.

Because reading other poets is such a powerful source of poems, many poets begin writing sessions by reading for an hour or so, or until some line, some image, some rhythm launches them into the mood of a poem's beginning. "Variations on a Text by Vallejo" illustrates how many streams flow together in a poem—one's imagination, intuition, ear for language, technical mastery, and knowledge of other poems.

We should make a distinction between imitations like Justice's "Variations" and parody. Strictly, **parody** is a deliberate, exaggerated imitation of another work or style. More loosely, parody is a form of criticism that exposes weaknesses in the original; as Anthony Hecht's "The Dover Bitch" skewers Matthew Arnold's "Dover Beach" (p. 275) or, more lightly, this takeoff by James Camp (b. 1923):

After the Philharmonic

Two paths diverged in a well-known park,
One well-lit, the other—dark
And since I did not wish to die,
I took the one more travelled by.

Writing a serious parody or an admiring imitation, following mannerisms of style (like Whitman's catalogues or Dickinson's breathless dashes) or of subject matter (like Frost's country matters), can let you explore another poet's technique or style. What, after all, makes Dickinson sound like Dickinson, or Frost sound like Frost? What makes an Elizabeth Bishop poem a Bishop poem?

Be careful of self-parody, the impulse when writing a poem to mock it, turn it against itself. Under the stress of trying to get your poem right, you may subconsciously feel tempted to deflate it, make it into a joke, annul your commitment to it. Be aware of this impulse; ask yourself what issues in the poem are making you uncomfortable and confront them in the poem.

SOURCES, CURRENTS

You may begin with a firm sense of what you want to write about, where you want to go with your poem, but don't hold too tightly to these notions. Stay open to fresh possibilities; allow your first impulses to shift and meander with new impulses. The poet Maxine Kumin says, "You write a poem to discover what you're thinking, feeling, where the truth is. You don't begin by saying, now this is the truth" and then start writing about it. Often your first impulses aren't the richest. They're merely the first. If you stick stubbornly to them, you may miss hidden springs or the discovery of a more tantalizing direction. For instance, maybe you first thought of writing about falling out of a treehouse when you were ten. Don't let the treehouse keep you from bringing in the smell of honeysuckle or your aunt's red Mustang convertible which you bled all over on the way to the emergency room. Perhaps you suddenly remember that your aunt pinched packages of saltines from restaurants to pass out to panhandlers in lieu of quarters. Perhaps your aunt didn't have a convertible, but when you started writing it suddenly seemed as if she *should have* one in the poem. Maybe it was really your sister who fell out of the tree.

Keeping yourself open to sources means also keeping your imagination open. We'll risk the obvious and say Justice doesn't *know* he'll die in Miami. He's not a clairvoyant, and Vallejo probably wasn't either. And unlike the reporter whose first loyalty is to the facts—accurately recording the details of an event—the poet's first loyalty is toward making the richest possible poem. Just because something happened a particular way in life doesn't mean it should happen that way in a poem. If your poem ultimately ends up celebrating the prosaic saltine cracker in crisp little rhymes, so be it. If falling from the treehouse keeps nudging you, you can bring it into another poem.

The power of this poem by Yusef Komunyakaa (b. 1947) may stem from the vitality of its sources, its openness toward many, even contradictory, ones:

Sunday Afternoons

They'd latch the screendoors
& pull venetian blinds,
Telling us not to leave the yard.
But we always got lost
Among mayhaw & crabapple.   5

Juice spilled from our mouths,
& soon we were drunk & brave
As birds diving through saw vines.
Each nest held three or four
Speckled eggs, blue as rage.   10

Where did we learn to be unkind,
There in the power of holding each egg
While watching dogs in June
Dust & heat, or when we followed
The hawk's slow, deliberate arc?   15

In the yard, we heard cries
Fused with gospel on the radio,
Loud as shattered glass
In a Saturday-night argument
About trust & money.   20

We were born between Oh Yeah
& Goddammit. I knew life
Began where I stood in the dark,
Looking out into the light,
& that sometimes I could see   25

Everything through nothing.
The backyard trees breathed
Like a man running from himself
As my brothers backed away
From the screendoor. I knew   30

If I held my right hand above my eyes
Like a gambler's visor, I could see
How their bedroom door halved
The dresser mirror like a moon
Held prisoner in the house.

Inexperienced, impressionable, time heavy on their hands, the boys can't sort out their emotions about their parents. They're shut out of the house and shut in the yard, stuck in the middle, between the intimate world inside the house and the dangerous world beyond the yard. They are powerless to enter either, though what holds them is flimsy—only a latched screen door and an admonishment to stay in the yard. And who has locked them out? Komunyakaa intensifies the power the parents hold over the children by identifying them only as "they": the others, the adults, the enemy.

Perhaps every detail here did not occur in Komunyakaa's childhood precisely as the poem lays it out. That's hardly the point. The details help to evoke the boys' pain and confusion. The image of the blue robin's eggs may have flowed into the poem from another day, another experience, and seemed relevant after he came up with the lines "We were born between O Yeah / & Goddammit"; the vandalism of the bird nests implies the boys' anger and confusion over their parents' vacillating fights and intimacy. Perhaps the mayhaw sprang into the poem not because Komunyakaa particularly remembered hiding in it on Sundays, but because "mayhaw" echoed "hawk" and "saw vines," or because unconsciously *mayhaw* recalled a phrase not even in the poem, "Mother, may I?" By linking robin's egg blue, normally a gentle color, with rage and connecting loud gospel music with shattered glass, Komunyakaa suggests violence submerged within the scene, the parents' violence and the boys', the violence of sex and the violence of anger.

In the early stages of a poem you naturally won't tap into all its potential sources, especially those hidden beneath the surface. The important thing is to cultivate a fluidity of vision, to remain receptive to everything. Let impressions, ideas, metaphors, half-forgotten memories, the rhythms of a well-loved poem flood into your poem to enrich your first notions and to surprise you—and your reader. As Frost put it, no surprise for the poet, no surprise for the reader.

Like Olds, Komunyakaa asks questions: "Where did we learn to be unkind?" Did they learn it there in the yard, "in the power of holding each egg"? By watching the hawk hunting? Or from their parents? By layering imagery of concealment, prey, and capture Komunyakaa shows the boys grappling with one of the great mysteries of childhood: adult sexuality. These images are oblique, implicit rather than explicit. We're not told exactly what the brothers see reflected in the mirror that makes them back away from the door. The speaker leaves the possibilities open and arrives at a surprising conclusion. He says he knew if he looked inside he'd see how "their bedroom door halved / the dresser mirror like a moon / held prisoner in the house." The moon itself has been captured. The speaker projects his feelings of imprisonment onto a normally innocuous mirror. It's as if the boys don't want to see, or can't see, what is really there. They're blinded by anger and confusion and innocence.

When something you hadn't been expecting enters your poem, allow it its full register. Allow it to grow and deepen. Don't be quick to judge it. The analytical, judging part of your thinking is essential to making poems, but don't turn it on too early, lest it dry up your sources. The analytical mind breaks things down into parts. At this stage you want to pull things together. Your analytical brain has the habit of saying, "No, that won't work. That doesn't make sense." You want to turn on the part of your brain that says, "Why not try it?" You want to synthesize, not analyze.

GETTING INTO WORDS

Besides reading other poets, many poets charge their engines by writing randomly at the beginning of a writing session. In a notebook (or at a typewriter or VDT) they set down whatever is swimming in their heads: phrases, rhymes, images, lists, weird words. Random writing is a writer's practice work, just as the NBA player shoots in the gym, or the pianist plays scales, or the painter sketches. In the free-play of the notebook, experiment with sentence rhythms, explore metaphors, rec-ollect scenes for future poems, try out new voices. Such random writing has a way of leading you into more, and then more possibilities. Tracing out a particular image can lead the way into a host of details you had forgotten which in turn lead into a new direction, to a fresh metaphor, perhaps, that surprises you with its inci-siveness. Drawing a connection between two or more unrelated passages in your notebook might give you the seed of a poem. For instance, in one place you've described a rugged hiking trail in Arizona, in another your grandfather's slow recovery from a stroke. How might the image of the trail inform the process of recovery? How might your grandfather's dry fingers be likened to that landscape?

Once you've begun to tap into the sources of poems, writing down what sur-faces helps channel those vague earliest musings into words. No matter how vivid a memory you have of honeysuckle crowding a creek bed, it remains locked away from a reader until you deliver it into language. You have to use words to make a reader smell the honeysuckle or hear the cellophane crinkle on a package of crackers.

Daily writing in a notebook can keep you in practice, get you in the habit of thinking in words, and let you keep track of the streams that feed your work. Your notebook can be your resource collection where during busy times you can stash your ruminations until you have time to take a look at them. Then later, you'll have something to begin with instead of having that oppressive blank page staring back at you.

If you're hooked on a word processor and can't fathom going back to pen and paper, regularly print out hard copies of your jottings to ensure you won't lose them. Be generous. If you only print out what you deem worthy, you're letting your analytical mind have too much say too early. For the earliest, sloppiest stages of writing, the notebook has many advantages: it's portable, quiet, always accessible, and no problem during a thunderstorm. Also, unlike the computer that obliterates deletions, the notebook allows you to reconstruct what you've crossed out. A note-book also keeps your writing together. When your notes are scattered under your bed and on your dashboard, you'll have a hard time bringing them together to start a poem.

In his book on poetry and writing, *The Triggering Town*, the poet Richard Hugo is probably speaking tongue-in-cheek when he advises student poets to use number

2 pencils, to cross out instead of erase, and to "write in a hard-covered notebook with green lined pages. Green is easy on the eyes. . . . The best notebooks I've found are National 48–581." That's what worked for him, and every poet will find a particular system that feels right and swear by it—notebook, computer, index cards with a felt-tip pen. The beginning poet will want to experiment drafting poems with typewriter and pencil, with different colors of ink, with script or printing, lined and unlined pages, single sheets, tablets, and notebooks. Such things may not be important, or they may. Poets have written with a nursing baby cradled in one arm, by flashlight on an army footlocker after lights-out, and under worse conditions. But the poet is entitled to prefer working wherever it feels right—at a desk or (like Frost) with a lapboard in an easy chair. We know one young poet who feels best writing in the bustling anonymity of airport terminals.

Whatever system you develop, when it no longer works, try something else. Write a lot and write often, whether you feel inspired or not. A carpenter who picks up a hammer every day will strike the nails truer than someone who picks up a hammer once a year. Better to write for an hour a day than write only when the feeling grabs you. The feeling may never grab you or, more likely, once you've got off your chest whatever sparked the desire to write, you'll have little interest in going back to what you wrote, crafting it, making it into a finished poem. Poets who don't revise are as rare as batters who hit every pitch.

The requirements of writing and rewriting and rewriting are rigorous. It's only human nature to avoid the painful and difficult, so set up a work schedule and stick with it. Writing at about the same time of day can give you a psychological edge— when you sit down at your scheduled time, your mind will get used to tuning in to the sources of your poems. Also, be protective of your writing schedule. Unplug the phone, draw the curtains, wake up before anyone else or stay up when they've turned in. Discipline may not be a substitute for talent (however one defines that), but talent will disappear without it.

Almost every writer goes through dry spells. Even the most disciplined come to a point where the streams look dry, the wells seem empty, and the blank page stares back. This can be particularly frustrating when you have a poem due Monday and don't have a clue where to begin. It sometimes helps to push yourself away from your desk for awhile; get away for a time, and you may find a new way to get started. Go for a drive, wander around a museum, get a haircut, page through a book of photographs. If that doesn't help, try looking through this text's Questions and Suggestions for a possibility, or if all else fails, maybe just set out to write a lousy poem. Make it as deliberately bad and awful as you can. Really work at that. Revise, expand, make it worse. At least you'll have fun, and maybe end up with something more appealing than you thought you would.

CHANNELING THE SOURCES

Whatever the sources, wherever it originates, the poem begins with a *given* in which the poet is aware of the possibility of a poem. Like the speck of dust that water molecules cling to in order to form a rain droplet, a poem needs a given, a speck around which impulses, words, memories can cohere. Sometimes the seed can be another poem—as with "Variations on a Text by Vallejo." At other times the poem begins with a controlling metaphor. Perhaps the seed of Olds's "Sex Without Love" was her drawing of that odd connection between ice-skating and lovemaking.

Often the seed is not much more than an idea coupled with an image or a line. The poem "Black Mulberry," by Michelle Boisseau, started when the poet jotted this in a notebook when she was eight months pregnant:

> Rel. betw. pregnant woman & child
>   Pyramus and Thisbe
>   the wall is the body, the self
>   the swollen mound, the wall they touch each other through

She was thinking about the myth of Pyramus and Thisbe: a young couple who live in adjoining houses, fall in love, and secretly whisper through the wall to each other. One night they arrange to meet each other face to face. When Pyramus arrives at the meeting place in the countryside, he finds a lion with Thisbe's scarf. Assuming she has been killed, he kills himself. When Thisbe, who had been hiding from the lion, returns and finds Pyramus dead, she too commits suicide.

After making the note about the lovers and the wall, the poet put the idea aside until, one night after the baby was born, she was paging through a reference book, trying to get back to sleep, when she was struck by an entry that described a myth of the mulberry tree: its red berries come from the spilled blood of the lovers. She wrote down in her notebook:

> Pyramus & Thisbe story—gave the
>   deep red color to mulberries
> Lived in Babylon
> Story in Ovid

For months she fiddled around trying to work this material into a poem, but it kept feeling flat and clunky. She was getting tangled up in so many details (like the blood spilled during the c-section) that she was missing richer possibilities. The actual events kept getting in the way.

Finally, sometime later (after the baby's first birthday), the poet saw on the evening news a report on water use in the desert states: the popularity of manicured lawns and mulberry trees that require gallons and gallons to flourish. Something sparked. Here's how the poem eventually turned out:

Black Mulberry

> Spindly sucker of the soil, lifting
> a whole pond into its crown, the mulberry
> stains the fence's whitewash
> luscious and pelts us with fine purple
> tones, notes not yet bundled into music.   5

I hold my daughter on my hip and nod
a branch down to us. A pluck
and it arcs away, more notes bouncing
off our heads. Berry in my fingers,
over her lips just to watch her squint   10
and pucker. I like to believe
experience can come this way, hand
to mouth and a minute explosion
follows on the tongue, like a word.
This is leaf and this and this,   15
and this transparency, stuff
you can touch but hardly grasp, is water,
on the windows, muttering into the bathtub,
far down in the yellow plastic cup.
Cinnamon, cloves, tarragon, pepper   20
I lift from the shelf for her to sniff:
What is it? What do you want from me?
All those months we answered each other
like those two who loved separated by a wall,
with her on that side knocking,   25
and me knocking back on this,
and the wall itself. I'd ease myself
behind the steering wheel, slide
in a cassette and drive hours through the hills
with Puccini pouring over us—   30
O dolci baci e languide carezze—
just to feel her tumbling inside me
like hunger, feel her brute music
inside the music, humming
back to me through the blood.   35
Pyramus, Thisbe, and the mulberry,
the old story of blood and natural sympathy.
The white berries went dark
in an instant, for the dead lovers
had soaked the earth through—   40
as if the recompense for sorrow
echoed in the trees, a narcissus
beside a puddle, a bracelet of stars,
fall and winter shriveled by a mother's loss.
It's the way I fool myself. Even when   45
we were close as rain and root,
and I could feel her head pressing
against the sky, it wasn't me she answered
so much as a farther rumbling,
some necessity already out of my hands.   50

Sometimes new poets believe you need everything figured out before you start writing. But writing the poem is often the only way to figure it out. Eudora Welty advises writers not to write about what they know, but to write about *what they don't know* about what they know. By burrowing into the initial sources of "Black Mulberry," asking where its metaphors led, digging after the subterranean meanings, the poet ended up finding more dimensions to the subject than Pyramus and Thisbe and thirsty mulberries. The imagery of music entered the poem, to balance the sadness associated with the myth and to link together images not normally associated with each other; the bond of music suggested other bonds between mother and daughter. Eating mulberries, learning words, smelling spices—some images invented, some not—led the poet to the notion that a parent's desire to guide a child's experience stems from the human impulse to make myths. Through them we explain the world to ourselves and give ourselves comfort for what we can't control.

KEEPING A POEM GOING

When the poem is coming, when the wind is in the sail, go with it. "And the secret of it all," Whitman noted, "is to write in the gush, the throb, the flood, of the moment—to put things down without deliberation—without worrying about their style." Writing the first draft all in one sitting, filling up the page, or pages, from top to bottom, pushing onward when you feel the growing poem resistant, can give a poem coherence and clarity, for you are writing under the influence of a single mood, following the notions of a particular time. Getting a whole first draft early, even if sketchy and sloppy and wordy, will give you something seemingly complete to work on and puzzle over.

Sometimes, however, the inspiration slackens and your poem drifts in the doldrums. Then you must turn to craft to keep the poem going. Being lucky is often knowing how to be lucky, how to coax more and then more of the poem out of the shadows. It is often like the skills of fishing, knowing where to look for a fish, how to play it, when to reel in, when to give slack, and when to jerk the line, set the hook, and finally bring the fish onto the boat.

Once you have what feels like it might be the *given* of a poem, a number of strategies can help you encourage its growth. One is simply to be very delicate about the moment you commit a line to paper. Poems often begin in the head and continue to develop there in the relatively free-floating mixture of thought, memory, and emotion. Putting something down on paper tends to fix it; and in the earliest stages of a poem, the shoots of the poem may be too tender for transplanting. Words that feel full and grand in the mind may look spindly and naked on the page. All that blankness can be intimidating, swallowing up the handful of words that try to break the silence. Some poets compose scores of lines in their heads before taking up the pen. Others need to get words down early, when a sentence, or line or just a phrase seems strong enough to withstand the scrutiny of the page.

Also, mull the idea for the poem over in your mind or mutter aloud the words or phrases you have. Go for a drive or a walk—something to keep your body busy and leave your mind free to wander. The trancelike states of listening to music and of drifting off to sleep can also be conducive to working through the poem. It's not bad advice to take the poem to bed, and keep a notebook handy.

Talking to oneself, *literally*, may also help a poem along. We usually talk to ourselves when we are upset. Worried by some complex choice or problem—like whether to move to a distant city—the talking takes the form of "If I do this, then .... But ... Or ... Then ..." Such brainstorming evaluates and projects uncertainties. Often, more significantly, talking to oneself is highly charged. Upset by an injustice, rejection, or unexpected flout—by an infuriating parent or bureaucrat, an unfaithful friend or lover—we go off by ourselves, talking *to* that person, making up a speech we might have made or still might make, if we ran into that person, a circumstance we also imagine. Angry and hurt, we rehearse the speech over and over until we get just the sharp, cutting "logic" that our frustration calls for. The fantasy speech usually doesn't get said, of course. What we end up with is a kind of resolution; we've defined, focused, and refocused the situation and our (just) response to satisfy ourselves. Similarly, as your poem develops, talk through your alternatives; verbalize; try out possible approaches to your "speech." In the early stages you don't know where your poem will end (unlike, say, the writer of an editorial); by literally talking through your options, testing and probing your choices, you can focus them toward a solution.

Early or later, at some stage in the process, seeing the words on the page becomes an important way to prompt fresh ideas and directions. The appearance of a poem on a page is part of its total effect. Early enough for a poem not to have jelled too much, type it up or print it out on a word processor. Since we read poems in print, seeing a young poem on the page can help you see clearly how it *looks*. Lines will be longer or shorter than you imagined, for instance, and the poem skinnier or chunkier or more graceful.

Sometimes while coaxing out the poem, considering its form, even if tentative, provisional, can help. The very first line you write (which need not survive into a final version) may *feel* right for the poem and provide a norm to build the poem from. Often the initial jottings, as in "Black Mulberry," will be more notelike and the poem will seem at first like random jigsaw pieces. You will be looking to discover what sort of poem will develop. A thin poem? A solid poem? Tight? Loose? Long? Short? When something confirms the first shadowy choices, this can become a standard by which to measure fresh possibilities, blanks into which newly arriving inspirations may be fitted. Determining line and form may open up a stuck poem, allowing it to spread and fill like water into a design.

In truth, even in the earliest stages of making a poem—when you put down whatever comes into your head—you are working your critical facilities, if often unconsciously. "Style," Susan Sontag notes, "is the principle of decision in a work of art, the signature of the artist's will." The writing of even a few lines may be a mingling of a hundred creative and critical acts in rapid-fire, usually invisible, succession. Every possibility that occurs to you for what might come next you either accept or ignore or abandon. The approval or rejection may be tentative; you may often hold parallel possibilities in your mind for a time, bracketed in the body of the poem or sketched out in the margin. You will find it useful to list several alternatives to a sentence or a word in the margin. Is the tulip *red, streaked, dangerous, smiling, barbed, bloody, yellow, fisted, squalid, a striped canopy*? At this stage the standard against which you test possibilities can hardly be more than a sketchy idea of the poem. But as your tentative choices accumulate, as the ideas of the poem clarify, as the poem seems to materialize on the page, it imposes more and more its own demands and necessities. Listen to the poem; follow where it wants to lead you.

As the look of a developing poem matters, so does its sound. When you can't seem to get a poem moving, try saying what you have so far aloud, over and over. Through repetition you can reveal both the awkward and graceful parts. Typing and retyping helps too. Repeating the poem from the beginning will improve the continuity of the rhythm as well as the sense. This going back to the poem's first sounds can give you the momentum to get across the hard spot, just as, coming upon a ditch, you must go back the way you came and get a running start to leap to the other side. You'll find that hearing the sound of your own voice saying the poem, sculpting, relishing, caressing the unfinished poem is part of the job, one of your tools.

To clarify the poem's intentions, it can pay to be belligerent with your words. Turn negative phrases into positives, positives into negatives. For instance, you've written, "The streets are shining back to me." Why not, "The streets *aren't* shining back to me," or "Those streets *don't* shine for me"? If the peacock's feathers were "beaten metal" try them out as "crayoned paper." By reversing your initial intentions, you will test your commitment to your words and may find that making the opposite assertion may be more productive for the growing poem than your first notion. At least you will stir up the soup pot.

Another strategy, when a poem is a stubborn knot that doesn't unravel, consider that you may have before you two (or more) poems. A poem can go in almost any direction, and in many directions at once; ask yourself if the poem's directions support each other or crowd each other out. "Kill your darlings," Faulkner advised. You must often get rid of those parts that feel most precious to you in order to let the whole flourish. Good writing is like good gardening; not only do you yank out the weeds, you thin out perfectly healthy plants to make room for the rest. You snip and prune to bring forth fruit and flower. When a poem is an intertwining of possibilities, you may need to unwind them, put some aside before you can proceed coherently. Walter Savage Landor advises:

> In every poem train the leading shoot;
> Break off the suckers. Thought erases thought,
> As numerous sheep erase each other's print
> When spongy moss they press or sterile sand.
> Blades thickly sown want nutriment and droop,
> Although the seed be sound and rich the soil;
> Thus healthy-born ideas, bedded close,
> By dreaming fondness perish overlain.

Training the leading shoot can help you when you arrive at an impasse. Look for the central thrust of the poem and prune out the rest. Find its central time and place, its key voice. Ask yourself, who is speaking? To whom? Why? When? Where? Bring the possibilities into focus. As she worked on "Black Mulberry," Boisseau realized that the poem had to be *placed* somewhere so that the images could cohere. Standing beside a mulberry tree, picking berries became the answer. She also realized she had to shift the poem's address from the second person to the third. Earlier drafts addressed her daughter and, at one point, her husband, confusing the poem's central direction. When the poem shifted toward referring to the daughter in the third person, Boisseau could see it wanted to operate like a meditation—the block shape the poem took is typical of a lyric meditation, like Coleridge's "Frost at Midnight" or Robert Hass's "Meditation at Lagunitas."

Just as each poem arrives from a unique set of sources, so too does each develop from a unique application of tools. If it comes in a rush, a waterfall down the page, it may then need you to go through it slowly, weighing each word, each sound. If the poem comes slowly, nail by nail and board by board, then try working out a new draft in one swift torrent. A strategy that works to get one poem going, may not work for another. Try out several strategies in a different order, at different times. See what works for you, but be elastic in the methods you try. Writing from formulas will only give you formulaic poems. At times, after hours of hard, focused work, the poem just doesn't come alive. Put it aside then; you may resuscitate it next week or next month. Or maybe not. Let it go then; you have other poems to write. The adventure—and the frustration—is that with each poem you begin all over again. But with each poem you'll have more skills to build your poem with— and more possibilities to choose from.

EMOTION

Every poem has a speaker and therefore a voice. The human voice, even when seemingly unmodulated, level, "emotionless," expresses a tone, an attitude toward the subject, and therefore an emotion, even if muted, unstated, or matter-of-fact. Handling emotion is a tricky aspect of bringing a poem to the page and can make an apprentice poet—or any poet—stumble. In the earliest stages of some poems, particularly those bound up with strong, upsetting emotions—grief, for instance, or inexplicable elation—achieving some emotional detachment may be the first step. Give yourself some time to gain control before trying to write about some sharp hurt or deep joy. Being too close to the material of a poem can keep you from putting it into perspective, giving it shape in a poem.

When the sharpness of your emotions has dulled a bit, you'll be capable of stepping back and taking a look; Wordsworth notes that poetry

> takes its origin from emotion recollected in tranquillity; the emotion is contemplated till, by a species of re-action, the tranquillity gradually disappears, and an emotion, kindred to that which was before the subject of contemplation, is gradually produced, and does itself actually exist in the mind. In this mood successful composition generally begins.

The more emotional the sources of a poem, the longer it may take to channel them into a poem. You don't stop feeling what's driving you to write the poem;

your relationship to your emotions changes. You are then able to do more than feel—you can explore, project, discover, discriminate: talk it out. Strong emotions are rarely pure. Grief gets mixed up with guilt and anger; bliss with hope and doubt.

Sorting out the multiplicity of our feelings, understanding them, editing them, coming to terms with them (whether in action or in art) is as much a moral process as it is an aesthetic one. How we do this stems from what kind of person we decide to be. For the poet, as later for the right reader, the poem (in Frost's words) "ends in a clarification of life—not necessarily a great clarification, such as sects and cults are founded on, but in a momentary stay against confusion."

In the earliest drafts of bringing a strong emotion to the page, get down in words the emotional nexus that urges you to write. Write random images, play out the metaphors that occur to you. At first you will likely put down only flat assertions and clichés: "You make me so happy." "My heart is heavy as lead." Such generalities are a kind of short-hand to our feelings; we use them automatically without considering what they really mean or what our *particular* feeling is.

To render an emotion your first impulse may be to describe the speaker or character's emotional *response* to a situation—someone weeping or giggling or moaning. But keep in mind that creating a response *in the reader* is what you're after. Sure, laughter and tears can be contagious, but consider that novels and films which deeply move us, bring us to tears—or crack us up—don't so much show someone crying or laughing but show someone *not* crying or laughing despite the dire or ridiculous circumstances. The grand comedy, and sadness, of Charlie Chaplin's Tramp was his imperturbability when feasting on a boiled boot and his dignity when receiving the scorn of the wealthy.

Don't be too dismayed if your early drafts are full of generalities and clichés; try getting them on the page and then exploring them. If there weren't a kernel of truth inside them, we wouldn't use clichés at all. At some time every cliché was a powerful metaphor, so sharp and memorable that those who heard it picked it up and began using it themselves. Eventually through overuse the metaphor became a dead metaphor, weak and meaningless. If you find yourself drawn to a particular cliché, if you feel you just can't get past it, try delving into it; examine its nuances. You may find a way of bringing the metaphor inside it back to life, of saving the cliché, as Emily Dickinson does in this poem:

> After great pain, a formal feeling comes—
> The Nerves sit ceremonious, like Tombs—
> The stiff Heart questions was it He, that bore,
> And Yesterday, or Centuries before?
>
> The Feet, mechanical, go round— 5
> Of Ground, or Air, or Ought—
> A Wooden way
> Regardless grown,
> A Quartz contentment, like a stone— 10
>
> This is the Hour of Lead—
> Remembered, if outlived,

> As Freezing persons, recollect the Snow—
> First—Chill—then Stupor—then the letting go—

Out of frustration to describe the pain we suffer, we talk about our heavy hearts, how we can't breathe or feel anything, how we feel dead. We point to our chests. We do feel made of stone. But all these feelings remain abstract to someone else and won't affect an objective reader. It doesn't count if your reader is a close friend and already knows what you've gone through.

Dickinson's poem makes the emotions of great pain vivid; she saves the metaphors. Lead, that deadly and heavy element, aptly describes the weight which grief and pain bear down on us. But "heavy as lead" means next to nothing. Dickinson makes the cliché fresh. She doesn't emphasize its weight—heaviness is a connotation of "lead" anyway. Instead she uses it to explore the eerie sense of time that pain creates. We feel locked in an eternity where we can't tell yesterday from the distant past: we exist in an "hour of lead." Dickinson's image of lead also excites our senses; we almost taste the dull metal on our tongues.

To achieve emotional detachment from a subject, you can also keep in mind that the speaker of a poem isn't precisely you, the living poet, but a version of you, a created self. This self needn't be false or disingenuous. After all, you are not exactly the same person when hanging out with your friends as you are when asking your boss for time off or when waiting on a dark road for a tow truck. Yeats called such versions of the self the poet's *masks*. In writing a poem the poet puts on a mask, adopts a *persona* who speaks the poem. Our words *person* and *persona* both come from the Latin word for the mask ancient Roman actors wore in performance. These masks served both as costume and as megaphone, enabling the actors both to become another character and to project their voices to crowds far up in the amphitheater. Keeping this in mind may help you find a perspective, a voice to write the poem in.

By putting on the poet's mask when we begin a poem, we can see past the emotional muddle we find ourselves in and gain insight. The stoic tone of Dickinson's "After great pain" speaks from such insight. In the space of their poems poets become noble, brave, brilliant, tolerant—better people than they normally are. And they can become worse—bitter, jealous, greedy, or vindictive. It's okay not to be "nice" in a poem. Sometimes you must forget good manners and get vicious to be true to the poem.

Besides the mask of the self, try the fiction writer's technique: focus the poem around another character in the situation. William Carlos Williams (1883–1963) expresses his concern for his newly widowed mother by writing in her voice:

The Widow's Lament in Springtime

> Sorrow is my own yard
> where the new grass
> flames as it has flamed
> often before but not
> with the cold fire

that closes round me this year.
Thirtyfive years
I lived with my husband.
The plumtree is white today
with masses of flowers.   10
Masses of flowers
load the cherry branches
and color some bushes
yellow and some red
but the grief in my heart   15
is stronger than they
for though they were my joy
formerly, today I notice them
and turn away forgetting.
Today my son told me   20
that in the meadows,
at the edge of the heavy woods
in the distance, he saw
trees of white flowers.
I feel that I would like   25
to go there
and fall into those flowers
and sink into the marsh near them.

Taking her perspective, Williams seems to realize how deep his mother's grief is and how small a part he plays in it. Through her eyes the gorgeous spring day loses its luster: the blades of new grass, the masses of plum and cherry blossoms, the forest trees don't touch her; she wants to leave it all. His efforts to cheer her up are futile. He tells her of the flowering trees he's seen, but she wants only to drown herself in them. By allowing her to express what she does feel—instead of how she ought to feel—Williams permits his mother the dignity of her grief.

Inventing a character to speak for you can also give you emotional distance. What might it feel like for another person to feel what you're feeling? Suppose you're angry and hurt because your girlfriend of three years dumped you. Imagine yourself a man married for thirty years who one day comes home to an empty house, the furniture cleared out, only a towel hanging on the pool fence. Invent a situation, emotionally similar to yours, and speak through that situation. Or become another character entirely. Amy Gerstler speaks in the voice of a mermaid (p. 311), Browning as the Duke of Ferrara (p. 166), Norman Dubie as a crazy farm woman (p. 228), and Louise Glück as a racer's widow (p. 15). These poets use their understanding of human emotion to create new characters and find the source of a poem.

SOME FINE LINES

A danger of the poet's using raw emotions is **sentimentality:** writing that indulges emotion in excess of what caused it or that doesn't earn—through imagery, metaphor, detail—the emotion it asks a reader to feel; writing burdened with clichés; writing more interested in crude self-expression than in moving a reader. Most often sentimentality is merely simplistic, cheap, easy: the schmaltz of saucer-eyed urchins in rags and cuddly-sad puppies. At its worst, sentimentality is dishonest. It masks the truth: if a writer depicts a ragged child as cute, how much of the child's actual situation has the writer really imagined? Will we be likely to see that child with all the subtleties and edges of a real human being?

At times we all enjoy letting our emotions run away with us. Who hasn't stood alone, late on a rainy night, looking out the window at the deserted street; then, feeling desolate, written a poem about the dark tragedy of everything? In the morning, however, with the sun out and the birds chittering, these gloomy pronouncements seem silly and empty. Self-pity is emotionally like taking a bath in warm syrup—"poor me"—and can be destructive when we let ourselves believe it.

Close kin to sentimentality is **overstatement.** Like the used-car salesperson's hard sell, overstatement, claiming too much, asserting something beyond what seems justified, makes a reader uncomfortable, then resistant. One fraction of an ounce over and the scales tip. The calm of **understatement,** on the other hand, carries a reassuring air of conviction. Your best reader won't miss anything. Consider a poem by Jane Kenyon (1947–1995).

The Suitor

We lie back to back. Curtains
lift and fall,
like the chest of someone sleeping.
Wind moves the leaves of the box elder;
they show their light undersides,   5
turning all at once
like a school of fish.
Suddenly I understand that I am happy.
For months this feeling
has been coming closer, stopping   10
for short visits, like a timid suitor.

How quietly, carefully, Kenyon picks her words. The details of the scene seem unobtrusive, the curtains' lifting and falling, the unitary motion of the leaves of the known tree observed through the window. These natural rhythms include the speaker's new awareness, which is similarly undramatic—not a discovery, not, for instance, "Suddenly I am happy." The happiness is already a settled and familiar feeling, and the moment is precisely distanced by line 8's main verb: now I understand that what I feel, and have been feeling, is happiness. Implicit in the poem's three similes is the fragility or transitoriness of the feeling. Any response beyond the poem's quiet one could disturb the sleeper, any movement cause the fish to turn again, any boldness repel this timid suitor. The poem's careful understatement guarantees its accuracy.

Brash, deliberate overstatement—**hyperbole**—has its uses. In Louise Glück's "The Racer's Widow" (p. 15), for instance, it reveals and measures the violence of the speaker's distress—"Spasms of violets," she says, or "I can hear . . . the crowd coagulate on asphalt." We are familiar with everyday hyperbole like "I'd give my right arm for a piece of that pie." We know that the claim isn't to be taken literally. This sort of understood overstatement appears in the witty exaggerations of Ted Kooser's "Looking for You, Barbara" (p. 59) or in this poem by Peter Klappert (b. 1942):

The Invention of the Telephone

The time it took he could have
crawled—on the hairs of his knuckles,
on his eyelids, on his teeth.

He could have chewed his way.
In a place without friction   5
he could have re-invented the wheel.

But he wanted you to be
proud of him, so he invented
the telephone before he called.

A word of caution—or of abandon. A poem that risks nothing is probably not worth writing. A poem that aims only at *not* being sentimental will be flat. The lines can be fine between overstatement and emotional accuracy, between sentimentality and sentiment, between understatement and obscurity. One person's proper outrage over a racist act may seem overblown to someone else. Dickinson's spare style baffled the first editor who published her. Walt Whitman's exhortations shocked some nineteenth century readers, delighted others. Handling emotions in poems involves a trade-off between the poet's fires and the reader's wish not to get scorched by wild rhetoric. A poem that convinces readers that its feelings are warranted and genuine—even if extreme and unpleasant—is not sentimental. Dancing on the fine line is often the highest art.

QUESTIONS AND SUGGESTIONS

1. Try random writing. Put a first phrase down; then another; keep going. Try to fill up a page without lifting your pen. Keep going.

2. Get up two hours before you usually do—it's best if it's not light out yet. Find a comfortable vantage-point (window, back steps, bus stop bench) and make

sentences for everything you notice. Metaphors are welcome ("The first light, blue as a gas flame . . . ").

3. Here is a poem by Robert Wallace with several words or images omitted. What words or images would *you* insert if it were your poem? Compare your suggestions with the original in Appendix II, p. 387. What gains or losses do you see?

In a Spring Still Not Written Of

This morning
with a class of girls outdoors, I saw
how frail poems are
in a world   with flowers,   *participle or adjective*
in which, overhead,   5
the great elms
—green, and tall—
stood   leaves in their arms.   *participle*

The girls listened equally
to my drone, reading, and to the bees'   10
ricocheting
among them for the   on the bone.   *noun*
or gazed off at a distant mower's
                of green   *noun*
and clover, flashing,   15
threshing in the new,   sunlight.   *adjective*

And all the while, dwindling,
tinier, the voices—Yeats, Marvell, Donne—
sank drowning
in a spring still not written of,   20
as only the sky
clear above the brick bell-tower
—blue, and white—
was shifting toward the hour.

Calm, indifferent, cross-legged   25
or on elbows half-lying in the grass—
how should the great dead
tell them of dying?
They will come to time for poems at last,
when they have found they are no more   30
the beautiful and young
all poems are for.

4. Here are possible first lines for some poems. Choose one that intrigues you and write a poem that the beginning suggests.

   a) One night my hometown shut down. The bankers

   b) The peonies shake their pompons

c) In the dark beneath the skin, in secret dark,

d) Take this mess from my plate, give me

e) We know, with a knowledge that rides the nerves

5. With your notebook open to a new page, think back to where you lived ten years ago. Look out your favorite window there. What do you see? Make it the first day of summer; it's raining. What does it smell like? What do you hear? Are you wearing shoes? Close your eyes and for five minutes look out that window. When you're finished, jot down what you saw. Now look out another window, twenty years or two years ago. It hasn't rained for weeks. Close your eyes, look, write it down. Then climb out the window and go for a walk. (And take notes.)

6. This poem by Wilfred Owen (1893–1918), who was killed in France just before World War I ended, takes the form of an argument against the glorification of war. The poem's scene—a soldier's death by mustard gas—supports a compelling argument against a phrase, from the Roman poet Horace, that was then popular: "Dulce et decorum est pro patria mori," which can be translated as "Sweet and fitting it is to die for one's country." Try your own hand at a poem that responds to some popular statement which you find unacceptable.

Dulce et Decorum Est

Bent double, like old beggars under sacks,
Knock-kneed, coughing like hags, we cursed through sludge,
Till on the haunting flares we turned our backs
And towards our distant rest began to trudge.
Men marched asleep. Many had lost their boots   5
But limped on, blood-shod. All went lame; all blind;
Drunk with fatigue; deaf even to the hoots
Of tired, outstripped Five-Nines° that dropped behind.

Gas! Gas! Quick, boys!—An ecstasy of fumbling,
Fitting the clumsy helmets just in time;   10
But someone still was yelling out and stumbling,
And flound'ring like a man in fire or lime . . .
Dim, through the misty panes° and thick green light,
As under a green sea, I saw him drowning.

In all my dreams, before my helpless sight,   15
He plunges at me, guttering, choking, drowning.

If in some smothering dreams you too could pace
Behind the wagon that we flung him in,
And watch the white eyes writhing in his face,
His hanging face, like a devil's sick of sin;   20
If you could hear, at every jolt, the blood

8 *Five-Nines:* 5.9 inch caliber shells; 13 *misty panes:* of the gas mask.

Come gargling from the froth-corrupted lungs,
Obscene as cancer, bitter as the cud
Of vile, incurable sores on innocent tongues,—
My friend, you would not tell with such high zest   25
To children ardent for some desperate glory,
The old Lie: Dulce et decorum est
Pro patria mori.

7. Translate this poem by César Vallejo. If your Spanish isn't strong, ask a friend to do a literal translation for you, then try to work the poem into idiomatic English, keeping with Vallejo's mood.

Piedra Negra sobre una Piedra Blanca

Me moriré en Paris con aguacero,
un día del cual tengo ya el recuerdo.
Me moriré en Paris—y no me corro—
tal vez un jueves, como es hoy, de otoño.

Jueves será, porque hoy, jueves, que proso   5
estos versos, los húmeros me he puesto
a la mala y, jamás como hoy, me he vuelto,
con todo mi camino, a verme solo.

César Vallejo ha muerto, le pegaban
todos sin que él les haga nada;   10
le daban duro con un palo y duro

también con una soga; son testigos
los días jueves y los huesos húmeros,
la soledad, la lluvia, los caminos . . .

8. "The Dover Bitch" written in 1959 by Anthony Hecht plays with the famous Victorian poem "Dover Beach," written about 1851 by Matthew Arnold (1822–1888). Is Hecht's point insightful? Fair? How do each of the poems stand up to time? Why not play with Hecht's poem—or another poem you'd like to comment on—as he does with Arnold's?

Dover Beach

The sea is calm tonight.
The tide is full, the moon lies fair
Upon the straits;—on the French coast the light
Gleams and is gone; the cliffs of England stand,
Glimmering and vast, out in the tranquil bay.   5
Come to the window, sweet is the night-air!
Only, from the long line of spray
Where the sea meets the moon-blanched land,
Listen! you hear the grating roar

Of pebbles which the waves draw back, and fling,   10
At their return, up the high strand,
Begin, and cease, and then again begin,
With tremulous cadence slow, and bring
The eternal note of sadness in.

Sophocles long ago   15
Heard it on the Aegean, and it brought
Into his mind the turbid ebb and flow
Of human misery; we
Find also in the sound a thought,
Hearing it by this distant northern sea.   20

The Sea of Faith
Was once, too, at the full, and round earth's shore
Lay like the folds of a bright girdle furled.

But now I only hear
Its melancholy, long, withdrawing roar,   25
Retreating, to the breath
Of the night-wind, down the vast edges drear
And naked shingles° of the world.

Ah, love, let us be true
To one another! for the world, which seems   30
To lie before us like a land of dreams,
So various, so beautiful, so new,
Hath really neither joy, nor love, nor light,
Nor certitude, nor peace, nor help for pain;
And we are here as on a darkling plain   35
Swept with confused alarms of struggle and flight,
Where ignorant armies clash by night.

28 *naked shingles:* gravel beaches

The Dover Bitch
(A Criticism of Life)

So there stood Matthew Arnold and this girl
With the cliffs of England crumbling away behind them,
And he said to her, "Try to be true to me,
And I'll do the same for you, for things are bad
All over, etc., etc."   5
Well now, I knew this girl. It's true she had read
Sophocles in a fairly good translation
And caught that bitter allusion to the sea,
But all the time he was talking she had in mind
The notion of what his whiskers would feel like   10
On the back of her neck. She told me later on

That after a while she got to looking out
At the lights across the channel, and really felt sad,
Thinking of all the wine and enormous beds
And blandishments in French and the perfumes.   15
And then she really got angry. To have been brought
All the way down from London, and then be addressed
As a sort of mournful cosmic last resort
Is really tough on a girl, and she was pretty.
Anyway, she watched him pace the room   20
And finger his watch-chain and seem to sweat a bit,
And then she said one or two unprintable things.
But you mustn't judge her by that. What I mean to say is,
She's really all right. I still see her once in a while
And she always treats me right. We have a drink   25
And I give her a good time, and perhaps it's a year
Before I see her again, but there she is,
Running to fat, but dependable as they come.
And sometimes I bring her a bottle of *Nuit d'Amour*.

POEMS TO CONSIDER

Performance   *1992*

BRUCE BENNETT (b. 1940)

You know the steps, the gestures, and the glance.
The music starts, and now you have your chance.
You do your imitation of a dance.

Ground Swell   *1988*

MARK JARMAN (b. 1952)

Is nothing real but when I was fifteen
going on sixteen, like a corny song?
I see myself so clearly then, and painfully—
knees bleeding through my usher's uniform
behind the candy counter in the theater   5
after a morning's surfing; paddling frantically
to top the brisk outsiders coming to wreck me,
trundle me gawkily along the beach floor's
gravel and sand; my knees ached with salt.

Is that all that I have to write about?   10
You write about the life that's vividest,
and if that is your own, that is your subject,
and if the years before and after sixteen
are colorless as salt and taste like sand—
return to those remembered chilly mornings,   15
the light spreading like a great skin on the water,
and the blue water scalloped with wind-ridges
and—what was it exactly?—that slow waiting
when, to invigorate yourself you peed
inside your bathing suit and felt the warmth   20
crawl all around your hips and thighs,
and the first set rolled in and the water level
rose in expectancy, and the sun struck
the water surface like a brassy palm,
flat and gonglike, and the wave face formed.   25
Yes. But that was a summer so removed
in time, so specially peculiar to my life,
why would I want to write about it again?
There was a day or two when, paddling out,
an older boy who had just graduated   30
and grown a great blond moustache, like a walrus,
skimmed past me like a smooth machine on the water,
and said my name. I was so much younger,
to be identified by one like him—
the easy deference of a kind of god   35
who also went to church where I did—made me
reconsider my worth. I had been noticed.
He soon was a small figure crossing waves,
the shawling crest surrounding him with spray,
whiter than gull feathers. He had said my name   40
without scorn, but just a bit surprised
to notice me among those trying the big waves
of the morning break. His name is carved now
on the black wall in Washington, the frozen wave
that grievers cross to find a name or names.   45
I knew him as I say I knew him, then,
which wasn't very well. My father preached
his funeral. He came home in a bag
that may have mixed in pieces of his squad.
Yes, I can write about a lot of things   50
besides the summer that I turned sixteen.
But that's my ground swell. I must start
where things began to happen and I knew it.

1920 Photo   1986

PATRICIA DOBLER (b. 1939)

Here is Grandpa, who did not want America,
flanked by children, wife and brother,
brother's wife and children . . . . Standing
to one side, a Chinese woman.

How did she get into this picture!   5
My mother can't, none of my aunts
can tell me, but they are children here,
see their rosy faces. The mustachioed men,
their women proud in white lace blouses,
a solemn occasion . . . and the Chinese woman   10

in a stiff bright robe, her eyes shining
into mine. Except for her, everyone touches
everyone else, all of them are making it
in America, even if Grandpa cries for Hungary
at harvest-time, even if he is a landless farmer   15
who shovels slag at the rolling mill.

Even the Chinese woman, who no one alive remembers,
who migrated into my family's picture
like a jungle bird among chickens,
looks happier to be here than Grandpa.   20

Woman on Twenty-second Eating Berries   1990

STANLEY PLUMLY (b. 1939)

She's not angry exactly but all business,
eating them right off the tree, with confidence,
the kind that lets her spit out the bad ones
clear of the sidewalk into the street. It's
sunny, though who can tell what she's tasting,   5
rowan or one of the service-berries—
the animal at work, so everybody,
save the traffic, keeps a distance. She's picking
clean what the birds have left, and even,
in her hurry, a few dark leaves. In the air   10
the dusting of exhaust that still turns pennies

green, the way the cloudy surfaces
of things obscure their differences,
like the mock-orange or the apple-rose that
cracks the paving stone, rooted in the plaza.   15
No one will say your name, and when you come to
the door no one will know you, a parable
of the afterlife on earth. Poor grapes, poor crabs,
wild black cherry trees, on which some forty-six
or so species of birds have fed, some boy's dead   20
weight or the tragic summer lightning killing
the seed, how boyish now that hunger
to bring those branches down to scale,
to eat of that which otherwise was waste,
how natural this woman eating berries, how alone.   25

Bread and Water   *1990*

SHIRLEY KAUFMAN (b. 1923)

After the Leningrad trials, after solitary confinement
most of eleven years in a Siberian *gulag*, he told us
this story. One slice of sour black bread a day.
He trimmed off the crust and saved it for the last
since it was the best part. Crunchy, even a little sweet.   5
Then he crumbled the slice into tiny pieces. And ate
them, one crumb at a time. So they lasted all day. Not
the cup of hot water. First he warmed his hands around it.
Then he rubbed the cup up and down his chest to warm his
body. And drank it fast. Why, we asked him, why not   10
like the bread? Sometimes, he said, there was more hot
water in the jug the guard wheeled around to the prisoners.
Sometimes a guard would ladle a second cup. It helped
to believe in such kindness.

Mosquito Nets   *1992*

MICHAEL WATERS (b. 1949)

Ios, 1989

How they dawdle in the sea
  breeze, water spouts
drawn to beds in stone cottages, furled now,

twisted and rising from the foam
   mattresses, spellbound through nightfall.   5

   Then, lamps extinguished, kerosene
fumes rending the honeysuckle,
the spumes open, dry leaves, dazzling webs
   that sift the air, sway, then
      begin to breathe, otherworldly.   10

   Who would expect safekeeping
from tissue so sheer, so easily
torn by an outthrust arm or heirloom ring?
   When sleepers succumb to the hazy
      laws of lovemaking, the mosquitoes   15

   pause in their trespassing
the precincts of lovers embraced all night
by the almost-invisible, lovers pleased
   to mend, each morning, if they must,
      their providential gauze.   20

 My Students Catch Me Dancing   *1990*

LESLIE ADRIENNE MILLER (b. 1956)

Only when I hear the knock
do I realize that what I've been doing
is probably odd: a few crooked pliés
and a variation on an arabesque
no dancer would recognize, after which   5
I arch my spine just to see
how far it will go, because it's spring
and my body's permutations are suddenly
as apparent to me as the shade
across the porch stair these two   10
young women ascend, glancing, as anyone would,
through the kitchen window to catch me
at the life I have without them.
When I open the door, they know better
than to giggle; they ask politely   15
if I *dance*, stretching the word
like a muscle to indicate art is meant.
They are not so much surprised by my dancing
as embarrassed to catch me concentrated

in my own grace, in the act of willing   20
myself beautiful. They would like
to apologize for something, but what?
Do you dance? one asks, as if I have
not been. *I have,* I say, as in not now,
not just now. They have seen how much   25
I liked the way my leg went up slowly
behind me, my breastbone forward, aloft
almost, as if a string were attached there.
They might have caught me at frying chicken
or sewing on a button; even trying faces   30
in the mirror would have been
less private, less sad, because I've said
too much about devotion, art, a whole life
concentrated in the movement of words
across a page, fingers across a keyboard,   35
so that the confinement of my dancing
to five square feet of dusk-lit kitchen
makes them too suddenly aware
of that place in us where art goes
when all the stages have gone dark.   40

 Fall   *1973*

ROBERT HASS (b. 1941)

Amateurs, we gathered mushrooms
near shaggy eucalyptus groves
which smelled of camphor and the fog-soaked earth.
Chanterelles, puffballs, chicken-of-the-woods,
we cooked in wine or butter,   5
beaten eggs or sour cream,
half expecting to be
killed by a mistake. "Intense perspiration,"
you said late at night,
quoting the terrifying field guide   10
while we lay tangled in our sheets and heavy limbs,
"is the first symptom of attack."

Friends called our aromatic fungi
"liebestoads" and only ate the ones
that we most certainly survived.   15
Death shook us more than once

those days and floating back
it felt like life. Earth-wet, slithery,
we drifted toward the names of things.
Spore prints littered our table   20
like nervous stars. Rotting caps
gave off a musky smell of loam.

 A narrow Fellow in the Grass   *1866*

EMILY DICKINSON (1830–1886)

A narrow Fellow in the Grass
Occasionally rides –
You may have met Him – did you not
His notice sudden is –

The Grass divides as with a Comb –   5
A spotted shaft is seen –
And then it closes at your feet
And opens further on –

He likes a Boggy Acre
A Floor too cool for Corn –   10
Yet when a Boy, and Barefoot –
I more than once at Noon
Have passed, I thought, a Whip lash
Unbraiding in the Sun
When stooping to secure it   15
It wrinkled, and it was gone –

Several of Nature's People
I know, and they know me –
I feel for them a transport
Of cordiality –   20

But never met this Fellow
Attended, or alone
Without a tighter breathing
And Zero at the Bone –

10

REVISING (I)
Both Ends of the Pencil

Craft completes magic; technique carries out inspiration. Sometimes poets claim otherwise, pretending that making poems is all too arcane and mysterious to be explicable. But as Edmund Waller (1606–1687) put it,

> Poets lose half the praise they should have got,
> Could it be known what they discreetly blot.

His contemporary, John Dryden, translating Boileau's *L'Art Poétique* (1674), offered this advice:

> Gently make haste, of labor not afraid;
> A hundred times consider what you've said:
> Polish, repolish, every color lay,
> And sometimes add, but oftener take away.
> 'Tis not enough, when swarming faults are writ,
> That here and there are scattered sparks of wit.

The secret of writing is rewriting. As W. H. Auden notes, "Literary composition in the twentieth century A.D. is pretty much what it was in the twentieth century B.C.: nearly everything has still to be done by hand." Rewriting is exploring, trying out. The poet uses both ends of the pencil. Luckily, unlike the sculptor or the painter, poets can go back to earlier versions if they make a mistake. A typical way is to scratch out and add, scratch out and add, scribbling alternatives in the margin, until the sheet is embroidered with corrections—and then to recopy the best version that can be sorted out of it. Then the poet goes on scratching out and adding on the draft. There are 175 worksheets for a poem by E. E. Cummings ("rosetree, rosetree"), and Donald Hall reports poems going through fifty or sixty drafts. Like simplicity, spontaneity and naturalness often spring from hard work.

Elizabeth Bishop's "The Moose" took twenty-six years from first draft to finished poem. Richard Wilbur reports that he waited fourteen years, occasionally jotting down a phrase "that might belong to a poem," before he started to write "The Mind-Reader"; he took another three years to finish the poem. Asked how long he was likely to work on a poem, he said, "Long enough." These are no doubt exceptional instances, and a lucky poem may sometimes appear without effort. But most poets would agree with Sir John Harington (1561–1612):

> Prose is like a fair green way, wherein a man may travel a great journey and not be weary; but verse is a miry lane, in which a man's horse puts out one leg after another with much ado, and often drives his master to alight to help him out.

This chapter and the next will mainly look at a number of poets' actual revisions—examples of the creative process, of the lucky leaps and the careful carpentry.

EXPLORING

First drafts will often be exploration. Is there a poem in this impulse? How would it begin? Hopeless blunders usually mix with useful clues, and in letting them begin to sort themselves out, the poet, like a prospector, pans for gold.

Richard Wilbur has generously published the first six drafts of the opening lines of "Love Calls Us to the Things of This World." In them we can follow the developing poem as it searches for both its language and its form. Consider first the finished poem.

Love Calls Us to the Things of This World

The eyes open to a cry of pulleys,
And spirited from sleep, the astounded soul
Hangs for a moment bodiless and simple
As false dawn.
       Outside the open window
The morning air is all awash with angels.   5

Some are in bed-sheets, some are in blouses,
Some are in smocks: but truly there they are.
Now they are rising together in calm swells
Of halcyon feeling, filling whatever they wear
With the deep joy of their impersonal breathing;   10

Now they are flying in place, conveying
The terrible speed of their omnipresence, moving
And staying like white water; and now of a sudden
They swoon down into so rapt a quiet
That nobody seems to be there.
       The soul shrinks   15

From all that it is about to remember,
From the punctual rape of every blessed day,
And cries,
      "Oh, let there be nothing on earth but laundry,
Nothing but rosy hands in the rising steam
And clear dances done in the sight of heaven."   20

      Yet, as the sun acknowledges
With a warm look the world's hunks and colors,
The soul descends once more in bitter love
To accept the waking body, saying now
In a changed voice as the man yawns and rises,   25

    "Bring them down from their ruddy gallows;
Let there be clean linen for the backs of thieves;
Let lovers go fresh and sweet to be undone,
And the heaviest nuns walk in a pure floating
Of dark habits,
          keeping their difficult balance."   30

This is a superb, passionate poem. The sight of laundry, drawn into the morning air between two buildings, becomes first a vision of wished-for angelic purity; and then, with accepting insight, of the mingled purity and impurity of the human condition. Seeing the pieces of laundry billowing in the breeze, the waking person momentarily mistakes them for angels. Not fully awake, he is an "astounded soul," "for a moment bodiless and simple." He "shrinks" from facing the dirtying reality of the world. As if answering the "cry of pulleys," the soul "cries":

      "Oh, let there be nothing on earth but laundry,
    Nothing but rosy hands in the rising steam
    And clear dances done in the sight of heaven."

But in stanza 5, reminded by the sun's "warm look," "The soul descends once more in bitter love / To accept the waking body"—its own inescapable attachment to physical reality—and, in the last stanza, to accept the world. The wish for purity is replaced by compassion for the ambiguities and precariousness of the human condition.

The poem's trajectory is psychological, dramatic; its theme, deeply Christian, though not in a doctrinal way; its title, from Saint Augustine. The initial mistaking of laundry for angels seems natural enough for the half-awakened consciousness; the speaker recognizes the whimsicality of the mistake soon enough, as the breeze slackens: "nobody seems to be there." But the universal desire for purity, the wish to avoid the inevitable sullying of "every blessed day," is real, and the colloquial emphatic "blessed" continues the religious theme. The poem's rich puns ("spirited from sleep," "awash with angels," "The soul shrinks") culminate in the nuns' "dark habits." Even "the heaviest" (most tempted and worldly) of them, nonetheless, walk "in a pure floating," "keeping their difficult balance," *in* but not *of* the world. With the somewhat biblical word "linen," the "ruddy gallows" suggests the crucifixion, and the "thieves" the two thieves on crosses on either side of Christ. Christ, the poem subtly reminds us, also descended in love into the world and into flesh. The soul's two speeches are, of course, prayers, recognizing that, although the world is imperfect, we must nonetheless live in it and love it.

Here are the poem's earliest drafts:

DRAFT 1

> My eyes came open to the squeak of pulleys
> My spirit, shocked from the brothel of itself

Lack of punctuation after line 1 suggests that the draft is preliminary, trying out possibilities for opening the poem. The lines are iambic pentameter, and we can guess that, before trying them on paper, the poet has been mulling them over in his head until they took on a distinct metrical shape. The oddity in the lines is the image "brothel." Sleep, the withdrawal of the soul from the body, is presented very forcefully as a self-indulgence on the soul's part. The implicit rebuke, which will soften in the final poem to an awareness of the soul's natural but mistaken repugnance for the "things of this world," shows that the thematic direction of the poem is already given. The paradox (or confusion) of a fleshly image for the soul's self-indulgence is striking. That the poet distrusts "brothel," however, is clear from the second draft, where the image is altered.

DRAFT 2

> My eyes came open to the shriek of pulleys,
> And the soul, spirited from its proper wallow,
> Hung in the air as bodiless and hollow

In place of the literal but uninteresting "squeak" of pulleys, the poet tries "shriek," which personifies them. The fairly straightforward "shocked" makes way for "spirited"—with the additional sense of something carried away mysteriously or secretly. Punctuated, the lines begin to be a sentence. Whichever word came first, a rhyme has suggested itself: "wallow-hollow," and so the poet engages a further formal possibility. In the third draft, perhaps foreseeing trouble in rhyming "pulleys," he reverses the word order and replaces "shriek" with "cry."

DRAFT 3

> My eyes came open to the pulleys' cry.
> The soul, spirited from its proper wallow,
> Hung in the air as bodiless and hollow
> As light that frothed upon the wall opposing;
> But what most caught my eyes at their unclosing

5

Was two gray ropes that yanked across the sky.
One after one into the window frame
. . . the hosts of laundry came

Apparently released by the possibility of rhyming, the poem makes a spurt forward. Without the negative connotations of "shriek" (and its too attention-getting personification), "cry" seems right, meaning ambiguously both to call out in grief or suffering and to announce. While "pulleys' cry" is awkward, it sets up the very usable rhyme of "sky"—which the poet may not yet know how he will use but which provides an easy target for a subsequent line. Again, whichever came first, the rhyme pairs "opposing-unclosing" and "frame-came" allow the draft to move toward the completion of its exposition and what sounds like the end of a stanza.

But the poet is plainly unsatisfied, as the unfinished and unpunctuated line 8 shows. In the fourth draft *all* the rhyme words except "cry" disappear from the poem, and "cry" moves back to a less clumsy place in its line. We can guess the causes, if not the order, of the poet's dissatisfactions. "Wallow" muted somewhat the comparison of the soul's weakness to fleshliness, but the confusion persists, along with an unfortunate animal connotation. Because "hollow" suggests the vacant interior of something solid, it isn't really accurate for the soul. Saying "the wall opposing," to set up the rhyme, is rather stagy—the normal phrase would be "the opposite wall." "At their unclosing" is mere padding. Lines 5–6 seem inaccurate or, at least, a digression, for the laundry, not the "two gray ropes," is surely what "most caught my eyes." The poet probably felt some pain giving up the nice detail of the ropes, and especially the word "yanked," which is the first word in the poem to strike naturally and unaffectedly the colloquial tone that the final version values in "awash," "shrinks," "blessed," "hunks," and "ruddy" (an English colloquialism meaning reddish, and suggesting "bloody"). The window "frame" distracts from what appears outside, and line 7 as a whole is open to the misreading of coming *into* the room through the window. "One after one" also limits the view of the laundry and, if allowed to stand, would preclude the panoramic view in the final version's second and third stanzas.

DRAFT 4

The eyes open to a cry of pulleys,
And the soul, so suddenly spirited from sleep,
Hangs in the air as bodiless and simple
As morning sunlight frothing on the floor,
While just outside the window
The air is solid with a dance of angels.

5

Freedom from rhyme now permits the poem to do in six lines what it had done in eight, and the first line has reached its final form. In line 2 the soul is now spirited merely from "sleep" instead of brothel or wallow. "Hollow" is replaced with the apt "simple" ("bodiless and simple"); that is, simply itself, uncomplicated, in its own nature. But "simple"also means ignorant or foolish, as in " simple-minded"; and the pun looks forward to the poem's ultimate judgment on the soul's natural but foolish desire to avoid the dirtying world. Lines 5–6 of this draft focus quickly and unceremoniously on the laundry/angels. The housecleaning between the third and fourth drafts sweeps away "the hosts of laundry," which was obviously an attempt to sneak up on the word "angels." The fourth draft is direct: "The air is solid with a dance of angels." The explanatory "laundry" is dropped. The bed-sheets, blouses, smocks of the second stanza will make the exposition perfectly clear; so the first stanza can end without apology on the startling appearance of "angels."

The tightening of this draft includes the tentative dropping of iambic pentameter. For the moment the lines will be left not only without rhymes but also free to be unequal in length. The possibility is a stanza of lines of differing lengths, such as Wilbur used in other poems. If indentations indicate relative line-length (as they conventionally do), the poet is counting loosely, perhaps waiting to see how things fall out before being more decisive.

Suggested by this metrical concession (or suggesting it), one of the major changes in the poem occurs here: the shift from past to present tense, with a consequent increase in immediacy. "Hangs" now looks forward to the "ruddy gallows" of the last stanza, as "hung" grammatically could not. (The past tense of *hang* meaning execution is "hanged," not "hung.") The other major change is from the first to the third person: "My eyes" become only "The eyes," opening the way to "the man yawns and rises" in stanza 5. The soul, rather than a first-person speaker, becomes the poem's protagonist. This change provides an important, measuring distance between the voice of the poem and the soul, whose fantasies and recognitions make up the central action. Having this central action occur entirely within the soul, at some remove from the man, who seems almost unaware of this drama—avoids any thorny questions about the relationship of body, mind, and soul—or who/what corrects the soul's mistaken wish for untainted purity. The poem's psychology is, thus, allegorized, simplified. The initial punitive tone toward the soul ("brothel") disappears, and it is the soul itself that, recognizing its understandable desire to disentangle itself from them, "descends in bitter love / To accept the waking body" and the world.

The soul's deflection from its true compassion lasts only for those few instants of waking before "the man yawns and rises." In the next draft the poet underlines this revision by altering line 3 from "Hangs in the air as bodiless and simple" to "Hangs for a moment bodiless and simple." Everything—vision of laundry as angels, the two prayers—in a moment; and the soul's momentary error is not a sinful lapse but a *simple* foolishness which it corrects quickly. (This change from first to third person was already implicit in the second draft's "My eyes . . . *the* soul," but it took two further drafts to respond to the cue.) Significant advance as the fourth draft is, the stanza is not finished.

DRAFT 5

> The eyes open to a cry of pulleys,
> And spirited from sleep, the astounded soul
> Hangs for a moment bodiless and simple

> As dawn light in the moment of its breaking:
>> Outside the open window   5
> The air is crowded with a

The unnecessary "so suddenly" in line 2 vanishes (being spirited away is always sudden to the victim); and "astounded" takes its place in the line, conveying the dramatic excitement one would feel at perceiving angels outside the bedroom window. It also, of course, prepares for making allowances for the soul's momentary error. With "for a moment" substituted in line 3, the poem's first three lines are complete. Line 4 gets rid of the "frothed" and "frothing" of the third and fourth drafts. Froth's bubbly airiness, whether on "wall opposing" or on the floor, may picture flickery early sunlight; but the connotations are so negative—foam, frothing at the mouth—that the possibility is discarded. The floor, as irrelevant as the wall opposing had been, disappears. Line 5 is sharpened: the rather empty "While just" is dropped and the window is made "open," which conveys the immediacy of the angels, as if they might indeed enter the room. Picking up the "open" (verb) of line 1, "the open window" (adjective) here makes the vision doubly close and surprising. In line 6 the poet discards the too static and dense adjective "solid"—"The air is solid with a dance of angels"—in favor of the plainer but more active "crowded." But, before he can add either "dance of angels" or "host of angels," the pending possibilities, the draft breaks off.

The most decisive thing the poet does in the fifth draft is to firm up the meter. The four lines that begin at the left margin are iambic pentameter, which is to become again the norm of the poem; the half indentation of line 1 indicates that it is tetrameter, the full indentation of line 5 that it is trimeter.

DRAFT 6

> The eyes open to a cry of pulleys,
> And spirited from sleep, the astounded soul
> Hangs for a moment bodiless and simple
> As false dawn.
>> Outside the open window,   5
> The air is leaping with a rout of angels.
>> Some are in bedsheets, some are in dresses,
>> it does not seem to matter

The weakest line in the fifth draft was line 4: "As dawn light in the moment of its breaking"—"in the moment" is niggling and lamely repeats "for a moment" in line 3; "of its breaking" is essentially empty. At a stroke in that sixth draft, the poet drops those phrases and alters "As dawn light" to "As false dawn"—period. The economy is complete. False dawn, the early light before sunrise, is itself "bodiless and simple," a vague, incomplete stage, eerie and somehow nonphysical. Like the soul's fanciful vision and its wish for utter and untested purity, it is "false dawn"; the soul's truer prayer is saved, like the sun's "warm look" itself, for the fifth and sixth stanzas. As the progression from false dawn to sunrise is natural, so, by implication, is the soul's from false prayer to true.

The other troublesome line in the fifth draft is line 6: "The air is crowded with a"—which is left unfinished. As "solid" was too heavy and static, so "crowded" is too flat. In the sixth draft the poet tries again for liveliness and surprise: "The air is leaping with a rout of angels." "Rout," which suggests unruliness, suitably describes the free-blowing laundry and adds the unexpected pleasure of imagining boisterous and disorderly angels. Heavenly fun, the word implies, needn't be dull. But the word is hardly serious enough for the variety of angelic attitudes and meanings that are to follow in stanzas 2 and 3 ("calm swells of halcyon feeling," "the terrible speed of their omnipresence," for example). And "The air is leaping" seems dyslexic, though perfectly clear. Presumably on the next try, the poet hits the mark of the line exactly: "The morning air is all awash with angels," with its multiple meanings.

Presumably, too, in the coming draft, the next two lines are properly put forward to stanza 2. (Why the poet alters "dresses" to "blouses" in the first line of stanza 2 is a puzzle the reader may consider.) With the poet's recognition that the two short lines, 4 and 5, together make a single pentameter line, the essential form of the poem's first stanza is set: one line of tetrameter, five of pentameter. Problems in maintaining that pattern in subsequent stanzas might have sent the poet back to rework stanza 1, but didn't. The decision whether to print "As false dawn. Outside the open window" as a continuous line or a dropped-line was presumably deferred. It was made only when other stanzas showed places where a dropped-line could be effective, especially in stanza 3 ("That nobody seems to be there. / The soul shrinks") and stanza 6 ("Of dark habits, / keeping their difficult balance"), where the dropped-line, along with the metrical irregularities, beautifully illustrates the precariousness in the line's meaning. Not incidentally, the drafts show the poet writing with practiced ease in metered lines, deftly using the trochaic "open" in line 1 for its surprise and positioning (after the first draft) the word "hangs" at the beginning of its line.

The poem is developing in several ways simultaneously. Its main idea, at first fuzzy and uncertain, clarifies with each successive draft. As the details of the scene are considered, then accepted or dropped, the visual impression sharpens. The diction becomes exact; tone and nuance focus with precision. And, after several trials, the form settles into a comfortable pattern.

TRYING OUT

In the early stages, the poet's job may well be looking for clues. Before a passage comes right and words click into place, it is often the poet's *dissatisfactions*—a sense of inaccuracy or weakness—that prove most helpful. Consider the two drafts and final version of the opening stanza of A. E. Housman's "Reveille." The images of dawn as a tide and of sunrise as a burning ship on the horizon don't change, but are *refocused* in language that, finally, leaps to exactitude. Revisions scribbled on the drafts appear in smaller italic type.

DRAFT 1:

> Yonder round the world returning   *Dusk in silver tides returning*
> Slow the tide of twilight spills   *On the brim of darkness spills*
> And the ship of sunrise burning
>   *beyond*
> Heaves behind the eastern hills
>   *Strands upon*

DRAFT 2:

> Dusk in silver tides returning
>   *bank*
>   *marge*   *brims*
> On the coast of darkness spills
> *Till*
> And the ship of sunrise burning
>   *rims*
> Strands upon the eastern hills.

FINAL VERSION:

> Wake: the silver dusk returning
> Up the beach of darkness brims,
> And the ship of sunrise burning
> Strands upon the eastern rims.

When the poet condenses the wordiness of lines 1–2 ("Yonder round the world," "Slow") in Draft 2, he opens space for both "silver" and "darkness," which make a sharper picture. The opportunity opens up, too, for a word to complete the picture of dusk as rising tide: *brim* (noun), then *coast, marge, bank,* and finally *beach.* Housman's first notion—*brim*—suggests the hidden dissatisfaction that continued to nag at him in Draft 2: the rhyme-word "spills." One can say properly that water spills up a beach, but spills is mainly a *downward* movement. Since the point here is dawn's inexorably rising, "spills" isn't the best word. "Brim" isn't a good choice for coast or beach, either, and is quickly dropped. But it was the clue needed: reenforced by "up" at the beginning of the line, use *brims* (verb) in place of *spills* at line's end! The rhyme-word that came to mind, "rims," also resolved a further awkwardness: having a metaphorical ship strand upon *hills.* The vaguer "rims," though the singular would do (rim of the world), smoothly replaces the sour note.

Notice also in the final version, as a measure of the elegance of Housman's revision, that the overly particular (and oddly plural) word "tides" has vanished from the poem. The idea is still there, but less crudely; it is expressed now with an insubstantiality proper to the gradual emergence of first light.

We watch similar trial-and-error in four successive versions of the opening of "Hyperion" by John Keats (1795–1821). The crux is his search for the right image in lines 8–9. Here is the passage, with the first version in italics:

Deep in the shady sadness of a vale
Far sunken from the healthy breath of morn,
Far from the fiery noon, and eve's one star,
Sat gray-haired Saturn°, quiet as a stone,
Still as the silence round about his lair;   5
Forest on forest hung about his head
Like cloud on cloud. No stir of air was there,
Not so much life as what an eagle's wing
Would spread upon a field of green eared corn,
But where the dead leaf fell, there did it rest.   10
A stream went voiceless by, still deadened more
By reason of his fallen divinity
Spreading a shade: the Naiad 'mid her reeds
Pressed her cold finger closer to her lips.

4 *Saturn:* an ancient Titan.

It is a melancholy scene: Saturn motionless in the silent, shading forest. The first phrase of the passage is exactly descriptive with its static internal off-rhyme: "stir-air-there." The trouble that Keats senses is in the image for this stillness in lines 8–9. From his next version we can see what particularly bothered him. The clumsy and unnecessary "what" was obviously used merely to keep the meter. An easy solution would have been to remove the word in favor of an adjective describing the eagle. He might then have written: "Not so much life as a young eagle's wing." But Keats was also unsatisfied with the eagle. Probably he sensed that it was an image too positive and vigorous to be appropriate to "fallen divinity." In the second version of the lines he exchanges the eagle for the tonally more relevant vulture.

No stir of air was there,
Not so much life as a young vulture's wing
Would spread upon a field of green eared corn

The image that Keats intends is apparently of a large, powerful bird of prey circling high in the sky, probably gliding rather than flapping; and the point is that its wing causes absolutely *no motion* in the field of easily swayed grain far below. (In British usage *corn* indicates wheat or some other grain, not American corn.) Perhaps Keats has in mind the shadow of the bird's wing passing over, but not moving, the limber stalks. The vulture might suit the picture of Saturn in his vale, and its youth contrast with Saturn's age and weakness.

As the third version reveals, however, Keats discards the entire image. Possibly, carrion or no, the strong, youthful bird spoils the unvarying tone of the mournful passage. Certainly, the "field of green eared corn"—sunny, spacious, and vital—does not fit the enclosed, "shady" forest scene of defeated Saturn. Interesting though the image is in itself, it seems a wrong choice.

So, in the third version, dropping the bird image altogether, Keats tries again:

> No stir of air was there,
> Not so much life as on a summer's day
> Robs not at all the dandelion's fleece

The substitution of the dandelion gone to seed for the "green eared corn" strikes a better note; and the light, easily dislodged, white-tufted seeds of the dandelion provide a good measure for the absolute stillness of air as well as, in their color and implicit ruin, a vivid parallel to the "gray-haired Saturn." The image has a literal rightness and consistent, useful overtones. The double negatives, "Not . . . not . . . ," may feel awkward at first, but they follow "No stir of air was there" with an emphatic absoluteness. Even the awkwardness seems, rhythmically, right for the utterly still air, unable to dislodge even a seed. For some months Keats let the lines stand so.

Several problems must have bothered him into another, final, revision. Possibly the lowly, common, near-comic dandelion came to seem inappropriate to a poem on a classical subject. More significantly, Keats must have recognized that "fleece," though visually accurate and fluffy enough for a head of dandelion seeds, is a poor image in the context. For one thing, fleece is really quite oily and rather heavy. For another, a fleece is not easily robbed (that would require taking the sheep whole or at least clipping it). Pieces of wool might be snagged from a fleece, but not by the wind—and ease of dislodgement is the point of the image. In any event, robbing a bit of wool from a fleece makes no sense. One other aspect of the image may have concerned Keats: the picture is of a single dandelion, close-up. Having the perspective farther away, so as to suggest the extent of the breezelessness, seems to have been a consideration in the revision:

> No stir of air was there,
> Not so much life as on a summer's day
> Robs not one light seed from the feathered grass

Like the dead leaf in the next line, the identity of the "seed from the feathered grass" is left abstract, generic. Visually, nothing is allowed to compete with the main pictorial presentation of Saturn. The rhythm of the revised line is masterful: "Róbs nót óne líght séed frŏm thĕ feáthĕred grás." The five utterly even, accented syllables at the beginning of the line suggest an evenly light, precarious balance without movement. After this, the slightly enhanced speed of "from the feathered grass" seems to pass like the looked for, but nonexistent, breath of air. Not the least of Keats's mastery is using spondees for an impression of lightness.

SHAPING

Another essential part of composition is **shaping.** As the words of a poem come, they must be deployed in lines. Sometimes the earliest verbalization carries with it an intuitive sense of form, but often the first phrases are a scattering, fragments with no certainty even as to which should come first. One consideration as a poem grows, then, is opting for some possible form, however tentative, which can be tested and altered as draft leads to draft. Meter? Rhyme? Free verse? Longer lines? Stanzas? We have seen Wilbur, keeping the form open, test lines of three, four, and five feet in the drafts of "Love Calls Us to the Things of This World." The initial preference may be habitual, as Dickinson or William Carlos Williams instinctively worked in very short lines, or Whitman in very long lines. But a given poem may want a different sort of form. In "Yachts," for instance, Williams elected to write in lines much longer than was his custom: "Today no race. Then the wind comes again. The yachts / move, jockeying for a start, the signal is set . . . ."

In choosing stanzaic forms, whether in free verse or in meter, the poet looks for a pattern that can be used fully, without slackening, in subsequent stanzas. Of "I Hoed and Trenched and Weeded," A. E. Housman commented: "Two of the stanzas, I do not say which, came into my head . . . . A third stanza came with a little coaxing after tea. One more was needed, but it did not come: I had to turn to and compose it myself, and that was a laborious business. I wrote it thirteen times, and it was more than a twelvemonth before I got it right." Poems don't always unwind from the top. Robert Lowell recalled that his well-known "Skunk Hour" was "written backwards," the last two stanzas first, then the next-to-last two, and finally the first four in reverse order.

Along with a tentative choice of form, shaping involves the experimental sculpting or fitting of further parts to the developing design. As Frost says, "I can have my first line any way I please. But once I say a line I am committed . . . . Every step you take is a further commitment."

William Stafford (1914–1993) wrote "Ask Me" in three drafts. Comparing the first draft with the finished poem shows Stafford's delicate skill in adjusting line-breaks. Here is the draft:

> Some time when the river is ice, ask me
> the mistakes, ask me whether what I have
> done is my life. Others have come
> in their slow way into the thoughts. And
> some have tried to help or to hurt.   5
> Ask me what differences their strongest efforts
> have made. You and I can then turn
> and look at the silent river and wait.
> We will know the current is there,
> hidden, and there are comings and goings   10
> miles away that hold the stillness
> exactly before us. If the river says anything,
> whatever it says is my answer.

And here is the finished poem:

> Some time when the river is ice ask me
> mistakes I have made. Ask me whether
> what I have done is my life. Others

have come in their slow way into
my thought, and some have tried to help   5
or to hurt—ask me what difference
their strongest love or hate has made.

I will listen to what you say.
You and I can turn and look
at the silent river and wait. We know   10
the current is there, hidden; and there
are comings and goings from miles away
that hold the stillness exactly before us.
What the river says, that is what I say.

Stafford has almost completely relined the poem. Only the first line remains the
same and keeps its line-break. Changes, however, are mostly small: "the mistakes"
in line 2 becomes "mistakes I have made," which is clarifying and emphatic; "their
strongest efforts / have made" in lines 6–7 becomes "their strongest love or hate
has made," turning a flat phrase into a sharp one and underlining the ironic level-
ing of "to help / or to hurt."

But the resentencing in lines 1–7 brings into clearer focus the three considerations: "mistakes I have made," "what I have done" or achieved nonetheless, and
the effect others have had. Three ideas, three sentences; and the invitations to
"ask me" now flow through the first seven lines, all of which are run-on until the
momentum comes to rest, properly, with the end-stopped line 7. In the draft, by
contrast, the end-stop of line 5 seems a false pause; and the end of the poem's thematic first half fell indecisively in the middle of a line. The more dramatic dash in
line 6, setting off the third "ask me," gives the invited questioning its climax.

Thus, in minor ways, Stafford prepares the major structural change: adding a
line, breaking the poem into two equal and balancing stanzas—the questioning,
the response. Like a sonnet, the poem "turns" at line 8.

Adding the phrase "I will listen to what you say," both focuses the imagined dialogue and implies that what the speaker would say is different from what the "you"
might say. After the end-stopped poise of the new line, the poem is run-on again
through line 13; and the final statement, "What the river says, that is what I say,"
now seems decisive and taut in its own line, unlike the merely conditional, rhythmically looser version of the draft. Flow and stasis, movement and poise are central
both to the poem's thematic acceptance and to its rhythm.

Interestingly, "Ask Me" seems to be free verse. The lines are, Stafford noted,
"generally just about equal." But most of them approximate iambic tetrameter.
Several, like line 7 ("their strongest love or hate has made"), are exactly metrical.
In an intermediate draft, the poem's last line would have been strongly metrical as
well: "What the river says is what I say." Stafford's final alteration of the line,
though still approximately countable, steers the rhythm away from the pat iambs—
suggesting that the speaker's firmness is not smooth or too easy. Stafford's instinct is
unerring.

Shaping as the discovery of a poem's form occurs startlingly in the published versions of Marianne Moore's "The Fish" (p. 46). Here is the earliest version, which appeared in a magazine in 1918:

The Fish

Wade through black jade.
Of the crow-blue mussel-shells, one
Keeps adjusting the ash-heaps;
Opening and shutting itself like

An injured fan.   5
The barnacles undermine the
Side of the wave—trained to hide
There—but the submerged shafts of the

Sun, split like spun   10
Glass, move themselves with spotlight swift-
Ness, into the crevices—
In and out, illuminating

The turquoise sea
Of bodies. The water drives a   15
Wedge of iron into the edge
Of the cliff, whereupon the stars,

Pink rice grains, ink
Bespattered jelly-fish, crabs like
Green lilies and submarine   20
Toadstools, slide each on the other.

All external
Marks of abuse are present on
This defiant edifice—
All the physical features of   25

Accident—lack
Of cornice, dynamite grooves, burns
And hatchet strokes, these things stand
Out on it; the chasm side is

Dead. Repeated   30
Evidence has proved that it can
Live on what cannot revive
Its youth. The sea grows old in it.

Despite its normal appearance, the poem is novel in form. Unmistakable rhyme-pairs—wade-jade, keeps-heaps, an-fan, and so on—*begin* and end lines 1 and 3 of each stanza. Self-enclosing in sound, laced tight, these lines seem to resist the otherwise fairly straightforward movement of the sentences, so that the poem alternates between this peculiar rigidity and a contrasting fluidity of run-ons (even over stanza-breaks). Perhaps the problem is only that a reader, unaccustomed to the device, finds the novelty more distracting than helpful. But the poem seems not to have its right form.

Whatever her reasons, Moore's own dissatisfaction with this 1918 version is clear from the appearance, in an anthology the next year and in her book *Observations* in 1924, of a quite different version of the poem:

The Fish

wade
through black jade.
   Of the crow-blue mussel shells, one
      keeps
         adjusting the ash heaps;   5
   opening and shutting itself like

an
injured fan.
   The barnacles which encrust the
      side   10
      of the wave, cannot hide
   there for the submerged shafts of the

sun,
split like spun
   glass, move themselves with spotlight swift-   15
      ness
         into the crevices—
   in and out, illuminating

the
turquoise sea   20
   of bodies. The water drives a
      wedge
      of iron through the iron edge
   of the cliff, whereupon the stars,

pink   25
rice grains, ink
   bespattered jelly-fish, crabs like
      green
      lilies and submarine
   toadstools, slide each on the other.   30

All
external
   marks of abuse are present on
      this
         defiant edifice—   35
   all the physical features of

```
    ac-
    cident—lack
        of cornice, dynamite grooves, burns
            and                                                    40
                hatchet strokes, these things stand
            out on it; the chasm side is

    dead.
    Repeated
      . evidence has proved that it can                           45
            live
                on what cannot revive
            its youth. The sea grows old in it.
```

Moore makes only two verbal changes, both improving. "The barnacles *undermine* the / Side of the wave—*trained to* hide / There—*but . . .*" becomes "The barnacles *which encrust* the / side / of the wave, *cannot* hide / there *for . . . .*" The simpler physical image of encrusting replaces the ambiguous idea of undermining, and focuses clearly the wit of reversing the usual way of seeing barnacles as belonging to, being attached to, the rock surface. The change also makes moot the possible questions of "trained how? by whom?"—a training which, in any case, doesn't prevent the shafts of sunlight from spotlighting them.

In stanza 4, "wedge of iron *into* the edge" becomes "wedge / of iron *through* the *iron* edge. . . ." The repetition of "iron" makes the opposed forces—sea, cliff—irreducibly equal; and the denser sound seems appropriate to this hard, unyielding opposition.

Excellent as these verbal adjustments are, the dramatic revision in 1924 is the opening up of the taut, flush-left, four-line stanzas into six-line stanzas with a pattern of indentation. The relining *in effect* moves each flush-left rhyme-syllable up to a line of its own. So,

    an injured fan

becomes

becomes

    an
    injured fan

This simple change, technically making both words *end*-rhymes, relieves the odd pressure in the 1918 version of the rhymes' seeming to bind or frame each line too tightly within itself. The 1924 stanzas rhyme *a a b c c d.*

The result might have been merely:

    an
    injured fan.
    The barnacles which encrust the
    side
    of the wave, cannot hide
    there for the submerged shafts of the

Moore, variably indenting the rhymed and unrhymed line-pairs, introduces a further flexibility into the stanza-shapes—a visual "in and out" that additionally suggests the interpenetrations of sea and cliff. Also dropping the line-capitals of the 1918 version, she increases the naturalness of the poem's appearance. In 1924, "The Fish" delightfully blends great fluidity and, in the unvaried syllabics and unremitting rhyming (which incorporates any word, however unimportant), great rigidity.

Reprinting the poem in 1935, with no verbal changes whatever, Moore made one further adjustment: moving the single-syllable lines 4 up to the end of lines 3, making a five-line stanza: *a a b b c*. Thus:

The Fish

wade
through black jade.
  Of the crow-blue mussel-shells, one keeps
  adjusting the ash-heaps;
    opening and shutting itself like   5

an
injured fan.
  The barnacles which encrust the side
  of the wave, cannot hide
    there for the submerged shafts of the   10

sun,
split like spun
  glass, move themselves with spotlight swiftness
  into the crevices—
    in and out, illuminating . . .   15

(The complete poem with this variant appears in full on p. 46.)

The poem gains in naturalness, avoiding the *two* monosyllabic rhyming lines of the 1924 stanza, which—as can be seen in the unindented form of it printed above—makes the pattern of lines 1–3 and 4–6 rhythmically duplicative. The 1924 stanza, by contrast, seems perhaps more brittle or fussy. If there is any pictorial quality in the stanzas at all, the 1935 stanzas' progressive indentation may make it the more just version.

Quite as successfully as William Stafford's in "Ask Me," Marianne Moore's changes in "The Fish" exemplify the power of shaping.

TITLES

Like the title above, titles may simply announce a poem's subject, as in "Peepers," "My Papa's Waltz," "Woman on Twenty-second Eating Berries," or its theme, as in "Delight in Disorder" or "Sex Without Love." Titles may also usefully set the scene, particularly for poems with a dramatic speaker, such as "Tuesday Morning, Loading Pigs," "Catania to Rome," or "The Widow's Lament in Springtime." Titles can also indicate a poem's tone, as in "Make Big Money at Home! Write Poems in Spare Time!" More technically, the title may function as a poem's effective first line, as in "The Fish."

Often, the title is the hardest part of a poem to write. Sometimes a poem seems complete in itself, and the title must be an afterthought. Since publishers need a title for contents or index and will promote the first line to serve as a title (as with poems by Emily Dickinson), the poet at a loss for a title can accept that expedient. Or, better, can often find one by looking through the poem's worksheets for a good phrase or image or detail that had been discarded. A title is also a convenient place to tuck information that does not fit easily *within* a poem, as in this poem by Miller Williams (b. 1930):

My Wife Reads the Paper at Breakfast on the Birthday of the Scottish Poet

Poet Burns To Be Honored, the headline read.
She put it down. "They found you out," she said.

Because the title is the first part of a poem the reader encounters, make it inter-esting—lest, thumbing through magazine or anthology, readers pass it by. Particu-larity is usually an advantage; one is more likely to be drawn to a poem called "Twila Jo and the Wrestler" (p. 312) than to a poem called "Jealousy." A title as general as "Jealousy" or "Hope," moreover, may promise more than the poem can deliver. What a good decision Christina Rossetti made in titling her poem "Up-Hill" (p. 372) instead of something like "Life's End" or "Salvation." The right title can also balance out a poem. For instance, a poem that seems burdened with the strange or the philosophical can be grounded with a definitive title like "A Guide to the Stone Age" (p. 225) or "Blackbirds" (p. 236). A highly concrete poem in which a reader might pass over a subtext may benefit from a more abstract title, like "Traveling Through the Dark" (p. 131) or "Politics" (p. 335). Searching for a title can often send the poet back to revision—suddenly aware of streams that the poem has yet to navigate.

Wallace Stevens was the master of intriguing titles: "Invective Against Swans," "The Revolutionists Stop for Orangeade," "On the Manner of Addressing Clouds," or—for a poem about a solipsistic rabbit whose inflated self-image gets him knocked off by a cat—"A Rabbit as King of the Ghosts." But simplicity is also good. John Updike notes that at one point he was thinking of calling his novel *Couples and Houses and Days*. "I asked Marianne Moore about it one noon when I found myself seated beside her at the Academy of Arts and Letters, and she promptly, in her tiny old lady's voice, said, '*Couples*. It's more mysterious.'"

A title may go beyond the poem, implying more than the poem directly states or reports, as in Michael Burns's "The First Time" (p. 338), where the suggestion of a wider perspective gives an ironic frame to the incident. Similarly, Claudia Rank-ine's "Out of Many, One" (p. 180), translating the Latin phrase that appears on our coins, *E Pluribus Unum*, quietly posits a political theme the narrative itself need never mention. Or consider the delicate way the title works in this wonderful poem by Gary Soto (b. 1952):

In the Madness of Love

Richard on the cold roof screams, I'm the eye
Of Omar, and a friend and I, with crumbs
Falling from our mouths, shout for him to get
Down, to remember that the rent is due
And it's no time to act silly.   5
Look, he says, and we look: a burst
Of sparrows. No, the clouds, he says,
They are coming. We plead with raisins,
Watery plums, but he's distant as the sky—
Dark with kites crossing over to rain.   10
We plead with a sandwich, car keys, albums;
Threaten him with a hose, our black neighbor
The drummer. No use. I climb on all fours
Over the roof, unsteady as a wobbly chair,
And when I touch him he shivers   15
Like a kicked dog. I take hold and rock him
In my arms, his jaw stiff with rage
And his eyes so wet we could drink from them
And be free. What is it? I ask.
There, he points. And the clouds begin to move.   20

The title both indicates and characterizes what is agitating the speaker's friend
Richard. In tone, though, it seems to be in a voice outside of or above the excited
and practical voice of the narration ("the rent is due / And it's no time to act
silly"). The tone is understanding, accepting. The madness of love is a condition,
known, something one can be *in*.

Omar of course is Omar Khayyám (d. 1123?), a Persian poet whose famed love
poems are familiar in English primarily in the great translation by Edward Fitzger-
ald (1809–1883), "Rubáiyát of Omar Khayyám of Naishápúr." For Omar, the transience of everything in nature was an emblem for the brevity and finality of human
life—"One thing is certain and the rest is Lies; / The Flower that once has blown
for ever dies." "I came like Water, and like Wind I go."

> The Moving Finger writes; and, having writ,
> Moves on: nor all your Piety nor Wit
>   Shall lure it back to cancel half a Line,
> Nor all your Tears wash out a Word of it.

Against such existential sorrow as grips Richard on the roof, bribes like "a sandwich, car keys, albums" or the threat of "our black neighbor / The drummer" are
useless.

Climbing out on the roof himself, the speaker holds and rocks Richard—"his
jaw stiff with rage / And his eyes so wet we could drink from them / And be free"—
until, in that pitying communion, he, too, shares the vision. "And," for the
speaker, "the clouds began to move."

It is the shadow of that understanding that we have already felt in the title.

The reader's first impression of a poem is usually made by its title; and, since titles are the way we refer to and remember poems, that impression may also be among the most enduring.

QUESTIONS AND SUGGESTIONS

1. Here are Yeats's initial sketches of the poem "After Long Silence" (p. 309) and a number of lines and alternatives from advancing drafts. Study them, noting the poem's growth, and compare them with the final version.

a) Recording a visit to Olivia Shakespeare in October 1929 as a proposed "Subject":

> Your hair is white
> My hair is white
> Come let us talk of love
> What other theme do we know
> When we were young
> We were in love with one another
> And then were ignorant.

b) Notes:

> 1) Your other lovers being dead and gone
> 2) Those other lovers being dead and gone
>
> friendly light
> hair is white
>
> 1) Upon the sole theme of art and song
> 2) Upon the supreme theme of art and song
> 3) Upon that theme so fitting for the aged; young
>   We loved each other and were ignorant
>
> Once more I have kissed your hand and it is right
> All other lovers being estranged or dead
>
> The heavy curtains drawn—the candle light
> Waging a doubtful battle with the shade
>
> 1) We call our wisdom up and descant
> 2) We call upon wisdom and descant
>   Upon the supreme theme of art and song
>   Decrepitude increases wisdom—young
>   We loved each other and were ignorant

The candle hidden by its friendly shade
The curtain drawn on the unfriendly night
That we descant and yet again descant
Upon the supreme theme of art and song

1) The friendly lamp light hidden by its shade
2) Unfriendly lamp light hidden by its shade

1) And shutters clipped upon the deepening night
2) Those curtains drawn upon the deepening night

That we descant and yet again descant
Upon the supreme theme of art and song—
Bodily decrepitude is wisdom—young

Once more I have kissed your hand and it is right
All other lovers being estranged or dead
Unfriendly lamplight hidden by its shade
The curtains drawn upon the deepening night—

2. Here are drafts and revisions of lines by William Wordsworth, Rupert Brooke (1887–1915), and W. B. Yeats; and of poems by Wilfred Owen, Robert Frost, and Don Welch (b. 1932). Consider why the poets made the changes and whether these changes involve gains or losses.

a)   from Wordsworth's *The Prelude:*

> Ere we retired,
> The cock had crow'd, the sky was bright with day.
> Two miles I had to walk along the fields
> Before I reached my home. Magnificent
> The morning was, in memorable pomp,
> More glorious than I ever had beheld.
> The Sea was laughing at a distance; all
> The solid Mountains were as bright as clouds.

> Magnificent
> The morning rose, in memorable pomp,
> Glorious as e'er I had beheld—in front,
> The sea lay laughing at a distance; near,
> The solid mountains shone, bright as the clouds.

b)   from Rupert Brooke's "The Soldier":

> If I should die think of me
> That in some corner of a foreign field
> Something of England lies.

If I should die, think only this of me:
That there's some corner of a foreign field
That is forever England. There shall be
In that rich earth a richer dust concealed.

c) from Yeats's "Adam's Curse" (p. 89):

There is one thing that all we women know,
Although we never heard of it at school—
That we must labor to be beautiful.

To be born woman is to know—
Although they do not talk of it at school—
That we must labor to be beautiful.

d) Wilfred Owen, "Anthem for Doomed Youth," *first draft*:

What mind's bells for these who die so fast?
—Only the monstrous anger of our guns.
Let the majestic insults of their iron mouths
Be as the priests' words at their burials.
Of choristers and holy music, none,   5
Nor any voice of mourning, save the wail,
The long-drawn wail of high, far-sailing shells.
What candles may we hold for these lost souls?
Not in the hands of boys, but in their eyes
Shall many candles shine, and He will light them: 10
Women's wide-spreaded arms shall be their wreaths,
And pallor of girls' cheeks shall be their palls.
The flowers, the tenderness of old men's minds,
And every dusk, a drawing down of blinds.

final version:

What passing-bells for these who die as cattle?
    Only the monstrous anger of the guns.
    Only the stuttering rifles' rapid rattle
Can patter out their hasty orisons.
No mockeries now for them; no prayers nor bells,   5
    Nor any voice of mourning save the choirs,—
The shrill, demented choirs of wailing shells;
    And bugles calling for them from sad shires.

What candles may be held to speed them all?
    Not in the hands of boys, but in their eyes   10
Shall shine the holy glimmers of good-byes.
    The pallor of girls' brows shall be their pall;
Their flowers the tenderness of patient minds,
And each slow dusk a drawing-down of blinds.

e)   Robert Frost:

In White   *1912*

A dented spider like a snowdrop white
On a white Heal-all, holding up a moth
Like a white piece of lifeless satin cloth—
Saw ever curious eye so strange a sight?
Portent in little, assorted death and blight   5
Like the ingredients of a witches' broth?
The beady spider, the flower like a froth,
And the moth carried like a paper kite.

What had that flower to do with being white,
The blue Brunella every child's delight?   10
What brought the kindred spider to that height?
(Make we no thesis of the miller's° plight.)
What but design of darkness and of night?
Design, design! Do I use the word aright?

12 *Miller:* Miller-moth.

Design   *1936*

I found a dimpled spider, fat and white,
On a white heal-all, holding up a moth
Like a white piece of rigid satin cloth—
Assorted characters of death and blight
Mixed ready to begin the morning right,   5
Like the ingredients of a witches' broth—
A snow-drop spider, a flower like a froth,
And dead wings carried like a paper kite.
What had that flower to do with being white,
The wayside blue and innocent heal-all?   10
What brought the kindred spider to that height,
Then steered the white moth thither in the night?
What but design of darkness to appall?—
If design govern in a thing so small.

f)   Don Welch, "There Is No Wind in Heaven," *first draft:*

There is no wind in heaven. Each leaf
simply greens in its own resplendence.

And there are no dead branches in heaven
combing the air, no moans in the eaves,
no whistling nor'westers anywhere.   5

God, how I'll miss the wind wherever
I am. I think the dead might like
a breath of it on the edge

of their porcelain souls;
or its strong palm slapped broadly   10
against their rich complexions.

Children love the wind, love it enough
to bundle up and let it in.
There must be someplace for the dead

where children's voices color every   15
part of winter, where their rigor
makes mortal every branch, however bare.

I've always thought the wind is the sky
come down, but there is no sky in heaven.
The only wind's the breath of the living dead.   20

final version: *1993*

There is no wind in heaven. Every leaf,
like every soul, never touches another.
Each greens in its own resplendence.

And there are no dead branches in heaven
combing the air, no moans in the eaves,   5
no whistling nor'westers in gold gutters.

God, how I'll miss the wind wherever
I am. I think the dead might like
a breath of it on the edge

of their porcelain souls;   10
or its strong palm slapped broadly
against their rich complexions.

Children love the wind. In the winter
they bundle up to let it in.
There must be someplace for the dead   15

where children's voices color every
extremity of winter, where their rigor
makes mortal every branch, however bare.

I've always thought the wind is the sky
come down, but there is no sky in heaven.   20

3. Choose a completed but somehow still unsatisfactory poem of your own and
have another try at revising it. Read it aloud several times. Does anything make
you wince—something you'd be embarrassed to show? (Maybe that's where the
trouble is.) Try taking out one or two words (the least effective) or, if the poem is
metered, a foot out of each line; does that open it up? Look back through the drafts
for a lost word, image, or detail that might start the poem moving again. Type it
over, varying the stanzas or breaking it into stanzas.

4. Write a sonnet, selecting all the rhyme words first and arranging them on the page. Then fill it in, keeping the meter. Write *anything,* don't worry whether it makes much sense. Read it aloud. How does it sound? Are there parts of it you like?

5. Here, set as prose, is Ezra Pound's translation of a Chinese poem, "Liu Ch'e." (The title is the name of the woman for whom it is an elegy.) Before looking at Pound's lining of it as verse (p. 309), experiment with your own ways of dividing it into lines.

> The rustling of the silk is discontinued, dust drifts over the court-yard, there is no sound of foot-fall, and the leaves scurry into heaps and lie still, and she the rejoicer of the heart is beneath them: a wet leaf that clings to the threshold.

6. An **abecedarian** is a variant of the acrostic in which each line begins, in order, with the letters of the alphabet. Poets have reported being helped by the device in getting a poem to flow out in composing. So, when you are stuck, give it a try. Copy the letters of the alphabet down the left side of a blank page, and begin filling in the lines, using each next letter as a clue for what might come next. (Once the poem is really going of course, you can diverge from the pattern.) Here is an example by Peter Meinke (b. 1932):

The ABC of Aerobics

Air seeps through alleys and our diaphragms
balloon blackly with this mix of
carbon monoxide and the thousand corrosives a city
doles out free to its constituents;
everyone's jogging through Edgemont Park,   5
frightened by death and fatty tissue,
gasping at the maximal heart rate,
hoping to outlive all the others streaming
in the lanes like lemmings lurching toward their last
jump. I join in despair   10
knowing my arteries jammed with
lint and tobacco, lard and bourbon—my
medical history a noxious marsh:
newts and moles slink through the sodden veins,
owls hoot in the lungs' dark branches;   15
probably I shall keel off the john like
queer Uncle George and lie on the bathroom floor
raging about Shirley Clark, my true love in
seventh grade, God bless her wherever she lives
tied to that turkey who hugely   20
undervalues the beauty of her tiny earlobes, one
view of which (either one: they are both perfect)
would add years to my life, and I could skip these
X-rays, turn in my insurance card, and trade
yoga and treadmills and jogging and zen and   25
zucchini for drinking and dreaming of her, breathing hard.

7. Make up three or four interesting, off-the-wall titles. Try to write a poem to follow one of them.

8. After reading Maura Stanton's "Song (After Shakespeare)" (p. 310), look up Shakespeare's winter song, "When icicles hang by the wall," at the very end of *Love's Labour's Lost*. How has Stanton drawn on and modernized the model? Compare the tones of each.

9. Recall an encounter with a wasp, spider, beetle, praying mantis, snail, or the like. Look the creature up in a good encyclopedia or natural history text, if possible one with color photographs. Might there be a poem in it?

POEMS TO CONSIDER

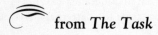 **from *The Task*** 1785

WILLIAM COWPER (1731–1800)

> There is a pleasure in poetic pains
> Which only poets know. The shifts and turns,
> Th' expedients and inventions, multiform,
> To which the mind resorts, in chase of terms
> Though apt, yet coy, and difficult to win—   5
> T'arrest the fleeting images that fill
> The mirror of the mind, and hold them fast,
> And force them sit till he has pencil'd off
> A faithful likeness of the forms he views;
> Then to dispose his copies with such art,   10
> That each may find its most propitious light,
> And shine by situation, hardly less
> Than by the labour and the skill it cost;
> Are occupations of the poet's mind
> So pleasing, and that steal away the thought   15
> With such address from themes of sad import,
> That, lost in his own musings, happy man!
> He feels th' anxieties of life, denied
> Their wonted entertainment, all retire.
> Such joys has he that sings. But ah! not such,   20
> Or seldom such, the hearers of his song.
> Fastidious, or else listless, or perhaps
> Aware of nothing arduous in a task
> They never undertook, they little note
> His dangers or escapes, and haply find   25
> There least amusement where he found the most.

After Long Silence   *1933*

WILLIAM BUTLER YEATS (1865–1939)

Speech after long silence; it is right,
All other lovers being estranged or dead,
Unfriendly lamplight hid under its shade,
The curtains drawn upon unfriendly night,
That we descant and yet again descant   5
Upon the supreme theme of Art and Song:
Bodily decrepitude is wisdom; young
We loved each other and were ignorant.

Liu Ch'e   *1914*

EZRA POUND (1885–1972)

The rustling of the silk is discontinued,
Dust drifts over the court-yard,
There is no sound of foot-fall, and the leaves
Scurry into heaps and lie still,
And she the rejoicer of the heart is beneath them: 5

A wet leaf that clings to the threshold.

Slugs   *1988*

MICHAEL HEFFERNAN (b. 1942)

There is an awful kindness in the way this cat
keeps his own counsel about these terrible slugs
curled in his dinner or draped from his waterbowl
or stalled at the end of a strand of belly-drool.
I wouldn't live that way. They would just make me mad.   5
My heart's in the wrong place. I am not any good
    at putting up with matters of this kind.

These nightly visitations from the Under-Slime,
the Ur-Spittle of the Creation, I couldn't
deal with them, even in my own way, even from   10
my end of the Cosmos of Animate Being.
They'd have to leave. I'd make their lives unliveable,
pry them with sticks, shove them in dust, send them packing

back where they came from I can tell you that.

As for the cat, what goes on in his heart of hearts?   15
Above him in the clouds most of the moon moves by,
while he steps amiably among these least of all
God's negligible beasts, these bloodless gastropods—
one crestfallen cat with his entourage of slugs,
and nothing for it but to hang around my yard,   20
    with me and my people fast in our dream.

 ### Poem for a New Cat   1988

ED OCHESTER (b. 1939)

Watching her stand on the first
joints of her hind legs like a kangaroo
peering over the edge of the bathtub
at my privates floating like a fungoid lilypad,
or her bouncy joy in pouncing on a crumpled   5
Pall Mall pack, or the way she wobbles walking
the back of the couch, I think when
was it we grew tired of everything?
Imagine the cat jogging, terrified
that her ass might droop, or studying   10
the effective annual interest paid
by the First Variable Rate Fund, the cat
feeling obliged to read those poems that
concentrate the sweetness of life like prunes.
O.K., that's ridiculous—though the cat   15
also kills for pleasure—but I find
myself in the middle of the way,
half the minutes of my sentient life
told out for greed and fear.
The cat's whiskers are covered with lint   20
from the back of the dryer.
                              Friend,
how it is with you I don't know
but I'm too old to die.

Song (After Shakespeare)   *1984*
MAURA STANTON (b. 1946)

When mist advances on the mountain
And Dick the postman shields his mail
And Tom adjusts the furnace fan
    And the cat mews with lowered tail
When the umbrella is our domain   5
Then softly calls the solemn rain,
                Oh-blue,
All-blue, Oh-blue: a dreary sound,
While lazy Joan creeps back to bed.

When leaves fall on the boulevard   10
    And quarrels begin among good men
And snails crisscross the sodden yard
    And Marian broods over maps again
When globed drops run down the pane
Then softly calls the solemn rain,   15
                Oh-blue,
All-blue, Oh-blue: a dreary sound,
While lazy Jack creeps in with Joan.

Siren   *1990*
AMY GERSTLER (b. 1956)

I have a fish's tail, so I'm not qualified to love you.
But I do. Pale as an August sky, pale as flour milled
a thousand times, pale as the icebergs I have never seen,
and twice as numb—my skin is such a contrast to the rough
rocks I lie on, that from far away it looks like I'm a baby   5
riding a dinosaur. The turn of centuries or the turn
of a page means the same to me, little or nothing.
I have teeth in places you'd never suspect. Come. Kiss me
and die soon. I slap my tail in the shallows—which is to say
I appreciate nature. You see my sisters and me perched   10
on rocks and tiny islands here and there for miles:
untangling our hair with our fingers, eating seaweed.

The Sea-Side Cave   1850

ALICE CARY (1820–1871)

> *for a bird of the air shall carry the voice, and that which*
> *hath wings shall tell the matter.*
> —*Ecclesiastes 10.20*

At the dead of night by the side of the Sea
I met my gray-haired enemy,—
The glittering light of his serpent eye
Was all I had to see him by.

At the dead of night, and stormy weather   5
We went into a cave together,—
Into a cave by the side of the Sea,
And—he never came out with me!

The flower that up through the April mould
Comes like a miser dragging his gold,   10
Never made spot of earth so bright
As was the ground in the cave that night.

Dead of night, and stormy weather!
Who should see us going together
Under the black and dripping stone   15
Of the cave from whence I came alone!

Next day as my boy sat on my knee
He picked the gray hairs off from me,
And told with eyes brimful of fear
How a bird in the meadow near   20

Over her clay-built nest had spread
Sticks and leaves all bloody red,
Brought from a cave by the side of the Sea
Where some murdered man must be.

Twila Jo and the Wrestler   1989

HEATHER ROSS MILLER (b. 1939)

Twila Jo, who was not a virgin,
wanted to run off with a Myrtle Beach wrestler,
tattoos on both his arms,
snaky green things with bicep eyelids

he raised and shut,   5
wonderful things, things she kissed.
She told her little sister, Faye,
the one who saved strings,
the one who crunched foil into big luminous coils,
and picked up cans along Ocean Hiway.   10
"You know better than that,"
the little sister smashed three Pepsis flat,
unraveled a long blue string
from Twila Jo's jeans.
"Look at the mess you already made,   15
sneaking out, acting weird, afraid of Daddy."
Little Faye jeered.
Twila Jo, stark, discordant, brutal,
said, "Daddy can die, and so can you.
I don't care. Don't you tell,"   20
and drove off to meet the wrestler.

Faye fingered her blue string,
sacked up her three dead Pepsis,
and squatted, pinching bright blisters in her foil.
She guessed Twila Jo halfway to Myrtle Beach,   25
somewhere along Ocean Hiway,
the stupid wrestler reaching across the seat,
flexing the snaky green things,
making Twila Jo squeal, and let go the wheel,
then a blue semi, FAYE'S EXPRESS,   30
flashy as foil,
flattening them both to a bloody blister,
the Myrtle Beach wrestler,
and her big sister.

Eyes   *1995*

LINDA TAYLOR (b. 1946)

We are blind, really. We cannot
open our eyes any deeper
than the skin around
the warm, jellied water.
We can see below, the angle   5
of nose, or the top of a cheek,
the hand and lip in front of us,
all we know of ourselves.
A mirror catches the full moon

in its hands.   10
A woman drowning sees yellow.

An eye is shaped like a fish
swimming through its own sight.
We can try to push a bird through,
a piece of furniture, a child's head,   15
hug them closer in our synapses,
but the eye can't caress a piece
of feathered wind or wood,
as Spinoza knew: matter could
not touch the mind. He spent   20
his life grinding lenses,
eventually went blind.

They say the eye is part
of the brain—the bridge that reaches
with hunger to the world,   25
and yet it is the receptive
lake that suffers rape
from the splash of any object
or scene, however undesired or cruel.
Or, of the softer lush of sunlit   30
leaves, green as light gently
moving toward us like
lovers' hands, or water.

11

REVISING (II)
Seven-Eighths of the Iceberg

One good rule of thumb is that any writing should be only as long as is necessary to do its job. There is leeway, of course, but as Shakespeare put it, "It is better to be brief than tedious." It takes time to read words. Any idea expressed in a hundred words that could have been said fully in fifty must be *less intense* because it is spread over a longer reading time. Redundancies, vague or empty epithets, and rhetorical roundabouts cause, second by second in the reading, a loss in impact; they inevitably lower interest and blur focus. Unnecessary words clutter, confuse, and distract. In his funny but practical essay on "Fenimore Cooper's Literary Offenses"—in the form of "mock" lectures to the Veterinary College of Arizona—Mark Twain (Samuel L. Clemens, 1835–1910) shows how several inflated passages from Cooper's novels might have been advantageously tightened. One he reduces from 320 words to 220, without loss in content. Another he reduces from eighty words to forty—a cut of 50 percent! Although Twain is discussing prose, his account is pertinent.

In studying Cooper you will find it profitable to study him in detail—word by word, sentence by sentence. For every sentence of his is interesting. Interesting because of its make-up; its peculiar make-up, its original make-up. Let us examine a sentence or two, and see. Here is a passage from Chapter XI of *The Last of the Mohicans*, one of the most famous and most admired of Cooper's books:

> Notwithstanding the swiftness of their flight, one of the Indians had found an opportunity to strike a straggling fawn with an arrow, and had borne the more preferable fragments of the victim, patiently on his shoulders, to the stopping-place. Without any aid from the science of cookery, he was

immediately employed, in common with his fellows, in gorging himself with this digestible sustenance. Magua alone sat apart, without participating in the revolting meal, and apparently buried in the deepest thought.

This little paragraph is full of matter for reflection and inquiry. The remark about the swiftness of the flight was unnecessary, as it was merely put in to forestall the possible objection of some overparticular reader that the Indian couldn't have found the needed "opportunity" while fleeing swiftly. The reader would not have made that objection. He would care nothing about having that small matter explained and justified. But that is Cooper's way; frequently he will explain and justify little things that do not need it and then make up for this by as frequently failing to explain important ones that do need it . . . .

No, the remark about the swiftness of their flight was not necessary; neither was the one which said that the Indian found an opportunity; neither was the one which said he *struck* the fawn; neither was the one which explained that it was a "straggling" fawn; neither was the one which said the striking was done with an arrow; neither was the one which said the Indian bore the "fragments"; nor the remark that they were preferable fragments; nor the remark that they were *more* preferable fragments; nor the explanation that they were fragments of the "victim"; nor the overparticular explanation that specifies the Indian's "shoulders" as the part of him that supported the fragments; nor the statement that the Indian bore the fragments patiently. None of those details has any value. We don't care what the Indian struck the fawn with; we don't care whether it was a straggling fawn or an unstraggling one; we don't care which fragments the Indian saved; we don't care why he saved the "more" preferable ones when the merely preferable ones would have amounted to just the same thing and couldn't have been told from the more preferable ones by anybody, dead or alive; we don't care whether the Indian carried them on his shoulders or in his handkerchief; and finally, we don't care whether he carried them patiently or struck for higher pay and shorter hours. We are indifferent to that Indian and all his affairs.

There was only one fact in that long sentence that was worth stating, and it could have been squeezed into these few words—and with advantage to the narrative, too: "During the flight one of the Indians had killed a fawn and he brought it into camp."

You will notice that "During the flight one of the Indians had killed a fawn and he brought it into camp," is more straightforward and businesslike, and less mincing and smirky, than it is to say, "Notwithstanding the swiftness of their flight, one of the Indians had found an opportunity to strike a straggling fawn with an arrow, and had borne the more preferable fragments of the victim, patiently on his shoulders, to the stopping-place." You will notice that the form "During the flight one of the Indians had killed a fawn and he brought it into camp" holds up its chin and moves to the front with the steady stride of a grenadier, whereas the form "Notwithstanding the swiftness of their flight, one of the Indians had found an opportunity to strike a straggling fawn with an arrow, and had borne the more preferable fragments of the victim, patiently on his shoulders, to the stopping-place" simpers along with an airy, complacent, monkey-with-a-parasol gait which is not suited to the transportation of raw meat.

I beg to remind you that an author's way of setting forth a matter is called his Style, and that an author's style is a main part of his equipment for business. The style of some authors has variety in it, but Cooper's style is remarkable for the absence of this feature. Cooper's style is always grand and stately and noble. Style may be likened to an army, the author to its general, the book to the campaign. Some authors proportion an attacking force to the strength or weakness, the importance or unimportance, of the object to be attacked; but Cooper doesn't. It doesn't make any difference to Cooper whether the object of attack is a hundred thousand men or a cow; he hurls his entire force against it. He comes thundering down with all his battalions at his back, cavalry in the van, artillery on the flanks, infantry massed in the middle, forty bands braying, a thousand banners streaming in the wind; and whether the object be an army or a cow you will see him come marching sublimely in, at the end of the engagement, bearing the more preferable fragments of the victim patiently on his shoulders, to the stopping-place. Cooper's style is grand, awful, beautiful; but it is sacred to Cooper, it is his very own, and no student of the Veterinary College of Arizona will be allowed to filch it from him.

In one of his chapters Cooper throws an ungentle slur at one Gamut because he is not exact enough in his choice of words. But Cooper has that failing himself. If the Indian had "struck" the fawn with a brick, or with a club, or with his fist, no one could find fault with the word used. And one cannot find much fault when he strikes it with an arrow; still it sounds affected, and it might have been a little better to lean to simplicity and say he shot it with an arrow.

"Fragments" is well enough, perhaps, when one is speaking of the parts of a dismembered deer, yet it hasn't just exactly the right sound—and sound is something; in fact sound is a good deal. It makes the difference between good music and poor music, and it can sometimes make the difference between good literature and indifferent literature. "Fragments" sounds all right when we are talking about the wreckage of a breakable thing that has been smashed; it also sounds all right when applied to cat's meat; but when we use it to describe large hunks and chunks like the fore- and hindquarters of a fawn, it grates upon the fastidious ear.

"Without any aid from the science of cookery, he was immediately employed, in common with his fellows, in gorging himself with this digestible sustenance."

This was a mere statistic; just a mere cold, colorless statistic; yet you see Cooper has made a chromo out of it. To use another figure, he has clothed a humble statistic in flowing, voluminous and costly raiment, whereas both good taste and economy suggest that he ought to have saved these splendors for a king, and dressed the humble statistic in a simple breech-clout. Cooper spent twenty-four words here on a thing not really worth more than eight. We will reduce the statistic to its proper proportions and state it in this way:

"He and the others ate the meat raw."

"Digestible sustenance" is a handsome phrase, but it was out of place there, because we do not know these Indians or care for them; and so it cannot interest us to know whether the meat was going to agree with them or not. Details which do not assist a story are better left out.

"Magua alone sat apart, without participating in the revolting meal" is a statement which we understand, but that is our merit, not Cooper's. Cooper is not clear. He does not say who it is that is revolted by the meal. It is really Cooper himself, but there is nothing in the statement to indicate that it isn't Magua. Magua is an Indian and likes raw meat.

The word "alone" could have been left out and space saved. It has no value where it is.

TIGHTENING

More than prose, poetry is an art of compression. This does not mean that all poems should be epigrams; nor that, at the expense of clarity or good manners, a poem should be clogged, crammed, or written in telegramese. But the poet should follow William Strunk's rule not to use two words when one will do and must continually weigh the effect of every word used.

In meter, padding a line to keep the form, instead of finding a necessary detail, results in slackness. The writer in meter may have an advantage, however, as, in a sense, form *tests* content; and he or she may, keeping at it, discover words, ideas, images, or details which the writer in free verse would not have considered. In free verse, having said something, it is all too easy never to look for a *better* way of saying it. Too readily satisfied, a writer in free verse may be like a cook whose only recipe is oatmeal.

In poetry every word should be doing more than one job. Its sound, as well as its sense, matters. Moreover, the feeling of mysterious depth in a good poem frequently comes from the implicit, from nuances and connotations, as in Burns's "red, red rose" and "melodie." Everything need not be *said*. As Ernest Hemingway notes:

> If a writer of prose knows enough about what he is writing about, he may omit things that he knows and the reader, if the writer is writing truly enough, will have a feeling of these things as strongly as though the writer had stated them. The dignity of movement of an iceberg is due to only one-eighth of it being above water.

This is, he adds, writing "with nothing that will go bad afterwards." What is *not* there—the implicit, the merely intimated, the nuance—will have its effect.

Tighten, then. Consider this draft by a student, D. A. Fantauzzi:

Moorings

A collection of white, yellow, red
hulks of sailboats—
bugs with wings
folded down their backs,
tucked out of the wind,
sitting still.

Through the heart
a tall pin
sticks each to the blue-green mat.

Sharply observed, the poem presents a colorful scene. Still, good instincts would test the poem. Here is the text again, with possible excisions shown by brackets:

[A collection of] white, yellow, red
[hulks of] sailboats—
bugs with wings
folded down their backs,
[tucked out of the wind,]
[sitting still.]

[Through the heart]
a tall pin
sticks each to the blue-green mat.

The plural "sailboats" might be sufficient without "A collection of." Though the comparison between sailboats and a display of pinned insects makes the word relevant, it has little force where it is, before the comparison is indicated. In line 2 "hulks of" seems unnecessary and misleading. "Hulks" both feels too large and clumsy for sailboats *and* suggests abandoned or battered vessels. The comparison of sails to wings is precise (both are means of propulsion by air) and necessary; the sails are literally "folded down their backs," as might also be the case of insects' wings. "Tucked out of the wind" seems needlessly explanatory, and the action seems too volitional because in the comparison the insects are obviously dead. Line 6 seems wasted as well as somewhat inaccurate. "Sitting" seems too flat and motionless for sailboats on open water, especially if there is wind; and it applies poorly to the lifeless, impaled insects. The feeling of "Through the heart" is right, but since neither sailboats nor insects have hearts, the line seems imprecise, sentimental, almost a cliché.

Each of these potential deletions raises a question the poet should consider. How necessary is this word, or detail, to the poem I am trying to write? Here is the poem as it might be arranged, with the cuts made:

White, yellow, red sailboats—
bugs with wings
folded down their backs.

A tall pin
sticks each to the blue-green mat.

Perhaps the unbalanced, low, flat shapes of the poem suggest the folded-down sails. Perhaps, at this stage, some other phrase or detail or other order will occur to the poet. Might the word "collection" go somehow into stanza 2? Might "away from the wind"—a slight alteration of "tucked out of the wind"—make a good final line and recover some of the pathos of "Through the heart"? How would that affect the rhythm? Asking and answering such questions is the process of writing a poem.

The poet's revision adds a detail—"in rows"— that both helps the picture and reenforces the comparison. He decided to keep the phrase "A collection of," which sets up the comparison and prevents a reader's imagining the sailboats as dispersed.

> A collection of white, yellow, red
> sailboats—bugs with wings
> folded down their backs,
> in rows.
>
> A tall pin
> sticks each to the blue-green mat.

Slackness (wasted words, wasted motions) goes against Anton Chekhov's belief, expressed in a letter to Maxim Gorki, that "when a person expends the least possible movement on a certain act, that is grace." A remark of Ezra Pound's in 1914 is tongue-in-cheek but not without point: "A Chinaman said long ago that if a man can't say what he has to say in twelve lines he had better keep quiet." Not all poems should be short, of course, nor as short as Pound's "In a Station of the Metro" (p. 208), which from a thirty-five line draft became a two-line poem! But every poem should be as short as it can be.

Tightening may become the occasion for a brilliant stroke that might never have occurred to the poet otherwise, as it does in the fourth stanza of this 1924 revision of Marianne Moore's "My Apish Cousins," which was retitled in 1935.

The Monkeys

> winked too much and were afraid of snakes. The zebras, supreme in
> their abnormality; the elephants with their fog-colored skin
>   and strictly practical appendages
>   were there, the small cats; and the parakeet—
>   trivial and humdrum on examination, destroying   5
>   bark and portions of the food it could not eat.
>
> I recall their magnificence, now not more magnificent
> than it is dim. It is difficult to recall the ornament,
>   speech, and precise manner of what one might
>   call the minor acquaintances twenty   10
>   years back; but I shall not forget him—that Gilgamesh among
>   the hairy carnivora—that cat with the

wedge-shaped, slate-gray marks on its forelegs and the resolute tail,
astringently remarking, "They have imposed on us with their pale
  half-fledged protestations, trembling about   15
    in inarticulate frenzy, saying
      it is not for us to understand art; finding it
      all so difficult, examining the thing

as if it were inconceivably arcanic, as symmet-
rically frigid as if it had been carved out of chrysoprase   20
  or marble—strict with tension, malignant
    in its power over us and deeper
      than the sea when it proffers flattery in exchange for hemp,
  rye, flax, horses, platinum, timber, and fur."

The evocation of a visit to the zoo some years earlier is both splendidly colorful and gently witty. The creatures, the ordinary and the odd and the grand, are all treated with affection as "minor acquaintances." (The slight coyness of "Apish Cousins" isn't really necessary to establish the affection or sense of kinship.) The admired big cat seems a Gilgamesh—that is, like the heroic king of a Babylonian epic.

The poem takes a dazzling leap at line 14, for the remark attributed to the cat turns out to be a vicious denunciation of the sort of high-flown, overly intellectual critic who would contend that it is not for ordinary readers or viewers "to understand art." Moore's admiration for the cat of course aligns her with its angry statement, and with the common readers whose portraits she has been amusedly sketching in the guise of zoo-creatures. In their variety, not so ordinary after all! And art then, in her view, is not some "inconceivably arcanic" thing, "malignant / in its power over us," which like the sea can take our practical goods in exchange for mere flattery or prettiness, deceiving us.

This marvelous poem first appeared in an anthology in 1917, where the fourth stanza went:

As if it were something inconceivably arcanic, as
Symmetrically frigid as something carved out of chrysoprase   20
  Or marble—strict with tension, malignant
    In its power over us and deeper
      Than the sea when it proffers flattery in exchange for hemp,
  Rye, flax, horses, platinum, timber and fur."

Aside from the dropping of line-capitals, the only change occurs in lines 19–20. Especially after "thing" in line 18, the repetition of "something" in both lines no doubt seemed both flat and wasteful. Without the word, line 19 could simply be closed up with no change in meaning at all. But the poem is in syllabics and that would leave the line two syllables short. Line 20 is a bit more problematic, but could be repaired merely in inserting "if": "frigid as *if* carved . . . ," but leaving the line a syllable short. In other poems such as "Poetry" and "Critics and Connoisseurs," Moore was content to leave the syllabics out of whack in making her precise revisions, and she could have done that here.

Her solution is brilliant. She repairs the syllable-count of line 20 by inserting "if it had been" and moving the first two syllables of "*symmet*rically" up to restore the syllable-count of line 19. It costs her the off-rhyme of "as-chrysoprase," but what better example could there be of fussy rigidity than thus "symmet- / rically" dividing the word! A minor chore of tightening leads to a fine discovery.

FOCUSING

As when we look at slides, when we read poems we want them brought *into clear focus*. Avoiding blur and fuzziness—unintentional ambiguity, private meanings, the omission of an essential detail, and especially purple passages—is part of the poet's job in revising. Because the words will always evoke the poet's original intention, it is often difficult for the poet to notice the blur. Sometimes more is involved: a reevaluation of the intention itself. As William Butler Yeats put it:

> The friends that have it I do wrong
> Whenever I remake a song,
> Should know what issue is at stake:
> It is myself that I remake.

He sometimes rewrote, years later, poems that had already been published, as Marianne Moore and W. H. Auden also did. Here, for example, as Yeats published it in 1892, is "The Sorrow of Love."

> The quarrel of the sparrows in the eaves,
>   The full round moon and the star-laden sky,
> And the loud song of the ever-singing leaves
>   Had hid away earth's old and weary cry.
>
> And then you came with those red mournful lips,   5
>   And with you came the whole of the world's tears,
> And all the sorrows of her labouring ships,
>   And all burden of her myriad years.
>
> And now the sparrows warring in the eaves,
>   The crumbling moon, the white stars in the sky,   10
> And the loud chanting of the unquiet leaves,
>   Are shaken with earth's old and weary cry.

Grave, languorous, and lovely, "The Sorrow of Love" shows the effect on the speaker of the woman "with those red mournful lips." Before her, he was unaware of "earth's old and weary cry"; and sparrows, moon, stars, and leaves had seemed only themselves. The quarreling sparrows keep this picture from seeming over-pretty. After the woman, all these things of the world are, for him, "shaken with earth's old and weary cry." The positive images become now negative: "the full round moon" decays and is "crumbling," "the ever-singing leaves" are now "unquiet." Even the sparrows' quarreling is worse, "warring."

With "those red mournful lips," the woman herself seems already to have suffered "the sorrow of love" and to bring with her, from the speaker's point of view, "the whole of the world's tears." Presumably because she rejects him, she is his induction into the "sorrow of love." It isn't quite clear what the "labouring ships" have to do with the sorrow of love, but like the sparrows, moon, stars, and leaves, they reflect the speaker's feelings about everything after the sad and beautiful woman.

When Yeats revised the poem in 1925, although only one of the rhyme words is altered ("years" to "peers"), he transformed it.

> The brawling of a sparrow in the eaves,
> The brilliant moon and all the milky sky,
> And all that famous harmony of leaves,
> Had blotted out man's image and his cry.
>
> A girl arose that had red mournful lips   5
> And seemed the greatness of the world in tears,
> Doomed like Odysseus and the labouring ships
> And proud as Priam murdered with his peers;
>
> Arose, and on the instant clamorous eaves,
> A climbing moon upon an empty sky,   10
> And all that lamentation of the leaves,
> Could but compose man's image and his cry.

In discussing the 1892 version, we used the word "woman." Although it does not appear in the text and there is nothing directly indicative of age, it seems more accurate to the history implied by her sorrowful experience of love than the word "girl" might. One of the major changes in the 1925 version, then, is the description of her as a "girl," which, at a single touch, increases the poem's pathos: so much sorrow in one so young is profoundly moving. Another major change is the depersonalization of the relationship in the poem. With the use of the third person—"girl" instead of "you"—the speaker's relationship to her (having been rejected or whatever) becomes irrelevant. In the later version, only his experience of her sorrow causes his darkened attitude. The poem loses much less in this playing down of the personal than it gains in poignancy. That gain is intensified by a third major change, in which "earth's old and weary cry" becomes "man's image and his cry." At best, the sorrow of love could have been associated only vaguely with the personified "earth." Dropping this rather weak elegance, Yeats accurately focuses the poem's tragic vision on the human. The natural details of sparrow, moon, stars, leaves (which, after all, exist apart from the human) seemed in stanza 1 to be sufficiently absorbing in themselves. After the girl has appeared, in stanza 3, their clamor, emptiness, and "lamentation" are felt by the speaker to express his feeling. The fourth major change, in lines 7–8, makes powerful use of the ships, which in the first version were a fuzzy image:

> Doomed like Odysseus and the labouring ships
> And proud as Priam murdered with his peers

Both epics of Homer, *Odyssey* and *Iliad*, act as evidence. Though Odysseus and Priam are mentioned, and though these comparisons characterize the doomed, proud girl, the effect is also to imply a comparison to the two heroic women of these epics, the beautiful and doomed Helen and the proud and faithful Penelope. The "labouring ships" suggest Agamemnon's fleet as much as Odysseus's hard travels. The image of the "murdered" Priam, last king of Troy, encompasses the destruction of Troy. Thus, in their allusive fashion, these two lines gather into Yeats's poem the whole of the heroic and amorous weight of *Iliad* and *Odyssey*. The poem's claim that the sorrow of love centers "man's image and his cry" thus gathers a convincing historical density.

The "And . . . And . . . And . . ." construction of the first version is replaced by more muscular syntax. Details in the first version that were somewhat misty or romantic, like "the ever-singing leaves," are hardened and sharpened. The plural quarreling and warring sparrows—which might now distract from the distinction between the natural and the human and offer a competing miniature to the vision of the Trojan War—become only a single brawling and clamorous sparrow. Yeats here accepts a small loss in order to clarify the shape of the whole poem, as perhaps he also does in letting go the image of the "crumbling" moon.

The reduction of the number of words in the poem makes it seem cleaner and more direct; compare the effect of "The full round moon and the star-laden sky" with the effect of "The brilliant moon and all the milky sky"; or the elimination of the redundant "song" and "singing" in line 3. Dropping the somewhat fussy indentation of lines increases the poem's directness visually. The sound of the final version is everywhere more resonant. Consider the alliteration of the last two lines of the two versions:

> And the loud chanting of the unquiet leaves,
>   Are shaken with earth's old and weary cry

and

> And all that lamentation of the leaves,
>   Could but compose man's image and his cry.

The diction in general becomes more dramatic: "you came" in the first version becomes the powerful "A girl arose" in the final version; and the dramatic repetition of "Arose" at the beginning of the third stanza gives a dynamic impetus to the poem's climax, which the flat "And now" did not. Though it may be a subjective response, "arose" and "red mournful lips" also seem somehow to exchange colors in a subtle resonance.

Only in the poem's final version did Yeats accomplish what he had intended more than thirty years earlier.

TESTING

One of a poet's most difficult jobs is assessing whether the words on the page, which seem right, will convey to a reader a feeling or impression identical to his or her own. If, for instance, your mother describes for you the house in which she lived at the age of five, she has in mind a picture of it, indeed, a whole set of pictures, and can with closed eyes still see it. But describing it to you, do words call up exactly the same picture? Obviously, they cannot. If she has chosen the right words, the significant details, the best she can hope is that you will visualize a house much *like* the house, on a street much like the street, and so on. Unless someone is describing a building we have also seen (the Empire State Building, say) there is no way we can have identical images in our minds. (Films made from novels we like often disappoint because they rarely reproduce things as we imagined them.)

As writers, we deal at best in impressions of visual scenes, people, ideas, or feelings. The poet's words will always call up, for her or him, the precise scene or feeling. But the poet must consider accurately the effect the words have on a reader if they are to evoke in the reader something sufficiently like.

Poets tend to become almost insatiable testers and tinkerers. The old saw has it that a poet never finishes a poem but merely abandons it. With good reason the poet learns to put a new poem away for a time, then to have another look. What may seem a stroke of genius at midnight may appear quite otherwise the following week. In this, poets are like manic-depressives—up, down, up—about what they are doing. Because the poem that seems great today can seem dumb tomorrow and wonderful again the day after, poets need friends, other members of a writing class, and eventually editors. What may be obvious to someone else, though not to the poet, may very well start the poet going again on the poem, or provide the clue to patching a thin spot or avoiding a clunker.

Friends are handy but are sometimes too well-meaning. Praise is always nice, but the poet wants (or should want in that heart of hearts) the unvarnished truth. Dryden's seventeenth-century advice still fits:

> . . . to yourself be critic most severe.
> Fantastic wits their darling follies love;
> But find you faithful friends that will reprove,
> That on your works may look with careful eyes,
> And of your faults be zealous enemies: 5
> Lay by an author's pride and vanity,
> And from a friend a flatterer descry . . .
> No fool can want a sot to praise his rhymes.
> The flattest work has ever in the court
> Met with some zealous ass for its support;   10
> And in all times a forward scribbling fop
> Has found some greater fool to cry him up.

Find those, as Pope says, "Who to a friend his faults can freely show."

Opposite is a facsimile of Draft 15 of Donald Hall's "Ox Cart Man." The comments, originally in longhand, are those of poet Louis Simpson, to whom Hall had sent the draft. Both of Simpson's insightful suggestions prompted good revisions by Hall. The awkward "He walks by ox head," perhaps natural enough in earlier versions where the poem was cast in first person as spoken by the character, becomes "He walks by his ox's head." (Why might Hall have preferred this to "by the ox's head"?)

Seeing that the activities that would complete the cycle in stanza 6 (back to potatoes, with which the poem began) are already implied, Hall dropped the stanza. Dissatisfied with the rhythm of "to build the cart again" for concluding the poem, however, he tried out several alternatives: "to make the new cart," then "building another cart," " building the cart again," and "building the new cart." Try to decide which you would choose before looking at the finished poem on p. 340.

Since few poems arrive from the imagination complete, in the clear (as cryptologists put it), revising is most of what a poet can *do*. It must be added, though, that poets have occasionally spoiled good poems by one revision too many. An alert editor, John Frederick Nims, saved one of James Wright's finest poems from a disastrous revision. Here is the poem in its final version, which, except for the changing of the title from the original "The Blessing," is the poem Wright submitted and Nims accepted in 1960:

A Blessing

Just off the highway to Rochester, Minnesota,
Twilight bounds softly forth on the grass.
And the eyes of those two Indian ponies
Darken with kindness.
They have come gladly out of the willows   5
To welcome my friend and me.
We step over the barbed wire into the pasture
Where they have been grazing all day, alone.
They ripple tensely, they can hardly contain their happiness
That we have come.   10
They bow shyly as wet swans. They love each other.
There is no loneliness like theirs.
At home once more,
They begin munching the young tufts of spring in the darkness.
I would like to hold the slenderer one in my arms,   15
For she has walked over to me
And nuzzled my left hand.
She is black and white,
Her mane falls wild on her forehead,
And the light breeze moves me to caress her long ear   20
That is delicate as the skin over a girl's wrist.
Suddenly I realize
That if I stepped out of my body I would break
Into blossom.

Ox Cart Man

In October of the year,
he counts potatoes dug from the brown fiedl,
counting the seed, counting
the cellar's portion out,
and bags the rest on the cart's floor.

He packs wool sheared in April, honey
in combs, linen, leather
tanned from deerhide
and vinegar in a barrel
hooped by hand at the forge's fire

He walks <u>by ox head</u>, ten days
to Portsmouth Market, and sells potatoes,
and the bag that carried potatoes,
flaxseed, birch brooms, maple sugar, goose
feathers, yarn.

An odd phrase.
Is it better than
"by the ox's head"?

When the cart is empty he sells the cart.
When the cart is sold he sells the ox,
harness and yoke, and walks
home, his pockets heavy
with the year's coin for salt and taxes,

and at home by fire's light in November cold
stritches new harness
for next year's ox in the barn,
and carves the yoke, and saws planks
to build the cart again.

This strikes me as
the place to stop.

and in March taps sugar trees,
and in April shears wool
from sheep that grew it all over again,
and in May plants potatoes
as bees wake, roused by the cry of lilac.

omit

Very well finished. No big cracks that I can see.
I'm pretty sure about omitting the last stanza—
it's fidgety. And redundant.

Before the poem could be published, however, Wright sent this revised version:

Just Off the Highway to Rochester, Minnesota

Twilight bounds softly out on the grass.
They have come gladly out of the willows
To welcome my friend and me.
We step over the barbed wire into the pasture
Where they have been grazing all day, alone.   5
And the eyes of those two Indian ponies
Darken.
I would like to hold the slenderer one in my arms,
For she has walked over to me
And nuzzled my left hand.   10
She is black and white,
Her mane falls wild on her forehead.
At home once more,
They begin munching the young tufts of spring in the darkness.
I think   15
That if I stepped out of my body I would break
Into blossom.

Wisely, Nims insisted on the original version and Wright agreed, changing only the title from "The Blessing" to "A Blessing" when the poem appeared in *The Branch Will Not Break* in 1963.

The revision is weaker in every particular. The main excisions (lines 9–12 and 20–21) not only flatten the description by removing two of the ponies' significant actions ("ripple tensely," "bow shyly"), but also omit the speaker's understanding of their eagerness in greeting the human visitors. Their "loneliness," moreover, is complex, for they also "love each other." They are sharing their own mutual affection, intimacy, with the visitors. The speaker understands this because he and his "friend" have come forward, presumably, in the same spirit. That the ponies "can hardly contain their happiness" prepares for the speaker's realization that his emotion, too, cannot be contained: "if I stepped out of my body I would break / Into blossom."

The ponies' sharing their love for each other with the visitors explains the speaker's curiously sexual, romantic response ("I would like to hold the slenderer one in my arms"). The revision also omits his caress, which completes the exchange of shared intimacies between the animals and the persons, and omits the simile ("delicate as the skin over a girl's wrist") that embodies and makes real the human half of this exchange.

In smaller ways, too, the revision is weaker. The delay in specifying "ponies" makes the opening exposition clumsily ambiguous. Omitting "with kindness" allows "Darken" to seem negative or even threatening. Moving "At home once more, / They begin munching the young tufts of spring in the darkness" down to precede the final three lines makes this action seem the culmination of the anecdote—whereas, in the original, it is this gesture of acceptance that draws from the speaker his longing "to hold the slenderer one in my arms." And the flatly rational "I think" loses the tone of surprise and excitement in "Suddenly I realize . . . "

The risks of spoiling a poem make the process of revising exciting and are, of course, less perilous than not revising at all. Happily, unlike the painter or sculptor, the poet can easily return to an earlier draft. Either way, "A hundred times consider what you've said."

A SET OF DRAFTS

So far in these chapters about revision we have been examining fair copies or transcriptions from poets' manuscripts, not actual working manuscripts with their scribbles and scrawls, scratchings out and interlinings, arrows, notations, jottings, marginal lists, and even phone numbers, doodles, or coffee stains. For the poet's own use, often set down in haste, actual manuscripts are usually a mess and often indecipherable. The four drafts of "Politics" by Miller Williams, however, are fairly legible and we can follow in them all the twists and turns in the writing of the poem.

DRAFT 1

The anecdote around which the poem will form seems complete. Its point is the parallel between the outside chores the man is doing—mowing, restraining some invasive ivy, knocking down a wasp nest—and the dog's making a comfortable

> He cuts the grass and ~~pulls~~ *pulls* the ivy back
> and ~~turns~~ to knock the wasp nest
> out of the eaves.
> He is imposing order, but he leaves
> some high grass in a corner of the yard
> where his dog turns intently clockwise
> first and then reverses itself
> and lies down.
> Thus man and dog shape the world
> to fit their individual ends.

place for itself in the unmowed grass. Albeit in differing ways, they "shape the world" to their own purposes. The similarity registers in the use of the same verb for both. In line 2 the man "turns to knock the wasp nest / out of the eaves," in line 5 the dog "turns intently clockwise," mashing the grass.

Williams began the poem in past tense, but changed in line 4 to present tense; and the only corrections on the manuscript are to alter the tense of "cut," "pulled," and "turned."

In form, the poem seems to have fallen out naturally enough in two stanzas, one devoted primarily to the man, one to the dog. The short third line in each, giving them a similarly distinctive shape, may have been felt by the poet as thematically relevant. The rhyme "eaves-leaves" in lines 3–4 appears casual or accidental (there is no sign of a further effort to rhyme), but it would be a reasonable guess that line 3 was initially left short, ending in "eaves," because the poet was aware of "leaves" coming just ahead. That present tense and potential rhyme, it may be, suggested the corrections in lines 1–2. What is clear is that the poet is alert to various formal possibilities in the unfolding poem.

As Williams usually writes in meter, it is not surprising that lines 1, 4, and 5 are distinct pentameters and several others tetrameters (or nearly). In this draft, however, he seems more to be listening to the poem than imposing formal choices.

DRAFT 2

So much is changed in this draft, with everything going on at once, that the poet must be doing much of the work in his head, rather than crossing out and revising on paper. Again, very few corrections appear on this draft; one correction—the insertion of "place" for the slightly inappropriate for daytime "bed" in line 7—was obviously made in the course of setting down the draft.

The most startling choices have been in form. The draft now blocks out the poem as three rhymed quatrains and a couplet, with little squiggles in lines 11, 12, and 13 to hold the form open for completion later. Except for a rhyme-word missing in line 11, a rhyme scheme is in place. Line 12 proposes somehow to end "please her" to rhyme with "Caesar." The poem is, or is rapidly becoming, a sonnet.

No less decisively, the draft is a leap forward in handling the subject matter. Drawing on the ideas of imposing order and shaping the world in Draft 1, the title "Politics" firmly asserts the theme. Though the word will disappear from the poem later, "civilize" is deeply suggestive; and the appearance in line 10 of Newton, Christ, and Caesar, in a poem about mowing the grass, makes a larger claim than one could have expected from Draft 1. Didn't these historical figures in their very different ways try to "reshape the world," just as the man and dog do, as everyone is bound to do? Caesar of course is a political figure, and Christ may be seen in this light, given his ethical teachings, as the change from the flat "they are friends" in line 13 to "help their friends" reminds us. The man, we recall, has left a corner of the yard uncut for the dog to use. Newton seems problematical, but the point must be that scientific discoveries often have political consequences.

POLITICS

[handwritten draft of a poem]

The other relevant insertion is, in line 2, that of "briar," which replaces the ivy of Draft 1. Less neutral than the ivy, briar with its thorns suggests (as does the wasp nest) a world that is hard to deal with, aggressive, and competitive. It would be far-fetched to see an allusion to the crown of thorns, but the harshness of nature after Eden may not be beside the point. The politics of force, the destruction of the wasps, protects the safety and comfort of the man's home. The insertion of the word "swarming" in line 7 extends the suggestion.

The issue of tense in lines 1–3 is now resolved by "having done with . . . ." Briar and wasp nest involve completed, past actions. This change allows the opening sentence to flow smoothly into line 3, incorporating "he imposes order . . ." as its main clause.

The advance of the draft, however, pays a price in wordiness. The insertion "because he always does" in line 4 is perhaps unnecessary (and the phrase will disappear in Draft 3). "To *take and* reshape the world" is awkward usage (though "reshape" improves upon "shape" in line 9 of Draft 1, now replaced there by "change"), and the same idea recurs somewhat redundantly in "civilize / a part of the world" in lines 8–9 and "to change the world they find" in line 14. The poet is no doubt aware of this, seeing the draft as very tentative, as is suggested by the squiggles in lines 11–13 and by the continuing casualness about meter. Although the sonnet form raises an expectation of pentameters, a number of lines remain tetrameters with no sign of metrical tinkering; and the limpid pentameter of line 4 in Draft 1, which will reappear in all further drafts—"he is imposing order, but he leaves"—is made (and kept) tetrameter here. The poet is roughing the poem in, still trying out and staying open to new possibilities that may alter its direction.

The not-very-convincing rhyme "mess-grass" is disconnected by scratching out "mess" for the firmer, more vivid "tangle." The poet notes a probable rhyme in a circle in the margin—"fence/angle"—but how to work out that change remains for the next draft.

DRAFT 3

Line 4, with the deletion of "because he always does," runs fluently to the rhyme on "angle." The correction of "ragged" for "high" is a useful clarification—high grass might well be a foot or more—and not incidentally smoothes the pentameter into regularity. In copying line 2, Williams had omitted the nest, so the sense is simply "having done . . . with wasps in the eaves." A change to "yellow jackets"— the insects themselves now rather than their nest—both makes the line more colorful and produces a graceful pentameter. Stanza 1 is now in its final form except

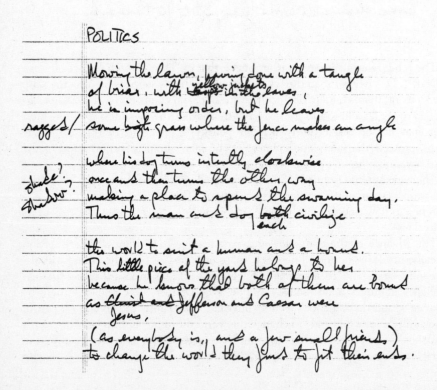

that "fence makes" will become more accurately plural after Draft 4: "where the fences make an angle."

The dog's complicated actions, circling first one way, then the other to mat the grass before lying down, have posed a problem since Draft 1. Even the omission of "around" in copying from Draft 2 doesn't get it right. The marginal queries—"shade? shadow?"—show the poet's continuing dissatisfaction with that stanza, but he leaves it to Draft 4 for further tinkering.

Stanza 3, in going to this draft, has been considerably reworked as well as filled in. The missing rhyme has been discovered: "hound." It is a brilliant choice, just light enough in tone, with an air of the humorous, to keep the poem's heavy theme in perspective. Along with the verbal cleverness in the ultimate version of line 10 ("A square *yard* of his *yard* . . . "), "hound" frees the pun that has all along been lurking in the last line: "to fit their ends." The poem is serious, but it is also not without an amused detachment about its claim.

But "hound" fits into line 9—they "civilize / the world to suit a human and a hound," with its tempting alliteration—thus requiring the pushing down of the two lines in Draft 2 about being "bound / as everyone is, Newton and Christ and Caesar."

Fortunately, the space marked by squiggles and wasted by the redundancy "to take and reshape the world" can absorb these displaced lines. Having at least personalized the dog ("*itself*" in Draft 1), the projected rhyme "Caesar-please her," which might have been problematic anyway, is replaced by "her-were," set up by the new line 10: "This little piece of the yard belongs to her . . . ." With "as everybody is" moved to line 13, the replacement of the dubious Newton—the poet obviously shared our discomfort—with Jefferson is easy. Further, the correction to "Jesus" is a fine stroke. As well as alliterating euphoniously (which helps compel a reader to accept the line's sense as inevitable), "Jesus" makes the line regularly metrical without the rather ponderous structure of "as Christ *and* Jefferson *and* Caesar were." The three historical figures are not arranged chronologically, as might seem natural, but the order interestingly suggests a spectrum from most altruistic to least. Jefferson, thus, with the ideals of democracy and equality, seems a balancing figure between Jesus and Caesar. The change to "Jesus" also emphasizes his human, rather than his divine, nature; and so reminds us of the radicalism of his teachings as well as of his own confrontations with political authority. The thorns of the "briar" are perhaps not so fanciful an echo, after all, if a reader thinks of them.

DRAFT 4

A new line 5, developing the marginal query of Draft 3, provides a fresh sense of the coziness of the dog's fence-corner, its shade: "trapping a small shadow most of the day." The rhyme scheme of the stanza is turned inside out—"day" moves from the second to the first line of the stanza, and "way" is then freed to serve as the connective from line 8 to line 9: "This is the way // she reshapes the world to suit a hound." Choosing between "civilize" and "reshape" from Draft 2 (dropped in Draft 3), Williams opts to reinsert the simpler. The redundancy in line 9 in both Drafts 2 and 3 ended up including *both* man and dog in the statement and so preempted the

POLITICS

Mowing the lawn, having done with a tangle
of briar, with yellow jackets in the eaves,
he is imposing order, but he leaves
some ragged grass where the fence makes an angle

trapping a shadow then most of the day.
On the swarming morning, circling clockwise twice
his dog turns herself intently clockwise
then lies on the flattened grass. This is the way

she reshapes the world to suit a hound.
He always leaves a square yard to her
because he knows that both of them are bound
as Jesus, Jefferson, and Caesar were

(as all people are, and some small friends)
to change the stubborn world to fit their ends.

conclusion in line 14 that properly brings them together. Note how the summarizing "Thus" of the last sentence of Draft 1 had moved up to line 8 in Draft 2 ("Thus the man and dog each civilize . . .") and persisted there in Draft 3. Line 9 now focuses on the dog only, thus keeping the sense from bunching up here into a full summary that short-circuits the poem's ending.

The idea of "because he always does" in Draft 2 reemerges here to fill out line 10: "He always leaves a square yard to her . . . ." The idea of the dog's possession ("belongs to her" in Draft 3) is dropped, as possibly problematic. In the final poem, a witty repetition of "yard" will displace the irrelevant "always"—it needn't matter that the concession is habitual—giving the line a fresh rhetorical snappiness: "A square yard of his yard he leaves to her . . . ."

The dog's actions are well sorted out. With the rhyme "civilize" out of the way, the right formulation occurs to the poet in re-copying line 6. He strikes out "clockwise" in favor of "circling *twice*," and lets "clockwise" end line 7. There is room to re-cast line 8, concluding the sentence: "then ~~lies~~ drops on the flattened grass." Her actually settling down had been in Draft 1 ("and lies down") and it seems clear now that that action is necessary to resolve or complete her painstaking circling, whose purpose, "flattened grass," is now for the very first time actually stated.

In line 13 "everybody is" gives way to "all people are," making "and some small friends" (including the dog) a more logical completion of the line. As he had edged away from "belongs to her" (in Draft 3), the poet here also keeps the human perspective at the center. If "some small friends" reminds a reader that others are enemies and must be excluded (the yellow jackets), it remains clear how difficult the world can be. Politics is essential to the continual re-adjustments the world requires. The plainer, matter-of-fact "world they find" of Draft 3 gives way to "the stubborn world" (and in the finished poem to "a stubborn world"), which provides a fitting emphasis.

Several other small but meaningful changes from Draft 4 to the published poem deserve comment. In line 2, for literal accuracy since yellow jackets nest in the ground, the insects in the eaves will be called "hornets"—and so space made for the nicely alliterating "buzzing."

In line 11, "because he knows that both of them" will become "because he sees that both of them . . . ." "Knows" has survived since Draft 2, but knowing is static, whereas "sees" suggests a realization. Cutting the grass, and thinking about it as he does, leads to a freshened sense of the world and what we do in it.

The somewhat plodding "This is the way" of line 8 will become, simply, "In this way // she reshapes . . . ." Interestingly, this good though minor change shows the poet roughing up the rhythm of a line that was closer to the metrical norm. Often we have observed the poet, in making some other useful change, *also* clicking the pentameter into regularity. Here, what clearly matters is that the line sound natural. Williams is listening to the *poem*, not following the cookbook. Similarly, he has been untroubled throughout that stanzas 1 and 2 rhyme *a b b a*, while stanza 3 rhymes *a b a b*, thus mingling qualities of Italian and Shakespearean sonnets.

A scribal error, instantly corrected, nonetheless leads to one further valuable revision. In copying line 13 into Draft 4, Williams began it *without* a stanza-space, realized the mistake and scratched it out, then re-started the line a space below. But the "mistake" was actually a poet's good instinct. In publishing the poem he closed up the stanza-breaks, pleased, as he commented, for the poem "to be secretly a sonnet, and not ostentatiously a sonnet."

Politics

Mowing the lawn, having done with a tangle
of briar, with hornets buzzing in the eaves,
he is imposing order, but he leaves
some ragged grass where fences make an angle,
trapping a small shadow most of the day.   5
There, in the swarming morning, circling twice,
his dog turns herself intently clockwise
then drops on the flattened grass. In this way

she reshapes the world to suit a hound.
A square yard of his yard he leaves to her   10
because he sees that both of them are bound
as Jesus, Jefferson, and Caesar were
(as all people are, and some small friends)
to change a stubborn world to fit their ends.

   The impulse for a poem is usually sudden, a luminous notion of it, a glimpse. As
with "Politics," the poet intuits the richness or complexities implied in that
glimpse. Writing the poem then is, as Philip Larkin noted in a letter, "like trying to
remember a tune you've forgotten. All corrections are attempts to get nearer the
forgotten tune."

QUESTIONS AND SUGGESTIONS

1. Here is the first draft of a poem called "In One Place." If it were your poem, how
would you revise it? (The poet's final version appears in Appendix II, p. 388.)

In One Place

The tree grows in one place.

A seed goes down, and something
holds up two or three leaves
the first year.

             Then the spindling   5
goes on climbing, branching,
up, up, up,

          until birds
live in it and no one can
remember it wasn't there.   10

The tree stands always here.

2. The most amusing instance of revision on record is John Keats's undressing of
his heroine, Madeline, in the manuscript of "The Eve of St. Agnes" (1819). As she
prepares for bed, she doesn't know that her young lover, Porphyro, watches or that
later, as she dreams of him, he will wake and rescue her to flee from the bad Baron's
castle "away into the storm." The first two stanzas in the passage set the scene,
describing the stained glass window through which the moonlight falls on
Madeline as she prays in her bedchamber. Keats's three attempts at the next stanza
follow—and then the finished version. Study these attempts to see why Keats
abandons each and how, finding new rhymes, he finally gets the stanza right. His

struggles also discover the epithets "warmèd" and "fragrant," which wonderfully imply the intimacy of the action.

> A casement high and triple-arched there was,
> All garlanded with carven imag'ries
> Of fruits, and flowers, and bunches of knot-grass,
> And diamonded with panes of quaint device,
> Innumerable of stains and splendid dyes,
> As are the tiger-moth's deep-damasked wings;
> And in the midst, 'mong thousand heraldries,
> And twilight saints, and dim emblazonings,
> A shielded scutcheon blushed with blood of queens and kings.
>
> Full on this casement shone the wintry moon,   .
> And threw warm gules° on Madeline's fair breast,
> As down she knelt for heaven's grace and boon;
> Rose-bloom fell on her hands, together pressed,
> And on her silver cross soft amethyst,
> And on her hair a glory, like a saint:
> She seemed a splendid angel, new dressed,
> Save wings, for heaven:—Porphyro grew faint:
> She knelt, so pure a thing, so free from mortal taint.

°*gules:* red colors.

a)   But soon his heart revives—her prayers done,
       Of all its wreathèd pearl she strips her hair;
       Unclasps her bosom jewels, one by one;

       Loosens {
           ~~bursting~~
           ~~her bodice~~
           ~~her bodice lace string~~
           ~~her bodice and her bosom bare~~
           ~~her~~
           her fragrant bodice and doth bare

       Her

b)   Anon his heart revives—her praying done,
       Of all its wreathèd pearl her hair she strips,
       Unclasps her warmèd jewels, one by one,
       Loosens her fragrant bodice: and down slips
       Her sweet attire

c)   Anon his heart revives: her vespers done,
       Of all its wreathèd pearls her hair she frees;
       Unclasps her warmèd jewels, one by one;
       Loosens her fragrant bodice; to her knees
       Her sweet attire falls light by slow degrees

Anon his heart revives: her vespers done,
Of all its wreathèd pearls her hair she frees;
Unclasps her warmèd jewels one by one;
Loosens her fragrant bodice; by degrees
Her rich attire creeps rustling to her knees:
Half-hidden, like a mermaid in seaweed,
Pensive awhile she dreams awake, and sees,
In fancy, fair St. Agnes in her bed,
But dares not look behind, or all the charm is fled.

3. This is an early draft of Walt Whitman's "A Noiseless Patient Spider." In what ways, if it were your poem, might you think of revising it? Then look again at Whitman's final version (p. 12). How has he revised it? In what way has he changed its central meaning?

The Soul, Reaching, Throwing Out for Love

The Soul, reaching, throwing out for love,
As the spider, from some little promontory, throwing out filament after
  filament, tirelessly out of itself, that one at least may catch and form a
  link, a bridge, a connection
O I saw one passing along, saying hardly a word—yet full of love I detected
  him, by certain signs
O eyes wishfully turning! O silent eyes!
For then I thought of you o'er the world,   5
O latent oceans, fathomless oceans of love!
O waiting oceans of love! yearning and fervid! and of you sweet souls perhaps
  in the future, delicious and long:
But Death, unknown on the earth—ungiven, dark here, unspoken, never
  born:
You fathomless latent souls of love—you pent and unknown oceans of love!

4. Here are two versions of "The First Time" by Michael Burns (b. 1953), as the poem appeared in *Laurel Review* in 1992 and as the poet revised it for his book, *The Secret Names* (1994). What considerations probably led to the changes?

a)   She slapped him. She screamed, Tell me why, why?
      And maybe he knew she didn't want an answer,
      only the lie that would keep them together,
      so he got out of the car and lay down in a dry ditch.

      There was sobbing, the quiet headlights in the fog,   5
      the motor running. He held his head in his hands
      and thought of the other woman's voice, full
      of rough pleasure, and the stain
      shaped like a ballerina on the motel's ceiling.

Listening to his own weeping, he felt something   10
in him was cast loose, adrift like the wooden boats
of children, or scorched and coasting, falling
like the spent phase of a rocket launched for the moon.

b)   She slapped him. She screamed, Tell me why, why?
And maybe he knew she didn't want an answer,
only the lie that would keep them together,
so he left the car and lay down in a ditch.

There was sobbing, the headlights in the fog,   5
the motor running.
He thought of the other woman
as she rode him under the stained motel ceiling.

Listening to his own weeping,
he felt something in him was cast loose,
adrift like the wooden boats of children,   10
or scorched and coasting,
falling like the spent phase of a rocket.

5. After considering the description and example of the sestina in Appendix I (p. 375), try your hand at this interesting and difficult form. In choosing the six recycling words, what problems or opportunities might you expect? For "Sestina" Elizabeth Bishop used: *house, grandmother, child, stove, almanac,* and *tears.* For "Hallelujah: A Sestina" Robert Francis managed: *Hallelujah, boy, hair, praise, father,* and *Ebenezer* (his father's given name). For "Farm Implements and Rutabagas in a Landscape" John Ashbery picked: *thunder, apartment, country, pleasant, scratched,* and *spinach.* Clearly, poets enjoy making trouble for themselves! (An in-class variant suggested by poet Susan Thornton: using the same six randomly chosen words, everyone, including the teacher, writes a sestina before the period ends and reads the result aloud. The words her class tried: *raining, chalkboard, watermelon, ordeal, zoo,* and *needle.*)

6. Also a good example of dramatic irony, this poem by Katharyn Howd Machan (b. 1952) exemplifies a dynamic relationship of speaking voice to line. Imagine a character as lively as Machan's charperson and work at catching his or her distinctive voice, perhaps in dialect.

Hazel Tells Laverne

last night
im cleanin out my
howard johnsons ladies room
when all of a sudden
up pops this frog   5

musta come from the sewer
swimmin aroun an tryin ta
climb up the sida the bowl
so i goes ta flushm down
but sohelpmegod he starts talkin   10
bout a golden ball
an how i can be a princess
me a princess
well my mouth drops
all the way to the floor   15
an he says
kiss me just kiss me
once on the nose
well i screams
ya little green pervert   20
an i hitsm with my mop
an has ta flush
the toilet down three times
me
a princess   25

7. Imagine a poem, *using an archeologist's eye*, about a drive-in movie in the
daytime, a marina in winter, a supermarket or department store after hours, a set of
tennis courts in snow, a graveyard of old boxcars, or the like. Forget what you
know. What might the place seem to an alien? What uses might be guessed? (For
example: A drive-in—a field of metal flowers or idols? A department store—some
sort of museum or temple?)

POEMS TO CONSIDER

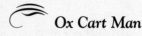 **Ox Cart Man**   1977

DONALD HALL (b.1928)

In October of the year,
he counts potatoes dug from the brown field,
counting the seed, counting
the cellar's portion out,
and bags the rest on the cart's floor.   5

He packs wool sheared in April, honey
in combs, linen, leather
tanned from deerhide,

and vinegar in a barrel
hooped by hand at the forge's fire.   10

He walks by his ox's head, ten days
to Portsmouth Market, and sells potatoes,
and the bag that carried potatoes,
flaxseed, birch brooms, maple sugar, goose
feathers, yarn.   15

When the cart is empty he sells the cart.
When the cart is sold he sells the ox,
harness and yoke, and walks
home, his pockets heavy
with the year's coin for salt and taxes,   20

and at home by fire's light in November cold
stitches new harness
for next year's ox in the barn,
and carves the yoke, and saws planks
building the cart again.   25

Disclaimer   *1985*

JOEL FERREE (b. 1947)

This poem, when written, contained 20 lines.
It is packaged according to weight, not length.
Some settling may have occurred due to handling,
or editing or last minute rewriting.

Titanic   *1983*

DAVID R. SLAVITT (b. 1935)

Who does not love the *Titanic*?
If they sold passage tomorrow for that same crossing,
who would not buy?

To go down . . . We all go down, mostly
alone. But with crowds of people, friends, servants,   5
well fed, with music, with lights! Ah!

And the world, shocked, mourns, as it ought to do
and almost never does. There will be the books and movies

to remind our grandchildren who we were
and how we died, and give them a good cry.   10

Not so bad, after all. The cold
water is anaesthetic and very quick.
The cries on all sides must be a comfort.

We all go: only a few, first-class.

 A Bird came down the Walk   *1891*

EMILY DICKINSON (1830–1886)

A Bird came down the Walk—
He did not know I saw—
He bit an Angleworm in halves
And ate the fellow, raw,

And then he drank a Dew   5
From a convenient Grass—
And then hopped sidewise to the Wall
To let a Beetle pass—

He glanced with rapid eyes
That hurried all around—   10
They looked like frightened Beads, I thought—
He stirred his Velvet Head

Like one in danger, Cautious,
I offered him a Crumb
And he unrolled his feathers   15
And rowed him softer home—

Than Oars divide the Ocean,
Too silver for a seam—
Or Butterflies, off Banks of Noon
Leap, plashless as they swim   20

 The Letter   *1919*

AMY LOWELL (1874–1925)

Little cramped words scrawling all over the paper
Like draggled fly's legs,
What can you tell of the flaring moon
Through the oak leaves?

Or of my uncurtained window and the bare floor   5
Spattered with moonlight?
Your silly quirks and twists have nothing in them
Of blossoming hawthorns,
And this paper is dull, crisp, smooth, virgin of loveliness
Beneath my hand.   10

I am tired, Beloved, of chafing my heart against
The want of you;
Of squeezing it into little inkdrops,
And posting it.
And I scald alone, here, under the fire   15
Of the great moon.

Sentimental Poem   *1978*

for Woody

MARGE PIERCY (b. 1936)

You are such a good cook.
I am such a good cook.
If we get involved
we'll both get fat.
Then nobody else will have us.   5
We'll be stuck, two
mounds of wet dough
baking high and fine
in the bed's slow oven.

Interim Report   *1984*

ELTON GLASER (b. 1945)

You could check out like the dandelion's
tatterdemalion, or like a fuel-injected starlet
wrecked in her Eldorado, blown away
with a choir of accountants piped in and
dismal wings squalling around the brain.   5

Might as well lie face down in the frogweed
and go peacefully. Let others drag their claws
across the blue back of the sky—it's all you can do
to keep your bowels out of a bowknot. Already
your heart is kicking the blood through with a curse.   10

And nothing now can save you, neither
the doctors nor the doctrines. Your bones rattle
like the spiel of an auctioneer, each sense
foreclosed and on the block, the creditors lining up
to claim what the beetle and the blowfly can salvage.   15

 ## Laws   1984

STEPHEN DUNN (b. 1939)

A black cat wanders out into
an open field. How vulnerable it is,
how even its own shadow
causes it to stop and hunch.
Mice come, hundreds of them,   5
forming a circle around the cat.
They've been waiting for months
to catch the cat like this.
But the cat is suddenly unafraid.
Though the mice have their plans,   10
have worked on tactics and tricks,
none of them moves.
The cat thinks: all I have to do
is be who I am. And it's right.
One quick move   15
and the mice scatter, go home.

After humiliation, home is a hole
where no one speaks. Mouse things
get done, and then there is
the impossibility of sleep.   20
They curse nature, they curse
their small legs and hearts.
We all know stories of how, after
great defeat, the powerless rise up.
But not if they're mice.   25
The cat waits for them in the tall grass.
The mice are constantly surprised.

Pesca de Esponjas°   1993

RICARDO PAU-LLOSA (b. 1954)

His slender legs kick him afloat
above the shallow citizens of a reef,

title: sponge fishing

sponges he picks off with a long trident.
He has a bucket already full, and above him
the mapmaker has painted a blow-up of his catch,   5
in case we can't read the vignette's label, Fishing
for Sponges. In other vignettes no one is sponging for
fish, so what is wrong with this young man, so tersely focused
on his craft that he will not cast off the indignities of language
so misused and misleading? Are the things he seeks or his actions   10
of greater consequence than their name? What if someone said
that a shark had bitten off his legs, or a giant wave had
engulfed him and his nearby dinghy spilling the sponges
back into the sea to live out their unblinking lives?
Or the witness swore that he was lost, not trying   15
to flee, but Castro's coast patrol fired at him
and no one knew? Why don't we think of him
as a sponge, happy beneath passing fins?

Our American Way of Life   1993

SUZANNE GARDINIER (b. 1961)

Smoking a cigarette in a classroom
a woman is copying sentences from
a book *Our American Way of Life*
the page marked Practice for Citizenship
The white lights flicker The others have gone   5
I want to be an American
citizen she writes and smiles *I have*
studied the American Constitution
I have a pen in my right hand
Today is a beautiful day I can   10
read write and speak simple English There are
many cars on the street I am working at
here is a blank to fill *Red Apple*
Supermarket It is raining now May
I write something else I will do my best   15
to be a worthy citizen I
enjoy my work She lays down the pen
rubs her eyes and turns to the section called
At Work and reads *This is a factory*
Many men work in this factory They   20
are factory workers This is an office
These women work in the office They are
office workers Everyone is smiling
She is left-handed and her back aches
from hours at the market stacking canned peaches   25

For the Women of Ancient Greece   1995

MEGGAN WATTERSON*

> *We come, then, to this strange paradox: man,*
> *wishing to find nature in woman, but nature*
> *transfigured, dooms woman to artifice.*
>
> —*Simone de Beauvoir*

I had not meant to pick up the scissors.
I was searching for something
I've now forgotten.
So it was by chance
That my skin touched steel   5
Sending chills into me.
I pulled them from deep within the drawer
Hidden beneath screwdrivers and batteries.
I slid fingers into place,
Taking control of the blades.   10
A glimmer of light reflecting from them
Invited me to crisscross
Swish . . . Swish . . . Swish . . .
The lopping, the not layering.
Here at last was my liberty.   15
We had finally met,
The shaking of hands had taken place
On my porch in the winter of my 20th year.

12

BECOMING A POET

A Hand at the Back of the Room

The owner of the hand wants to know, "How does someone become a poet?" The answer is that anyone who writes a poem is a poet—which means almost everybody at one time or another. But that isn't what the student means.

Becoming a poet is almost always unpredictable, a sort of accident. Liking poems turns into writing poems; writing poems leads to reading more poets and, influenced by these poets, the beginning poet continues to experiment, struggling to get each new poem right, learning, draft to draft, poem to poem.

Sooner or later the beginner shows some work to a friend or a teacher, enrolls in a writing class, perhaps has a few poems published in the school or college literary magazine. Then one day, with some encouragement and determination, the poet takes a chance and sends some poems off to one of the literary magazines he or she has been reading. And probably the editor sends the poems back because they aren't quite good enough—yet. And sometimes—only sometimes—despite all the discouragements . . . .

What drives poets to write? Is it a love of words, of ideas, of discovery through language? Is it because nothing else is quite as challenging and fulfilling? Or are poets driven by less noble motives like power and fame? Poets are often hard put to say for themselves, and surely every poet writes for a unique combination of motives. For some writers the issue may be as simple as Flannery O'Connor's response to a student who asked "Why do you write?" "Because I'm good at it," she answered.

The growth of a poet usually takes years, and if the poet is lucky and determined, that growth continues. Reading the early writing of poets like Dickinson and Whitman can be tremendously reassuring. One of Dickinson's earliest poems, written when she was about nineteen, is an unremarkable valentine. Here are a couple of lines:

> Oh the Earth was *made* for lovers, for damsel, and hopeless swain,
> For sighing, and gentle whispering, and *unity* made of twain.

Fuzzy, sentimental images, slack lines, wooden rhythms, pedestrian or inflated diction—no arresting noun or verb in either line—make it typical of the drawing room poems of its time and in many ways typical of most poets' early work. It merely makes pretty a commonplace notion. It doesn't explore. It doesn't grapple. It certainly doesn't—to use Dickinson's later definition of poetry—make a reader "feel physically as if the top of my head were taken off." Reading it one could not predict that in her early thirties she would be writing some of the most powerful and distinctive poems in our language.

Whitman's early poems are as trivial as Dickinson's valentine. Here is a stanza of "Our Future Lot," published in a newspaper in 1838 when Whitman was nineteen:

> O, powerless is this struggling brain
>   To pierce the mighty mystery;
> In dark, uncertain awe it waits,
>   The common doom—to die!

Egads! This doggerel hardly predicts the poet who would pierce the mystery in poems like his elegy for Abraham Lincoln, "When Lilacs Last in the Dooryard Bloom'd" (even the title tells us how far Whitman had come from his "Our Future Lot"). Dickinson's and Whitman's early work share at least one problem: the poems aim to decorate a fact or a feeling rather than to discover or explore. They don't take chances. They are unadventurous. Language appears to act as a servant to a preordained "meaning." The poems are written from the outside in, instead of from the inside out: through exploration, trusting in the poem.

Obviously both beginning poets grew dissatisfied with their early efforts; they wrote more poems and read more poems. They read the journals of their age and immersed themselves in the world around them—even if that world, in Dickinson's case, was centered in a house and garden in Amherst. Dickinson found guides in Shakespeare, George Herbert, and her older contemporary, Elizabeth Barrett Browning. Whitman found guides in the Bible, Shakespeare, and his older contemporary, Ralph Waldo Emerson. They grew up, and they became, in the great mystery of such things, our great foremother and forefather of American poetry.

Don't be too hard on yourself when a poem fails—failed poems can teach you much. And don't be embarrassed to be a beginner. Had there been creative writing classes in the sixteenth century, who knows, the hand in the back of the room might have belonged to a sophomore named Will Shakespeare.

THE GROWTH OF A POET

Poets grow in the struggle, draft to draft, to make each poem fulfill itself. But "fixing" poems may not be the most important thing. Often, as Marvin Bell remarked, "revision means writing the next poem." For it is in the zigzag progress from poem to poem that the beginning poet develops. In this section we will follow the development of a recent student, C. Lynn Shaffer, through several poems over time.

Here is one of the first poems Lynn wrote:

A Baglady's Plea

Another stretch of city street—
I turn to you but your eyes don't meet
Mine.
Can you not feel?

My heart beats,   5
With love,
With grief,
As yours does; do you see me in the rain?

My clothes are tatters; my shoes are worn,
But flesh and blood are things with which we both were born.   10
It's useless,
I won't lay blame.

If you would but try
Looking into my eyes you would see
Yourself in disguise—   15
Our souls are exactly the same.

A clear strength of this poem is that instead of talking generally about homelessness, Lynn has created a dramatic situation to embody the problem, with a character (though a generalized one) as speaker. A phrase ("a stretch of city street") succinctly draws the scene. The poem also generalizes the "you"; we learn nothing specific about the age, sex, or class of the person whom the speaker encounters and who apparently ignores her. We see only the gesture of this person's refusal to meet the speaker's eyes.

The appearance of the poem on the page—free verse in four end-stopped quatrains—shows Lynn's trying to give it shapeliness. But several lines fit awkwardly. Several seem needlessly abrupt (like line 3) or gangly (particularly line 10), forced to obey the quatrain form. Only in stanza 4, as if with practice, do the lines begin to move with poise and precision. Elsewhere the poem seems off-balance, as in line 8, where the end of the stanza's first main clause seems jammed in with its second main clause, "do you see me in the rain?" Lynn manages beautifully the line break at line 15 ("Looking into my eyes you would see"), demonstrating that she knows how line breaks can give sentences multiple meanings. Perhaps in line 3 she intended the isolated "Mine" to highlight the speaker's loneliness. As the only one-word line in the poem, however, the line seems an obvious contrivance; and it creates an awkward line break in line 2 ("your eyes don't meet") that offers the odd reading that the addressee has an eye problem of some sort.

The couplet rhymes *street-meet* and *worn-born* (lines 1–2, 9–10) are perhaps too pronounced for free verse or, at any rate, create an expectation of a pattern that seems abandoned, erratically resumed, then abandoned again. A reader may not even notice *blame-same* (lines 12, 16) or, worse, will conclude that the poem's rhymes are merely opportunistic. But the poem skillfully handles the inexact and internal rhymes in stanza 4 *try-[eyes]-disguise*, stressing the similarity between the addressee and the homeless speaker. These inexact and internal rhymes seem appropriate to the poem's free verse as the couplet rhymes do not. In emphasizing the eyes in the opening and closing stanzas, Lynn brings the poem full circle and helps it cohere. We sense a whole work before us, not just bits and pieces thrown together.

Admirably, the poem takes risks, dealing with a weighty theme: that if we look beyond appearances the homeless are like the rest of us and deserve the same respect. Decent people would agree with this statement. But does the poem do more than merely appeal to our sense of decency? Does it make the character *interesting* so the theme awakens in us a fresh response? Does the poem resist easy paraphrasing? If we summarize it, do we hazard leaving out some essential nuance?

The problem may lie in the poem's approach. Labeling the speaker a "baglady" undermines the attempt to show the speaker's essential dignity. The generic (even scornful) term and her tattered clothes are all we know of her. Whom she loves or for whom she grieves, remains unknown. Nothing suggests even how it might feel to be forced to carry all one's belongings around in shopping bags. The poem doesn't delve deeply and explore. The speaker asks, "do you see me in the rain?" If we're honest, we must answer, "No." We see only a blurry figure and one (notice) ready to assign blame. Might not the passerby's averted eyes mean, not indifference or repugnance, but an all too vivid awareness of how human, and painful, an exchange of looks would be when one can do nothing meaningful to change the situation? Perhaps even the poem's momentary drama is too simplistic, undeveloped.

Now look at a poem Lynn wrote for her first creative writing class a few months later.

A Butterfly Lands on the Grave of My Friend

Two pieces of translucent blue silk,
the same blue as pieces of her car on Route 7,
stir its own little breeze
in the somber sunlight.

It seems to hang in front of me   5
like a waterfall in air.
I reach out to grasp it.
It feels alive, an unreal blue powder
lingers on my fingertips.

I think life is like the wispy wings of the Wood Nymph   10
(Giant Swallowtail or Long-dash Skipper)
—delicate, memorable.

> The missionary disappears beyond the tombstones.
> Its distinct colors
> (like her intentional unfeminine stagger and cackle-snort laugh)   15
> remain in my mind, vivid, permanent
> as water flowing over stone.

Finding consolation in nature is typical of elegies, but Lynn's developing craft allows her to treat the subject with some originality and to make it fresh. We might first notice that Lynn has grown as a poet in her attention to details: "translucent blue silk," "Route 7," "Wood Nymph," and "cackle-snort laugh." These details help clarify the implicit narrative and, equally important, offer her avenues to explore the situation. For example, in drawing the connection between the color of the butterfly and the color of the wrecked car, the speaker can also indicate how the friend died, and through her exploration of the image of the butterfly, she can give us a secondary impression that the friend was a young and energetic person. Notice, too, her sharper use of verbs, like "stir" and "grasp," which makes the scene feel immediate and dynamic.

Not all the details, however, appear significant. The "Giant Swallowtail" and "Long-dash Skipper" seem to enter the poem only because the poet likes the names. The heavily modified details of line 15 ("her intentional unfeminine stagger and cackle-snort laugh") seem more personally important than crucial to the poem; and the line's length makes it clumsy. The word "missionary" in line 13 is confusing. Is this a literal missionary (where did he or she come from?) or—as we gather after being momentarily distracted—is this the butterfly? Yet what is the butterfly a *missionary* of? Death? But that would seem to contradict the simile that likens the butterfly to life. Also, the word "missionary" prompts a religious reading which nothing else in the poem clearly supports.

But the quality of attention Lynn pays to the subject shows her growing skills. The speaker carefully examines the butterfly—noticing it stirs "its own little breeze," likening it to a "waterfall in the air," and feeling its "unreal blue powder"—and then she makes this examination central to the poem; it means something. In trying to clearly perceive the butterfly, the speaker gropes for a new understanding of her friend's short life and of how she remembers her: "I think that life is like . . . ." Here Lynn borrows a move from a Mary Oliver poem that she admired ("White Owl Flying Into and Out of a Field": "so I thought: / maybe death"), and she tries to push the implications of her metaphors. That *pushing* is what is important for a beginning poet. The result may seem a bit forced and contrived, a bit too easy (for example, the complicated nature of a survivor's memory, which she describes as "vivid, permanent," gets glossed over), but the result isn't very critical; more crucial here is that Lynn is trying to make the images *work*, do the work of the imagination. In the final line her pushing pays off; she arrives at the fitting simile, "as water flowing over stone." This metaphor doesn't feel strained; it seems to have grown out of the imagery of waterfall (line 6) and tombstones (line 11) and suggests that the speaker contemplates the relationship between the permanent and the mutable: water often implies life and life-forces; stone often implies permanence and death. Yet flowing water erodes stone. The images aren't easy to sort out, yet their complexity makes possible an emotionally complex poem which resists easy paraphrasing.

Rhythmically the final line sounds right, too. As a line of iambic tetrameter in a free-verse poem, it lends authority to the speaker's final words; it sounds measured and thoughtful, giving us a sense that some truth has been won. Line 10 begins to be metrical; line 11 is exact:

> rĕmáin | ĭn mў mínd, vív|ĭd, pĕr|mănĕnt
> ăs wa|tĕr flŏw|ĭng o|vĕr stŏne.

Even the run-on, "*permanent* / as water flowing," has the air of a graceful paradox. As the last sound in the line, the word "stone" receives extra emphasis and touches a dark note which is slightly undercut by the lulling assonance of the *o*'s in "flow-ing," "over" and "stone." Throughout the poem, Lynn's use of internal rhyme, allit-eration, and assonance give the poem cohesion and a rich texture. In the first line, the *u* sounds in "two," "translucent," and "blue" offer musical unity. The counter-pointed *r*'s, light *i*'s and long *i*'s in lines 8 and 9, along with the internal rhyme of "lingers" and "fingertips," help to underline the delicate, ephemeral qualities of the butterfly and set up the coming exploration of life in terms of the butterfly. Some-times, however, Lynn's alliteration seems to go too far. The phrase "wispy wings of the Wood Nymph" (nearly impossible to say aloud) sounds overwrought and self-conscious, as though—to use a pun—she were gilding the butterfly.

Notice other small ways, too (like the less formal choice of not using line-capi-tals) that indicate that the poem is an advance in the poet's development. Espe-cially remarkable is Lynn's confidence that the *plural* "Two pieces of translucent blue silk" in line 1 can take the *singular* pronoun of "stir *its* own little breeze" in line 2 without confusion—of course, she's using her title to good advantage.

Like Lynn's earlier poem, this one also has some trouble getting the pace of the lines right. The awkward line 15 may echo the friend's lovable gawky manner, but its seventeen syllables throw the stanza, even the poem, off-balance. We sense that the poet is suddenly trying to stretch the line out to fit in everything.

As Lynn continued writing and reading, she grew more aware of how to con-sider and control her lines' inner structure. That attention shows in a poem she wrote the next year.

To Dust

The earth sucks the life right out of you,
Dad told me once, because it has to.
He had to make the dirt bleed rich
in his fields, and the dust stirred
to cling to him for spite. When he ripped   5
the onions from the ground, their roots
hung pale like bloodless veins.

We found him sitting against a sycamore.
He died while the corn stalks waved

in the distance, to the wailing of the pregnant   10
cow, her hooves stomping up poofs of dust.
He must have been watching to make sure
she made it, must have sat to rest
while the nose of the calf squeezed
out towards the light, heart twitching in its chest.   15

They carried him up from the field on a stretcher.
I held the newborn Black Angus, hot birth stink
rubbing into my clothes, and I buried my face
in the slick black squirming flesh.
Its spindly legs hung over my arms like grass.   20

What a leap! The suppleness of this poem reveals Lynn's maturing skills. Lynn's deft handling of balance and imbalance in the lines help her emphasize a farmer's struggle and quiet acceptance of fate. An impression of alternating force and release pervades the poem and supports its two major themes of birth and death and the congruent images of farming.

The poem opens with a harsh assertion, "The earth sucks the life right out of you," but the next line moderates the assertion: the laws of nature may seem personally malevolent, but are only necessary. The end-stop of line 1 sharpens the emphatic opening line—six stressed and three unstressed syllables—but the sentence runs on to the relatively balanced and more lightly stressed line 2 which closes the sentence as if getting in the last word. Line 3 begins evenly, with a regular pattern of unstressed and stressed syllables, then ends with two stressed syllables. This strong beat is somewhat modulated by the enjambment into the fourth—more lightly accented—line. The first phrase of line 3 echoes the end of line 2 ("because it has to. / He had to . . . ."), suggesting the interconnection between the earth and the father, between birth and death, plowing and harvesting, grass and dust.

Lynn's images and metaphors also draw this connection. The first stanza's closing image of the onions' "bloodless veins," which the father ripped from the ground, recalls how "the earth sucks the life right out of you." Closing her poem, Lynn touches on this image through the calf to create a subtle resolution: "Its spindly legs hung over my arms like grass": visually the long leaves of spring onions are akin to the grass. Like the poem's first line, the last line uses six accented syllables but is more rhythmically balanced: we might say it scans as beginning and closing with two iambs with a rhythmic glitch in the middle; therefore the rhythm suggests a pattern of order-disturbance-order, corresponding perhaps to the thematic cycle life-death-life.

Somewhere along the way the reader may realize with surprise that the poem is in meter. (The little arrhythmia in line 20 scans as a dactyl—"húng over | my arms . . .") Yet the poem so flexibly deploys the meter—with frequent anapests and double-iambs—that it may pass unnoticed; its pace underlies the assured, measured flow of the poem's sentences. Lines 1, 8, 10–11, 15–18, and 20 are pentameters; lines 2–3, 5–6, and 12–13, tetrameters; and lines 4, 7, 9, 14, and 19, trimeters. Only the lame foot in line 1, focusing the harsh verb—

The earth | sucks | the life | right out | of you,

—is irregular; and perhaps that anomaly, along with the quick variation of line length in lines 1–4 (pentameter, tetrameter, tetrameter, trimeter) works to conceal the poem's formal undercurrent.

Although a striking poem, "To Dust" might still profit from some fiddling. In writing about death—or any other intense subject—one risks sentimentality and melodrama. Some readers might find the title an example of such heavy-handedness, even though Lynn has indirectly called up the too familiar "dust to dust" and has made dust integral to the poem by weaving it into the first two stanzas. Is a similar risky allusion ("all flesh is grass") meant in "flesh" and "grass" in lines 19–20? The danger is perhaps greater as the somewhat mechanical reference may seem decorative and undercut the daring of the final simile. Is "flesh" exactly the right word anyway?

Some refocusing might help lines 9–10. The phrase "the corn stalks waved" in context permits the silly possibility that the corn is waving *goodbye* to the father. Even if unintentional, the pathetic fallacy hazards undercutting the tone of somber acceptance and trivializing the farmer's death. (**Pathetic fallacy:** crediting nature with human feelings or behavior.)

And in lines 10–11 the breaking of the phrase "the pregnant / cow," which jams the flow against the caesura, seems awkward and puts undue emphasis on "pregnant." The point is not that the cow is pregnant—she is *giving birth*. Lynn tried moving "cow" back to the end of line 10—

> in the distance, to the wailing of the pregnant cow,
> her hooves stomping up poofs of dust.

—but was dissatisfied. End-stopped, the lines seem flat, passive. Without the strong emphasis the run-on creates, the cow is merely pregnant, uncomfortable, not in labor. The solution may be in recasting the syntax of the passage so the muscular run-on carries the meaning with a truer emphasis, something like ". . . in the distance and the pregnant *cow / wailed*, her hooves . . . ."

These are niggling imperfections in a fine poem. Lynn has created a vividly imagined world and peopled it. Lynn herself isn't the speaker, and the father in the poem bears very little resemblance to her own father, who is still alive. In her growth as a poet, Lynn has come far from the thinly imagined character in "A Baglady's Plea."

PO' BIZ

Professional Poet

Someone the other day called me a professional poet to my face.

"Don't call me that," I cried. "Don't call anyone that. As well talk about a professional friend."

"Oh!" he said.

"Or a professional lover."

"Oh!"

Most poets and readers share Robert Francis's reverence for poetry's intimacy and its often lonely devotion to truth. Trust the poem.

But there is a practical side. For one thing, as we have been saying all along, respect for the poem means getting it right. To make it new, as Pound urges, you must learn not only the trade or craft, but also the traditions which gave birth to the poets who preceded you. Dickinson and Whitman became the poets they became partly because they knew earlier traditions so well they could challenge them, change them, bring other traditions to them to create new traditions. Poets like Joy Harjo, Garrett Hongo, M. Scott Momaday, and Rita Dove have found new ways to marry the European traditions of poetry to the oral and musical traditions of their ancestral cultures—to line singing, jazz rhythms, ceremonial chants—to the multifarious aspects of the world's traditions, past and present. Knowing the great (and even the not-so-great) work of other poets both humbles and thrills any poet. John Dryden scolds poets who, rashly deciding they know all about poetry before they have immersed themselves in it, conclude that "Virgil, compared to them, is flat and dry; / And Homer understood not poetry." Don't be too quick to grab a theory about poetry; theories—like the knowledge of craft—must be earned through practice.

And remember not to be in a rush, either, to finish a poem and judge it. As William Stafford remarks, "Writing is a reckless encounter with whatever comes along . . . . A writer must write bad poems, as they come, amongst the better—and not scorn the 'bad' ones. Finicky ways can dry up the sources." If you write enough poems, good ones will happen. Try having several poems going at once; then, as a class due-date approaches, you'll have choices. Pounding out a poem the night before will usually produce something misshapen or frail, likely to wither under the strong light of public scrutiny. Baudelaire described inspiration as working every day.

Respect for the poem also includes finding for it the readers who complete the equation. Later, as you grow as a poet, you will think of submitting to magazines and journals, perhaps eventually of gathering your poems in a book. For now, though, your audience is your class. Put your best foot forward, as they say. Type or print out the poems neatly. Proofread—carefully—to prevent mistakes creeping in and to check for oversights. Anything that distracts for even the tiniest flicker of a second—a grammatical error, mispunctuation, cloudy bit of syntax, misspelling, typo—costs your poem a momentary loss of your reader's attention. Do a surgical job. Don't leave clamps in the patient.

When you discuss another poet's work in class, be fair. Give the poem and the discussion your full attention. You will learn much, almost by osmosis, by listening to others talk about a fellow poet's work. Read the poem on its own terms. What is the poem trying to do? What are the ways it is trying to do it? How are they working? Be honest, but never cruel or patronizing. Your responsibility as a poet-reader means you respect and trust the poet's effort. By the same measure, when your poem comes up for discussion, do *hear* what people are saying. Some of it won't be helpful, but you can think that through later. And don't rush to explain or defend. A poem that needs explaining isn't doing its job.

Here is Robert Francis again—a chilling, charming little essay called "The Indeciferable Poem":

> I have no love for the indecipherable poem, but for the indecipherable poet I have often a warm friendly feeling. He is usually a bright chap, perhaps brilliant, a good talker, someone worth knowing and worth watching. He is also often a college undergraduate majoring in English and in love with writing.
>
> In his literature and writing courses it is taken for granted that the significant poets are the difficult ones. So, what less can an undergraduate poet do than be difficult himself?
>
> Difficulty, of course, is not the only virtue of great poets. They give us passion, vision, originality. None of these the undergraduate poet probably has, but he *can* be difficult. He can be as difficult as he wants to be. He can be as difficult as anybody else. He need only give the words he uses a private set of meanings. It is not difficult to be difficult.
>
> What I mean is, a poem that is very difficult to read may not have been at all difficult to write.
>
> One poem sufficiently difficult can keep a creative writing class busy a whole hour. If its young author feels pleased with himself, can we blame him? He is human. He has produced something as difficult as anything by Ezra Pound. Why shouldn't he be pleased?
>
> If he wants to, he can let his classmates pick away at his poem indefinitely and never set them straight. If his teacher ventures to criticize a phrase or a line, the author can say that the passage is exactly as he wants it. Is it awkward? Well, he intended it to be awkward since awkwardness was needed at that point. This would be clear, he murmurs, to anyone who understood the poem.
>
> Nobody can touch him. Nobody at all. He is safe. In an ever-threatening world full of old perils and new, such security is to be envied. To be able to sit tight and pretty on top of your poem, impregnable like a little castle perched on a steep rock.

GETTING ORGANIZED

Keep the drafts of your poems; you never know what will be useful. Clip the sheets together, latest version on top. Always make a copy when you submit poems for class (or to a magazine).

As poems multiply, a system of manila folders will keep things straight: a folder labeled NEW for poems you are currently working on, one marked FINISHED, and maybe one for NOTES—ideas, stray lines or images, interesting words, clippings, and so on. Soon an OLD MSS folder will be useful to collect fragments and poems that seem no longer promising; it may turn up a treasure on a rainy Saturday morning when you are looking for ideas. And soon, too, perhaps a folder marked PUBLISHED. Think of your work as an assembly line with poems moving along it in all the varying stages of the process.

When should a beginning poet begin sending poems out to magazines? If your school has a literary magazine, start readying a group of poems now—apply the finishing touches and away they go!

In general, a sensible answer is: as soon as you have three or four good, really finished poems *and* know several magazines or journals that would be appropriate for the poems. A rule of thumb: stick to magazines you have seen and read. If you like the poems in a magazine, odds are, you and the editors are on a similar wavelength. If you don't like the poems in a magazine, you would probably be wasting stamps to send a manuscript there. So the first thing is to get acquainted with magazines that publish poetry: literary quarterlies, poetry journals, little magazines, as well as *The New Yorker, The Atlantic,* and *The Nation.* Start browsing at the library. Writer's Digest Books publishes *Poet's Market,* an annual, which lists some 1,700 periodicals and presses that print poems, specifying the kind of poetry each wants, what they pay, and how to submit manuscripts. Dustbooks' *The International Directory of Little Magazines and Small Presses* lists more than 4,000 markets. *Poets & Writers* and *The AWP Chronicle* are journals that print announcements from editors wanting poems. If you can't find a magazine in the library, write for a sample copy (enclosing the single copy price). Magazines that pay should be higher among your possibilities.

When you are ready, send a sheaf of three or four poems to the first magazine on your list. Type each poem cleanly, single-spaced, in the center of a sheet of regular 8 1/2 X 11-inch bond paper, with your name and address in the upper left corner. There is no need for a cover letter, but *always enclose a self-addressed, stamped envelope* (SASE) for the return of your poems. Address the packet to the editor by name if you know it, or to Poetry Editor. Keep a log: poems, date sent, and, later, the response.

The probability, of course, is rejection. Even very good poets get enough rejection slips to wallpaper a den. But don't be discouraged easily. If the poems still look pretty good to you, put them in another envelope and ship them off to the next magazine on your list. Sooner or later, a rejection slip will carry a scribbled note: "Sorry" or "Fine work" or "Liked 'Apples.'" Sooner or later, there will appear a letter of acceptance and perhaps a small check. (Checks for poems are usually small checks.)

Sending poems around may be exciting as well as part of learning the trade. And it can be a stimulus to finishing poems. So never mind Horace's classical advice to wait nine years before publishing. Learning from mistakes may be more useful in the long run than trying not to make them.

If anyone wants money to publish or consider your poems, beware. Odds are, unless you know the journal or press to be reputable, it is a scam.

The copyright law (Title 17, USC) that went into effect in 1978 gives copyright protection to a work for the author's lifetime plus fifty years. That protection begins with its creation, so the penciled poem on your desk is included. An author *may* register unpublished work (Form TX, one copy of the work, and the fee), but there is no need to go to this trouble. The publisher of any reputable periodical or book will register the work on publication. Even though the registration is made in the publisher's or magazine's name, the copyright belongs to the author—*unless there is a written agreement to the contrary.* In the absence of such a written agreement, a magazine acquires only the right to initial publication in one of its issues.

The author retains copyright and full control. So don't sign anything, except a check. If in doubt, consult someone who knows about such things. (For information or forms: Copyright Office, Library of Congress, Washington, DC 20559.)

MONEY

Most little magazines usually pay in copies—two copies. Some pay a dollar or two per line. A poem that will last as long as the English language might bring fifty bucks. The commercial magazines that publish poetry do better, but not by much. Few books of poems sell more than 1,000 copies, though sales of 30,000 aren't unheard of. Poetry *has* made the bestseller lists, once upon a time with Dorothy Parker, and recently with Shel Silverstein's *A Light in the Attic*. Poets usually earn more from giving readings than from publishing. Someday there may be, too, occasional prizes and grants—several hundred dollars, or even twenty-five thousand dollars.

If you make any money to speak of, the Internal Revenue Service must regard you, albeit with suspicion, as a small business. Form C of the 1040: "Profit (or Loss) from Business or Professions (Sole Proprietorships)" will let you deduct expenses, from paperclips and postage to the cost of desk and books, and sometimes even a portion of rent and utilities. For you are, willy-nilly, a business every bit as much as IBM or General Motors. "What is good for the poet," you may freely declare, "is good for the country." But very few poets earn a living by poetry. Williams was a doctor, Stevens was an attorney for an insurance company, and Frost himself did a lot of teaching. Money (like honors, if they come) is likely to come too late to do much good. Get a job.

More important than money, though, is freedom. Since in our society poetry doesn't pay much, poets are free to write pretty much as they wish.

And more important still is the art of poetry, in which the least of us is for a time companion to Geoffrey Chaucer and John Milton and Alexander Pope and Marianne Moore. Every poet may share the hope of the Roman poet Sextus Propertius (died 15 B.C.) that, in Ezra Pound's elegant translation, he or she may write a few pages that will not "go to rack ruin beneath the thud of the years."

As Ben Jonson advised, "Live merrily, and trust to good verses."

QUESTIONS AND SUGGESTIONS

1. In the library browse among the poetry in magazines like *Poetry, Kenyon Review, Hudson Review, Paris Review, Callaloo, Poetry Northwest, Yankee Magazine, Agni, Ploughshares, Field, American Poetry Review, North American Review, New Republic, Cream City Review, Iowa Review, Ohio Review, Georgia Review, Gettysburg Review, Carolina Quarterly, Nimrod, Prairie Schooner, Epoch, Hanging Loose, New Letters, Tar River Poetry, Southern Review, Crazyhorse, Boulevard, Pembroke Magazine, Negative Capability, Laurel Review, DoubleTake,* or *Salamagundi.*

2. Buy a book of poems.

3. Here are three accomplished poems by students. If you were an editorial assistant for a poetry magazine, would you recommend any for publication? (See Appendix II.)

a)   *The Invention of the Snowman*

MARK IRWIN*

Somewhere beyond the bounds of sleep,
my bones undressed, rising from their flesh
to become this selfless, falling dust.

It was then that I wanted ears
with which to hear the familiar cries   5
of those children building me.

And of course, I had no eyes—
only this unfailing bandage of light,
the snow sewing its colorless view.

But worst of all, this thirst to be living—   10
to understand those small, clumsy hands
making the same careless mistakes as gods.

b)   *Howard*

GLENN BROOKE*

A fisherman, Howard goes down to the Ohio River
every day; there is nothing else.
He cuts a fresh willow rod, and settles himself
by the same muddy pool below the B&O tracks,
on his usual knob of damp slate.   5

Howard never baits his hook. He waits.
He looks at the dimple where his twill line
disappears into the brown water,
hardly looking up or down or away.
"Tis enough," he says.   10

My mother says Howard is crazy;
our preacher, who has prayed earnestly,
says Howard is the greatest fisherman in the world.
We accept Howard with the patience of farmers,
with the faith of great depths in rivers.   15

Howard has never caught a fish.
There, in his cord coat and patch cap,
he endures season upon season, the comings and goings
of barges and children, and the backwater fogs
drifting in and out, like doubts, like legends.   20

c)   *Mrs. Bradley's Dilemma*

AMY B. KESEGICH*

His underwear is the last thing
in the dryer—
the cotton folds stay damp
long after
the socks become electric,   5
the sheets hot.
What can I do with these—
loose and white as puppy skins?
No one I know is poor enough
for a dead man's underwear.   10
Our sons won't take them.
They have his watch
and ties, his belts and coins,
things with value to pass on.
And yet, I can't toss the cloth   15
that held him close
into the trash with chicken bones.
He's not in them anymore—
his egret legs don't poke
through these hemmed holes,   20
nor does this elastic loop
hug his wrinkled waist.
Maybe I'll tuck them in my drawer,
nuzzling against my socks.
Should I hide them from myself—   25
what if they surprise me?
I'm scared enough of ghosts
not to plant them
in my own house.

4. The **clerihew** is a comic form named for its inventor, Edmund C. (for Clerihew) Bentley (1875–1956). It consists of four lines of irregular length, of which the first is the name of a famous person or historical character; the rhyme scheme is *a a b b*. The fun is rhyming on the proper name; and the challenge is making the rest of the poem a pointed comment on the personage. After looking at these examples, try a clerihew of your own.

> St. Jerome
> abandoned brush and comb
> and bread and jam and everything nice.
> He did it on divine advice.
>
> *Vonna Adrian (1906–1987)*

> Percy Bysshe Shelley
> Thought all fish smelly
> And never learned to swim—

Unfortunately for him.

> *Roberta Simone (b. 1935)*

Dorthy Parker
Knew the darker
Side of wit
And made the *mots* of it.

> *Martha H. Freedman (b. 1915)*

How Sweet the Sound

Mr. Zane————
And Lady Jane————
Were, in rather different ways,
Amazing Greys.

> *Edmund Conti (b. 1929)*

5. Write a poem about writing poems. Use metaphors and particulars to make it colorful. Is it like planning, planting, tending, and harvesting a garden? Like manufacturing a machine tool? Perhaps focus on some detail of the process of writing (the padding sheet you use to protect the platen of your typewriter, or the miles of words stored in the tiny cylinder of a pencil lead).

6. Look over three or four poems you have written during the past few months. What has changed in your work? How have you grown as a poet? In what ways would you like to see your work develop further?

7. Prepare and send out a group of poems to the first magazine on your list.

POEMS TO CONSIDER

Realism   1994
CZESLAW MILOSZ (b. 1911)

We are not so badly off if we can
Admire Dutch painting. For that means
We shrug off what we have been told
For a hundred, two hundred years. Though we lost
Much of our previous confidence. Now we agree   5
That those trees outside the window, which probably exist,
Only pretend to greenness and treeness
And that the language loses when it tries to cope
With clusters of molecules. And yet this here:
A jar, a tin plate, a half-peeled lemon,   10

Walnuts, a loaf of bread—last, and so strongly
It is hard not to believe in their lastingness.
And thus abstract art is brought to shame,
Even if we do not deserve any other.
Therefore I enter those landscapes   15
Under a cloudy sky from which a ray
Shoots out, and in the middle of dark plains
A spot of brightness glows. Or the shore
With huts, boats, and, on yellowish ice,
Tiny figures skating. All this   20
Is here eternally, just because once it was.
Splendor (certainly incomprehensible)
Touches a cracked wall, a refuse heap,
The floor of an inn, jerkins of the rustics,
A broom, and two fish bleeding on a board.   25
Rejoice! Give thanks! I raised my voice
To join them in their choral singing,
Amid their ruffles, collets, and silk skirts,
One of them already, who vanished long ago.
And our song soared up like smoke from a censer.   30

Translated, from the Polish, by the author and Robert Hass.

 Dancing with Poets   *1987*

ELLEN BRYANT VOIGT (b. 1943)

"The accident" is what he calls the time
he threw himself from a window four floors up,
breaking his back and both ankles, so that walking
became the direst labor for this man
who takes my hand, invites me to the empty strip of floor   5
that fronts the instruments, a length of polished wood
the shape of a grave. *Unsuited for this world*—
his body bears the marks of it, his hand
is tense with effort and with shame, and I shy away
from any audience, but I love to dance, and soon   10
we find a way to move, drifting apart as each
effects a different ripple across the floor,
a plaid and a stripe to match the solid navy of the band.
And suddenly the band is getting better, so pleased
to have this pair of dancers, since we make evident   15
the music in the noise—and the dull pulse
leaps with unexpected riffs and turns, we can hear

how good the keyboard really is, the bright cresting
of another major key as others join us: a strict
block of a man, a formidable cliff of mind, dancing   20
as if melted, as if unhinged; his partner a gift of brave
elegance to those who watch her dance; and at her elbow,
Berryman back from the bridge, and Frost, relieved
of grievances, Dickinson waltzing there with lavish Keats,
who coughs into a borrowed handkerchief—all the poets of exile   25
and despair, unfit for this life, all those who cannot speak
but only sing, all those who cannot walk
who strut and spin until the waiting citizens at the bar,
aloof, judgmental, begin to sway or drum their straws
or hum, leave their seats to crowd the narrow floor   30
and now we are one body, sweating and foolish,
one body with its clear pathetic grace, not
lifted out of grief but dancing it, transforming
for one night this local bar, before we're turned back out
to our separate selves, to the dangerous streets and houses,   35
to the overwhelming drone of the living world.

 ## Stepping Out of Poetry   *1977*

GERALD STERN (b. 1925)

What would you give for one of the old yellow streetcars
rocking toward you again through the thick snow?

What would you give for the feeling of joy as you climbed
up the three iron steps and took your place by the cold window?

Oh, what would you give to pick up your stack of books   5
and walk down the icy path in front of the library?

What would you give for your dream
to be as clear and simple as it was then
in the dark afternoons, at the old scarred tables?

 ## Like Miles Said   *1994*

ALVIN AUBERT (b. 1930)

my memory aint too good
i trouble the past, like, crazy
maybe i'm crazy like they say miles was
maybe i don't half know what i'm doing

like miles said if you don't know what you're   5
doing chances are you ain't doing nothin'

quoting the old drummer he played with
when he first started playin'
who was dead when miles said that about him

now miles is dead and i'm sure every mf   10
and his mama is going to be lyin'
about stuff miles said like maybe i'm doin'
right now but miles won't mind
miles was hip to all that shit

like every time you put a mouthpiece   15
to your lips you bound to lie some.

The Supremes   *1991*

CORNELIUS EADY (b. 1954)

We were born to be gray. We went to school,
Sat in rows, ate white bread,
Looked at the floor a lot. In the back
Of our small heads

A long scream. We did what we could,   5
And all we could do was
Turn on each other. How the fat kids suffered!
Not even being jolly could save them.

And then there were the anal retentives,
The terrified brown-noses, the desperately   10
Athletic or popular. This, of course,
Was training. At home

Our parents shook their heads and waited.
We learned of the industrial revolution,
The sectioning of the clock into pie slices.   15
We drank cokes and twiddled our thumbs. In the
Back of our minds

A long scream. We snapped butts in the showers,
Froze out shy girls on the dance floor,
Pin-pointed flaws like radar.   20
Slowly we understood: this was to be the world.

We were born insurance salesmen and secretaries,
Housewives and short order cooks,
Stock room boys and repairmen,
And it wouldn't be a bad life, they promised,   25
In a tone of voice that would force some of us
To reach in self-defense for wigs,
Lipstick,

Sequins.

Selecting a Reader   *1974*

TED KOOSER (b. 1939)

First, I would have her be beautiful,
and walking carefully up on my poetry
at the loneliest moment of an afternoon,
her hair still damp at the neck
from washing it. She should be wearing   5
a raincoat, an old one, dirty
from not having money enough for the cleaners.
She will take out her glasses, and there
in the bookstore, she will thumb
over my poems, then put the book back   10
up on its shelf. She will say to herself,
"For that kind of money, I can get
my raincoat cleaned." And she will.

Building an Outhouse   *1991*

RONALD WALLACE (b. 1945)

Is not unlike building a poem: the pure
mathematics of shape; the music of hammer
and tenpenny nail, of floor joist, stud wall,
and sill; the cut wood's sweet smell.

If the Skil saw rear up in your unpracticed hand,   5
cussing, hawking its chaw of dust,
and you're lost in the pounding particulars
of fly rafters, siding, hypotenuse, and load,
until nothing seems level or true
but the scorn of the tape's clucked tongue,   10

let the nub of your plainspoken pencil prevail
and it's up! Function. Tight as a sonnet.
It will last forever (or at least for awhile)
though the critics come sit on it, and sit on it.

Make Big Money at Home!
Write Poems in Spare Time!   1962

HOWARD NEMEROV (1920–1991)

Oliver wanted to write about reality.
He sat before a wooden table,
He poised his wooden pencil
Above his pad of wooden paper,
And attempted to think about agony   5
And history, and the meaning of history,
And all stuff like that there.

Suddenly this wooden thought got in his head:
A Tree. That's all, no more than that,
Just one tree, not even a note   10
As to whether it was deciduous
Or evergreen, or even where it stood.
Still, because it came unbidden,
It was inspiration, and had to be dealt with.

Oliver hoped that this particular tree   15
Would turn out to be fashionable,
The axle of the universe, maybe,
Or some other mythologically
Respectable tree-contraption
With dryads, or having to do   20
With the knowledge of Good and Evil, and the Fall.

"A Tree," he wrote down with his wooden pencil
Upon his pad of wooden paper
Supported by the wooden table.
And while he sat there waiting   25
For what would come next to come next,
The whole wooden house began to become
Silent, particularly silent, sinisterly so.

The Next Poem 1985

DANA GIOIA (b. 1950)

How much better it seems now
than when it is finally done—
the unforgettable first line,
the cunning way the stanzas run.

The rhymes (for, yes, it will have rhymes) 5
almost inaudible at first,
an appetite not yet acknowledged
like the inkling of a thirst.

While gradually the form appears
as each line is coaxed aloud— 10
the architecture of a room
seen from the middle of a crowd.

The music that of common speech
but slanted so that each detail
sounds unexpected as a sharp 15
inserted in a simple scale.

No jumble box of imagery
dumped glumly in the reader's lap
or elegantly packaged junk
the unsuspecting must unwrap. 20

But words that could direct a friend
precisely to an unknown place,
those few unshakeable details
no confusion can erase.

And the real subject left unspoken 25
but unmistakable to those
who don't expect a jungle parrot
in the black and white of prose.

How much better it seems now
than when it is finally written. 30
How hungrily one waits to feel
the bright lure seized, the old hook bitten.

Raptures   *1994*

DAVID R. SLAVITT (b. 1935)

To claim the poem as mine would be to tell
only that half-truth that's worse than a lie.
The other, the missing half, which is true as well,
is the poem's claim on me: I know how I

was lured, held for a brief spell in a rapture.   5
I wasn't myself, but a vessel, a plain tin cup
filled and then suddenly emptied, and cannot recapture
the dazzle of those droplets. I look up

from the poem and can't remember, or only barely,
what it felt like, and what I have lost. What you   10
approve the most is what afflicts most sorely,
not being me but something I went through

and want not to resent. Enlivened by birds
migrating south, the sky they wheeled upon
is emptier for their passing. These spates of words   15
leave similar vacancies when they've gone.

APPENDIX I

A Glossary of Forms

GENERIC FORMS

couplet The most elementary stanza, two lines; when rhymed, *a a*. Flexible, it has served for narrative (Chaucer's *The Canterbury Tales*), but is also capable of succinctness and epigrammatic punch, as in Pope's

> The hungry judges soon the sentence sign
> And wretches hang that jurymen may dine.

triplet (tercet) Stanza of three lines. Triple-rhyming (*a a a*) is possible in shorter poems, such as Herrick's "Upon Julia's Clothes" (p. 18). Both *a b b* (Marianne Moore's "Nevertheless") and *a b a* are alternatives. The Italian form **terza rima** follows the *a b a* scheme *and* uses the unrhymed line for the double rhymes of the next stanza: *a b a, b c b, c d c*, and so on. Shelley's "Ode to the West Wind" is the most familiar example in English.

quatrain Stanza of four lines. Although in "Cadence" (p. 210) Robert Francis succeeds with *a a a a*, the usual schemes are: *a b c b* (often used in ballads, hymns, and popular songs), *a b a b, a a b b*, and *a b b a*. Rhyming on only two of the four lines, *a b c b* is of course the simplest; and when the lines alternate tetrameter and trimeter, as in "Western Wind" (p. 5) or Dickinson's "I heard a Fly buzz" (p. 168), it is sometimes called a **ballad stanza.**

Beyond the quatrain, stanzaic variation increases exponentially. Three longer stanzas have been employed with frequency: **rime royal** (seven lines of iambic pentameter, *a b a b b c c*), **ottava rima** (eight lines, *a b a b a b c c*), and the **Spenserian stanza** (nine lines: eight of iambic pentameter and the last iambic hexameter, *a b a b b c b c c*; used by Keats in "The Eve of St. Agnes," p. 337). With such patterns, the poet must be continually looking forward for possible rhymes in the sense that lies ahead, and backward to bring other rhyme words into place, as each stanza is laced together. A **nonce stanza** is one made up for a particular poem, like that invented by Marianne Moore for "The Fish" (p. 46) or John Donne for "Song" (p. 85). The challenge is to repeat the form naturally and effectively throughout the poem.

refrain   A phrase, line, or group of lines repeated from stanza to stanza, usually at the end. This device recalls one of the origins of the short poem: in song. It is a small step from the merry "Hey nonny, nonny" of a Shakespearean song (p. 84) to the delicious solemnity of Yeats's "Mad as the Mist and Snow" (p. 99) in the twentieth century. In "Recuerdo" (Spanish for a recollection or memory), Edna St. Vincent Millay organizes the poem by beginning the stanzas with a refrain:

> We were very tired, we were very merry—
> We had gone back and forth all night on the ferry.
> It was bare and bright, and smelled like a stable—
> But we looked into a fire, we leaned across a table,
> We lay on a hill-top underneath the moon;   5
> And the whistles kept blowing, and the dawn came soon.
>
> We were very tired, we were very merry—
> We had gone back and forth all night on the ferry;
> And you ate an apple, and I ate a pear,
> From a dozen of each we had bought somewhere;   10
> And the sky went wan, and the wind came cold,
> And the sun rose dripping, a bucketful of gold.
>
> We were very tired, we were very merry,
> We had gone back and forth all night on the ferry.
> We hailed, "Good morrow, mother!" to a shawl-covered head,   15
> And bought a morning paper, which neither of us read;
> And she wept, "God bless you!" for the apples and pears,
> And we gave her all our money but our subway fares.

ballad   A narrative song in traditional forms (like ballad stanza). Historically, ballads were composed and passed along orally among a non-literate people, often with successive modifications. Thus, when they came to be written down (or collected), the same story-song might appear in remarkably differing versions in diverse locales. Appalachian folk songs, like "Barbary Ellen" (in the version popularized by John Jacob Niles), often turn out to be variants of traditional British ballads, brought over long ago by immigrants from the British Isles. As Edwin Muir notes in *The Estate of Poetry*, the communal nature of ballads produces a style of startling brevity and strength. "It may take hundreds of years to bring a ballad to its perfection, and many generations may participate in its making." Here is "Bonny Barbara Allan" (about 1500):

> It was in and about the Martinmas° time,
>   When the green leaves were a falling,
> That Sir John Græme, in the West Country,
>   Fell in love with Barbara Allan.
>
> He sent his men down through the town,   5
>   To the place where she was dwelling.
> "O haste and come to my master dear,
>   Gin° ye be Barbara Allan."

1 *Martinmas:* a church festival in November; 8 *Gin:* if.

O hooly,° hooly rose she up,
   To the place where he was lying,   10
And when she drew the curtain by:
   "Young man, I think you're dying."

"O it's I'm sick, and very, very sick,
   And 'tis a'° for Barbara Allan."
"O the better for me ye s'° never be,   15
   Though your heart's blood were a-spilling.

"O dinna ye mind,° young man," said she,
   "When ye was in the tavern a drinking,
That ye made the healths gae° round and round,
   And slighted Barbara Allan?"   20

He turned his face unto the wall,
   And death was with him dealing:
"Adieu, adieu, my dear friends all,
   And be kind to Barbara Allan."

And slowly, slowly raise she up,   25
   And slowly, slowly left him,   25
And sighing said she could not stay,
   Since death of life had reft him.

She had not gane° a mile but twa,°
   When she heard the dead-bell ringing,
And every jow° that the dead-bell geid,°   30
   It cried, "Woe to Barbara Allan!"

"O mother, mother, make my bed!
   O make it saft° and narrow!
Since my love died for me to-day,   35
   I'll die for him to-morrow."

9 *hooly:* slowly; 14 *a':* all; 15 *s':* shall; 17 *dinna ye mind:* do you not recall; 19 *gae:* go;
29 *gane:* gone; 29 *twa:* two; 31 *jow:* stroke; 31 *geid:* gave; 34 *saft:* soft.

Expanding, contracting as variations are tried out, accepted, or discarded, a ballad
may also change to fit local circumstances. In American versions of "Bonny Barbara Allan," the action sometimes occurs in the spring; and the young man who
literally dies of love for a woman he had earlier spurned, and who in turn spurns
him, is variously identified as Sweet William or Jemmy Grove. One version ends
fancifully:

They buried her in the old churchyard,
Sweet William's grave was nigh her,
And from his heart grew a red, red rose,
And from her heart a briar.

They grew themselves to the old church wall,
Twill they couldn't grow no higher;

They grew twill they tied a true-lovers' knot,
The red rose round the briar.

blank verse   Unrhymed iambic pentameter. Since the seventeenth century, it has been a formal workhorse for longer poems—Shakespeare's tragedies, Milton's *Paradise Lost*, Wordsworth's *The Prelude*, Browning's and Frost's dramatic monologues, Stevens's "Sunday Morning" or "The Idea of Order at Key West."

dropped-line   A convention perhaps originating in dramatic usage. In printing Shakespeare, for instance, when a single pentameter line is divided between two speakers, the second part of the line is shown as "dropped":

Brutus: What means this shouting? I do fear, the people
          Choose Caesar for their king.
Cassius: Ay, do you fear it?
          Then must I think you would not have it so.

The Tragedy of Julius Caesar, I, ii, 79–81

Dropped-line may be used for rhythmical variation or emphasis, as Richard Wilbur does in "Love Calls Us to the Things of This World" (p. 284):

And the heaviest nuns walk in a pure floating
Of dark habits,
          keeping their difficult balance.

Dropped-line is a principal organizing device in this poem by E. E. Cummings, which seems to evoke the mythological story of the beautiful Persephone who, gathering flowers in that fair field of Enna, "Herself a fairer Flow'r," as Milton says, was carried off by Pluto to be queen of Hades:

Tumbling-hair
          picker of buttercups
                    violets
dandelions
And the big bullying daisies
                    through the field wonderful
with eyes a little sorry
Another comes
          also picking flowers

stichomythia   A convention of dialogue, from Greek drama, in which two characters speak in exactly alternating lines of verse. The device is useful for contrast or dispute or, as in "Up-Hill" by Christina Rossetti (1830–1894), question and answer:

Does the road wind up-hill all the way?
     Yes, to the very end.

Will the day's journey take the whole long day?
    From morn to night, my friend.

But is there for the night a resting-place?   5
    A roof for when the slow dark hours begin.
May not the darkness hide it from my face?
    You cannot miss that inn.

Shall I meet other wayfarers at night?
    Those who have gone before.   10
Then must I knock, or call when just in sight?
    They will not keep you standing at that door.

Shall I find comfort, travel-sore and weak?
    Of labour you shall find the sum.
Will there be beds for me and all who seek?   15
    Yea, beds for all who come.

light verse   Comic or funny poetry, especially of a witty sort like John Updike's "Player Piano" (p. 95). The term, coined in 1867 by Frederick Locker-Lampson, comes from a Victorian distinction that tried to reserve the term *poetry* for the serious and lofty, though no one ever called *it* "heavy verse." Light verse may be merely playful, as in the punning by William Rossa Cole (b. 1919) of "A River Rhyme":

It was floodtime on the Seine:
Flotsam, jetsam, garbage, then
Five cats clinging to a plank—
Un, deux, trois cats sank!

(**Pun:** using a word so as to suggest two quite incongruous meanings or applications at once. Example: telling a condemned man at the gibbet that he'll get the *hang* of it.) Equally, funny poems may have an underlying point, as does this sophisticated parody of an Elizabethan sonnet by Wendy Cope (b. 1945). Strugnell is a fictitious poet; Sir Philip Sidney, of course, was the Elizabethan sonneteer.

Strugnell's Bargain

My true love hath my heart and I have hers:
We swapped last Tuesday and we felt elated
But now, whenever one of us refers
To "my heart," things get rather complicated.
Just now, when she complained "My heart is racing,"   5
"You mean *my* heart is racing," I replied.
"That's what I said." "You mean the heart replacing
Your heart my love." "Oh piss off, Jake!" she cried.
I ask you, do you think Sir Philip Sidney
Got spoken to like that? And I suspect   10
If I threw in my liver and a kidney

She'd still address me with as scant respect.
Therefore do I revoke my opening line:
My love can keep her heart and I'll have mine.

COMPLEX WHOLE-POEM FORMS

sonnet   Both familiar and useful: fourteen lines of iambic pentameter. The **Shakespearean** (or **Elizabethan**) **sonnet** is rhymed in three quatrains and a couplet: *a b a b, c d c d, e f e f, g g.* Shakespeare's Sonnet 73 (p. 10) is a good example in which the sense corresponds to the four divisions. The **Italian** (or **Petrarchan**) **sonnet** is rhymed: *a b b a a b b a, c d e c d e* (or *c d c d c d*) in units of eight and six lines: **octave** and **sestet.** The sense, statement and resolution, usually conforms to this division. Although its "turn" does not come exactly between the octave and the sestet, John Milton's sonnet typifies the form:

On His Blindness

When I consider how my light is spent,
Ere half my days, in this dark world and wide,
And that one talent which is death to hide,
Lodged with me useless, though my soul more bent
To serve therewith my Maker, and present   5
My true account, lest he returning chide;
Doth God exact day-labor, light denied?
I fondly ask. But patience to prevent
That murmur, soon replies, God doth not need
Either man's work or his own gifts; who best   10
Bear his mild yoke, they serve him best; his state
Is kingly. Thousands at his bidding speed
And post o'er land and ocean without rest:
They also serve who only stand and wait.

Poets have worked any number of successful variations on the rhyme schemes of both kinds of sonnet. Edmund Spenser used an interlocking *a b a b, b c b c, c d c d, e e.* Frost, who wrote more sonnets than might be supposed, tried numerous variations, including: *a a a b b b c c c d d d e e.* His "Acquainted with the Night" is a variation on terza rima, with the final couplet made by simply "omitting" the unrhymed line in the last "triplet": *a b a, b c b, c d c, d e d, e e.*

In the twentieth century, the sonnet has ranged far beyond the traditional subject matter, as will appear from a look at Marilyn Nelson Waniek's "Balance" (p. 115), T. R. Hummer's "The Rural Carrier Discovers That Love Is Everywhere" (p. 185), or perhaps David Wojahn's "The Assassination of John Lennon as Depicted by the Madame Tussaud Wax Museum, Niagara Falls, Ontario, 1987" (p. 143).

villanelle   Borrowed from the French, a poem of six stanzas—five triplets and a quatrain. It employs only *two* rhymes throughout: *a b a, a b a, a b a, a b a, a b a, a b a a.* Moreover, the first and third lines are repeated entirely, three times, as a refrain. Line 1 appears again as lines 6, 12, and 18. Line 3, as lines 9, 15, and 19. See Dylan Thomas's "Do Not Go Gentle into That Good Night" (p. 100).

sestina Even more complicated: six six-line stanzas and one three-line stanza. Instead of rhyme, the *six words* at the ends of lines in the first stanza are repeated in a specific, shifting order as line-end words in the other five six-line stanzas. Then all six words are used again in the final triplet, three of them at line-ends, three of them in midline. The order of the line-end words in the stanzas may be transcribed this way: 1–2–3–4–5–6, 6–1–5–2–4–3, 3–6–4–1–2–5, 5–3–2–6–1–4, 4–5–1–3–6–2, 2–4–6–5–3–1; and in the triplet, (2)–5–(4)–3–(6)–1. Poets since Sir Philip Sidney have used the sestina successfully. Note the round and round, spiraling-in quality of the form. Here is a contemporary example by David Evett (b. 1936):

Popcorn

It seems so right to sit here eating some popcorn,
dipping out handfuls of gentle white explosions,
relishing the contrast between cold bourbon and warm salt,
at ease with the world here within this ring of lamplight,
not yet satisfied but certainly no longer hungry,   5
selecting a last few morsels from among the old maids.

Another nice contrast: the small smooth brown old maids
against the white puffed irregularity of the popcorn.
When they're all that's left I'm glad I'm not hungry—
taut they are, swollen, threatening small explosions,   10
but held in by the comfortable circle of lamplight,
and the bowl, and pacified by fine small jewels of salt.

Of course, one of you is bound to observe that so much salt
provokes high blood pressure, and that hard old maids
break teeth, that scarce fuels burned to make my lamplight   15
and were processed into fertilizer to grow the popcorn.
While I indulge myself, the population explosion
booms: my pleasure against the misery of the truly hungry.

Of course, about now some woman among you's hungry
for justice, every word I say rubbing coarse salt   20
into an old wound, on the verge of a real explosion
at my thoughtless endorsement of the phrase "old maid":
a long history of exploitation trivialized by popcorn,
suffering in the shadows beyond the comfy male lamplight.

To say nothing of that definitive intense lamplight   25
ready to gather in its expanding ring both hungry
and fed, ready to shadow under clouds like monster popcorn
all of us, ready when we're finally sick of futile SALT
talks to gather us by handfuls, young, old, maids
and men, dissolving all contrast in one ghastly explosion.   30

All right, all right: I'll try to stop the explosion,
illuminate that darkness there beyond my lamplight.

But don't the rest of you in contrast sit there like old maids:
get out there, heal the sick, clothe the naked, feed the hungry,
battle indifference and injustice and discrimination, assault   35
fear, persuade the Others to trade guns for buttered popcorn.

First, though, we old maids and health freaks are a bit hungry.
Gathering forces by lamplight, even the very best, the salt
of the earth's explosion, can use the sustenance of a little popcorn.

pantoum   A Malayan form: an indefinite number of *a b a b* quatrain stanzas, with this restriction: lines 2 and 4 of each stanza, *in their entirety*, become lines 1 and 3 of the following stanza, and so on. The carry-over lines are called *repetons*. The sequence is ended in a quatrain whose repetons are lines 1 and 3 of the *first* stanza *in reversed order*. This example by Vonna Adrian will make it clearer:

A *Plaguey Thing*

If I were you I'd just forget it:
A pantoum is a plaguey thing.
It drives you crazy if you let it;
It haunts you, dawn and evening.

A pantoum is a plaguey thing.   5
My friend, can you define *pantoum*?
It haunts you, dawn and evening.
Does it belong in a drawing room?

My friend, can you define *pantoum*?
Do you strum it or pluck it or beat it?   10
Does it belong in a drawing room?
If fruit or veg, then you could eat it.

Do you strum it or pluck it or beat it?
Dare mail it to a little mag?
If fruit or veg, then you could eat it.   15
Producing it can be a drag.

Dare mail it to a little mag,
It drives you crazy if you let it.
Producing it can be a drag;
If I were you I'd just forget it.   20

For the poet who enjoys the challenge of complicated forms, there are many more, like the French rondeau and rondel, the Welsh cywydd llosgyrnog, or the Arabic rubaiyat, all of which have been successfully adapted to English.

SHORT WHOLE-POEM FORMS

haiku (hokku)   A Japanese form, three lines of five, seven, and five syllables. The essence of the haiku, however, is not its syllabic form (which is virtually meaningless in English), but its tone or touch, influenced by Zen Buddhism. Haiku are, in general, very brief natural descriptions or observations that carry some implicit spiritual insight. The most famous is by Matsuo Basho (1644–1694), translated (without the syllabics) by Nobuyuki Yuasa:

> Breaking the silence
> Of an ancient pond,
> A frog jumped into water—
> A deep resonance.

Nearly as famous are these tender poems by Kobayashi Issa (1763–1827), translated by Robert Bly:

> Cricket, be
> careful! I'm rolling
> over!

> The old dog bends his head listening . . .
> I guess the singing
> of the earthworms gets to him.

epigram   A very brief, aphoristic, usually satiric poem like Alexander Pope's "Epigram from the French":

> Sir, I admit your gen'ral rule
> That every poet is a fool.
> But you yourself may serve to show it,
> That every fool is not a poet.

This anonymous poem characterizes the form:

> Three things must epigrams, like bees, have all,
> A sting, and honey, and a body small.

The Greek word *epigramma* meant "inscription," and primarily implies brevity and pith.

epitaph (literally, "on a tomb")   A commemoration suitable for inscribing on a gravestone. But epitaphs, especially comic ones, are a literary convention that has little to do with chisels or real marble—as in Thomas Hardy's

> *Epitaph on a Pessimist*

> I'm Smith of Stoke, aged sixty-odd,
>   I've lived without a dame
> From youth-time on; and would to God
>   My dad had done the same.

limerick   Five lines, of which the first, second, and fifth are trimeter; the (usually indented) third and fourth, dimeter. Rhymed *a a b b a*. The dominant rhythm is anapestic. The first limericks, published in London in 1821 by John Harris, in *The History of Sixteen Wonderful Old Women*, were not humorous:

> There was an old woman of Leeds
> Who spent all her life in good deeds;
>   She worked for the poor
>   Till her fingers were sore,
> This pious old woman of Leeds.

Edward Lear (1812–1888) saw the comic potential and in 1846 published his first *Book of Nonsense* (verses and drawings) which started the craze:

> There was an Old Man with a beard,
> Who said, "It is just as I feared—
>   Two Owls and a Hen,
>   Four Larks and a Wren,
> Have all built their nests in my beard!"

Lear kept the model's fifth line as a recycling of the first line, though other poets didn't, and by the end of the century an almost classical literature existed in the form—mostly by the versatile Anonymous:

> There was a young fellow named Hall,
> Who fell in the spring in the fall;
>   'Twould have been a sad thing
>   If he'd died in the spring,
> But he didn't—he died in the fall.

The fun often is using a proper name, preferably polysyllabic, to end the first line and then getting the second and fifth lines to rhyme with it:

> There was an old man of Nantucket
> Who kept all his cash in a bucket;
>   But his daughter, named Nan,
>   Ran away with a man,
> And as for the bucket, Nantucket.

monostich   A one-line poem. Technically, it can't be verse—it doesn't "turn." One-liners, nonetheless, make a delightful mini-genre. Titles often provide an essential juxtaposition, and so the gap across which a spark can leap, as in this monostich by Eric Torgersen (b. 1943):

> *Wearing Mittens*
>
> You remember the sea.

"Frankenstein in the Cemetery" by Mike Finley (b. 1950) has a lovely comic pathos: "Here is where I ought to be. And here. And here. And here. And here.

And here." Tiniest of these tiny knots is by Joseph Napora (b. 1944), with a palindromic title:

Sore Eros

tOUCH

(A **palindrome** is a word, phrase, or sentence that reads the same backward as forward: "Rats live on no evil star" or "Madam, I'm Adam.")

prose poem   A composition in prose that asks for the concentrated attention usually given to poetry rather than the more discursive attention usually given to prose. Shorter in length than the short story or essay. "Swimmers" by Jay Meek (p. 54) or this prose poem by Robert Bly, for instance, act in subject, tone, and imagery as we expect a poem to do:

Looking at a Dead Wren in My Hand

Forgive the hours spent listening to radios, and the words of gratitude I did not say to teachers. I love your tiny rice-like legs, that are bars of music played in an empty church, and the feminine tail, where no worms of Empire have ever slept, and the intense yellow chest that makes tears come. Your tail feathers open like a picket fence, and your bill is brown, with the sorrow of an old Jew whose daughter has married an athlete. The black spot on your head is your own mourning cap.

APPENDIX II

Notes to the Questions and Suggestions

CHAPTER 1

1. *a)*   *Theology*

PAUL LAURENCE DUNBAR (1872–1906)

There is a heaven, for ever, day by day,
The upward longing of my soul doth tell me so.
There is a hell, I'm quite as sure; for pray,
If there were not, where would my neighbors go?

b)   *Braille*

GERALD COSTANZO (b. 1945)

The blind folding their dollar
bills in half. Giving the fives
a crease on each corner; leaving
the tens smooth as a knuckle.

There are ways, even in trust
among the rank and file
of the seeing,
not to be bilked.

The blind leading the blind
is not so bad—

how it is lost on us every day
that you can learn all
of the world you need to know
by tapping it gently
with a stick.

CHAPTER 3

1. *a)*　*Death of the Day*

My píc|tŭres bláck|ĕn 'in | thĕir fråmes

Ăs níght | cómes ón,

Ănd yóuth|fŭl máids | ănd wrínk|lĕd dámes

Ăre nów | áll óne.

Déath ŏf | thĕ dáy! | ă stérn|ĕr Déath

Dĭd wórse | bĕfóre;

Thĕ fáir|ĕst fórm, | thĕ swéet|ĕst bréath,

Ăwáy | hĕ bóre.

b)　*Epitaph*

Hĕre líes | Sĭr Táct, | ă díp|lŏmát|ĭc fél|lŏw

Whŏse sí|lĕnce wás | nŏt góld|ĕn, bút | jŭst yél|lŏw.

c)　*Anecdote of the Jar*

Ĭ plácced | ă jár | ĭn Tén|nĕsşée

Ănd róund | ĭt wás, | ŭpón | ă híll.

Ĭt máde | thĕ slóv|ĕnlў wíl|dĕrnéss

Sŭrróund | thăt híll.

Thĕ wíl|dĕrnéss | róse úp | tŏ ít,

Ănd spráwled | ăróund, | nŏ lóng|ĕr wíld.

Thĕ jár | wăs róund | ŭpón | thĕ gróund

Ănd táll | ănd óf | ă pórt | ĭn áir.

Ĭt tóok | dŏmín|ĭon év|ĕ̆rўwhére.

Thĕ jár | wăs gráy | ănd báre.

Ĭt díd | nŏt gíve | ŏf bírd | ŏr búsh,

Lĭke nóth|ĭng élse | ĭn Tén|nĕssée.

d)   *If I should learn, in some quite casual way*

Ĭf Í | shŏuld léarn, | ĭn sóme | qŭite cás|ŭ̆ăl wáy,

Thăt yóu | wĕre góne, | nŏt tŏ | rĕtúrn | ăgáin—

Réad frŏm | thĕ báck-|páge ŏf | ă páp|ĕr, sáy,

Héld bў | ă néigh|bŏr (ĭ́n) | ă súb|wăy tráin,

Hów ăt | thĕ córn|ĕr ó̆f | thĭs áv|ĕnúe

Ănd súch | ă stréet | (só̆ áre | thĕ páp|ĕrs fílled)

Ă húr|rў̆ĭng mán, | whŏ háp|pĕnĕd tŏ bé yóu,

Ăt nóon | tŏdáy | hăd háp|pĕned tó̆ | bĕ kílled—

Ĭ shóuld | nŏt crý | ălóud—|Ĭ cóuld | nŏt crý

Ălóud, | ŏr wríng | mў́ hánds | ĭn súch | ă pláce—

Ĭ shóuld | bŭt wátch | thĕ stá|tĭon líghts | rúsh bў́

Wíth ă | móre cáre|fŭl ín|tĕrĕst ón | mў́ fáce;

Ŏr ráise | mў́ éyes | ănd réad | wĭth gréat|ĕr cáre

Whére tŏ | stóre fúrs | ănd hów | tŏ tréat | thĕ háir.

e)   *Delight in Disorder*

Ă swéet | dĭsór|dĕr ín | thĕ dréss

Kíndlĕs | ĭn clóthes | ă wán|tŏnnéss;

Ă láwn | ăbóut | thĕ shóul|dĕrs thrówn

Íntŏ | ă fíne |dĭstrác|tĭón,

Ăn érr|ĭng láce, | whĭch hére | ănd thére

Ĕnthrálls | thĕ crím|sŏn stóm|ăchĕr,

Ă cúff | nĕgléct|fŭl, ánd | thĕrebý

Ríbbănds | tŏ flów | cŏnfús|ĕdlý,

Ă wín|nĭng wáve, | dĕsérv|ĭng nóte,

Ín thĕ | témpés|tŭoŭs pét|tĭcóat,

Ă cáre|lĕss shóe-|strĭng, ĭn | whŏse tíe

Ĭ sée | ă wíld | cĭvíl|ĭtý,

Dŏ móre | bĕwítch | mĕ thán | whĕn árt

Ĭs tóo | prĕcíse | ĭn év|ĕrý párt.

f)   *In the Field Forever*

Sún's | ă róar|ĭng dán|dĕlí|ŏn, hóur | bў hóur.

Sŏmetímes | thĕ móon's | ă scýthe, | sŏmetímes | ă síl|vĕr flówer.

Bút thĕ | stárs! áll | níght lóng | thĕ stárs | ăre clóv|ĕr,

Óvĕr, | ănd óv|ĕr, ănd óv|ĕr!

2.   Version of the Lewis Thomas passage:

Afield, a single ant of any kind
Cannot be said to have much on his mind;

Indeed, it would be hard by rights to call
His neurons, few, loose-strung, a mind at all,

Or say he had a thought half-way complete.
He is more like a ganglion with feet.

Circling a moth that's dead, four ants—or ten—
Will seem more like a real idea then,

Fumbling and shoving, Hill-ward, bit by bit,
As if by blind chance slowly moving it.

But only when you watch, in crowded dance
Around their Hill, a thousand massing ants

As black and purposeful as scribbling ink,
Do you first see the whole beast, see it think,

Plan, calculate—a live computer's bits
Of dark intelligence, its crawling wits.

CHAPTER 4

1. Housman tried "sunny," "pleasant," "checkered," "patterned," and "painted" before he hit on the word he finally chose: "colored." Why do you think he preferred "colored" to the other adjectives? Consider the qualities of the scene each suggests. Might alliteration have influenced his choice?

2. Possible rhymes might include:

> circle = *work'll*
> stop-sign = *drop mine*
> rhinoceros = If ever, outside a zoo,
> > You meet a rhinoceros
> > And you *cross her, fuss*
> > Is exactly what she'll do.
>
> > > *Anonymous*

> evergreen = *never seen*
> broccoli = Look at the *clock! Oh, me!*
> pelican = Ogden Nash used "belly can" and "hell he can."
> umbrella = The rain it raineth every day,
> > upon the just and unjust *fella*,
> > but more upon the just, because
> > the unjust hath the just's umbrella.
>
> > > *Anonymous*

4.   *The Fourth of July*

HOWARD NEMEROV (1920–1991)

Because I am drunk, this Independence Night,
I watch the fireworks from far away,
From a high hill, across the moony green
Of lakes and other hills to the town harbor,
Where stately illuminations are flung aloft,   5
One light shattering in a hundred lights
Minute by minute. The reason I am crying,
Aside from only being country drunk,
That is, may be that I have just remembered
The sparklers, rockets, roman candles, and   10

So on, we used to be allowed to buy
When I was a boy, and set off by ourselves
At some peril to life and property.
Our freedom to abuse our freedom thus
Has since, I understand, been remedied   15
By legislation. Now the authorities
Arrange a perfectly safe public display
To be watched at a distance; and now also
The contribution of all the taxpayers
Together makes a more spectacular   20
Result than any could achieve alone
(A few pale pinwheels, or a firecracker
Fused at the dog's tail). It is, indeed, splendid:
Showers of roses in the sky, fountains
Of emeralds, and those profusely scattered zircons   25
Falling and falling, flowering as they fall
And followed distantly by a noise of thunder.
My eyes are half-afloat in happy tears.
God bless our Nation on a night like this,
And bless the careful and secure officials   30
Who celebrate our independence now.

6.   There is a big, old wooden box,
            Without a thing inside.
        It therefore needs, and has, no locks.
            The top is open wide.

        Here is a big, old wooden box
            Which needs, and has, no locks.
        Because it holds nothing inside,
            Its top is opened wide.

        The top is open wide;
            There are no locks.
        For nothing's kept inside
            This wooden box.

CHAPTER 5

4.   *Eavesdropping*

        MICHELLE BOISSEAU (b. 1955)

        It was Mrs. Garvin, the doctor's wife,
        who told my mother, Well if you're that broke

put the kids up for adoption.
Out under the porch light that summer
we slapped at mosquitoes and invented   5
our brave escape—luminous sheets
knotted out the window
were the lines of a highway down the house.
We would know the way,
like ingenious animals, to go   10
quietly toward the river,
but we could imagine no further
than the shacks on stilts
shivering the water,
the Kentucky hills on the other side.   15
Denise, the youngest, took to sleepwalking,
wading room to room for the place
one of us—curled up in a bed's corner—
might have left her. I'd wake
with her face pressed against my back,   20
her hands reining the edges of my nightgown.
I didn't tuck her into my shoulder
but loosened her fingers and led her
back to her own bed, her fear
already seeping into me like water   25
or like the light spilling
from the milk truck
as it backfired down the street.

CHAPTER 7

2.   a) Raspberries *splash*, redly in their leaves
         b) Four cars like a *kite's tail* / behind the hearse
         c) droning, *unzipping* the halves of the air
         d) will shower its peaceful *rockets* / all over the towns
         e) The clarinet, a dark tube / *tallowed* in silver
         f) Big as *wedding cakes*, / two white launches
         g) whirled by a boat's wash / into *Queen Anne's lace*
         h) Dreams are the soul's *home movies*

CHAPTER 9

3. The original words in "In a Spring Still Not Written Of" are: "burning up" in
line 4, "carrying" in line 8, "blossom" in line 12, "astronomies" in line 14, and
"untarnished" in line 16.

CHAPTER 11

2.   *In One Place*

ROBERT WALLACE (b. 1932)

—something
holds up two or three leaves
the first year,

and climbs
and branches, summer
by summer,

till birds
in it don't remember
it wasn't there.

CHAPTER 12

3. All three poems have been published.

APPENDIX III

Select Bibliography

In addition to a good dictionary:

ANTHOLOGIES

Marjorie Agosan, ed., *These Are Not Sweet Girls: Poetry by Latin American Women*, White Pine, 1994.

A.R. Ammons, ed., David Lehman, series ed., *The Best American Poetry 1994*, Simon & Schuster, 1994.

Aliki Barnstone & Willis Barnstone, eds., *Women Poets from Antiquity to Now*, Schocken, 1992.

Michael Benedikt, ed., *The Poetry of Surrealism*, Little, Brown, 1974.

Laura Chester and Sharon Barba, eds., *Rising Tides: 20th Century American Women Poets*, Washington Square Press, 1973.

Nicholas Christopher, ed., *Under 35: The New Generation of American Poets*, Anchor, 1989.

Gerald Costanzo & Jim Daniels, eds., *The Carnegie Mellon Anthology of Poetry*, Carnegie Mellon University Press, 1993.

Philip Dacey & David Jauss, eds., *Strong Measures: Contemporary American Poetry in Traditional Forms*, Harper & Row, 1986.

Richard Ellmann & Robert O'Clair, eds., *The Norton Anthology of Modern Poetry*, 2d ed., Norton, 1988.

Peter Fallon & Derek Mahon, eds., *The Penguin Book of Contemporary Irish Poetry*, Penguin, 1990.

Edward Field, Gerald Locklin, & Charles Stetler, eds., *A New Geography of Poets*, University of Arkansas Press, 1992.

Annie Finch, ed., *A Formal Feeling Comes: Poems in Form by Contemporary Women*, Story Line Press, 1994.

Carolyn Forché, ed., *Against Forgetting: Twentieth Century Poetry of Witness*, Norton, 1993.

Ray Gonzalez, ed., *After Aztlan: Latino Poets of the Nineties*, Godine, 1992.

R. S. Gwynn, ed., *Poetry: A HarperCollins Pocket Anthology*, HarperCollins, 1993.

Michael S. Harper & Anthony Walton, eds., *Every Shut Eye Ain't Asleep: Poetry by African Americans Since 1945*, Little, Brown, 1994.

Jane Hirshfield, ed., *Women in Praise of the Sacred: 43 Centuries of Spiritual Poetry by Women*, Harper Perennial, 1994.

Garrett Hongo, ed., *The Open Boat: Poems from Asian America*, Anchor, 1993.

Paul Hoover, ed., *Postmodern American Poetry*, Norton, 1994.

Florence Howe, ed., *No More Masks! An Anthology of Twentieth-Century Women Poets*, revised, Harper Perennial, 1993.

X. J. Kennedy & Dana Gioia, *An Introduction to Poetry*, 8th ed., HarperCollins, 1994.

Michael Klein, ed., *Poets for Life: Seventy-Six Poets Respond to AIDS*, Persea, 1992.

Jack Myers & Roger Weingarten, eds., *New American Poets of the '90s*, Godine, 1991.

Duane Niatum, ed., *Harper's Anthology of Twentieth-Century Native American Poetry*, Harper & Row, 1988.

Ed Ochester & Peter Oresick, eds., *The Pittsburgh Book of Contemporary Poetry*, University of Pittsburgh Press, 1993.

Dudley Randall, ed., *The Black Poets*, Bantam, 1971.

Kenneth Rosen, ed., *Voices of the Rainbow: Contemporary Poetry by Native Americans*, Arcade, 1993.

Ronald Wallace, ed., *Vital Signs: Contemporary American Poetry from the University Presses*, University of Wisconsin Press, 1989.

ON POETRY, WRITING POETRY, AND POETS

W. H. Auden, *The Dyer's Hand and Other Essays*, Random House, 1962.

David Baker, ed., *Meter in English: A Symposium*, University of Arkansas Press, 1996.

Robin Behn & Chase Twichell, eds., *The Practice of Poetry*, Harper Perennial, 1992.

Sven Birkerts, *The Electric Life: Essays on Modern Poetry*, Morrow, 1989.

Robert Bly, *American Poetry: Wildness and Domesticity*, Harper Perennial, 1991.

Sharon Bryan, ed., *Where We Stand: Women Poets on Literary Tradition*, Norton, 1993.

Michael Burns, ed., *Miller Williams and the Poetry of the Particular*, University of Missouri Press, 1991.

Frederick Feirstein, ed., *Expansive Poetry: Essays on the New Narrative & the New Formalism*, Story Line Press, 1989.

Annie Finch, *The Ghost of Meter: Culture and Prosody in American Free Verse*, University of Michigan Press, 1993.

Robert Francis, *The Satirical Rogue on Poetry*, University of Massachusetts Press, 1968.

Stuart Friebert & David Young, eds., *A Field Guide to Contemporary Poetry and Poetics*, Longman, 1980.

Tess Gallagher, *A Concert of Tenses: Essays on Poetry*, University of Michigan Press, 1986.

Dana Gioia, *Can Poetry Matter?* Graywolf, 1992.

Thom Gunn, *Shelf Life: Essays, Memoirs, and an Interview*, University of Michigan Press, 1993.

Donald Hall, *Death to the Death of Poetry: Essays, Reviews, Notes, Interviews*, University of Michigan Press, 1994.

Charles O. Hartman, *Free Verse: An Essay on Prosody*, Princeton University Press, 1980.

Robert Hass, *Twentieth Century Pleasures*, Ecco Press, 1984.

Richard Hugo, *The Triggering Town*, Norton, 1982.

Randall Jarrell, *Poetry and the Age*, Knopf, 1953.

David Kalstone, *Becoming a Poet: Elizabeth Bishop with Marianne Moore and Robert Lowell*, Farrar Straus Giroux, 1989.

Mary Kinzie, *The Cure of Poetry in an Age of Prose*, University of Chicago Press, 1993.

David Lehman, ed., *Ecstatic Occasions, Expedient Forms*, Macmillan, 1987.

Robert McDowell, ed., *Poetry After Modernism*, Story Line Press, 1991.

Edwin Muir, *The Estate of Poetry*, Harvard University Press, 1962; Graywolf, 1993.

Charles Newman, *The Post-Modern Aura*, Northwestern University Press, 1985.

Alex Preminger & T.V.F. Brogan, eds., *The New Princeton Encyclopedia of Poetry and Poetics*, Princeton University Press, 1993.

Adrienne Rich, *What Is Found There: Notebooks on Poetry and Politics*, Norton, 1993.

George Saintsbury, *A History of English Prosody*, Macmillan, 1910.

Barbara Herrnstein Smith, *Poetic Closure: A Study of How Poems End*, University of Chicago Press, 1968.

Timothy Steele, *Missing Measures: Modern Poetry and the Revolt Against Meter*, University of Arkansas Press, 1990.

Alberta T. Turner, ed., *45 Contemporary Poems: The Creative Process*, Longman, 1985.

Miller Williams, *Patterns of Poetry*, Louisiana State University Press, 1986.

Clement Wood, *The Complete Rhyming Dictionary*, revised, Doubleday, 1992.

Acknowledgments

Adeyemon, Omoteji, "Saviour." Copyright © 1995 by Omoteji Adeyemon. Reprinted by permission.

Adrian, Vonna, "St. Jerome" and "A Plaguey Thing": From *A Gaggle of Verses*, Bits Press. Copyright © 1986, 1988 by Vonna Adrian. Reprinted by permission.

Alexander, Pamela, "Look Here." Copyright © 1994 by Pamela Alexander. First appeared in *The Atlantic*. Reprinted by permission.

Allbery, Debra, "Outings." From *Walking Distance*. Copyright © 1991 by Debra Allbery. Reprinted by permission of the University of Pittsburgh Press.

Andrews, Tom, "Cinema Vérité: The Death of Alfred, Lord Tennyson." Copyright © 1993 by Tom Andrews. First appeared in *Field*. Reprinted by permission of the author.

Armour, Richard, "Going to Extremes." From *Light Armour* by Richard Armour. Reprinted by permission of the author and McGraw–Hill Book Company.

Ashley, Renée, "Crow." From *Salt*. © 1991 by The Board of Regents of the University of Wisconsin System. Reprinted by permission of The University of Wisconsin Press, Madison, Wisconsin.

Aubert, Alvin, "Like Miles Said." From *If Winter Come*. Copyright © 1994 by Alvin Aubert. Reprinted by permission of Carnegie Mellon University Press.

Baker, David, "The Plain Style." Copyright © 1991 by David Baker. First appeared in *The Gettysburg Review*. In *After the Reunion*, 1994, The University of Arkansas Press. Reprinted by permission of the author.

Barrax, Gerald, "Eagle. Tiger. Whale." From *Leaning Against the Sun*. Copyright © 1992 by Gerald Barrax. Reprinted by permission of The University of Arkansas Press.

Basho, "Breaking the silence." From *The Narrow Road to the Deep North & Other Travel Sketches*, translated by Nobuyuki Yuasa. Copyright © 1966 by Nobuyuki Yuasa. Reprinted by permission of Penguin Books, Ltd.

Bennett, Bruce, "Smart." Copyright © 1978 by Bruce Bennett. "Performance." Copyright © 1992 by Bruce Bennett. From *Taking Off*, Orchises Press. Reprinted by permission of the author.

Bishop, Elizabeth, "First Death in Nova Scotia." From *The Complete Poems 1927–1979* by Elizabeth Bishop. Copyright © 1979, 1983 by Alice Helen Methfessel. Reprinted by permission of Farrar, Straus & Giroux, Inc.

Bly, Robert, "Looking at a Dead Wren in My Hand." From *The Morning Glory* by Robert Bly. Copyright © 1970 by Robert Bly. Translations of two haiku by Issa. Copyright © 1969 by Robert Bly. "Waking from Sleep." From *Silence in the Snowy Fields*. Copyright © 1962 by Wesleyan University Press. All reprinted by permission of Robert Bly.

Boisseau, Michelle, "Eavesdropping." From *No Private Life*, Vanderbilt University Press. Copyright © 1990 by Michelle Boisseau. "Black Mulberry." Copyright © 1993 by Michelle Boisseau. First appeared in *Green Mountains Review*. "Against the Muse." Copyright © 1995 by Michelle Boisseau. All reprinted by permission of the author.

Brooke, Glenn, "Howard." Copyright © 1986 by Glenn Brooke. Reprinted by permission.

Brooks, Gwendolyn, "We Real Cool." From *Blacks*, The David Company, Chicago. Copyright © 1987 by Gwendolyn Brooks. Reprinted by permission.

Buckley, Christopher, "Sparrows." From *Dust Light, Leaves*, Vanderbilt University Press. Copyright © 1986 by Christopher Buckley. Reprinted by permission of the author.

Burns, Michael, "The First Time." From *The Secret Names: Poems*. Copyright © 1994 by Michael Burns. Reprinted by permission of the University of Missouri Press and the author.

Camp, James, "After the Philharmonic." First appeared in *Open Places*. Copyright © 1978 by James Camp. Reprinted by permission.

Cassian, Nina, "Ordeal." Translation copyright © by Michael Impey and Brian Swann. Originally published in *An Anthology of Contemporary Romanian Poetry*, London. Reprinted by permission of Michael Impey.

Ciardi, John, "True or False." From *The Birds of Pompeii*. Copyright © 1985 by John Ciardi. Reprinted by permission of The University of Arkansas Press.

Cole, William, "A River Rhyme." Copyright © 1985 by William Rossa Cole. Reprinted by permission.

Conoley, Gillian, "The Woman on the Homecoming Float." From *Tall Stranger*. Copyright © 1991 by Gillian Conoley. Reprinted by permission of Carnegie Mellon University Press.

Conti, Edmund, "How Sweet the Sound." Copyright © 1985, 1988 by Edmund Conti. Reprinted by permission.

Cope, Wendy, "Strugnell's Bargain." Copyright © 1984 by Wendy Cope. Reprinted by permission.

Costanzo, Gerald, "Braille" and "The Sacred Cows of Los Angeles." Copyright © 1992 by Gerald Costanzo. Reprinted from *Nobody Lives on Arthur Godfrey Boulevard*, by Gerald Costanzo, with the permission of BOA Editions, Ltd., 92 Park Ave., Brockport, NY 14420.

Coulette, Henri, "The Sickness of Friends." From *The Poems of Henri Coulette*. Copyright © 1990 by Donald Justice and Robert Mezey. Reprinted by permission of The University of Arkansas Press.

Cunningham, J. V., "For My Contemporaries." From *The Exclusions of a Rhyme*. Copyright © 1960 by J.V. Cunningham. Reprinted with the permission of the Ohio University Press, Athens.

Daniels, Jim, "Short-order Cook." From *Places/Everyone*. Copyright © 1985 by Jim Daniels. Reprinted by permission of the University of Wisconsin Press.

Derricotte, Toi, "The Weakness." From *Captivity*. Copyright © 1989 by Toi Derricotte. Reprinted by permission of the University of Pittsburgh Press.

Dickey, James, "Cherrylog Road." From *Helmets*. Copyright © 1964 by James Dickey. Wesleyan University Press. Reprinted by permission of the University Press of New England.

Dickinson, Emily, "After great pain, a formal feeling comes," "A Bird came down the Walk—," "I heard a Fly buzz—when I died—," and "A narrow Fellow in the Grass." Reprinted by permission of the publishers and the Trustees of Amherst College from *The Poems of Emily Dickinson*, Thomas H. Johnson, ed., Cambridge, Mass.: The Belknap Press of Harvard University Press, Copyright © 1951, 1955, 1979, 1983 by the President and Fellows of Harvard College. "After great pain, a formal feeling comes." From *The Complete Poems of Emily Dickinson* edited by Thomas H. Johnson. Copyright © 1929 by Martha Dickinson Bianchi; copyright © renewed 1957 by Mary L. Hampson. By permission of Little, Brown and Company.

Dobler, Patricia, "1920 Photo." From *Talking to Strangers*. Copyright © 1986 by The Board of Regents of the University of Wisconsin System. Reprinted by permission of the University of Wisconsin Press, Madison, Wisconsin.

Dobyns, Stephen, "Bleeder." From *Black Dog, Red Dog*. Copyright © 1984 by Stephen Dobyns. Reprinted by permission of Carnegie Mellon University Press.

Döhl, Reinhard, "Apfel." Reprinted by permission of the author.

Dove, Rita, "The House Slave." From *The Yellow House on the Corner* by Rita Dove. Copyright © 1980 by Rita Dove. "A Hill of Beans." From *Thomas and Beulah*. Copyright © 1986 by Rita Dove. Reprinted by permission of Carnegie Mellon University Press.

Dubie, Norman, "A Blue Hog." Reprinted with the permission of W. W. Norton & Company, Inc. from *Radio Sky* by Norman Dubie. Copyright © 1991 by Norman Dubie. Originally published in *The Mississippi Review*.

Dunn, Stephen, "Laws." From *Not Dancing*. Copyright © 1984 by Stephen Dunn. Reprinted by permission of Carnegie Mellon University Press.

Eady, Cornelius, "The Supremes" and "The Wrong Street." From *The Gathering of My Name*. Copyright © 1991 by Cornelius Eady. Reprinted by permission of Carnegie Mellon University Press.

Eimers, Nancy, "Training Films, Nevada, 1953." From *Destroying Angels*. Copyright © 1991 by Nancy Eimers. Wesleyan University Press. Reprinted by permission of the University Press of New England.

Éluard, Paul, "The Deaf and Blind." Translation by Paul Auster in *The Random House Book of Twentieth Century French Poetry*. Copyright © 1982 by Paul Auster. Reprinted by permission.

Emanuel, Lynn, "One Summer Hurricane Lynn Spawns Tornados as Far West as Ely." From *The Dig*. Copyright © 1992 by Lynn Emanuel. Reprinted by permission of the University of Illinois Press.

Estés, Clarissa Pinkola, "La Muerte, Patron Saint of Writers." Copyright © 1990 by Clarissa Pinkola Estés. First appeared in *Colorado Review*, Fall 1993. Reprinted by permission.

Evett, David, "Popcorn." Copyright © 1985 by David Evett. Reprinted by permission.

Ewart, Gavin, "Miss Twye." From *The Collected Ewart: 1933–1980*. Copyright © 1980 by Gavin Ewart. Reprinted by permission of Century Hutchinson, Ltd., and the author.

Fantauzzi, David A., "Moorings" and draft of same. Copyright © 1977 by David A. Fantauzzi. Reprinted by permission.

Ferree, Joel, "Disclaimer." Copyright © 1985 by Joel Ferree. Reprinted by permission.

Finley, Michael, "Frankenstein in the Cemetery." Copyright © 1977 by Michael Finley. Reprinted by permission.

Flanders, Jane, "Shopping in Tuckahoe." From *Timepiece*. Copyright © 1988 by Jane Flanders.

Reprinted by permission of the University of Pittsburgh Press.

Francis, Robert, "Cadence." From *Butter Hill.* Copyright © 1984 by Paul W. Carman. Reprinted by permission. "Professional Poet" and "The Indecipherable Poem." From *The Satirical Rogue on Poetry.* Copyright © 1965 by Robert Francis. Reprinted by permission of the University of Massachusetts Press. "Excellence" and "Glass." From *Robert Francis: Collected Poems, 1936–1976.* Copyright © 1976 by Robert Francis. Reprinted by permission of the University of Massachusetts Press.

Freedman, Martha H., "Dorothy Parker." Copyright © 1988 by Martha H. Freedman. Reprinted by permission.

Freshley, Jill, "Woman's Work." Copyright © 1981 by Jill Freshley. Reprinted by permission.

Frost, Robert, "Design." From *The Poetry of Robert Frost* edited by Edward Connery Lathem. Copyright © 1936 by Robert Frost. Copyright © 1964 by Lesley Frost Ballantine. Copyright © 1969 by Henry Holt and Company, Inc. "In White." From *The Dimensions of Robert Frost* by Reginald L. Cook. Copyright © 1958 by Reginald L. Cook. Reprinted by permission of Henry Holt and Company, Inc.

Fulton, Alice, "The Orthodox Waltz." From *The Powers of Congress.* Copyright © 1990 by Alice Fulton. Reprinted by permission of David R. Godine, Publisher.

Gallagher, Tess, "Kidnaper." From *Instructions to the Double* by Tess Gallagher. Copyright © 1976 by Tess Gallagher. Reprinted by permission of Graywolf Press.

Gardinier, Suzanne, "Our American Way of Life." From *The New World.* Copyright © 1993 by Suzanne Gardinier. Reprinted by permission of the University of Pittsburgh Press.

Gerstler, Amy, "Siren." From *Bitter Angel.* Copyright © 1990 by Amy Gerstler. Reprinted by permission.

Gioia, Dana, "The Next Poem." Copyright © 1985 by Dana Gioia. First appeared in *Poetry.* Reprinted by permission.

Glaser, Elton, "Interim Report." From *Relics.* Copyright © 1984 by Elton Glaser. Wesleyan University Press. Reprinted by permission of the University Press of New England.

Glück, Louise, "The Racer's Widow." Copyright © 1968 by Louise Glück. Reprinted by permission. "The Gold Lily" by Louise Glück. Copyright © 1992 by Louise Glück. From *The Wild Iris,* first published by The Ecco Press in 1992. Reprinted by permission.

Greenway, William, "Pit Pony." From *Where We've Been.* Copyright © 1987 by William Greenway. Reprinted by permission of Theodore W. Macri, agent for Breitenbush Books.

Hall, Donald, "Names of Horses." From *Kicking the Leaves.* Copyright © 1978 by Donald Hall. Reprinted by permission of the author. "Ox Cart Man." From *Old and New Poems.* Copyright © 1990 by Donald Hall. Reprinted by permission of Ticknor & Fields / Houghton Mifflin Company. All rights reserved. Draft of "Ox Cart Man." From *A Piece of Work: Five Writers Discuss Their Revisions,* edited by Jay Woodruff. Copyright © 1993 by Jay Woodruff and Donald Hall. Reprinted by permission of the University of Iowa Press and Donald Hall.

Hass, Robert, "Fall." From *Field Guide.* Copyright © 1973 by Robert Hass. Reprinted by permission of Yale University Press.

Hayden, Robert, "Those Winter Sundays" and "Bone–Flower Elegy." From *Collected Poems of Robert Hayden,* edited by Frederick Glaysher. Reprinted with the permission of W. W. Norton & Company, Inc. Copyright © 1985 by Emma Hayden.

Hecht, Anthony, "The Dover Bitch." From *The Hard Hours.* Copyright © 1967 by Anthony Hecht. Reprinted by permission of the author.

Heffernan, Michael, "Slugs." From *The Man at Home.* Copyright © 1988 by Michael Heffernan. Reprinted by permission of The University of Arkansas Press.

Heinrich, Sheila, "disappearances." Copyright © 1975 by Sheila Heinrich. Reprinted by permission.

Hilberry, Conrad, "Storm Window." Copyright © 1980 by Conrad Hilberry. Reprinted by permission.

Hogan, Linda, "Potholes." First appeared in *Savings* by Linda Hogan, Coffee House Press, 1988. Reprinted by permission of the publisher. Copyright © 1988 by Linda Hogan.

Holley, Margaret, "The Fireflies" and "Peepers." From *Morning Star.* Copyright © 1992 by Margaret Holley. Reprinted by permission of Cooper Beech Press.

Howe, Marie, "The Good Reason for Our Forgetting." From *The Good Thief,* Persea Books. Copyright © 1988 by Marie Howe. Reprinted by permission.

Hudgins, Andrew, "My Father's Rage." Copyright © 1992 by Andrew Hudgins. First appeared in *The Hudson Review.* Reprinted by permission.

Hummer, T. R., "The Rural Carrier Discovers That Love Is Everywhere." From *The Angelic Orders,* Louisiana State University Press, 1982. Copyright © 1980 by *Commonweal.* Reprinted by permission of *Commonweal.*

Irwin, Mark, "Icicles." Copyright © 1978 by Mark Irwin. Reprinted by permission. "The Invention of the Snowman." From *Shenandoah: The Washington and Lee University Review.* Copyright © 1980 by Washington and Lee

University. Reprinted with the permission of the Editor.

Jackson, Fleda Brown, "Kitten." Copyright © 1994 by Fleda Brown Jackson. First appeared in *Indiana Review.* Reprinted by permission.

Jacobson, Bonnie, "On Being Served Apples." Copyright © 1980 by Bonnie Jacobson. Reprinted by permission.

Jarman, Mark, "Ground Swell." Copyright © 1991 by Mark Jarman. First appeared in *New American Poets of the 90s.* Reprinted by permission.

Justice, Donald, "Variations on a Text by Vallejo." From *Selected Poems.* Copyright © 1979 by Donald Justice. Reprinted by permission.

Karp, Vickie, "Getting Dressed in the Dark." Copyright © 1989 by Vickie Karp. Appeared in *The New York Review of Books,* November 10, 1988, and in *The Best American Poetry 1989,* Collier Books, Macmillan. Reprinted by permission.

Kaufman, Shirley, "Bread and Water." From *Rivers of Salt,* Copper Canyon Press. Copyright © 1990 by Shirley Kaufman. First appeared in *Ploughshares.* Reprinted by permission of the author.

Kennedy, X. J., "In a Prominent Bar in Secaucus One Day." From *Cross Ties,* University of Georgia Press. Copyright © 1985 by X. J. Kennedy. Reprinted by permission of Curtis Brown, Ltd.

Kenyon, Jane, "The Suitor." From *From Room to Room,* Alicejamesbooks. Copyright © 1978 by Jane Kenyon. Reprinted by permission.

Kesegich, Amy B., "Mrs. Bradley's Dilemma." Copyright © 1991 by Amy B. Kesegich. Reprinted by permission.

Kinzie, Mary, "The Quest." From *The Threshold of the Year.* Copyright © 1982 by Mary Kinzie. Reprinted by permission.

Kirschner, Elizabeth, "These Heady Flowers." From *Twenty Colors.* Copyright © 1992 by Elizabeth Kirschner. Reprinted by permission of Carnegie Mellon University Press.

Klappert, Peter, "The Trapper." From *Circular Stairs, Distress in the Mirrors* by Peter Klappert. Copyright © 1975 by Peter Klappert. Reprinted by permission of The Griffin Press and the author. "The Invention of the Telephone." From *Lugging Vegetables to Nantucket* by Peter Klappert. Copyright © 1971 by Peter Klappert. Reprinted by permission.

Knight, Etheridge, "A Poem of Attrition." From *The Essential Etheridge Knight.* Copyright © 1986 by Etheridge Knight. Reprinted by permission of the University of Pittsburgh Press.

Komunyakaa, Yusef, "Sunday Afternoons." From *Magic City.* First appeared in *New American Poets of the 90s.* Copyright © 1991 by Yusef Komunyakaa. Reprinted by permission of the author.

Kooser, Ted, "Selecting a Reader." From *Sure Signs: New and Selected Poems* by Ted Kooser. Copyright © 1980 by Ted Kooser. Reprinted by permission of the University of Pittsburgh Press. "Looking for You, Barbara." Copyright © 1976 by Ted Kooser. Reprinted by permission of the author and The Best Cellar Press.

Lake, Paul, "Blue Jay." From *Catches.* Copyright © 1986 by Paul Lake. Reprinted by permission of the publisher, R. L. Barth.

Lattimore, Richmond, "Catania to Rome." From *Poems of Three Decades* by Richmond Lattimore. Copyright © 1972 by Richmond Lattimore. Reprinted by permission of The University of Chicago Press.

Lee, David, "Tuesday Morning, Loading Pigs." From *The Porcine Canticles* by David Lee. Copyright © 1984 by David Lee. Reprinted by permission of Copper Canyon Press and the author.

Levine, Philip, "Animals Are Passing from Our Lives." From *Not This Pig.* Copyright © 1968 by Philip Levine. Wesleyan University Press. Reprinted by permission of the University Press of New England. "The Return: Orihuela, 1965." Copyright © 1994 by Philip Levine. First appeared in *The Nation.* Reprinted by permission.

Lux, Thomas, "Tarantulas on the Lifebuoy." From *Half Promised Land.* Copyright © 1986 by Thomas Lux. Reprinted by permission.

Machan, Katharyn Howd, "Hazel Tells Laverne." Copyright © 1981 by Katharyn Howd Machan. Reprinted by permission.

Matthews, William, "Men at My Father's Funeral." Copyright © 1992 by William Matthews. First appeared in *The Ohio Review.* Reprinted by permission.

McBride, Mekeel, "As She Has Been Taught." From *The Going Under of the Evening Land* by Mekeel McBride. Copyright © 1983 by Mekeel McBride. Reprinted by permission of Carnegie Mellon University Press.

McPherson, Sandra, "The Study of Genius." Copyright © 1994 by Sandra McPherson. First appeared in *Poetry.* Reprinted by permission.

Meek, Jay, "Swimmers." From *Windows.* Copyright © 1994 by Jay Meek. Reprinted by permission of Carnegie Mellon University Press.

Meinke, Peter, "The ABC of Aerobics." From *Night Watch on the Chesapeake.* Copyright © 1987 by Peter Meinke. Reprinted by permission of the University of Pittsburgh Press.

Miller, Heather Ross, "Twila Jo and the Wrestler." Copyright © 1989 by Heather Ross Miller. First appeared in *The Laurel Review.* Reprinted by permission.

Miller, Leslie Adrienne, "My Students Catch Me Dancing." From *Staying Up for Love.* Copyright © 1990 by Leslie Adrienne Miller.

Reprinted by permission of Carnegie Mellon University Press.

Milosz, Czeslaw, "Realism." Copyright © 1994 by Czeslaw Milosz. First appeared in *The New Yorker*. Reprinted by permission of Robert Hass.

Mitchell, Susan, "Blackbirds." From *The Water Inside the Water*. Copyright © 1983 by Susan Mitchell. Wesleyan University Press. Reprinted by permission of the University Press of New England.

Moore, Marianne, "The Fish" and "My Apish Cousins" ("The Monkeys"). Permission to reprint two versions of Marianne Moore's poem, "The Fish" (1918 and 1924), and Moore's poem, "My Apish Cousins" (full text [1924] and in part [1917]) granted by Marianne Craig Moore, Literary Executor for the Estate of Marianne Moore. All rights reserved.

Moss, Thylias, "Those Men at Redbones." From *At Redbones*. Copyright © 1990 by Thylias Moss. Reprinted by permission of Cleveland State University Poetry Center.

Napora, Joseph S., "Sore Eros." Copyright © 1979 by Joseph S. Napora. Reprinted by permission.

Nelson, Warren, "Loan." Copyright © 1978 by Warren Nelson. Reprinted by permission.

Nemerov, Howard, "Power to the People," "Learning by Doing," "Make Big Money at Home! Write Poems in Spare time!," "The Fourth of July." Copyright © 1973 by Howard Nemerov. Reprinted by permission.

Nye, Naomi Shihab, "Famous." From *Hugging the Jukebox*. Copyright © 1982 by Naomi Shihab Nye. Reprinted by permission of Theodore W. Macri, agent for Breitenbush Books.

Ochester, Ed, "Poem for a New Cat." From *Changing the Name to Ochester*. Copyright © 1988 by Ed Ochester. Reprinted by permission of Carnegie Mellon University Press.

Olds, Sharon, "Sex without Love." From *The Dead and the Living*. Copyright © 1983 by Sharon Olds. Reprinted by permission of Alfred A. Knopf, Inc.

Oliver, Mary, "Music at Night." From *The Night Traveler*. Copyright © 1978 by Mary Oliver. Reprinted by permission of Bits Press and the author.

Olsen, William, "The Dead Monkey." From *The Hand of God and a Few Bright Flowers*. Copyright © 1988 by William Olsen. Reprinted by permission of the author.

Ostriker, Alicia, "Dissolve in Slow Motion." From *The Imaginary Lover*. Copyright © 1986 by Alicia Ostriker. Reprinted by permission of the University of Pittsburgh Press.

Otis, Emily, "Mother-in-Law." Copyright © 1985 by Emily Otis. Reprinted by permission.

Owen, Wilfred, "Arms and the Boy." From *Collected Poems of Wilfred Owen*. Copyright © 1963 by Chatto & Windus, Ltd. Reprinted by permission of New Directions Publishing Corporation.

Pape, Greg, "Children of Sacaton." From *Storm Pattern*. Copyright © 1992 by Greg Pape. Reprinted by permission of the University of Pittsburgh Press.

Pastan, Linda, "Mother Eve." First appeared in *The Georgia Review*. Copyright © 1985 by Linda Pastan. Reprinted by permission.

Patchen, Kenneth, "The Murder of Two Young Men by a Kid Wearing Lemon–colored Gloves." From *Collected Poems of Kenneth Patchen*. Copyright © 1945 by Kenneth Patchen. Reprinted by permission of New Directions Publishing Corporation.

Pau-Llosa, Ricardo, "Pesca de Esponjas." From *Cuba*. Copyright © 1993 by Ricardo Pau-Llosa. Reprinted by permission of Carnegie Mellon University Press.

Piercy, Marge, "Sentimental Poem." Copyright © 1978 by Marge Piercy. Reprinted by permission.

Plumly, Stanley, "Woman on Twenty–second Eating Berries." Copyright © 1990 by Stanley Plumly. First appeared in *Antaeus*. Reprinted by permission.

Porritt, Ruth, "Read This Poem from the Bottom Up." Copyright © 1987 by Ruth Porritt. First appeared in *The Laurel Review*. Reprinted by permission.

Pound, Ezra, "In a Station of the Metro" and lines from "The Return." From *Personae*. Copyright © 1926 by Ezra Pound. Reprinted by permission of New Directions Publishing Corporation.

Prospere, Susan, "Ministering Angels." From *Sub Rosa*. Reprinted with the permission of W. W. Norton & Company, Inc. Copyright © 1991 by Susan Prospere. Originally published in *Poetry*.

Rankine, Claudia, "The Man. His Bowl. His Raspberries." and "Out of Many, One." From *Nothing in Nature Is Private*, Cleveland State University Poetry Center. Copyright © 1994 by Claudia Rankine. Reprinted by permission of the author.

Rich, Adrienne, "The Slides." Reprinted from *Time's Power, Poems 1985–1988*, by Adrienne Rich, by permission of the author and W. W. Norton & Company, Inc. Copyright © 1989 by Adrienne Rich.

Roethke, Theodore, "My Papa's Waltz." Copyright © 1942 by Hearst Magazines, Inc. From *The Collected Poems of Theodore Roethke* by Theodore Roethke. Used by permission of Doubleday, a division of Bantam, Doubleday, Dell Publishing Group, Inc.

Root, Judith, "Insomnia." From *Weaving the Sheets*. Copyright © 1988 by Judith Root. Reprinted by permission of Carnegie Mellon University Press.

Rose, Jan M. W., "Spider." Copyright © 1977 by Jan M. W. Rose. Reprinted by permission.

Rosenberg, Liz, "The Silence of Women." From *Children of Paradise*. Copyright © 1994 by Liz Rosenberg. Reprinted by permission of the University of Pittsburgh Press.

Rosser, J. Allyn, "Letter to the Cracker Company." From *Bright Moves*. Copyright © 1990 by J. Allyn Rosser. Reprinted by permission of Northeastern University Press, Boston.

St. John, David, "Iris." From *Hush*. Copyright © 1976 by David St. John. Reprinted by permission of John Hopkins University Press.

Shaffer, C. Lynn, "A Baglady's Plea," "A Butterfly Lands on the Grave of My Friend," and "To Dust." Copyright © 1995 by C. Lynn Shaffer. Reprinted by permission.

Shomer, Enid, "Among the Cows." From *This Close to Earth*. Copyright © 1992 by Enid Shomer. Reprinted by permission of The University of Arkansas Press.

Shumaker, Peggy, "Chinese Print: No Translation." From *Esperanza's Hair*. Copyright © 1985 by Peggy Shumaker. Reprinted by permission.

Simic, Charles, "The Prisoner." From *Charon's Cosmology* by Charles Simic. Copyright © 1977 by Charles Simic. Reprinted by permission of George Braziller, Inc. "Stone." From *Dismantling the Silence* by Charles Simic. Copyright © 1971 by Charles Simic. Reprinted by permission of George Braziller, Inc. "Watermelons." From *Return to a Place Lit by a Glass of Milk* by Charles Simic. Copyright © 1974 by Charles Simic. Reprinted by permission of George Braziller, Inc.

Simone, Roberta, "Percy Bysshe Shelley." Copyright © 1984 by Roberta Simone. Reprinted by permission.

Simpson, Louis, "American Classic." From *Caviare at the Funeral*. Copyright © 1981 by Louis Simpson. Reprinted by permission of Grolier, Inc.

Slavitt, David R., "Titanic." From *Big Nose* by David R. Slavitt. Copyright © 1983 by David R. Slavitt. Reprinted by permission of Louisiana State University Press. "Raptures." From *Crossroads*. Copyright © 1994 by the author, published by Louisiana State University Press. Used with permission.

Smith, Dave, "Parkersburg, W. Va." From *The Fisherman's Whore*. Copyright © 1989 by Dave Smith. Reprinted by permission of Carnegie Mellon University Press.

Snodgrass, W. D., "Leaving the Motel." From *After Experience* by W. D. Snodgrass. Copyright © 1968 by W. D. Snodgrass. Reprinted by permission of the author.

Song, Cathy, "Primary Colors." From *Picture Bride*. Copyright © 1983 by Yale University Press. Reprinted by permission of Yale University Press.

Soto, Gary, "In the Madness of Love." Copyright © 1985 by Gary Soto. Used by permission of the author.

Spires, Elizabeth, "Letter in July." Copyright © 1992 by Elizabeth Spires. First appeared in *Poetry*. Reprinted by permission.

Stafford, William, "Traveling Through the Dark." From *Stories that Could Be True* by William Stafford. Copyright © 1960 by William Stafford. Reprinted by permission of Harper & Row, Publishers, Inc. "Ask Me." From *50 Contemporary Poets*, edited by Alberta T. Turner. Copyright © 1977 by Longman, Inc. Reprinted by permission.

Stanton, Maura, "Song (After Shakespeare)." From *Cries of Swimmers*. Copyright © 1984 by Maura Stanton. Reprinted by permission of Carnegie Mellon University Press.

Steele, Timothy, "Epitaph" and "Jogging in the Presidio." From *Uncertainties and Rest*. Copyright © 1979 by Timothy Steele. Reprinted by permission of the author.

Stern, Gerald, "Stepping Out of Poetry." From *Lucky Life*. Copyright © 1977 by Gerald Stern. Reprinted by permission.

Stuckey, Tricia, "In the Mirror." Copyright © 1995 by Tricia Stuckey. Reprinted by permission.

Tate, James, "A Guide to the Stone Age." From *Absences*. Copyright © 1972 by James Tate. Reprinted by permission of Carnegie Mellon University Press.

Taylor, Henry, "Barbed Wire." Reprinted by permission of Louisiana State University Press from *The Flying Change* by Henry Taylor. Copyright © 1985 by Henry Taylor.

Taylor, Linda, "Eyes." Copyright © 1995 by Linda Taylor. First appeared in *Poetry Northwest*. Reprinted by permission.

Thomas, Dylan, "Do not go gentle into that good night." From *Poems of Dylan Thomas*. Copyright © 1939 by New Directions Publishing Corporation, 1945 by the Trustees for the Copyrights of Dylan Thomas, 1952 by Dylan Thomas. Reprinted by permission of New Directions Publishing Corporation and of David Higham Associates for J. M. Dent & Sons, Ltd.

Thomas, Lewis, excerpt from *The Lives of a Cell* by Lewis Thomas. Copyright © 1974 by Lewis Thomas. All rights reserved. Reprinted by permission of Viking Penguin, a division of Penguin Books USA, Inc.

Tomes, Marta, "The Kiss." Copyright © 1995 by Marta Tomes. Reprinted by permission.

Torgersen, Eric, "Wearing Mittens." Copyright © 1976 by Eric Torgersen. Reprinted by permission.

Trawick, Leonard, "At the Flying School." First appeared in *The Beloit Poetry Journal*. Copyright © 1987 by Leonard Trawick. Reprinted by permission.

Trowbridge, William, "Enter Dark Stranger." Copyright © 1985 by William Trowbridge. From *Enter Dark Stranger*, The University of Arkansas Press, 1989. Reprinted by permission.

Twichell, Chase, "Evening, Herron's Farm." From *The Odds*. Copyright © 1986 by Chase Twichell. Reprinted by permission of the University of Pittsburgh Press.

Updike, John, "Player Piano." Copyright © 1958 by John Updike. Reprinted by permission.

Voigt, Ellen Bryant, "Dancing with Poets." From *The Lotus Flowers*. Reprinted with the permission of W. W. Norton & Company, Inc. Copyright © 1987 by Ellen Bryant Voigt. Originally published in *The New Yorker*.

Wallace, Robert, "In a Spring Still Not Written Of," "In the Field Forever," and "In One Place." Copyright © 1965, 1968, 1979 by Robert Wallace. From *The Common Summer: New and Selected Poems*, Carnegie Mellon University Press, 1989. Reprinted by permission.

Wallace, Ronald, "Building an Outhouse." From *The Makings of Happiness*. Copyright © 1991 by Ronald Wallace. Reprinted by permission of the University of Pittsburgh Press.

Waniek, Marilyn Nelson, "Balance." From *The Homeplace*. Copyright © 1990 by the author, published by Louisiana State University Press. Used with permission.

Waters, Michael, "Mosquito Nets." From *Bountiful*, Carnegie Mellon University Press. Copyright © 1992 by Michael Waters. Reprinted by permission.

Watterson, Meggan, "For the Women of Ancient Greece." Copyright © 1995 by Meggan Watterson. Reprinted by permission.

Welch, Don, "There Is No Wind in Heaven." Copyright © 1993 by Don Welch. First appeared in *Georgia Review*. Poem and draft reprinted by permission.

Wier, Dara, "Daytrip to Paradox." From *The Book of Knowledge*. Copyright © 1988 by Dara Wier. Reprinted by permission of Carnegie Mellon University Press.

Wilbur, Richard, "Hamlen Brook." First appeared in *The New Yorker*. Copyright © 1985 by Richard Wilbur. Reprinted by permission of the author. "Love Calls Us to the Things of This World." From *Things of This World* by Richard Wilbur. Copyright © 1956 and renewed 1984 by Richard Wilbur. Reprinted by permission of Harcourt Brace & Company. Six drafts of the opening lines of "Love Calls Us to the Things of This World." Copyright © 1964 by Richard Wilbur. Reprinted by permission.

Wild, Peter, "Natural Gas." From *The Lost Tribe* by Peter Wild. Copyright © 1978 by Peter Wild. Reprinted by permission of Wolfsong Press and the author.

Williams, Miller, "My Wife Reads the Paper at Breakfast on the Birthday of the Scottish Poet." Copyright © 1985 by Miller Williams. Reprinted by permission. "The Curator." From *Adjusting to the Light*. Copyright © 1992 by Miller Williams. Reprinted by permission of the University of Missouri Press. Drafts of "Politics." Copyright © 1995 by Miller Williams. Reprinted by permission of the author.

Williams, William Carlos, "To Waken an Old Lady," "Poem (As the cat)," and "The Red Wheelbarrow." From *Collected Poems Volume I 1909–1939*. Copyright © 1938 by New Directions Publishing Corporation. Reprinted by permission of New Directions Publishing Corporation. Lines from "Asphodel, That Greeny Flower." From *Collected Poems Volume II 1939–1962*. Copyright © 1944, 1962 by William Carlos Williams. Reprinted by permission of New Directions Publishing Corporation.

Wojahn, David, "The Assassination of John Lennon." From *Mystery Train*. Copyright © 1990 by David Wojahn. Reprinted by permission of the University of Pittsburgh Press.

Wright, James, "A Blessing." From *The Branch Will Not Break*. Copyright © 1963 by James Wright. Wesleyan University Press. Reprinted by permission of the University Press of New England. The version, "Just Off the Highway to Rochester, Minnesota," is reprinted by permission of Mrs. James Wright.

Yeats, William Butler, "After Long Silence." Reprinted with permission of Macmillan Publishing Co., Inc., from *Collected Poems* by W. B. Yeats. Copyright © 1933 by Macmillan Publishing Co., Inc., renewed 1961 by Bertha Georgie Yeats.

Index of Authors and Titles

Index of Terms